The Role of Sustainability and Artificial Intelligence in Education Improvement

This book is devoted to the issues faced by universities in the field of distance learning during and after COVID, as well as in digitalization times. The book devotes a lot of space to the issues of Web 3.0 in university e-learning, Industry 4.0, artificial intelligence and digital equity.

The aim and scope of this book is to draw a holistic picture of education before and after COVID, the psychological effects of COVID in education, and using modern technologies application in education, taking into consideration aspects of sustainability development, Industry 4.0 and Society 5.0. The authors also raise the issue of artificial intelligence investigation in learner-instructor interaction.

Features:

- To elaborate the functions of online education and numerous pedagogical strategies based on electronic learning to aid teachers and students with the tools required to succeed in the 21st century via engaging virtual experiences
- To analyze tools provided by Ed-Tech firms and the effect of digital tools on maintaining the educational process in times of crisis and after pandemic
- To create a roadmap for higher education institutions and provide tips regarding how to improve the effectiveness of the hybrid learning system
- To understand e-learning characteristic in the era of Industry 4.0 and Society 5.0 and characteristics of the different web generations
- To use AI applications to improve connections and relationships between students and teachers and in education in the future

The book is both scientific and educational. It can be used at the university level and by anyone interested in the topics it covers.

The Role of Sustainability and Artificial Intelligence in Education Improvement

Edited by
Joanna Rosak-Szyrocka
Justyna Żywiołek
Anand Nayyar
Mohd Naved

CRC Press
Taylor & Francis Group
Boca Raton London New York

CRC Press is an imprint of the
Taylor & Francis Group, an **informa** business
A CHAPMAN & HALL BOOK

First edition published 2024
by CRC Press
2385 NW Executive Center Dr. Suite 320, Boca Raton, FL 33431

and by CRC Press
4 Park Square, Milton Park, Abingdon, Oxon, OX14 4RN

CRC Press is an imprint of Taylor & Francis Group, LLC

ISBN: 978-1-032-54464-9 (hbk)
ISBN: 978-1-032-54614-8 (pbk)
ISBN: 978-1-003-42577-9 (ebk)

DOI: 10.1201/9781003425779

Typeset in Times
by Apex CoVantage, LLC

Contents

About the Editors xiii
List of Contributors xv
Preface xvii

Chapter 1 Hybrid Learning in Higher Education Institutions: Pathway, Implementation and Challenges 1

V. Harish and Thiyagarajan R.

1.1 Introduction 1
1.1.1 Objectives of the Chapter 2
1.1.2 Organization of the Chapter 2
1.2 Need for Hybrid Learning 2
1.3 Challenges in Teaching and Learning during Covid 2
1.3.1 Paradigm Shift 3
1.3.2 Aspiring for Interaction 3
1.3.3 Paucity of Infrastructure and Resources 3
1.3.4 Lack of Training 4
1.4 Hybrid Learning 4
1.5 Literature Review: Hybrid Learning 4
1.6 Elements of Hybrid Learning 8
1.6.1 Traditional Elements 8
1.6.2 New Elements 9
1.7 Benefits of Hybrid Learning 9
1.8 Hybrid Learning Pathway 10
1.8.1 Understand and Conceive 11
1.8.2 Determine and Design 11
1.8.3 Planned Execution 11
1.8.4 Evaluate and Act 11
1.9 Implementation Roadmap of Hybrid Learning 12
1.10 Tips to Effective Hybrid Learning Engagement 14
1.11 Challenges in Hybrid Learning System 16
1.12 Conclusion and Future Scope 18
References 18

Chapter 2 The Psychological Effects of COVID 19 on College Students due to the Digital Divide via Online Education 22

Ravi Kumar Gupta, Udit Maheshwari and Dhirendra Bahadur Singh

2.1 Introduction 22
2.1.1 Objectives of the Chapter 26
2.1.2 Organization of the Chapter 26
2.2 Literature Review 27
2.2.1 Research Gap 28
2.3 Methodology 29
2.3.1 Research Methods 29
2.3.2 Target Population 29

2.3.3 Sample Collection 29
2.3.4 Study Area 29
2.3.5 Tools for Data Collection 29
2.3.6 Online Forms 29
2.3.7 In-Depth Interview 30
2.3.8 Ethical Consideration 30
2.3.9 Tools for Data Analysis 30
2.4 Results 31
2.4.1 Implementation of Online Methods of Education in an Emergency during the Pandemic 31
2.4.2 Influence of Online Classes during the COVID-19 Period on Mental Stress of College Students, Problems Encountered and Experience of Online Learning 34
2.5 Discussion 36
2.5.1 Execution Procedure of Online Education 36
2.5.2 Opinions of College Students and Level of Satisfaction 37
2.5.3 Mental Status 37
2.5.4 Plan of Action to Keep Good Mental Health during Pandemic (COVID-19) 38
2.5.5 Limitation of the Research Study 38
2.6 Conclusion and Future Scope 38
References 39

Chapter 3 Investigation of Students' Intention and Related Determinants for E-Learning Continuance in Education after COVID-19 42

Diksha Khera

3.1 Introduction 42
3.1.1 Organization of the Chapter 44
3.2 Literature Review 44
3.2.1 E-Learning Continuance Intention 44
3.2.2 Technology Continuance Theory (TCT) 47
3.2.3 Information System Success Model (ISSM) 48
3.2.4 Task-Technology-Fit (TTF) 48
3.2.5 Unified Theory of Acceptance and Use of Technology (UTAUT) 49
3.3 Research Methodology 49
3.4 Data Analysis and Interpretation 53
3.5 Discussion 58
3.6 Conclusion, Limitations and Recommendations 59
References 60

Chapter 4 Education 4.0 and Web 3.0 Technologies Application for Enhancement of Distance Learning Management Systems in the Post–COVID-19 Era 66

Aditya Kumar Gupta, Vivek Aggarwal, Vinita Sharma, and Mohd Naved

4.1 Introduction 66
4.1.1 Background 66
4.1.2 Scope 67

4.1.3 Objectives of the Chapter ... 67
4.1.4 Organization of the Chapter ... 67
4.2 Impact of COVID-19 over Education ... 67
4.3 Web Evolution (1.0 to 3.0) ... 68
4.3.1 Web 1.0 (Read-Only Web) ... 68
4.3.2 Web 2.0 Read-Write (Social Web) ... 68
4.3.3 Web 2.5 Social and Semantic Web (Cloud Based) ... 69
4.3.4 Web 3.0 (Semantic Web) ... 69
4.4 Education 4.0 ... 72
4.4.1 Education 4.0 and Students ... 72
4.4.2 Education 4.0 and Educators ... 72
4.4.3 Education 4.0 and E-Learning Enhancement ... 74
4.4.4 Advancements in E-Learning with Education 4.0 ... 74
4.5 E-Learning Definition ... 74
4.5.1 E-Learning Environment ... 75
4.5.2 Developing E-Learning Framework ... 75
4.5.3 E-Learning Evolution ... 76
4.6 Critical Success Factors of Web Technologies for E-Learning ... 77
4.6.1 Technology ... 78
4.6.2 Content ... 79
4.6.3 Stakeholders ... 79
4.7 Influence of Web 3.0 on E-Learning ... 79
4.7.1 The Impact of Web 3.0/Semantic Web–Based Learning for Instructors ... 80
4.7.2 The Impact of Web 3.0/Semantic Web–Based Learning for Learners ... 80
4.7.3 Benefits of Web 3.0 in Distance Learning ... 81
4.8 Challenges ... 81
4.9 Conclusion and Future Scope ... 82
References ... 83

Chapter 5 Undergraduate Perception towards E-Learning during the Pandemic: Evidence from State Universities in Sri Lanka ... 87

E.W. Biyiri, J.A.P.M. Jayasinghe, and S.N.S. Dahanayake

5.1 Introduction ... 87
5.1.1 Objectives of the Chapter ... 88
5.1.2 Organization of the Chapter ... 89
5.2 Background ... 89
5.3 Literature Review ... 90
5.3.1 E-learning during Covid-19 ... 90
5.3.2 Social Presence ... 91
5.3.3 Collaborative Learning ... 91
5.3.4 Student Satisfaction with E-Learning ... 92
5.3.5 Online Learning Experience ... 92
5.4 Methodology ... 93
5.4.1 Model ... 93
5.4.2 Study Population and Sample ... 93
5.4.3 Instrument ... 93
5.4.4 Data Analysis ... 94

5.5 Results and Discussion ... 94
5.5.1 Respondents Profile ... 94
5.5.2 Undergraduates' Perception towards E-Learning ... 96
5.5.3 Undergraduates' Learning Preference ... 97
5.5.4 Reasons for Preferring Face-to-Face Learning ... 98
5.5.5 Reasons for Preferring E-Learning ... 99
5.6 Conclusion and Recommendations ... 100
References ... 101

Chapter 6 Online Teaching Sustainability and Strategies during the COVID-19 Epidemic ... 106

Gbemisola Janet Ajamu, Joseph Bamidele Awotunde, Taibat Bolanle Jimoh, Emmanuel Abidemi Adeniyi, Kazeem Moses Abiodun, Idowu Dauda Oladipo, and Muyideen Abdulraheem

6.1 Introduction ... 106
6.1.1 Objectives of the Chapter ... 108
6.1.2 Organization of the Chapter ... 108
6.2 Review of Higher Education for Sustainability ... 108
6.3 Importance of Online Teaching and Learning Technology Adoption during COVID-19 ... 110
6.3.1 Online Learning Sustainability ... 111
6.4 Instructional Strategies and Potential Implications for COVID-19 ... 113
6.4.1 Course Content ... 113
6.4.2 Learning Activities ... 114
6.4.3 Learning Supports ... 114
6.5 Information and Communication Technology (ICT)-Based Approach to Assist Education and Teaching during a Pandemic ... 115
6.5.1 Types of Online Learning ... 116
6.5.2 Commonly Used Online Learning Applications ... 117
6.6 The Application of Online Teaching and Learning during COVID-19: A Case Study in Nigeria ... 119
6.6.1 Methods and Materials ... 120
6.6.2 Results ... 121
6.7 Discussion of the Findings ... 123
6.7.1 Online Platforms Used in Teaching/Learning ... 123
6.7.2 Benefits of Online Platforms during COVID-19 Pandemic in Nigerian Universities ... 123
6.7.3 Challenges Related to Online Teaching and Learning ... 124
6.8 Conclusions and Future Scope ... 124
References ... 125

Chapter 7 Inclusiveness and Sustainability of Teaching and Learning Technologies amidst the COVID-19 Pandemic in Higher Education: An Indian Perspective ... 133

Anil Kumar and Subhanshu Goyal

7.1 Introduction ... 133
7.1.1 Objective of the Chapter ... 134
7.1.2 Organization of the Chapter ... 134

7.2 Quantitative View of COVID-19 Pandemic ... 134
7.3 Evolution of Web-Based Learning Systems ... 135
7.3.1 Latest Tools by Ed-Tech Companies ... 136
7.4 Paradigm Shift towards Online Learning ... 137
7.4.1 Government of India Initiatives ... 137
7.4.2 Initiatives of Indian States ... 141
7.5 Schemes of Higher Education ... 142
7.5.1 Rashtriya Uchatter Sikasha Abhiyan (RUSA) ... 142
7.5.2 Integration of Persons with Disabilities in the Mainstream ... 142
7.5.3 Pandit Madan Mohan Malviya Mission on Teachers and Training (PMMMNMTT) ... 142
7.6 National Education Policy 2020 and Sustainability in Technology-Driven Education ... 142
7.6.1 Overview of National Education Policy 2020 ... 142
7.6.2 Objectives of National Education Policy ... 143
7.6.3 Regulatory Bodies of Higher Education in India ... 144
7.6.4 Challenges before National Education Policy ... 145
7.7 Major Challenges and Gains due to Web-Based Learning ... 146
7.7.1 Digital Infrastructure ... 146
7.7.2 Uninterrupted Internet Connection ... 146
7.7.3 Digital Illiteracy and Lack of Motivation among Learners ... 147
7.7.4 Lack of Trained Teachers ... 147
7.7.5 Interaction and Engagement in E-Learning Environment ... 147
7.7.6 Evaluation and Feedback of Learning Process ... 147
7.7.7 Decline in Soft Skills of Learners ... 147
7.7.8 Practical Implementation through Virtual Labs ... 148
7.7.9 Lack of Comprehensive Educational Suite for the Web-Based Learning Model ... 148
7.8 Major Gains Due to Web-Based Learning ... 148
7.8.1 Anytime, Anywhere, Anyone Approach ... 148
7.8.2 Remove the Psychological Barriers between Tutor and Learner ... 148
7.8.3 Continuous Learning in Times of Crisis ... 148
7.8.4 Objective Evaluation of Learners and Prompt Feedback ... 149
7.8.5 Enhancing the International Dimension of Educational Services ... 149
7.9 Conclusion and Future Scope ... 149
References ... 149

Chapter 8 Framework to Integrate Education 4.0 to Enhance the E-Learning Model for Industry 4.0 and Society 5.0 ... 151

Aditya Kumar Gupta, Vivek Aggarwal, Vinita Sharma, and Mohd Naved

8.1 Introduction ... 151
8.1.1 Scope of the Study ... 152
8.1.2 Background of the Study ... 152
8.1.3 Objectives of the Study ... 152
8.1.4 Organization of the Chapter ... 153
8.2 Education 4.0 ... 153
8.2.1 Education 4.0 to Educational Innovation ... 153

8.3 Society 5.0 ... 154
8.3.1 Significance of Society 5.0 ... 155
8.3.2 Evolution of Society 1.0 to Society 5.0 ... 156
8.4 Theoretical Model for Online Teaching-Learning ... 156
8.4.1 Anderson's Model ... 156
8.4.2 An Integrated Framework for E-Learning ... 157
8.4.3 Effect of Industry 4.0 over Online Teaching-Learning Methods ... 158
8.5 Education 4.0 Framework ... 161
8.6 Evolution of Industry 1.0 to Industry 4.0 ... 162
8.7 LMS Systems Used in Technically Oriented Education ... 163
8.7.1 Chamilo ... 163
8.7.2 Google Classroom ... 164
8.7.3 Moodle ... 164
8.8 Conclusion and Future Scope ... 164
References ... 165

Chapter 9 Towards Digital Equity: Reimagining Digital Learning through the Lens of Bloom's Taxonomy ... 168

Chanel L. Fort and Samaa Haniya

9.1 Introduction ... 168
9.1.1 Organization of the Chapter ... 169
9.2 Evolution of the Knowledge Economy in the Information and Digital Age ... 169
9.2.1 The Digital Divide ... 170
9.2.2 The Digital Learner ... 172
9.3 The Need for Transformative Learning ... 173
9.4 Understanding Bloom's Contributions to Learning ... 174
9.5 Digital Equity through the Lens of Bloom's Taxonomy ... 175
9.5.1 Student Development ... 175
9.5.2 Faculty Development ... 176
9.5.3 Lifelong Organizational Learning and the Future of Work ... 178
9.6 New Perspectives of Bloom's Taxonomy ... 178
9.6.1 Opposing Perspective of Bloom's Cognitive Domain ... 178
9.6.2 Revision of Bloom's Taxonomy ... 179
9.7 Discussion ... 180
9.8 Conclusion and Future Scope ... 181
References ... 181

Chapter 10 The Empirical Investigation of Artificial Intelligence for Enhancing the Learner–Instructor Interaction towards Online Learning Using Multiple Regression Analysis ... 185

Ajay Sidana and Neeru Sidana

10.1 Introduction ... 185
10.1.1 Organization of the Chapter ... 187
10.2 Literature Review ... 187
10.2.1 Nature of AI in Learning ... 187
10.2.2 Impact of AI Implementation in Online Learning ... 189
10.2.3 The Negative Impact of AI Implementation in Learning ... 190

10.2.4 AI Implementation and the Instructor's Perspective 190
10.2.5 AI Implementation and the Learner's Perspective 193
10.2.6 Learner-Instructor Interactions 194
10.3 Research Methodology 195
10.4 Analysis and Interpretation 196
10.5 Discussion and Findings 199
10.6 Conclusion and Future Scope 200
References 200

Chapter 11 Effect of Digital Competence and Pedagogies on Gender Orientation of Pedagogues: A Quantitative Study with Regression Modeling of Higher Education Institutions 203

Muhammad Mujtaba Asad, Syeda Sumbul Shah, Prathamesh Churi, Norah Almusharraf, and Anand Nayyar

11.1 Introduction 203
11.1.1 Objectives of the Chapter 204
11.1.2 Organization of the Chapter 204
11.2 Problem Statement 204
11.3 Theoretical Framework 205
11.3.1 European Digital Competence Framework for Educators 205
11.4 Literature Review 208
11.5 Methodology 212
11.6 Results and Findings 212
11.7 Discussion 213
11.8 Conclusion and Future Scope 215
References 215

Chapter 12 Artificial Intelligence in Sustainable Education: Benefits, Applications, Framework, and Potential Barriers 219

V. Harish, Ravindra Sharma, Geeta Rana, and Anand Nayyar

12.1 Introduction 219
12.1.1 Objectives of the Chapter 220
12.1.2 Organisation of the Chapter 220
12.2 Literature Review 220
12.2.1 Historical Overview of Education: From Ancient Times to Modernity 220
12.2.2 Technology and Education 221
12.2.3 Significant Studies in the Area of AI in Sustainable Education 222
12.2.4 Additional Studies in 2022 223
12.3 Benefits of AI in Sustainable Education 223
12.4 Potential of AI to Solve Sustainability-Related Problems in Education 227
12.5 Applications of AI in Sustainable Education 228
12.6 Framework for Integrating AI into Sustainable Education: Meeting Future Demands 230
12.6.1 Needs Assessment and Goal Setting 230
12.6.2 Data Collection and Analysis 230
12.6.3 AI-Enabled Teaching and Learning 230

12.6.4 AI-Enabled Curriculum Development 230
12.6.5 AI-Enabled Resource Allocation 231
12.6.6 AI-Enabled Monitoring and Evaluation 231
12.6.7 Ethical Considerations 231
12.7 Potential Barriers of Implementing AI in Sustainable Education 232
12.8 Conclusion and Future Scope 233
References 234

Index 237

About the Editors

Dr. Joanna Rosak-Szyrocka, Assistant Professor, Erasmus+ coordinator at the Faculty of Management, Czestochowa University of Technology, Poland. She specialized in the fields of digitalization, industry 5.0, quality 4.0, education, IoT, AI, and quality management. She completed a research internship at the University of Żilina, Slovakia, and at Silesia University of Technology, Poland. Participant in multiple Erasmus+ teacher mobility programs: Italy, UK, Slovenia, Hungary, Czech Republic, Slovakia, and France. She held a series of lectures on Quality Management at universities in countries such as Great Britain, the Czech Republic, Slovakia, Slovenia, France, Hungary, and Italy. She cooperates with many universities both in the country (University of Szczecin, Rzeszów University of Technology, Silesian University of Technology), and abroad (including the University of Tabuk, Saudi Arabia; Széchenyi István University, Hungary; University Faisalabad, Pakistan; University of Humanities, China, University of Technology Sydney, Australia; Bucharest University of Economic Studies, Romania; and Federal University Dutse, Nigeria). Editorial Board: *Plos One, PeerJ*, and *IJQR* (ISSN 1800-6450). Reviewer Board: IJERPH MdPI (ISSN 1660-4601) IF: 4.614. Associate Editor for *Cogent Business and Management*, Taylor & Francis (ISSN: 2331-1975). Guest Editor of: Resources MdPI, IJERPH MdPI, Energies MdPI, Sustainability MdPI, *Springer Discover Sustainability Journal, Frontiers Journal*, and *Elsevier Measurement Journal*. Reviewer for a number of prestigious journals like IEEE, Elsevier, MdPI, Frontiers, Sage, and Emerald.

Justyna Żywiołek completed her master's studies in the field of metallurgy in 2010. In 2014, she defended her doctoral dissertation with honors in the field of management science, specializing in security science, titled: *The Impact of Information Process Management on the Security of Knowledge Resources in the Enterprise*, at the Faculty of Organization and Management of the Lodz University of Technology. Since January 2015, she has been working as an assistant professor at the Faculty of Management at the Technical University of Czestochowa. She is a respected researcher in Poland and abroad for her experience in management issues: knowledge and information management and their security. She has published over 160 articles and is the author/co-author/editor of seven books. She actively participated in presenting research results at various international conferences. She deals with data protection, is an inspector of personal data protection, and is a leading ISO 27001:2018 auditor. She is a member of ICAA (Intellectual Capital Association) and EU-OSHA, as well as in organizations operating in Poland promoting information and knowledge security. Guest editor of *Energies MDPI* and *International Journal of Environmental Research and Public Health MDPI*, and *Computer Modeling in Engineering and Sciences*. Early Career Editorial Board of the *Journal of Strategic Information Systems* (IF 14.682) and Editorial Advisory Board of *International Journal of Management and Applied Research* (IF 3.508). Participant in multiple Erasmus+ teacher mobility, including Slovenia, Hungary, Czech Republic, Slovakia and France.

Anand Nayyar received Ph.D (Computer Science) from Desh Bhagat University in 2017 in the area of Wireless Sensor Networks, Swarm Intelligence and Network Simulation. He is currently working in School of Computer Science-Duy Tan University, Da Nang, Viet Nam as **Assistant Professor, Scientist, Vice-Chairman (Research) and Director-IoT and Intelligent Systems Lab**. A Certified Professional with **100+ Professional certifications** from CISCO, Microsoft, Amazon, EC-Council, Oracle, Google, Beingcert, EXIN, GAQM, Cyberoam and many more. Published more than **150+ Research Papers** in various High-Quality ISI-SCI/SCIE/SSCI Impact Factor Journals cum Scopus/ESCI indexed Journals, 70+ Papers in International Conferences indexed with Springer, IEEE and ACM Digital Library, 40+ Book Chapters in various SCOPUS/WEB OF SCIENCE Indexed Books with Springer, CRC Press, Wiley, IET, Elsevier with Citations: **10500+, H-Index: 55 and I-Index: 200**. Member of more than 60+ Associations as Senior and Life Member including IEEE, ACM. He has authored/co-authored cum Edited **50+ Books of Computer Science**. Associated with more than 500+ International Conferences as Programme Committee/Chair/Advisory Board/Review Board member. He has 18 Australian Patents, 7 German Patents, 4 Japanese Patents, 34 Indian Design cum Utility Patents, 1 USA Patent, 3 Indian Copyrights and 2 Canadian Copyrights to his credit in the area of Wireless Communications, Artificial Intelligence, Cloud Computing, IoT and Image Processing. Awarded **44 Awards for Teaching and Research**—Young Scientist, Best Scientist, Best Senior Scientist, **Asia Top 50 Academicians and Researchers**, Young Researcher Award, Outstanding Researcher Award, Excellence in Teaching, Best Senior Scientist Award, **DTU Best Professor and Researcher Award-2019, 2020–2021, 2022** and many more. **He is listed in Top 2% Scientists as per Stanford University (2020, 2021, 2022)** and **Listed on Research.com (Top Scientist of Computer Science in Viet Nam-National Ranking: 2; D-Index: 31).** He is acting as Associate Editor for Wireless Networks (Springer), Computer Communications (Elsevier), International Journal of Sensor Networks (IJSNET) (Inderscience), Frontiers in Computer Science, PeerJ Computer Science, Human Centric Computing and Information Sciences (HCIS), Tech Science Press-CSSE, IASC, IET-Quantum Communications, IET Wireless Sensor Systems, IET Networks, IJDST, IJISP, IJCINI, IJGC, IJSIR. He is acting as Editor-in-Chief of IGI-Global, USA Journal titled "***International Journal of Smart Vehicles and Smart Transportation (IJSVST)***". He has reviewed more than 2500+ Articles for diverse Web of Science and Scopus Indexed Journals. He is currently researching in the area of Wireless Sensor Networks, Internet of Things, Swarm Intelligence, Cloud Computing, Artificial Intelligence, Drones, Blockchain, Cyber Security, Healthcare Informatics, Big Data and Wireless Communications.

Dr. Mohd Naved is a distinguished Associate Professor with an impressive career spanning over 16 years in the fields of Business Analytics, Data Science, and Artificial Intelligence. As an educator, Dr. Naved has consistently demonstrated a commitment to the highest standards of teaching and mentoring, ensuring that his students receive an education that is both cutting-edge and grounded in real-world experience. His dedication to helping students achieve their full potential extends beyond the classroom, as he has been an active participant in the university's Mentor-Mentee Program, providing guidance and support to over 150 undergraduate and postgraduate students. In addition to his teaching prowess, Dr. Naved has excelled in the areas of education management, research, and curriculum development. As a researcher, Dr. Naved has made significant contributions to the fields of Business Analytics, Data Science, and Artificial Intelligence, with over 80+ publications in reputed scholarly journals and books. His research focuses on the applications of these disciplines in various industries, and he has supervised numerous research projects and dissertations, guiding students to successful outcomes.

Contributors

Abdulraheem, Muyideen
University of Ilorin
Kwara State, Ilorin, Nigeria

Abiodun, Kazeem Moses
Landmark University
Omu Aran, Nigeria

Adeniyi, Emmanuel Abidemi
Landmark University
Omu Aran, Nigeria

Aggarwal, Vivek
Galgotias University
Uttar Pradesh, India

Ajamu, Gbemisola Janet
Landmark University
Omu Aran, Nigeria

Almusharraf, Norah
Prince Sultan University
Riyadh, Saudi Arabia

Asad, Muhammad Mujtaba
Sukkur IBA University
Pakistan

Awotunde, Joseph Bamidele
University of Ilorin
Kwara State, Ilorin, Nigeria

Biyiri, E.W.
Rajarata University of Sri Lanka
Sri Lanka

Churi, Prathamesh
Mukesh Patel School of Technology Management and Engineering
Mumbai, India

Dahanayake, S.N.S.
Rajarata University of Sri Lanka
Sri Lanka

Fort, Chanel L.
Pepperdine University
Malibu, California

Goyal, Subhanshu
Marwadi University
Gujarat, India

Gupta, Aditya Kumar
AIBS, Amity University
Noida, India

Gupta, Ravi Kumar
Madan Mohan Malaviya University of Technology
India

Haniya, M.S. Samaa
Pepperdine University
Malibu, California

Harish, V.
PSG Institute of Management
Tamil Nadu, India

Jayasinghe, J.A.P.M.
Rajarata University of Sri Lanka
Sri Lanka

Jimoh, Taibat Bolanle
National Examinations Council, Ilorin Zonal Office
Kwara State, Ilorin, Nigeria

Khera, Diksha
Guru Gobind Singh Indraprastha University
India

Kumar, Anil
Deen Dayal Upadhyaya College, University of Delhi
India

Maheshwari, Udit
Madan Mohan Malaviya University of Technology
India

Naved, Mohd
School of Inspired Leadership (SOIL)
Gurgoan, India

Nayyar, Anand
Duy Tan University
Da Nang, Viet Nam

Oladipo, Idowu Dauda
University of Ilorin
Kwara State, Ilorin, Nigeria

R., Thiyagarajan
PSG Institute of Management
Tamil Nadu, India

Rana, Geeta
Swami Rama Himalayan University
Dehradun, India

Shah, Syeda Sumbul
Sukkur IBA University
Pakistan

Sharma, Ravindra
Swami Rama Himalayan University
Dehradun, India

Sharma, Vinita
AIBS, Amity University
Uttar Pradesh, India

Sidana, Ajay
Amity International Business School, Amity University
Noida, India

Sidana, Neeru
Amity International Business School, Amity University
Noida, India

Singh, Dhirendra Bahadur
Madan Mohan Malaviya University of Technology
India

Preface

Education is the most powerful weapon which you can use to change the world.

—Nelson Mandela

In an era of global climate action, higher education institutions may be essential in advancing sustainable development. Only a few of the more complex demands that higher education institutions must simultaneously fulfill are those of massification, globalization, marketization, and digitalization. University 4.0, which would use hybrid technologies and cooperative intelligence, would be an example of a "cognitive society". They become "a highly open environment—a hub for multiple communications, a node at the intersection of numerous networks" as a consequence. These communications, research projects, and development activities engage a wide range of outside partners in addition to academics and students. Education is the driving force behind advancing sustainability since it is a vital instrument for communication and the basis of the "sustainable attitude". The next generation of sustainability leaders must be developed by higher education institutions, who must also spearhead significant global, regional, and local initiatives and play a critical role in accomplishing the sustainable development goals.

The aim of the book is to present the situation of education both before and after the pandemic, together with its psychological effects after the pandemic. The authors analyze many different perspectives towards e-learning: students' intention, e-learning implementation, and using applications and artificial intelligence (AI) during lessons. The book is a reference point for readers to seriously think and research distance learning with regard to Industry 4.0 in order to improve education quality, university development, and knowledge management because the book provides solutions to various problems faced by universities that are of key importance to their functioning in the world of Society 5.0, Industry 4.0, and sustainability development environment.

The book consists of 12 chapters. Chapter 1 highlights the elements, benefits pathway, and implementation of hybrid learning. In addition, this chapter also identifies the tips for effective hybrid management and challenges in hybrid learning system. Chapter 2 intends to investigate the causes of the declining mental health of college students in Gorakhpur city, as well as implementation strategies, issues with online learning, and college students' perspectives on online learning during the epidemic. Chapter 3 seeks to examine, using its determinants, students' desire to continue using e-learning while enrolled in higher education institutions in the states of Punjab and Haryana. Chapter 4 evaluates various versions of Web 3.0 technology, reflects the application of Web 3.0 technologies in Education 4.0, and stresses on latest ICT technologies in order to enhance operational procedures and students' social presence in online higher education via a framework for social software use. Chapter 5 investigates how undergraduates perceive e-learning in relation to social presence, collaborative learning, online learning experience, and satisfaction. In addition, the chapter also illustrates the preferences of undergraduate students for e-learning and face-to-face learning. Chapter 6 discusses online teaching sustainability especially in higher institution during the COVID-19 pandemic, explores online learning strategies that can be deployed during a pandemic, stresses the significance of online learning during pandemic times, and discusses COVID-19's potential consequences for the education sector and instructional methodologies. Chapter 7 explores the various applications offered by Ed-Tech companies as an alternative to the physical mode of learning during the time of crisis as well as the schemes of the central and state government in India to aid and improve the online teaching-learning process. In addition, the chapter also highlights the benefits offered by web-based learning along with the challenges for inclusiveness of online learning by different colleges or/and universities from an Indian perspective. Chapter 8 investigates influence of Industry 4.0 on e-learning teaching and learning and explains Education 4.0 for new technology-based e-learning enhancement and stresses on Industry 4.0 and Society 5.0

integration in education for lifelong skills. Chapter 9 goes into great depth about diverse education reforms and throws light on creative strategies for utilizing Bloom's Taxonomy to improve educational equity. Chapter 10 illustrates how successful AI applications may simultaneously improve learner-instructor relationships and interactions while carrying out efficient online learning and suggests the potential uses of AI in education in the future. Chapter 11 identifies the level of digital competencies of male and female teachers at public universities of Pakistan and analyzes the effect of innovative pedagogies on developing male and female teacher's digital skills in public universities of Pakistan. Chapter 12 investigates the potential of AI in promoting sustainable education and learning; provides an overview of the various AI applications that can be used to promote sustainable practices, as well as the benefits and potential barriers associated with its adoption; discusses a variety of technologies and their potential applications in sustainable education, including individualized instruction, the creation of curricula, the evaluation of student progress, the distribution of resources, and environmental monitoring; and provides a framework for educational institutions to integrate AI into their teaching and learning processes, while also addressing the ethical and responsible use of AI to ensure that its adoption will not have unintended consequences.

We hope that the readers will like the book because it was written with passion and love for the education and learning process.

Joanna Rosak-Szyrocka
Justyna Żywiołek
Anand Nayyar
Mohd Naved

1 Hybrid Learning in Higher Education Institutions

Pathway, Implementation and Challenges

V. Harish and Thiyagarajan R.

1.1 INTRODUCTION

One of the most vital aspects of human civilization since ages is not only to gain skills and knowledge but also to transfer the gained skill and knowledge to future generations. One of the ways that the humans have adopted to achieve the above objective is learning, which is a situation where a qualified person imparts knowledge to others by lecture or by action or any other form. Learning in the past decades has prominently been an in-class and in-person, instructor-led phenomenon where the instructor/teacher imparts knowledge to a group of learners (Thornton & Raihani, 2008). Although this teaching-learning methodology has been proved effective for years, in recent years there have been significant changes in the system especially due to the advent of various technologies. The teaching-learning process no longer aims to stick to the physical presence of both the instructor and the learner but aims to offer a learning system wherein the learner and teacher can be apart while the transfer of the knowledge happens (Shadiev & Yang, 2020). The launch of distance learning has enabled learners to acquire the necessary knowledge from anywhere, and the drawback of geographical boundaries is being eliminated leading to a greater opportunity and increased flexibility.

The concept of learning from a distance has evolved across the globe as it provides an opportunity for people from different countries and regions to learn from the best instructors who are located elsewhere (Park & Shea, 2020). This concept of learning from a distance has been significantly supported by the advances in various digital platforms and technologies. Various technologies have facilitated the delivery of courses in various forms and has assisted in an improved and efficient system of delivery. While the learning from a distance mode has various benefits, it also has some serious drawbacks as it lacks the personal touch which helps in effective learning (Soto et al., 2019). This has resulted in combining the system of deliveries, where essentially the instructors use a combination of both physical teaching-learning as well as online instruction in order to deliver content. The term used for the adoption of physical as well as online delivered process is *hybrid learning* (Raes et al., 2020).

Hybrid learning is a combination of the distance learning mode and in-person class delivery (Ora et al., 2018). Hybrid learning offers huge potential not only in educational institutions but also among corporate learning and training institutes. While the educationalists were comprehending the various drawbacks of the hybrid learning methodology and were hesitant to adopt the new system of teaching-learning, the onset of Covid created a huge disruption across all industries and also in the field of education. While the educationalists were apprehensive of the drawbacks of the hybrid learning, the recent pandemic has made it clear that hybrid learning is the way forward (Li et al., 2021).

DOI: 10.1201/9781003425779-1

1.1.1 Objectives of the Chapter

The following are the objectives of the chapter:

- To understand the elements of hybrid learning;
- To understand the benefits of hybrid learning;
- To understand the hybrid learning pathway;
- To design a implementation roadmap for hybrid learning;
- To identify tips for effective hybrid learning engagement;
- And, to identify the challenges faced in the hybrid learning system.

1.1.2 Organization of the Chapter

The rest of the chapter is organized as follows: Section 1.2 deals with the need for hybrid learning, and section 1.3 elaborates the challenges faced in teaching and learning during the Covid pandemic. Section 1.4 elaborates the definition of hybrid learning; Section 1.5 illustrates literature review on the topic. Section 1.6 discusses the various elements involved in hybrid learning, and section 1.7 stresses the benefits of hybrid learning. Section 1.8 focuses on the hybrid learning pathway for educational institutions. Section 1.9 deals with the implementation roadmap of hybrid learning for higher educational institutions. Section 10 discusses various tips to improve hybrid learning for institutions and teachers. Section 1.11 discusses the various challenges in the hybrid learning system, and, finally section 1.12 concludes the chapter with future scope.

1.2 NEED FOR HYBRID LEARNING

The students of today are unique to the previous generation of students (Hwang, 2018). These students, commonly known as Gen Z, have not seen a world without computers and cannot imagine a world without internet and see these technologies as an integral part of them. They use mobile phones (or smartphones) constantly and feel very comfortable with the use of various applications on their phones (Serbanescu, 2022). They often resort to using the technologies for reading and educational purposes.

The Covid pandemic has disrupted the education system across the globe in a scale unheard of, impacting nearly 1.6 billion students and learners (Tadesse & Muluye, 2020). The Covid pandemic resulted in closure of educational institutions including schools, colleges, universities and all other learning institutions. The crisis further impacted the disparities by reducing the opportunities for learning, thereby creating a dent in the educational space. The disruption it has created is not a one-time affair and it has made a permanent impact on the process of teaching-learning (Burgess & Sievertsen, 2020).

Now with the pandemic curfews being relaxed, educational institutions worldwide are slowly transitioning from complete remote or online learning to back in the classroom, at the same time facing challenges such as following safety protocols making it challenging, with the biggest challenge being the constant danger of a mutant variant of Covid (Neuwirth et al., 2021). This forces government, educational institutions and all concerned stakeholders to think and develop a resilient and easy hybrid approach to the teaching-learning system (Zhao & Watterston, 2021). The challenges explode when they have to address the challenges of distance learning, such as student engagement with the existing challenges of infrastructure, scarcity of teachers and so on (Dumont & Raggo, 2018).

1.3 CHALLENGES IN TEACHING AND LEARNING DURING COVID

There were a lot of challenges faced by educational institutions, teachers and students resulting from the pandemic. The pandemic created a severe disruption in the education sector, and institutions had to resort to alternative ways to continue the teaching-learning process. Some of the challenges the pandemic created in education field are highlighted in Figure 1.1. and discussed as follows.

1.3.1 Paradigm Shift

There was a sudden shift for institutions with the announcement of lockdowns across countries. Lockdown led to a sudden stoppage of physical teaching, a process which people were comfortable with (Jena, 2020). There was a sudden stoppage in the functioning of educational institutions and this led instructors to jump into the unknown territory of online learning with limited or no know-how and infrastructure resources (Naik et al., 2021). There was no time to prepare or experiment with the system resulting in lots of mistakes. The institutions and instructors had to get ready for a different way of delivery in a short span of time. This sudden shift not only created the geographic space but also resulted in changes in the entire teaching process, such as preparation, delivering, assessment, and grading and conducting tests (Rashid & Yadav, 2020).

1.3.2 Aspiring for Interaction

The traditional teaching-learning system has always stood on the foundation of the interaction between the teacher and the student. There has been a constant need for interaction and variety for students with faculty for better understanding (Li et al., 2019). Online education created a distance in the form of pre-recorded lectures or virtual sessions, thereby reducing interaction and motivation, resulting in low student engagement. The digital tools were quite monotonous for the students, and to listen to the same kind of delivery became boring for the students after a few days (Johnson et al., 2018). Even certain innovative features such as breakout rooms did not give the required interaction for the students. In spite of all the tools, students and teachers felt that the levels of communication, engagement and interaction were severely limited. Irrespective of all the efforts by teachers in aiming to integrate various tools and approaches, the students always felt that it was ineffective (Mumford & Dikilitaş, 2020).

1.3.3 Paucity of Infrastructure and Resources

Teachers and students were finding it difficult to adjust to the new way of learning on the onset of the pandemic due to the sudden shift in the mode of the delivery, but they also had a different kind

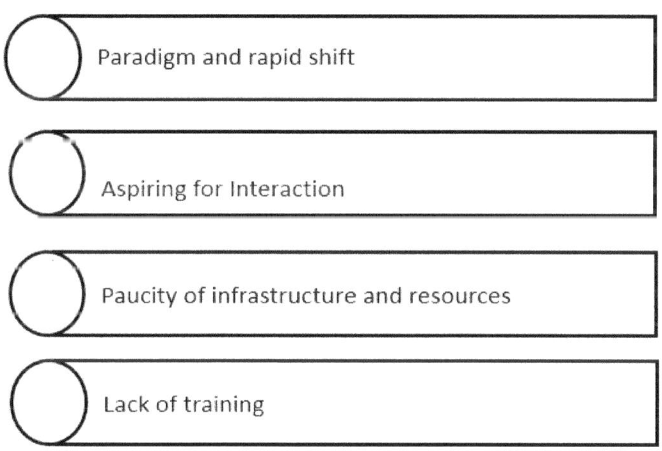

FIGURE 1.1 Challenges in teaching and learning during Covid.

of problem, which is more of an institutional challenge (Shirrell et al., 2019). As much as there are a lot of studies and literature works in the pre-Covid times, a majority of the institutions were unprepared for the new norm. There were huge gaps seen in terms of the teacher's preparedness as they had little or no training in using online resources; as also, there were severe shortages in terms of infrastructure and technology (Ma & Hall, 2018). Some of the common challenges faced were inadequate internet bandwidth, lack of cameras, headsets and proper workspace at home using the various digital methodologies.

1.3.4 Lack of Training

The sudden onset of the Covid pandemic was a massive jolt to the teaching community more so than the student community. This was primarily because before the pandemic there was a lot of apprehension in going for online education or hybrid learning. There was a scarcity of resources, infrastructure and institutions; in addition, faculty did not feel the need to undergo training.

1.4 HYBRID LEARNING

Hybrid learning can be explained as a teaching-learning approach which combines in-person face-to-face learning and online learning with the objective of improving student engagement and experience (Bennett et al., 2020). The advent of internet in the educational arena has impacted the traditional learning set-up. The objective of hybrid learning is to combine the face-to-face traditional education and the new age, internet-based system in order to reap the benefits of both. The content, assessment and delivery of the content is designed in such a way that it combines both physical teaching and an engaging online mode of teaching and learning (Sulistyanto, 2021).

Hybrid learning has been explained by different researchers in different contexts in different situations, and some of them are as follows. Hybrid learning is the process of integrating both traditional and internet-based online systems (Rao, 2019). In general, it is the mix of instruction (online or self-paced study), delivering the content (classroom as well as live or recorded online classes) and adopting various internet-based technologies (which can include both synchronous as well as asynchronous tools) to teach. There is no distinctive definition of hybrid learning as the choice of what resources to use and how much of technology is to be used, which part of the delivery should be face-to-face and how much should happen online; these factors all depend on the teacher, the students and the environment (Hariadi et al., 2019). Figure 1.2 highlights the components of hybrid learning.

1.5 LITERATURE REVIEW: HYBRID LEARNING

Table 1.1 illustrates literature review from various authors in Hybrid Learning. Sorden (2012) defined hybrid teaching and learning not only as a combination of online teaching-learning and

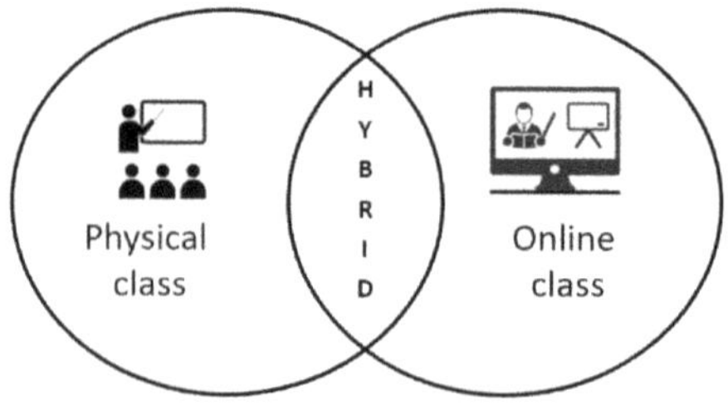

FIGURE 1.2 Components of hybrid learning.

face-to-face learning but also as combining trading methodologies using appropriate delivery models to achieve a higher level of teaching-learning outcomes. There have been various definitions given by many researchers resulting in varied understanding of the concept of hybrid teaching and learning. A common understanding of the term explains hybrid learning as a methodology which combines both in-person physical class and remote learning (Aristika & Juandi, 2021). Remote learning refers to teachers teaching students through online or remote instruction which are dealt simultaneously. This means that the students learn a part of their course face-to-face in a physical class setup while they do a greater part of their course online, which can be synchronous and/or asynchronous (Dumont & Raggo, 2018).

Some researchers used the terms *hybrid learning* and *blended learning* interchangeably. For example, Boora et al. (2010) used the terms synonymously as, according to them, both teaching processes adopt a combination of online and physical activities. Other researchers distinguish the terms. According to (Nortvig 2013), hybrid learning is a process where there is simultaneous application of physical class and online teaching, whereas a blended learning scenario refers to the asynchronous method of teaching and learning. Hybrid learning has various benefits over traditional teaching and blended learning as it incorporates an in-person learning experience (Fadde & Vu, 2014).

Hybrid learning refers to the mixing of the two different learning situations, the physical classroom and the online experience. Hybrid learning has been defined as a mix of face-to-face learning where the teacher and the students are in the same physical place, where they meet, discuss and the teacher imparts knowledge to the student, while the students at the same time also access educational resources through online and digital platforms that are contributed/posted by the teacher. This flexible and personalized learning model with a combination of online as well as offline learning allows students to access materials at their own pace, accommodating various learning styles and schedules (Grant & Cheon, 2007). Hybrid learning provides an atmosphere where the student can explore and learn the content that is supported through an online learning experience. Hybrid learning clubs the physical learning experience with the online content delivery system. The objective of having a hybrid learning approach is to provide an effective teaching-learning experience by mixing the two delivery methods (Burgess & Sievertsen, 2020).

The hybrid learning methodology involves a system which facilitates one set of students attending the class in person and another set of students attending the same class in an online mode or in a virtual mode (Bennett et al., 2020). Hybrid learning involves both synchronous and asynchronous learning methods based on the teacher's preference. Synchronous learning refers to students attending classes and learning at the same time as the instructor teaches. Although the class happens online, the instructor and the students interact in live sessions. As in the case of on-campus studies, students must read and prepare for the online class and then come together and meet with the teacher for efficient discussion (Mumford & Dikilitaş, 2020). There is a lot of planning involved in having a synchronous learning session for a class to be more meaningful. The discussion becomes a two-way interaction, where the teacher instructs the online live classes, and at certain times students might make presentations and discuss.

In the case of asynchronous learning the student has a flexibility to learn on their own schedule, and class assignments must be completed within a specific timeframe. A student will be given the access to the recorded lectures, the assignments given and reading materials at any time within the specific time duration. The asynchronous form of learning has many benefits. For example, a student has total flexibility to learn at any time of their choice. The student need not attend the class at the same time as when the faculty is teaching or when their classmates are studying (Olt, 2018). The student has a choice to view the recorded sessions as many times as desired and have the subject clarified. There are certain drawbacks to asynchronous learning as well. For example, the student does not get a chance to interact with the teacher and clarify their doubts. The student also misses the feel of a classroom experience and the peer learning aspect (Rao, 2019). Hybrid learning often uses a mix of both asynchronous and synchronous

TABLE 1.1
Literature Review—Hybrid Learning

No.	Author(s)	Year	Context of the Research	Respondents	Research Design	Research Objective
1	Rasmussen	2003	Hybrid teaching-learning	6 (remote) + 11 (face-to-face)	Qualitative case study	Quantity and quality of human interaction between instructor and students
2	Grant & Cheon	2007	Hybrid teaching in higher education institutions using both audio and video in blended classes	18 (video) + 11 (audio)	Mixed-method	How video conferencing affects teaching and learning
3	Shen et al.	2008	Distance learning classroom	250 (on campus) + 750 (online)	Mixed-method	Evaluation of students' experiences
4	McGovern & Barnes	2009	Hybrid teaching-learning—PG program in healthcare	16	Mixed-method	Impact of the virtual classroom on learning
5	White et al.	2010	Hybrid teaching-learning among higher education institutions	10	Mixed-method	Feasibility of delivering a course on-campus and virtually at the same time
6	Hastie et al.	2010	Hybrid teaching-learning among two institutions in two countries		Qualitative study	Explains the nine modes of synchronous hybrid learning
7	Stewart et al.	2011	Hybrid teaching-learning	46 (graduate students)	Mixed-method	Evaluates students' online learning experiences
8	Wiles & Ball	2013	Hybrid teaching-learning among undergraduate students	3707	Longitudinal mixed-methods	Elaborates hybrid learning benefits and challenges
9	Roseth et al.	2013	Hybrid teaching-learning in a doctoral seminar		Conceptual study	Various pedagogical choices in a hybrid teaching system
10	Fadde & Vu	2014	Hybrid teaching-learning in a graduate level course	15 (sem 1) + 13 (sem 2)	Mixed-method	Students' preference for hybrid learning setup
11	Nortvig	2013	Hybrid teaching-learning bachelor program in Denmark		Conceptual study	Impact of hybrid learning on teachers and students
12	Noesgaard & Ørngreen	2015	Hybrid teaching-learning bachelor program		Qualitative case study	Challenges and barriers in hybrid learning
13	Renner et al.	2015	Hybrid teaching-learning in adult learning	10 + 26	Mixed-method	Experiences of students and teachers in hybrid learning
14	Ramsey et al.	2016	Hybrid teaching-learning in a public university	19	Mixed-method	Hybrid learning experiences of students

15	Lightner & Lightner-Laws	2016	Remote classroom in higher education		Empirical study	How environmental factors impact student learning experience
16	Szeto & Cheng	2016	Remote classroom	28	Qualitative case study	Students' hybrid learning experiences
17	Lakhal et al.	2017	Hybrid teaching-learning in higher education		Review study	Advantages, barriers, influencing factors
18	Zhang & Zhu	2017	Hybrid teaching-learning		Mixed-method	Identifying categories of hybrid learning
19	Romero-Hall and Vicentini	2017	Hybrid teaching-learning at graduate level	3	Qualitative case study	Effectiveness and efficiency of hybrid learning
20	Wang et al.	2018	Hybrid teaching-learning	24 (graduate students)	Design-based research	Benefits, barriers and suggestions on pedagogical methods for hybrid learning
21	Liu et al.	2018	Hybrid teaching-learning at four universities		Case study	Technologies assisting course development and delivery across locations
22	Olt	2018	Hybrid teaching-learning	9 (remote)	Qualitative case	Phenomenon of adopting hybrid learning from remote participants' perspective
23	Zydney et al.	2019	Hybrid teaching-learning at two universities		Multiple case study	Explains varied models, approaches and best practices
24	Aristika & Juandi	2021	Hybrid teaching—teacher-student relationship	2 classes, 40 per group	Quasi-experimental design	Relationship of teacher and students in terms of learning motivation in hybrid learning setup
25	Liu et al.	2020	Hybrid teaching	Teachers (76) and students (163)	Mixed method	Pedagogy for hybrid teaching in arts setup
26	Mutmainnah et al.	2021	Hybrid teaching	10 students and teachers	Mixed method–qualitative method	Perceptions of English teachers and students in hybrid learning
27	Pavlidou et al.	2021	Hybrid teaching-learning in business education	74 students	Mixed method	Knowledge dimensions perspective in business education setup
28	Rahim et al.	2022	Hybrid teaching in school	84 students and 5 teachers	Mixed method	Effectiveness of using Google Classroom in hybrid learning
29	Ironsi	2023	Hybrid teaching-learning	70 students	Mixed method	Mixed method efficacy in improving writing skills

learning approaches based on the teacher's preference, the infrastructure available, the student's needs and so on.

1.6 ELEMENTS OF HYBRID LEARNING

Hybrid learning adopts various elements from the traditional or physical classroom teaching-learning scenario and also includes some new elements into the ecosystem to facilitate the process. Figure 1.3 highlights both traditional and new elements on hybrid learning.

1.6.1 Traditional Elements

Hybrid learning includes certain traditional elements of the conventional classroom learning such as the following:

Students: As an integral part of the educational system, students have needs and requirements that must be kept in mind at all times, especially when designing a course, be it a physical class or a hybrid class (Nortvig, 2013).

Teachers: As the content developers and the content delivery people, teachers are the critical resources required for an efficient teaching-learning system. The delivery aspect has been evolving from physical mode to blended learning with various new technologies coming in. The teachers will have to be trained and made comfortable in using the various technologies (Liu et al., 2010).

Curriculum: Curriculum design and the delivery of the curriculum are crucial factors in the success or failure of the teaching-learning process. The curriculum for a hybrid course will have to be modified for the hybrid learning process. The curriculum design should be drafted such that it meets the requirements of the students (Ma & Hall, 2018).

Education regulators and administrative bodies: These play an important role in providing the necessary guidelines for educational institutions in order to maintain a standard and quantity in the education field. They play a critical role in drafting policies and guidelines to pave the way for higher educational institutions in meeting the standards (Ironsi, 2021).

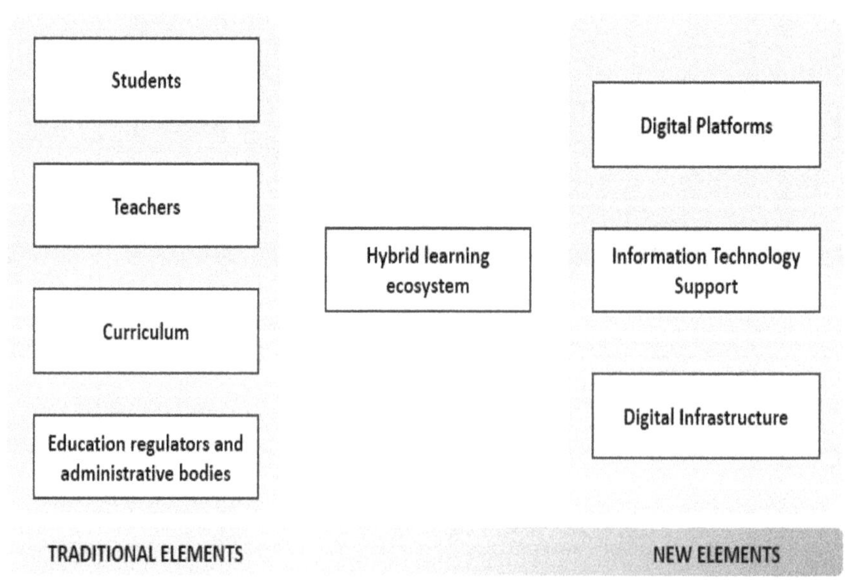

FIGURE 1.3 Elements of hybrid learning.

1.6.2 New Elements

With the development of various technologies, certain new elements have been added as a part of the education system. These elements have been introduced in a short span of time and have become integral parts of the education system today across the world.

Digital platforms: The curriculum or the knowledge transfer has to happen through a medium, unlike in a physical class where it happens face-to-face. Digital platforms such as Webex, Google Meet, and Zoom play the role of the medium where the knowledge transfer happens. They serve as the means of delivery and thus become crucial in the hybrid teaching-learning scenario (Jena, 2020).

Information technology support: The foundation for a digital platform is the required information technology support. The information technology team manages the various digital platforms and ensures they are used in an optimized way. The team must also ensure that these digital platforms and tools functions continuously without any hindrances (Aristika & Juandi, 2021).

Digital infrastructure: The adequacy of the necessary infrastructure is to be monitored and validated by the digital infrastructure team. The team enables and monitors the usage of the various digital tools and technologies. It also ensures that there is adequate network bandwidth to ensure a fast and reliable network connection to facilitate hybrid teaching and learning (Hwang, 2018).

1.7 BENEFITS OF HYBRID LEARNING

Figure 1.4 highlights the benefits of hybrid learning and all the benefits are enlightened as follows:

- *Convenience and flexibility*
  One of the most cited benefits of hybrid learning is the convenience it offers. It moves away from the strict requirements of date, place and time. One can work at their own convenience, thereby they are able to manage many responsibilities and tasks (Hastie et al., 2010). The student can learn from the convenience of their home or office or anywhere else at a time suitable for them.
- *Low cost*
  Hybrid teaching is a relatively low-cost model of education when compared to physical classes as it can reach out to many students at the same time. It also provides the

FIGURE 1.4 Benefits of hybrid learning.

necessary connection and interaction as needed, and can negate the costs incurred by both the student and the institution. There has been a boom of technologies which have reduced the costs of tools to teach and learn in the online space with minimum disturbance to the stakeholders (Johnson et al., 2018).

- *Reduced travel*
  On the same lines of convenience and flexibility, another advantage is the reduced travel needed by teachers and students. When classes happen in both modes, both online and offline, the commute for the teachers and the students is reduced considerably. This not only saves time for the commuters but also improves on the sustainability front (Li et al., 2021).
- *Learning does not stop within the walls*
  In the case of the traditional classroom, the teaching-learning process stops once the class is over, whereas in the case of hybrid learning the teaching-learning is not confined to the physical classroom but can happen even once the class is over. This can happen by teacher-student engagement even after class hours (Rahim et al., 2022). A great advantage of the hybrid system is that learning after the class hours need not happen only with the teacher but also can happen with peers and classmates. This engages all the students and helps in better understanding of the concepts taught.
- *Effective and engaging*
  The biggest advantage that the hybrid teaching-learning can provide is the effective and engaging learning that it can offer, which ultimately provides deeper learning for the student. Many researchers have complimented the benefits of the hybrid learning system across different levels of institutions (Rao, 2019). Many of the studies conclude that the students felt at ease and also acknowledged that the hybrid form of learning was the most effective form of learning for them.
- *Making the best of both worlds*
  Another advantage of hybrid learning is the variety it has to offer in the form of delivery of classes. While the theory part of the course could be dealt online, the much more required hands-on application of the concepts can happen in person for much more effective delivery and provides opportunity for clarification and better tutoring (Rashid & Yadav, 2020). Hybrid learning provides the best of both worlds of physical classroom session and an online classroom session, thereby bringing a great deal of benefit for both the teacher and the student.
- *Anytime anywhere access*
  Hybrid learning offers the student to access study materials anytime and anywhere. This provides the opportunity for the student to learn at their comfort and choice and is not restricted by the lack of access to study materials. This results in a better learning experience for the student (Rao, 2019).

1.8 HYBRID LEARNING PATHWAY

Implementing a hybrid learning system involves a structured approach with a continuous effort to monitor and adjust continuously. Institutions will have to undergo a structured process in order to achieve excellence. The following are the key steps in the hybrid learning pathway:

- Understand and conceive;
- Determine and design;
- Planned execution;
- Evaluate and act.

1.8.1 Understand and Conceive

The instructor first has to make an assessment of the of the requirements and the existing capabilities of the learners in order to have an effective hybrid system. The steps involved in the process of understand and conceive are as follows:

- Determine the foundation principles for a hybrid strategy:
  - Should the course be designed for today or considering the future?
  - Should the delivery be self-paced or class paced?
  - Should the curriculum be easy or heavy on the student?
- Make an assessment of the student's requirements for a hybrid learning approach;
- Make an assessment of the student's remote access and the efficiency of the system;
- Make an assessment of the teacher's capability to teach in a hybrid way;
- Make an assessment of the infrastructure (physical and online technologies);
- Make an assessment of the environmental factors such as internet bandwidth, budget availability and so on.

1.8.2 Determine and Design

The instructor in assistance with the team will have to build the hybrid teaching and learning model in a way so that it minimizes the impact of the disruption in the existing system. Some of the key points to consider in this stage would be:

- Which part of the course should be prioritized and how to manage to different segments of the class;
- Which segments of the course grading are to be done in person and which ones online;
- How to address the question of tackling the weaker sections of the class;
- Decide on the final course content, delivery aspect and evaluation criteria.

1.8.3 Planned Execution

The most important aspect in the implementation of the hybrid learning is the execution phase, as this is the stage in which all the issues and the barriers crop up and solutions are to be arrived at. The operationalizing of the hybrid teaching-learning method brings new challenges, and it should be ensured that the risks are managed in an effective way. Some of the important aspects of the operational part of the hybrid learning would be what aspects of the educational system would be online and which part would be offline, when do the different modes happen, who are the faculty who will be instrumental in making it happen, and how will it happen.

Some of the points to be determined in this stage would be as follows:

- Decide which courses or content will be taught in physical class and which will be taught virtually;
- Establish the priorities of the content in terms of delivery and evaluation;
- Ensure the teething problems are addressed to ensure minimum disturbance in the system;
- Provide the necessary teachers, training and infrastructure.

1.8.4 Evaluate and Act

As many institutions and key stakeholders are new to the concept of hybrid learning, there has to be a proper monitoring mechanism to make necessary refinements to improve the learning process. This becomes an important aspect as it assists in evaluating the hybrid teaching-learning experience from the teachers and the students and making necessary improvements in order to improve the efficiency of the system. Two important aspects are:

- Monitoring the key parameters of hybrid learning from both the teacher and student's perspective;
- Making necessary refinements or adjustments to adopt a continuous improvement philosophy to meet the requirements of the stakeholders.

1.9 IMPLEMENTATION ROADMAP OF HYBRID LEARNING

There are certain steps which an institution has to follow while implementing hybrid learning approach. Figure 1.5 highlights the steps for successful implementation of hybrid learning.

- *Start with a big bang*
  The first step in launching a hybrid learning system is to start with a specific problem to be resolved or the objective that is to be met. The hybrid learning programs are often successful if they are started to resolve a problem faced by institutions, teachers and students. Once the specific problems or the objectives to be achieved are defined, the next stage is to develop a goal that is based on the "SMART" principles. SMART stands for "Specific, Measurable, Actionable, Realistic and Time specific". Unless goals are not specific and measurable, they become difficult to achieve.
- *Form a team*
  Having the right team is one of the most important criteria in order to be successful in creating and delivering a quality and robust hybrid team. The team composition should be a mix of subject matter experts and people understanding the technology part. This team must work on the pedagogical aspects of teaching the course in a hybrid way, and also address the problems that require architectural changes in the system itself. This can be implemented only by people who have the necessary authority to make strong decisions. There is also a need to have a dynamic team to experiment with notional aspects such as allocating staff, the budget allocation and the scheduling of the delivery.
- *Motivate stakeholders*
  In the designing of the hybrid learning system, one of the most important factors to be considered is to design a system which motivates the stakeholders, namely the students

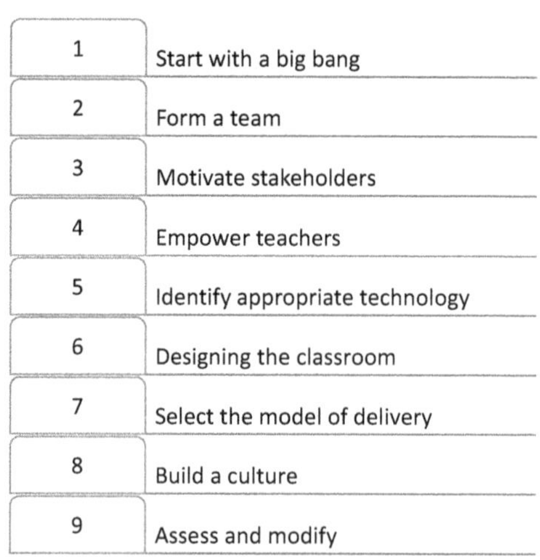

FIGURE 1.5 Implementation steps for hybrid learning.

and the teacher. In order to do this, their requirements have to be understood. There has to be clear conception of what the students want and what the teachers want, and the gap has to be bridged. The design has to be in such a way that it can integrate the experiences of the stakeholders to provide a rich teaching-learning experience. The final hybrid model should integrate the various teaching-learning resources and the operational part of the online and offline classroom experience, which will motivate the stakeholders.

- *Empower teachers*
  The success of any hybrid teaching-learning system greatly depends on the level of interaction of the teacher and the students. This is largely driven by the teacher's role and their capabilities. This can be achieved by finding ways to improve the satisfaction levels of the teachers by empowering them. Their satisfaction can be improved by working on factors such as recognition given, responsibilities assigned to them, growth prospects and support offered. Institutions should find an optimized way to integrate these factors into the hybrid learning program. Empowered teachers will be in a better position to provide a better and enriching experience to the students.
- *Identify appropriate technology*
  With the onset of Covid on one side and the technology advancements on the other side, there has been a flood of various technologies and tools available in the market. Educational institutions will have to rely on technology experts to understand what is the right technology for them. More often than not, institutions select a technology that is a misfit and do not reap the expected benefits, which leads to disinterest in adoption of new technology. This process will have to be given enough thought, and it is always better to have own content as well as own infrastructure. A specific technology has to be adopted not because of the availability of the technology or because others have implemented, but the technology is to be adopted as it would satisfy the need of the institution or solve a problem.
- *Designing the classroom*
  The classroom should be designed in such a way that it promotes the hybrid learning program. The physical classroom should align with the requirements of the teachers and the students. The classroom should facilitate the expectations of the student and the teacher. The classrooms of hybrid learning can have tables and desks that are movable in order to provide an atmosphere conducive for efficient teaching and learning. The infrastructure should be such that it is adaptable for both face-to-face teaching and learning as well as virtual teaching. The classroom should be flexible to incorporate changes and not be fixed as in the case of the physical classroom.
- *Select the model of delivery*
  There are various types of models of delivery in a hybrid learning approach, such as:
  - *The homework approach*: In this model the teachers teach at the institution and the students are given practice work to be completed after physical class, supported by the teacher.
  - *Flipped classroom*: This model works in the opposite way as the homework model. In the flipped classroom the students learn about the concepts in their home and practice the concepts at the institutions under the review of the teacher.
  - *Synchronous class*: This follows a mix of class where the instructor teaches some of the students in the class in physical mode while some students attend the same session virtually at the same time.
  - *Asynchronous class*: This model adopts from the flipped model and the homework model in which the online aspect happens asynchronously. This is done usually by recording the sessions or instructions of the teacher which can be used as a reference by the student later.

- *Completely remote learning*: This model adopts a strategy where the student completely learns the course in an online way with a mix of both synchronous and asynchronous learning.

  The institution and the teacher together will have to identify the model best suited for them and their students. Each of the models has certain benefits and disadvantages, and based on the needs and requirements, a proper mix has to be adopted to provide a rich experience for the student and teacher.

- *Build a culture*

  Institutions will have to create a strong culture in order to support the hybrid learning system. A hybrid culture can be useful if it provides the students more flexibility and control over the learning process. The benefit of creating a culture is that it can help in resolving the common and recurring issues in an efficient way. The culture of an organization cannot be built in a short span of time but will have to evolve over a period of time, and care should be taken to ensure that it does not poison the organization's workspace.

- *Assess and modify*

  An efficient hybrid learning system can be built only over a period of time as it can evolve as a process and cannot be a one-time affair. The process will have to start and continuously monitored and adapted continuously. Over a period of time there will be many challenges encountered, and they will have to be addressed and refined constantly aiming at continuous improvement process. Institutions will have to adopt the "plan-do-check-act" philosophy in order to improve the system.

1.10 TIPS TO EFFECTIVE HYBRID LEARNING ENGAGEMENT

Figure 1.6 enlightens the tips to improve hybrid learning engagement which are illustrated as follows:

1. *Have an alternative plan*

   It is a good practice to have an alternative plan that will work when synchronous learning fails at some point in time. The student should not be left stranded due to a technical glitch or technology failure. There always has to be an alternative plan in the form of content in the campus learning management system (LMS) or the institution's web portal or any other place where the remote student can access the content and thereby does not feel left out.
2. *Adopt synchronous as well as asynchronous learning together*

   While a hybrid learning approach should incline towards synchronous learning, spending more together, it should be designed to incorporate asynchronous learning as well. The student should be given time to understand the content and do the preparatory work that will enable them to participate in an engaged manner in the hybrid learning process.
3. *Have a tested, clear course plan*

   The course plan for a hybrid learning class will have to be a detailed one with very clear instructions, especially for the asynchronous part of the class. The instruction, unlike in the case of a physical class where there is the constant presence of the teacher to guide the students, has to be clear so that the students can understand and perform the required tasks as needed. Try out the course plan with a small group to test its effectiveness and then deploy to a larger group.
4. *Ensure you have the right technology promoting interaction*

   There has to be a right technology adopted to facilitate interaction and the devices have to be tested to check the audio and video feeds so that the students are able to see and hear and—more importantly—can be seen and heard in the classroom. This becomes critical as this will ensure a high level of interaction and engagement among students. Constant feedback has to be obtained during the sessions and post sessions for the effectiveness of the hybrid learning system.

1	Have an alternative plan
2	Adopt synchronous as well as asynchronous learning together
3	Have a tested, clear course plan
4	Ensure you have the right technology promoting interaction
5	Project your screen and see students as well
6	Ensure all students are on video call instead of audio call
7	Use engaging tools as chat, breakout rooms, etc.
8	Have a robust network connection
9	Ensure a strong thinking process for students
10	Have a session wise course plan given well ahead to students
11	Ensure interactive teaching plans
12	Often have conference calls with individuals or small groups of online students
13	Give specific attention for online students
14	Learn continuously
15	Have fun

FIGURE 1.6 Tips to improve hybrid learning engagement.

5. *Project your screen and see students as well*
   One of the most important element in the hybrid learning is the ability to see the students and the students get to see the teacher and their classmates who have opted for physical class. The teacher before the class has to ensure that the screen is working and the students are able to see and hear the teacher clearly. Without the video feeds the effectiveness and the engagement of the students drop drastically.
6. *Ensure all students are on video call instead of audio call*
   Experience indicates that the engagement level as well as the understanding of the student's increase when there is video call instead of audio calls. The teacher will have to ensure that the teacher as well as the students are available on video feed on a continuous basis. This will provide instant feedback for the teacher and also have a great enriching experience for the student.
7. *Use engaging tools as chat, breakout rooms, etc.*
   The teacher, apart from getting all students on video, can also engage the students by using chat features in the platform adopted for online or hybrid learning. The student can either discuss one on one or in small groups using features such as breakout rooms or chats. By doing this the teacher can engage the remote students who are distracted and/or not clear in the concept.
8. *Have a robust network connection*
   One of the basic requirements of the entire premise of hybrid learning is a robust internet connection to engage in video calls. In the absence of a high-speed internet connection the whole system of hybrid learning will fail, as the students might not be in a position to

hear and see what the teacher is doing. The disturbance in the connection or the delay in the relay will create a negative impact for the learner as well as the teacher.

9. *Ensure a strong thinking process for students*

   Teachers have always inclined into having meaningful discussions in the physical space and this practice will also have to extend into the hybrid world also. Teachers should encourage students to document and work collaboratively by sharing their work. This will develop the thinking process of the students, which is critical for the student development. The teachers will have to inculcate a framework which will enable the students to think more and work as a team.

10. *Have a session-wise course plan given well ahead to students*

    To make the student more comfortable and ease the students' minds, it becomes important to share what is in store for the student or what is to be expected. The teacher can share with the class what the plan of study is upfront so that the student can prepare and the teacher can also at the beginning of the class spell out the agenda for the day or session. This will help the students to plan and prepare for the class.

11. *Ensure interactive teaching plans*

    The entire teaching process has to be designed in such a way that it has to be interactive. A hybrid teaching process cannot happen monotonously and should be designed so that it is interactive. In order to achieve this the teachers will have to think of the same from the inception of designing the course. The teaching plans or the course plan will have to embed ways and mechanisms that ensure that the student remains interactive in the sessions.

12. *Have frequent conference calls with individuals or small groups of online students*

    There has to be periodic validations or checks done by the teacher to understand the pulse of the students, especially the ones taking the remote sessions. By getting instant feedback there can be corrections made by the teacher as well as identify slow learners or the ones having difficulty in understanding or having any technical difficulties and offer customized support where ever possible and required. This will improve the student experience to a great level.

13. *Give specific attention to online students*

    While all students will have to be dealt with equally, in the case of hybrid learning the teacher will have to pay little bit more attention to the students who engage online or study remotely. This can be done by allocating some time at the end of the class for the students who are studying online and can use the time to take their questions and resolve their issues. This will reduce the imbalance between the students studying in physical class and those studying online.

14. *Learn continuously*

    When trying or experimenting something it becomes always important that learning is the most important outcome achieved. This is more relevant and applicable to teachers where they have to take each opportunity to learn from what they are doing correctly as well as the mistakes they have made so that they can learn from their mistakes and continue what they are doing correctly. The teachers as well as the institutions will have to learn continuously in order to make significant progress and improvement in the hybrid learning system.

15. *Have fun*

    The final tip for an efficient hybrid learning system is for teachers as well as students to have fun on the go. It is imperative that there will be technology failures, disturbances and slow network connections but the stakeholders will have to manage on the go and ensure that they have fun and enjoy the experience.

1.11 CHALLENGES IN HYBRID LEARNING SYSTEM

While the hybrid learning system boasts of many benefits, it also has certain challenges for the teachers and learners. These challenges can be classified into two broad categories as the challenges that are faced by the institution or the teacher and the challenges faced by the student as shown in Figure 1.7.

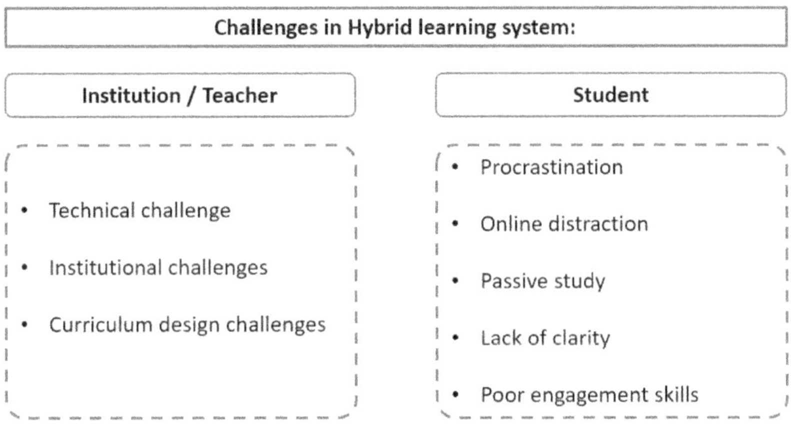

FIGURE 1.7 Challenges in hybrid learning system.

- *Challenges faced by the institution/teacher*

There are a set of challenges that are faced by the teachers or the institutions which are seen across the various educational institutions. Some of them are:

  - *Technical challenges*: One of the main challenges faced is the technical challenge, which is not only about acquiring the said technology but is about getting the technology to work continuously ensuring the success of the hybrid learning. Some of the difficulties would be ensuring that the teachers and learners are in a stage where they can use the technology without any assistance or difficulty.
  - *Institutional challenges*: There are certain institutional challenges such as allocation of budget, providing assistance for training the teachers and not expecting instant results that create roadblocks in implementing a hybrid system. Some of the institutional challenges would include handling shortage of resources, allocating necessary budget for acquiring technology and motivating the teachers.
  - *Curriculum design challenges*: The biggest challenge faced in implementing the hybrid learning would the high level of attention paid to the technology rather than the curriculum itself. Some of the other challenges would include what to teach online, matching the curriculum with the delivery system, ensuring student participation in the class and coordination across all elements.

- *Challenges faced by the student*

There are various challenges that the student faces while undergoing a hybrid learning. Some of the major ones are:

  - *Procrastination*: With a part of the learning being in online mode and some modules being asynchronous, the student faces a big challenge of procrastinating the work and not completing the reading or finishing the assigned tasks on time. The students might also not have the necessary motivation to take part in the discussion and they might feel forced into the hybrid mode.
  - *Online distractions*: The student can easily get distracted with so many online temptations available on the internet and with very few monitoring mechanisms. The student taking a hybrid learning module can easily get distracted by various social media platforms, online internet games, social websites and many more. There are no foolproof mechanisms to monitor the progress or attention of the students in the class.

- *Passive study*: Another challenge faced by the students is the passive learning approach, where some of the students who do not have interest might not take the course seriously and might do only what is the bare minimum. The students who do not engage or participate in active learning have a higher probability to fail in the hybrid learning course.
- *Lack of clarity*: Online or hybrid learning can cause misunderstanding and lack of clarity on the subject as the student feels he or she is not a part of the class. The student does not have the elements of a physical class such as eye contact, understanding body language, voice reach and humor, and this might lead to lack of clarity.
- *Poor engagement skills*: The students in an online setup will have a challenge of having a poor engagement in the classroom. The student will miss out on the various elements of interacting socially and thereby have a low engagement level in the class. Lower engagement will lead to a low level of understanding, resulting in the failure of the hybrid learning process.

1.12 CONCLUSION AND FUTURE SCOPE

The rate of change in teaching and learning historically has been incremental and slow, but the pandemic created a digital shock, and educational institutions had to make a radical transition in a very short period of time. On top of the rapid change, the institutions as well as the teachers and students were not prepared, and did not have the adequate technology or training for the onset of online teaching and learning. With the pandemic extending into years the concept of hybrid learning has become the new normal, and governments and educational institutions across the globe have accepted the concept of hybrid learning and are making arrangements to make the concept of hybrid learning a permanent feature in the teaching-learning process. For a robust and successful hybrid learning system the support of the entire educational ecosystem support is required. Educationalists across have accepted hybrid learning as the way of the future and are working to have a process which can deliver value for the students as well as the teachers. While there are certain challenges faced in implementing a hybrid learning system there will be ways to mitigate these challenges and have a successful hybrid learning process in the future.

In spite of much research work done over the past decade on hybrid learning, there is huge potential for advanced research in this area, especially post pandemic and once the lockdowns have begun to ease. Some of the areas of scope for future research are as follows:

- In-depth exploration of how higher educational institutions have adopted hybrid learning;
- Study the best practices adopted by institutions for effective implementation and practice of hybrid learning;
- How HEI have managed to mitigate the challenges faced by teachers and students in adopting hybrid learning;
- Detailed study on the cost-benefit analysis on the implementation of hybrid learning;
- Obtain detailed feedback on student and faculty experiences on implementing hybrid learning;
- Impact of hybrid learning on students and teachers on its adoption.

REFERENCES

Aristika, A., & Juandi, D. (2021). The effectiveness of hybrid learning in improving of teacher-student relationship in terms of learning motivation. Emerging Science Journal, 5(4), 443–456.

Bennett, D., Knight, E., & Rowley, J. (2020). The role of hybrid learning spaces in enhancing higher education students' employability. British Journal of Educational Technology, 51(4), 1188–1202.

Boora, R., Church, J., Madill, H., Brown, W., & Chykerda, M. (2010). Ramping up to hybrid teaching and learning. In Handbook of research on hybrid learning models: Advanced tools, technologies, and applications (pp. 406–423). IGI Global.

Burgess, S., & Sievertsen, H. H. (2020). Schools, skills, and learning: The impact of COVID-19 on education. VoxEu. org, 1(2).

Dumont, G., & Raggo, P. (2018). Faculty perspectives about distance teaching in the virtual classroom. Journal of Nonprofit Education and Leadership, 8(1).

Fadde, P. J., & Vu, P. (2014). Blended online learning: Benefits, challenges, and misconceptions. Online Learning: Common Misconceptions, Benefits and Challenges, 33–48.

Grant, M. M., & Cheon, J. (2007). The value of using synchronous conferencing for instruction and students. Journal of Interactive Online Learning, 6(3), 211–226.

Hariadi, B., Sunarto, M. J., & Sudarmaningtyas, P. (2019). Hybrid learning by using brilian applications as one of the learning alternatives to improve learning outcomes in college. International Journal of Emerging Technologies in Learning, 14(10), 34–45.

Hastie, M., Hung, I. C., Chen, N. S., & Kinshuk, (2010). A blended synchronous learning model for educational international collaboration. Innovations in Education and Teaching International, 47(1), 9–24. https://doi.org/10.1080/14703290903525812.

Hwang, A. (2018). Online and hybrid learning. Journal of Management Education, 42(4), 557–563.

Ironsi, C. S. (2021). Google meet as a synchronous language learning tool for emergency online distant learning during the COVID-19 pandemic: Perceptions of language instructors and preservice teachers. Journal of Applied Research in Higher Education, 14(2), 640–659.

Ironsi, C. S. (2023). Efficacy of blended interactive educational resources in improving writing skills in a hybrid learning environment. Quality Assurance in Education, 31(1), 107–120.

Jena, P. K. (2020). Online learning during lockdown period for covid-19 in India. International Journal of Multidisciplinary Educational Research (IJMER), 9.

Johnson, E., Morwane, R., Dada, S., Pretorius, G., & Lotriet, M. (2018). Adult learners' perspectives on their engagement in a hybrid learning postgraduate programme. The Journal of Continuing Higher Education, 66(2), 88–105.

Lakhal, S., Bateman, D., & Bédard, J. (2017). Blended synchronous delivery modes in graduate programs: A literature review and its implementation in the master teacher program. Collected Essays on Learning and Teaching, 10, 47–60.

Li, G., Sun, Z., & Jee, Y. (2019). The more technology the better? A comparison of teacher-student interaction in high and low technology use elementary EFL classrooms in China. System, 84, 24–40.

Li, Q., Li, Z., & Han, J. (2021). A hybrid learning pedagogy for surmounting the challenges of the COVID-19 pandemic in the performing arts education. Education and Information Technologies, 26(6), 7635–7655.

Lightner, C. A., & Lightner-Laws, C. A. (2016). A blended model: Simultaneously teaching a quantitative course traditionally, online, and remotely. Interactive Learning Environments, 24, 224–238.

Liu, H., Spector, J. M., & Ikle, M. (2018). Computer technologies for model-based collaborative learning: A research-based approach with initial findings. Computer Applications in Engineering Education, 26(5, SI), 1383–1392.

Liu, Y., Han, S., & Li, H. (2010). Understanding the factors driving m-learning adoption: A literature review. Campus-Wide Information Systems, 27(4), 210–226. https://doi.org/10.1108/10650741011073761

Ma, J. Y., & Hall, R. (2018). Learning a part together: Ensemble learning and infrastructure in a competitive high school marching band. Instructional Science, 46(4), 507–532.

McGovern, N., & Barnes, K. (2009). Lectures from my living room: A pilot study of hybrid learning from the students' perspective. In F. L. Wang, J. Fong, L. Zhang, & V. S. K. Lee (eds.), Hybrid learning and education (pp. 284–298). Second International Conference, ICHL, Macau, China, August 25–27.

Mumford, S., & Dikilitaş, K. (2020). Pre-service language teachers reflection development through online interaction in a hybrid learning course. Computers & Education, 144, 103706.

Mutmainnah, M., Samtidar, S., & Korompot, C. A. Study of perceptions on Hybrid Learning in the teaching of English at Mtsn 4 bone during the covid-19 pandemic. JTechLP: Journal of Technology in Language Pedagogy, 1(1), 27–37.

Naik, G. L., Deshpande, M., Shivananda, D. C., Ajey, C. P., & Manjunath Patel, G. C. (2021). Online teaching and learning of higher education in India during COVID-19 emergency lockdown. Pedagogical Research, 6(1).

Neuwirth, L. S., Jović, S., & Mukherji, B. R. (2021). Reimagining higher education during and post-COVID-19: Challenges and opportunities. Journal of Adult and Continuing Education, 27(2), 141–156. Reimagining higher education during and post-COVID-19: Challenges and opportunities. Journal of Adult and Continuing Education, 27(2), 141–156.

Noesgaard, S. S., & Ørngreen, R. (2015). The effectiveness of e-Learning: An explorative and integrative review of the definitions, methodologies and factors that promote e-Learning effectiveness. Electronic Journal of e-Learning, 13(4), 277–289.

Nortvig, A.-M. (2013). In the presence of technology—Teaching in hybrid synchronous classrooms. In Proceedings of the European conference on E-learning, ECEL (pp. 347–353). Academic Conferences and Publishing International. http://academic-conferences.org/ecel/ecel2013/ecel13-proceedings.htm

Olt, P. A. (2018). Virtually there: Distant freshmen blended in classes through synchronous online education. Innovative Higher Education, 43(5), 381–395.

Ora, A., Sahatcija, R., & Ferhataj, A. (2018). Learning styles and the hybrid learning: An empirical study about the impact of learning styles on the perception of the hybrid learning. Mediterranean Journal of Social Sciences, 9(1), 137.

Park, H., & Shea, P. (2020). A review of ten-year research through Co-citation analysis: Online learning, distance learning, and blended learning. Online Learning, 24(2), 225–244.

Pavlidou, I., Dragicevic, N., & Tsui, E. (2021). A multi-dimensional hybrid learning environment for business education: A knowledge dynamics perspective. Sustainability, 13(7), 3889.

Raes, A., Detienne, L., Windey, I., & Depaepe, F. (2020). A systematic literature review on synchronous hybrid learning: Gaps identified. Learning Environments Research, 23(3), 269–290.

Rahim, R., Lundeto, A., Elihami, E., & Riyanto, A. (2022). The effectiveness of google classroom on hybrid learning in junior high school. AL-ISHLAH: Jurnal Pendidikan, 14(2), 1241–1250.

Ramsey, D., Evans, J., & Levy, M. (2016). Preserving the seminar experience. Journal of Political Science Education, 12(3), 256–267.

Rao, V. (2019). Blended learning: A new hybrid teaching methodology. Online Submission, 3(13).

Rashid, S., & Yadav, S. S. (2020). Impact of Covid-19 pandemic on higher education and research. Indian Journal of Human Development, 14(2), 340–343.

Rasmussen, R. C. (2003). The quantity and quality of human interaction in a synchronous blended learning environment. Doctoral dissertation, Brigham Young University. Available from ProQuest Dissertations & theses (UMI No. 305345928).

Renner, D., Laumer, S., & Weitzel, T. (2015). Blended learning success: Cultural and learning style impacts. In Wirtschaftsinformatik Proceedings, Germany, 92. https://aisel.aisnet.org/wi2015/92

Romero-Hall, E., & Vicentini, C. (2017). Examining distance learners in hybrid synchronous instruction: Successes and challenges. Online Learning, 21(4, SI), 141–157.

Roseth, C., Akcaoglu, M., & Zellner, A. (2013). Blending synchronous face-to-face and computer supported cooperative learning in a hybrid doctoral seminar. TechTrends, 57(3), 54–59. https://doi. org/10.1007/s11528–013–0663-z.

Serbanescu, A. (2022). Millennials and the Gen Z in the era of social media. Social Media, Technology, and New Generations: Digital Millennial Generation and Generation Z, 61.

Shadiev, R., & Yang, M. (2020). Review of studies on technology-enhanced language learning and teaching. Sustainability, 12(2), 524.

Shen, R. M., Wang, M. J., & Pan, X. (2008). Increasing interactivity in large blended classrooms through a cutting-edge mobile learning system. British Journal of Educational Technology, 39(6), 1073–1086. https://doi.org/10.1109/ITICT.2008.4806642.

Shirrell, M., Hopkins, M., & Spillane, J. P. (2019). Educational infrastructure, professional learning, and changes in teachers' instructional practices and beliefs. Professional Development in Education, 45(4), 599–613.

Sorden, S. D. (2012). The cognitive theory of multimedia learning. Handbook of Educational Theories, 1(2012), 1–22.

Soto, M., Gupta, D., Dick, L., & Appelgate, M. (2019). Bridging distances: Professional development for higher education faculty through technology-facilitated lesson study. Journal of University Teaching & Learning Practice, 16(3), 7.

Stewart, A. R., Harlow, D. B., & DeBacco, K. (2011). Students' experience of synchronous learning in distributed environments. Distance Education, 32(3), 357–381. https://doi.org/10.1080/01587 919.2011.610289.

Sulistyanto, H. (2021). The potential of hybrid learning models in improving students' critical thinking ability. Urecol Journal. Part A: Education and Training, 1(1), 1–8.

Szeto, E., & Cheng, A. Y. N. (2016). Towards a framework of interactions in a blended synchronous learning environment: What effects are there on students' social presence experience? Interactive Learning Environments, 24(3), 487–503.

Tadesse, S., & Muluye, W. (2020). The impact of COVID-19 pandemic on education system in developing countries: A review. Open Journal of Social Sciences, 8(10), 159–170.

Thornton, A., & Raihani, N. J. (2008). The evolution of teaching. Animal Behaviour, 75(6), 1823–1836.

Wang, Q., Huang, C., & Quek, C. L. (2018). Students' perspectives on the design and implementation of a blended synchronous learning environment. Australasian Journal of Educational Technology, 34(1), 1–13.

White, C. P., Ramirez, R., Smith, J. G., & Plonowski, L. (2010). Simultaneous delivery of a face-to-face course to on-campus and remote off-campus students. TechTrends, 54(4), 34–40. https://doi. org/10.1007/s11528–010–0418-z.

Wiles, G. L., & Ball, T. R. (2013, June 23–26). The converged classroom. Paper presented at ASEE Annual Conference: Improving course effectiveness, Atlanta, Georgia. https://peer.asee.org/22561.

Zhang, W., & Zhu, C. (2017). Review on blended learning: Identifying the key themes and categories. International Journal of Information and Education Technology, 7(9), 673–678.

Zhao, Y., & Watterston, J. (2021). The changes we need: Education post COVID-19. Journal of Educational Change, 22(1), 3–12.

Zydney, J. M., McKimm, P., Lindberg, R., & Schmidt, M. (2019). Here or there instruction: Lessons learned in implementing innovative approaches to blended synchronous learning. TechTrends. https://doi. org/10.1007/s11528–018–0344-z.

2 The Psychological Effects of COVID-19 on College Students due to the Digital Divide via Online Education

Ravi Kumar Gupta, Udit Maheshwari and Dhirendra Bahadur Singh

2.1 INTRODUCTION

A sudden breakout of COVID-19 has made many countries halt all their economic activities. The World Health Organization Emergency Committee on 30 January 2020 proclaimed it a worldwide health emergency due to many cases registered in many countries. Coronavirus got its name because of the physical structure, as in Latin *corona* means "crown". This virus has a severe influence on both social factors like health and economic factors like financial implications (Velavan & Meyer, 2020). COVID-19 has affected global production, and the demand and supply chain, which has created many problems among different sectors of the economy (McKibbi & Fernando, 2020). To contain the propagation of the virus the Indian government has taken many preventative steps such as stringent lockdown imposed for a long period with exceptions of only essential commodities. The education sector was among those critically affected as it is always conducted in an offline manner but due to strict lockdown, educational institutions couldn't operate so many institutes conducted their operations in online mode, which is again a hurdle for both teachers and students to cope with. Students learn various things from school as they get the chance to enhance their social skills. Inequalities among students were also a problem as many students do not have proper access to digital devices to participate in online classes, which reveals many lacunas in online education and schools, with low-income government and private schools at a disadvantage due to insufficient resources available, which is creating various foundational problems (Butnaru et al., 2021). Higher education has a prominent role to play in future economic development, but the sudden outbreak of the pandemic had a huge negative impact on it (Tarkar, 2020). Many businesses and educational institutes shifted their operations to a teleworking basis, which has provided many advantages and disadvantages to both employees and companies. This was the only feasible option open during the whole pandemic and, according to estimated data that dependable employment of around 37% is in state to be conducted through the teleworking methodology which means there is enough scope for work-from-home–related activities, but this percentage can be increased with some training of employees, teleworking allows employees to have time for leisure activities, a more balanced work-life balance (Kumar et al., 2021), provide more freedom to individual discretion; also this contributes towards lower pollution level and diminished traffic on roads. The most affected areas are the tourism sector in which international tourism is at greatest disadvantage. Many restaurants had to face huge losses due to complete lockdown and other related hospitably sector has also suffered as people were fearful to take part in any physical activity involving physical interaction, the service sector was the only sector which was able to survive during this pandemic, as operations in this sector are mostly dependent on rigorous computer networks, and simultaneously workers related to

 DOI: 10.1201/9781003425779-2

service sectors are in much more ease even in the situation of pandemic due to a strong flexibility of work from home without any disturbance in official work. Before the advent of pandemic people were not that much ready to welcome the work-from-home culture, but due to this pandemic the only possible option was teleworking, which has saved many workers from losing their jobs and also supported many workers to sustain their jobs for the time being. According to data of the year 2019, only a single person out of 20 employees was able to conduct their work from home on a regular basis (Sostero et al., 2020).

The digital divide is a kind of inequality in terms of usage of digital technologies. Its meaning is the diversion created between those people who have an opportunity of access to various information and communication technologies and other people who are unable to have any access to usage of digital technologies like computer and internet (Doyumgaç et al., 2021). The various barriers to the digital divide can be classified into mental aspects (attractiveness and interest), based on skills (social support, education and friendliness), related to material devices such as various hardware-related devices and other activities related to usage. There are nine kinds of negative effects of the digital divide: economic, social, personal (such as perception regarding risk and motivations) and demographic aspects, kind of technology used (such as dependence on mobile devices and dearth of equipment), social support, training in using digital technologies (such as information and communication technology training and other technologies of assistive nature), various rights (such as net neutrality and civil liberties), related infrastructure (such as access to electricity) and outcomes which are of large scale. Due to the collection of various pieces of evidence, the factors which have a prominent kind of role to play in the contribution of the digital divide are age, gender, quality of support, concerns relating to privacy, and education. The prominence of this outcome reveals serious kinds of overlap among social inequalities and the digital divide (Pokhrel & Chhetri, 2021). It can also be the digital divide and inequalities which are social and these two factors are interconnected. At the time of the pandemic (COVID-19), this can be understood with the help of an example regarding an event on a large scale. While a review of presently available evidence indicates the extensive negative impact of COVID-19, it contributed an immense role in expanding the digital divide and other inequalities related to social aspects.

As technology is becoming more advanced day-by-day, which is bringing more digital and technological revolutions, the inequalities related to social aspects are also intensifying daily, as happened in the case of the urban and rural divide. This expanding digital divide is putting people belonging to vulnerable and marginalized section into a much worse and disadvantageous situation. On the other side, inequalities related to social aspects also enhance the digital divide as both are indirectly related in terms of an overlapping set of determinants, antecedents, results and contextual factors toward the same negative outcomes, such as social exclusion and more severe discrimination among the population who are vulnerable to the digital divide (Asgari et al., 2021). Current studies indicate that available infrastructure is also responsible for the intensification of the digital divide. The studies conducted at the time of the COVID-19 pandemic also show that barriers to the digital divide encompass similar challenges encountered by the population vulnerable to the digital divide, such as aged people and people living in rural areas; barriers related to knowledge, communication and study; biases related to gender; and discrimination regarding technologies. The severity of the digital divide, COVID-19 and conventional inequalities related to social aspects greatly impacted the same people. These findings bring a direct relationship between social inequalities and barriers to the digital divide (Muthuprasad et al., 2021).

These outcomes are alarming and depict an explicit picture. Many studies indicate COVID-19 resulted in psychological issues due mental issues such as depression, anxiety and suicidal thoughts. A survey which is based in the United Kingdom regarding an index of digital various digital aspects shows that about 78% of those surveyed showed that COVID-19 fuelled the demand and usage of skills regarding usage of digital technologies (Adedoyin & Soykan, 2020). The outcome of a survey conducted showed that 37% of participants out of a total number of participants agreed that they utilized technological devices for coping with various challenges concerning COVID-19 and issues concerning mental health. The overall understanding indicates these technologies have many positive aspects as well as some negative aspects also, in the case of those people who are facing the digital divide, are more likely to face more negative impacts and will not be in a situation to enjoy various related advantages, which will have a direct bearing on mental and physical aspects of peoples both tangibly and intangibly.

In considering psychological health, for example, the meaning of psychological health is "a rational condition in which a person can utilize his abilities to full potential, can handle the usual level of stress in his life, and also in a condition to give optimum productivity at work while also be contributing towards society". Due to the influence of COVID-19, the situation of the digital divide has become worse as it has helped to expand the social and digital exclusion which has negatively impacted the mental health of ordinary people. Studies also examined the negative influence of COVID-19 on adolescents and children concerning many factors, such as level of education, age, psychological influences and economic status. Additionally, many people dealing with abnormal psychological conditions have experienced much more depression, greater levels of loneliness and inequalities of health because of restricted access to social and health services, which has a severe impact on people already belonging to the vulnerable section (Teymori & Fardin, 2020). However, researchers also suggested the impact of the digital divide on mental health because COVID-19 is not limited. Research also indicated that the gap between genders is also expanded due to the digital divide, which is supported by data obtained in a survey based on learning through online mode, which is based on data collected from five developing countries. The outcomes of this research indicated that learning through digital mode causes an increased burden of responsibilities on households due to COVID-19, leading to a rising level of stress among female students. Female students agreed that they have faced inequalities related to gender, which is causing more marginalization on a social level because of simultaneous effect of the digital divide and gender discrimination. Other researchers investigated the psychological influences of the digital divide which happened due to the adoption of the online method of teaching to cope with COVID-19 and to provide uninterrupted teaching to students by education institutions. The findings based on the data analysed in the study using the Kessler distress scale (K-10) suggested that around 40% of college students are facing the issues regarding a medium level of psychological stress. Some researchers state that problems concerning mental issues are mainly an outcome of a huge gap in the digital divide, in which people belonging to vulnerable sections are badly impacted. The vulnerable group includes those people in developing countries who fall into the vulnerable category, such as children who are under-privileged economically, people who are more than 60 years old, and elderly females. There are higher chances of a dearth of information, social isolation of people, more distress, higher stress, fear and anxiety, and so on (Adnan & Anwar, 2020).

Researchers also analysed children who are falling into a vulnerable category such as higher anxiety and trauma. The findings of the research indicated a proper action plan should be formulated which can work for children who are vulnerable and mental and psychological requirements of the health of adolescents. The outcomes also suggest that proper dedicated centres should be established to tackle mental issues and provide a kind of physical and mental level of support to adolescents and children in such a situation of pandemics (Qazi et al., 2020).

The data published in March 2020, according to the United Nations Educational, Scientific and Cultural Organization (UNESCO) for the protection of the safety and health of the public, the majority of the educational institutions were shut down to halt the propagation of COVID-19 virus so that death rates can be brought to least numbers. UNESCO reported that around 87% of students at the global level were impacted by enormous closures of schools and university, which accounts for about 1.5 billion students studying and living in 165 countries (Alam, 2020).

The only way left to carry out education in the various educational institution was through online mode as conducting in-person classes was impossible for any educational institution (Xie et al., 2020). About 90% of educational institutions moved toward online education methods or remote learning started from December 2019 and impacted around 55 million school and college students.

The online learning and teaching method has gained momentum after the advent of the pandemic, which has made it necessary for educational institutions to adopt online teaching and learning methods. According to data of 11th March 2020 of 192 countries, around 1725 million students have faced the impact of COVID-19 which caused the sudden closure of the majority of institutions at the global level. All the face-to-face learning courses are suddenly transformed into the online method of teaching and learning, which has also created various difficulties for all the educational institutions as they all were in a completely new scenario of online teaching and learning, and they were not aware of efficient usage of new technical devices which has created many difficulties for those teachers who have never used the digital devices for teaching their students (Kontoangelos et al., 2020; Ha et al., 2019). This pandemic has revealed various problems in the existing educational system concerning the online method of education, which were hidden earlier (Mukhopadhyay et al., 2020). It has also revealed the potential of the online methodology of education, while simultaneously it has played an important role in putting many questions about the traditional method of teaching and learning, which means that, is the traditional method sufficient method in various situations? Or is this the time to move towards the online method of learning and teaching to keep ourselves in a better situation to deal with a new potential threat? There are some positive aspects of online education, but it has some negative aspects as well, like the majority of the educational institutions were not in a condition to implement and manage the online teaching and learning process, which had become a prime cause for the ineffectiveness of online education method as reported by various pieces of evidence of many educational institutions (Amerio et al., 2020). While students were also not able to cope with the new methodologies of online education and they faced many challenges, both at the time of attending online classes and also while writing and submitting their assignments on time, which made them less competent at the time of learning and teaching. The traditional method of learning and teaching is used for a long time, which has made them habitual their dependency on the traditional method. So, after the introduction of the new method, it has worked much like destructive creation concerning the online education system. Most of the students have reported that they do not have any positive perception regarding online education, which is because of bad experiences in the past which have fuelled a greater number of dropouts, and most of the students also face less motivation for studies. Satisfaction levels among the majority of students were not satisfactory. Despite that, research also indicates that instructors and students are easily able to cope with new methods of online education as they are with the offline method of education. The factors responsible for satisfaction among students are the contribution of students and teachers, method regarding assessment, related content, the environment of learning and various materials used. All the educational institutions, from grade schools to universities, were closed because they were considered potential places for larger propagation of COVID-19 (Giorgi et al., 2020).

Online education was not just a substitute for the offline method of education, but it was the last option and a need at the time of the pandemic for every educational institution all around the world. Every educational institution, whether it is private or public, faces an enormous impact at the global level. This sudden shift has created too much of a workload on staff and faculty members of educational institutions and forced these institutions to work with a lesser number of staff, faculties and resources (Lee, 2020).

Many types of research indicated some problems in online education, which include improper infrastructure for teaching online, the dearth of exposure regarding online teaching methods among teachers, an information gap, an ineffective learning environment as students were at their homes, and academic excellence and equity regarding education. Those students who have a static mindset regarding the offline method of teaching and learning have faced many difficulties while accepting the online method of teaching and learning, while the students who possess a flexible mindset towards the learning method or have any experience with the online method of teaching and learning face few or no issues regarding the online method (Liu et al., 2020). The online education system helped physically disabled students as it has a leverage of lesser movement compared to the physical method of education, which shows that online education has much potential for some aspects also. The majority of students who have been a part of online education in India have faced issues related to emotional and psychological stress, and they were not in a condition to show their productivity at the time of engagement in studies. With time, more methods to engage effectively in online education will emerge as teachers and students will gain more experience and expertise. But at the present time, because of the emergent implementation of the online method of education, both students and teachers are not in a condition to engage effectively in online education (Iqbal et al., 2020).

Many decisions were taken by government and educational institutions to tackle the situation of COVID-19, but the majority of policies failed because of this new virus which has created various problems in a very short period of time and created a sudden pressure on the educational system and policymakers. This pressure has made them make decisions which were made without any preparedness. The online method of teaching was also taken to tackle this pandemic situation; the majority of educational institutions and students were not ready to accept and use this medium of instruction, which made this online method an ineffective method for teaching and learning (Cullen et al., 2020). The unpreparedness element has an important role in the ineffectiveness of the online method of the education system. The effectiveness of the online method of education among students was found to be less than 50% in a survey of college students regarding the effectiveness of learning and teaching methods among various higher educational institutes. The online technique of teaching and learning is the most appropriate technique in the case of distance education students, but the COVID-19 has proved that this can also play a significant role in substituting offline education techniques in case of any emergency or for the regular use under normal conditions. Network quality has a direct effect on the quality of online education. The learning and teaching process is happening effectively, but if the quality of the network is poor at either the teacher's side or student's side, the outcome of teaching and learning will not be effective and suitable for both students and teachers (Gualano et al., 2020). The major problem with online teaching and learning methodologies is the immediate implementation of this technique which leaves no space for training either for the students and teacher, and the educational institutions were not able to chalk out any plan for tackling the problems of the pandemic (Chakraborty et al., 2021). Due to online classes, many students have faced many physical and mental issues which may have a long-term effect on the physical and mental health of students. Many students have reported that they have faced severe irritation in their eyes and headaches due to the overuse of smartphones, tablets and laptops because of the high amount of radiation these devices emit (Campion et al., 2020).

2.1.1 Objectives of the Chapter

The objectives of the chapter are as follows:

- To understand the plan of action of application for online education system due to the outbreak of COVID-19 at educational institutes of Gorakhpur district of Uttar Pradesh state (India) and simultaneously give attention to the current situation of college students studying at the undergraduate and postgraduate levels;
- To find the difficulties and efficacy of online education on college students based on slow internet speed, electricity disruptions and unfavourable surroundings for study;
- And, to observe the mental effects on college students and effectiveness of an online method of education during COVID-19 from the standpoint of college students.

2.1.2 Organization of the Chapter

The rest of the chapter is organized as: Section 2.2 elaborates a literature review concerning the psychological impact on students during the pandemic period which is majorly influenced by the sudden expansion of the digital divide due to the immediate adoption of the online education method. Section 2.3 highlights the justification and elaboration of the adopted research methodology, research methods utilized, target population of the study, sample collection, study area, tools used for data collection, details about questionnaire and in-depth interviews, ethical consideration and tools used for data analysis. Section 2.4 discusses the results found during this research study, the implementation of the online method of education in an emergency during the pandemic and influences of online classes during COVID-19 period on mental stress of college students, problems encountered and the experience of online learning. Section 2.5 highlights discussion and elaborates about execution procedure of online education, opinions of college students and level of satisfaction, mental status, plan of action to keep good mental health during pandemic (COVID-19) and limitation of the research study. And, finally section 2.6 concludes the chapter with future scope.

2.2 LITERATURE REVIEW

Since the use of digital services has risen especially during the pandemic (COVID-19), the digital divide is emerging as an important problem that needs to be tackled. This concept has come into the limelight at the global level due to COVID-19, and the digital divide has a significant and positive relationship with the income levels of households (Alradhawi et al., 2020). In those households with lower income levels, there is a higher chance of a greater digital divide. Other factors which have also contributed to a larger digital divide are the age of students and teachers, social status, gender, geography of the educational institution, and the home of the student. The concept of the digital divide gained importance in second half of the 1990s. "Digital divide" means the gap among those people who have resources for access to use the internet services and those who do not. The digital divide can also be defined as a kind of social inequality among concerning dissimilar access regarding internet and other required devices. This pandemic has halted the offline method of work which has given rise to use of online method of work, which again contributes to further extending the gap of digital divide. Common indicators used in digital divide are socio-economic and socio-demographic factors like age, income, geographical location and gender, which are used to explain different kinds of digital divides. This pandemic has forced to educational institutes to adopt digital methods to carry out their educational activities. The internet has played an inevitable role during the pandemic as it provided a backbone for economy to carry out different business activities, educational facilities and other social services but also created a digital divide among those who have good internet facility with high-speed data and among those who do (Lai & Widmar, 2021), and this has imposed a negative impact on those students who are unable to access the internet and live in rural and remote areas. This has also made many underprivileged students leave the education system, while richer household with access to internet connection were not impacted much in this pandemic situation. For those belonging to poor backgrounds, which are mostly rural areas, the factors responsible for the extended digital divide are deficiency of digital literacy, education facilities that are not up to the mark at various educational institutes, and lack of proper internet facilities either at educational institutes or at their homes, which makes them more vulnerable in the digital divide (Azubuike et al., 2021). Many countries do not have proper access to digital infrastructure which mostly falls into developing countries and lower developing counties, while in the case of developed countries they have proper access to digital infrastructure which makes them capable of online services. The countries which have been impacted severely are the ones which fall into the category of either developing country or less developed country, as they were not even prepared for such kind of sudden pandemic or they normally do not have that kind of digital infrastructure to support online education at different schools and universities. These factors contribute for social inequality in respective countries. Major concerns for countries post COVID-19 are filling digital gaps among rural and urban peoples in various countries and problems related to mobility, accessibility and adaptability of information and communication technology. The Asian nations have been ranked the second number in terms of internet penetration, but still, these countries show considerable signs of unequal distribution of wealth and social inequalities in terms of digital infrastructure. These countries do not have enough income to acquire internet services, which also creates an added disadvantage in combatting the pandemic (Alvarez Jr, 2021). This pandemic also sets the students apart from the social environment, which contributes a significant part to child development. Online education may compensate for offline education to some extent, but it is not a perfect substitute for offline education as it cannot provide the students with such conducive educational environment. Many students lack the equipment required to carry out the education online at their home, which again creates a kind of digital divide among different students. Especially those students who lack motivation to study generally will also find it difficult to study with online teaching methods (Daniel, 2020). Digital technologies have a wide scope for use as they are used in education, communication, healthcare, office work and other daily life activities. They have many users like students, government, teachers, patients and the general public, so we can explicitly conclude that digital technologies have occupied a prominent place in our lives. Countries that have sufficient technological penetration are not impacted much by such pandemics. These digital technologies have also been a lifesaver in the hospital system by providing support to patients and doctors and helping them to control the situation. These technologies not only help to detect medical problems but also help to cure them (Vargo et al., 2021). Problems are faced by educational institutes in online educational techniques because of unpreparedness of government and other educational institutes from such kind of pandemic not even as a precaution. Another prominent reason was inequality in the distribution of resources among different regions of a particular country (Batubara, 2021). Many doctors have adopted telehealth facilities to carry out their medical services which have supported the whole medical system, as the offline meetings with doctors were not possible and may create problems for both doctors and patients. Many peoples in rural areas do not have the economic ability to purchase these electronic gadgets, making them economically unequal to others (Ramsetty & Adams, 2020). All students have been impacted by measures taken to contain the virus, which has given a rise to an emergent online method of teaching. About one-fourth of students encountered anxiety; a positive association is found between anxiety, mental and economic stress, and detained academic activities, while there is a negative relationship between anxiety and support from social groups (Pragholapati, 2020). College students are not ready to accept online education in just one go, as the offline method is a traditional method, so students have developed a habit of that educational method. Now that they are finding it difficult to accept the online learning techniques, students see online teaching methods with lower motivation and satisfaction because of their past experiences are not favourable. Challenges with online education are technical, social, administrative and academic (Aboagye et al., 2021). The majority of college students reported that they have faced anxiety and stress which can be attributed to the security of health and health of their family members, which has resulted in less social interaction and disturbed sleeping patterns (Son et al., 2020). Those people who are living in rural areas have faced severe effects of the digital divide, they were deprived in terms of education and terms of required hardware and software devices. The schools in rural areas are not even able to conduct online classes, while schools in urban areas have the ability and capacity to provide online classes with less effectiveness. Students in rural areas were not able to join any kind of educational facilities provided by educational institutions (Thakur, 2020).

2.2.1 Research Gap

The COVID-19 pandemic has created an immediate and severe digital divide. There are only limited number of studies which cover the problem of digital divide among college students. Previous studies conducted on online learning and teaching methods were not involved in examining the effect of the digital divide on college students regarding stress created among due to extension of the digital divide due to pandemic. The above literature lacks the use of both kinds of data (qualitative and quantitative), and the majority of studies focus on secondary data and lack the insight from primary data and qualitative data. These gaps in existing literature form the basis of this research study which focuses on mental stress among college students with the help of qualitative and quantitative data.

2.3 METHODOLOGY

2.3.1 Research Methods

This study is based on a descriptive analysis method of college students of Gorakhpur city. Hence, different kinds of methods were adopted in this study to obtain plausible responses to research questions. As this research aimed to examine the efficacy, outlook and mental effects encountered during the pandemic, it uses both qualitative and quantitative data to provide a better understanding of college students' outlook and efficiency of online educational methods.

2.3.2 Target Population

Since this research aimed to examine the plan of action for the application procedure, efficacy, difficulties and mental effects from the standpoint of college student's personal experience and satisfaction levels, the sample size for primary data collection was 210 college students currently pursuing degree courses from various colleges of Gorakhpur city.

2.3.3 Sample Collection

The sample units were chosen through the non–probability-based purposive sampling method. The main focus of this study was on college students of Gorakhpur city of Uttar Pradesh state.

2.3.4 Study Area

This research includes study areas based on college students from Gorakhpur city. The results obtained from primary data have appropriately represented the entire population of the country (India). Data was collected from students of two universities (Madan Mohan Malaviya University of Technology and Deen Dayal Upadhyaya, Gorakhpur) to get wider representative primary data covering the whole city.

2.3.5 Tools for Data Collection

Data was acquired from both sources, secondary and primary, for this research study. The sources of secondary data included research articles and research papers. The analysis of secondary data was done in terms of the point of view of college students, a pattern of events and themes. Data was examined based on the pattern of events and themes, and the examination of data was conducted concerning data available in the relevant available literature. Since this study looks for the perception of feasible answers and attitude of college students, efficacy, mental problems and other problems from the outlook of college students' real-life experiences and efficiency regarding the online education system, for collection of primary data an online questionnaire was provided and interviews were also conducted. Tools used in primary data collection are discussed later.

2.3.6 Online Forms

A total of 210 college students were selected on a random basis from both universities situated in Gorakhpur city of Uttar Pradesh state (India). These students were contacted through Gmail and social media websites (WhatsApp and Instagram). Online questionnaires were distributed in college class groups identified randomly in Gorakhpur city for 15 days. Due to the pandemic (COVID-19) online questionnaires were prepared through Google Forms and included 25 items divide into three sections concerning the different objectives of the research study. The first section of the online questionnaire included four kinds of closed-ended questions concerning different aspects of the implementation of online methods of education. The questions covered different procedures, the speed of internet connections, various online platforms and different devices used in online education adopted by college students of Gorakhpur city. The second section includes eight questions of the closed-ended type enquiring about the behaviour of college students and their satisfaction level with various aspects of online education methods such as favourable study environment at their home, compatibility of devices, electricity disruptions, technical know-how and different online teaching methods used by teachers. A 5-point Likert scale ranging from strongly satisfied to strongly dissatisfied was used to measure different factors, such as technological efficacy of students and engagement level during online classes. Furthermore, three different categories of responses created (effective, partly effective and ineffective) were in a separate section of the online questionnaire to obtain experience of online education among undergraduate and postgraduate college students. The third section of the questionnaire contained questions related to problems encountered by college students, measurement of mental effects while online education and choice of learning in future. In this study, the Kessler-10 distress scale (K10) (Slade et al., 2011) was used as an instrument. This K-10 includes ten questions that emphasize symptoms associated with anxiety and depression experienced by college students during the pandemic while attending online classes. The respondents who responded on the Likert scale revealed that college students under 20 years of age do not feel any mental effects, students aged between 18 to 22 years felt moderate mental stress, and students above 23 years of age group faced higher mental stress. The online questionnaire also included a future preference for teaching methods and it included their methods offline (face-to-face method), completely online method and a blended method of teaching and learning.

2.3.7 In-Depth Interview

The interview method provides in-depth insight into the sample unit regarding their viewpoint concerning a particular situation and is also helpful in the collection of comprehensive information regarding any specific event or situation. It also gives answers beyond the surface level which provide more in-depth valuable information based on individual's point of view. This research includes data from 15 in-depth interviews taken over the phone. Participants were selected through purposive sampling based on a non-probability sampling of 210 college students through an online survey. Proper care of the confidentiality of respondents was assured before the conduction of interviews.

2.3.8 Ethical Consideration

Proper care was taken for the written consent of respondents while filling out the online questionnaire, and all the information was provided to the respondents participating in the online survey.

2.3.9 Tools for Data Analysis

To measure the mental stress among college students, the K-10 distress scale was used. The Likert scale, frequency distribution, percentage analysis and bar graphs were also used. This study analysed various platforms used by various teachers to teach their students, such as Google Meet, YouTube, Zoom, Webex, WhatsApp, Facebook, and Microsoft Teams. It also analysed various methods adopted for online learning and teaching such as PowerPoint presentations, PDF files, assignments, recorded videos, live classes, online quizzes, module and voice calls. It also studied various electronic devices used for learning and teaching such as tablets, smartphones, laptops and desktops. It also threw light on various types of internet connection such as Wi-Fi, broadband, mobile data and people who use all type internet of connections. This study also examined the factors encountered while online learning such as electricity supply, internet speed, compatibility of devices, student's technical efficiency, training for studying in online class, teaching methodology, engagement during online class and comfort of surroundings for study.

2.4 RESULTS

The research study is categorized under three sections based on the different objectives through tables and graphs. This research also includes findings from comprehensive interviews of participants.

2.4.1 Implementation of Online Methods of Education in an Emergency during the Pandemic

Analysis of data obtained through an online questionnaire, which is presented in Table 2.1, showed that the most preferred online platform for the study is Google Meet during the period of the pandemic with a response rate of 95.23%. Google Meet is followed by YouTube and Zoom, which have a response rate of 85.71% and 71.42% out of total responses, respectively. The most renowned companies in the information technology sector are Facebook and WhatsApp, but they are not much preferred as a medium for online education, having a response rate of 42.85% and 51.42%, respectively.

The findings of Table 2.2 and Figure 2.1 indicated that the most preferred method of online teaching and learning is through live classes with a 100% response rate. PowerPoint

TABLE 2.1
Various Applications Used for Online Teaching during the Pandemic

Applications	Frequency (*N*)	Percentage Out of Entire *N*
Google Meet	200	95.23
YouTube	180	85.71
Zoom	150	71.42
Webex	126	60
WhatsApp	108	51.42
Facebook	90	42.85
Microsoft Teams	45	21.42

Source: Analysis of primary data collected by author.

TABLE 2.2
Methods Adopted for Online Learning and Teaching during the Pandemic

Methods	Frequency (*N*)	Percentage Out of Entire *N*
PowerPoint presentations	205	97.61
PDF files	182	86.66
Assignments	195	92.85
Recorded videos	155	73.80
Live classes	210	100
Online quizzes	128	60.95
Modules	105	50
Voice calls	165	78.57

Source: Analysis of primary data collected by author.

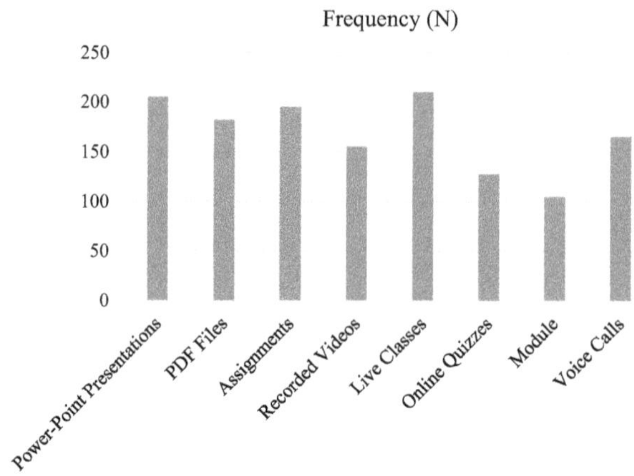

FIGURE 2.1 Methods adopted for online learning and teaching during the pandemic.

Source: Analysis of primary data collected by author.

presentations with a response rate of 97.61%, assignments with a response rate of 92.85%, PDF files with a response rate of 86.66% and voice calls with a response rate of 78.57% are mostly used methods adopted for online learning and teaching during the pandemic period (COVID-19). Other methods adopted for online teaching and learning during pandemics that are less preferred are recorded videos, online quizzes and modules according to the responses received from respondents.

The findings of the closed-ended question of devices utilized for online learning and teaching during the time of pandemic situation are shown in Table 2.3 and Figure 2.2. The data show that most of the respondents (96.19%) use their smartphone as a primary device to attend online classes. Other devices used for online classes are laptops with a response rate of 75.23%; desktops are used by 49.52% of respondents and some respondents (25.71%) also used tablets to attend online classes, so tablet is the least used electronic device utilized to attend online classes.

Seven respondents expressed in the interview that their devices (smartphones) do not have adequate features to attend online classes effectively, and they are not able to complete their assignments on time which creates unnecessary mental stress for the college students to manage the online education system. They have also stated that a phone is making them fetch fewer marks, which may impact their future career negatively.

The data of college students in Table 2.4 and Figure 2.3 show the type of internet connection utilized by college students to attend during the pandemic. A majority of respondents (49.52%) used a broadband connection to attend online classes in college. Thirty percent of respondents used Wi-Fi as their primary source of internet connection. The number of respondents who used all kinds of devices to attend online classes is 10.48%, and the least used device to attend online classes is mobile data with a response rate of 10% from respondents.

Table 2.5 measures the opinions of respondents regarding various factors encountered while online classes during the pandemic. The findings reflect that the majority of college students are satisfied with the internet speed they are getting at their home to attend online classes (30.95% of respondents are strongly satisfied and 30.95% of respondents are just satisfied), and electricity supply facility required for properly attending online classes (24.76% of respondents are strongly satisfied and 30.47% of respondents are just satisfied).

Although contrasting beliefs among respondents are reported concerning the compatibility of different devices used to attend online classes by college students (36.66% of respondents are neutral, 16.66% of respondents are dissatisfied and 12.38% of respondents are strongly dissatisfied);

TABLE 2.3
Devices Used for Online Teaching and Learning during the Pandemic

Devices	Frequency (N)	Percentage Out of Entire N
Tablet	54	25.71
Smartphones	202	96.19
Laptops	158	75.23
Desktops	104	49.52

Source: Analysis of primary data collected by author.

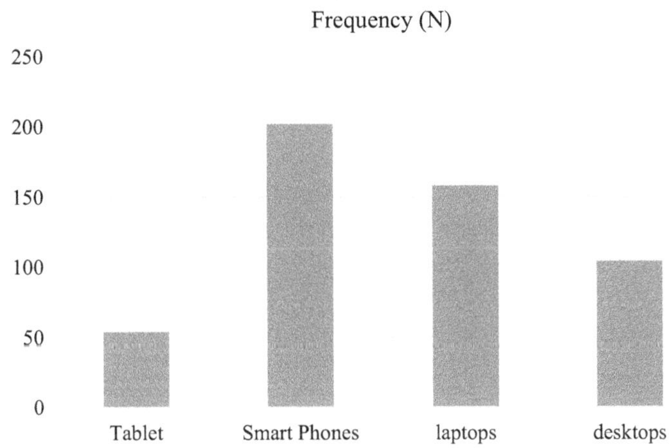

FIGURE 2.2 Devices utilized for online teaching and learning during pandemics.

Source: Analysis of primary data collected by author.

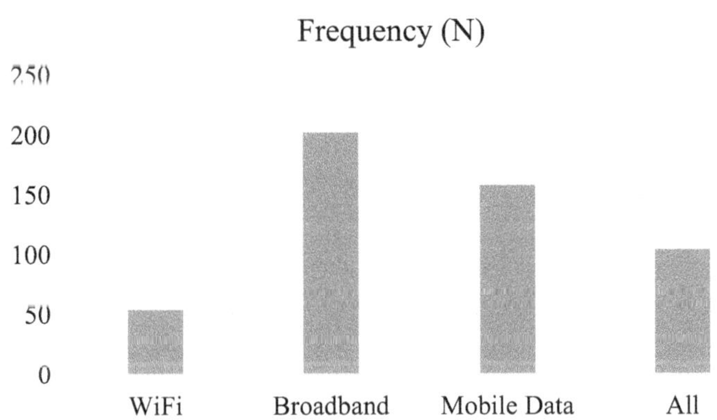

FIGURE 2.3 Type of internet connection used to attend by students during the pandemic.

Source: Analysis of primary data collected by author.

students' technical efficiency (56.19% of respondents are neutral, 7.61% of respondents are dissatisfied and 0.03% of respondents are strongly dissatisfied); and training for studying in online classes to college students (40.47% of respondents are neutral, 20.47% of respondents are dissatisfied and 21.90% of respondents are strongly dissatisfied).

TABLE 2.4
Type of Internet Connection Used to Attend by Students during the Pandemic

Type of Internet Connection	Frequency (*N*)	Percentage Out of Entire *N*
Wi-Fi	63	30
Broadband	104	49.52
Mobile data	21	10
All	22	10.48

Source: Analysis of primary data collected by author.

TABLE 2.5
Opinions of Respondents Regarding Various Factors Encountered While in Online Classes during the Pandemic

	Responses (*N* = 210; Percentages in Parentheses)				
Factors Encountered While Online Learning	Strongly Satisfied	Satisfied	Neutral	Dissatisfied	Strongly Dissatisfied
Electricity supply	52 (24.76)	64 (30.47)	39 (18.57)	32 (15.23)	23 (10.95)
Internet speed	65 (30.95)	65 (30.95)	30 (14.28)	34 (16.19)	16 (7.61)
Compatibility of device	40 (19.04)	32 (15.23)	77 (36.66)	35 (16.66)	26 (12.38)
Students' technical efficiency	38 (18.09)	30 (14.28)	118 (56.19)	16 (7.61)	8 (0.03)
Training for studying in online class	15 (7.14)	21 (10)	85 (40.47)	43 (20.47)	46 (21.90)
Teaching methodology	36 (17.14)	47 (22.38)	68 (32.38)	52 (24.76)	7 (3.33)
Engagement during online class	24 (11.42)	58 (27.61)	32 (15.23)	77 (36.66)	19 (9.04)
Unfavourable surroundings for study	35 (16.66)	39 (18.57)	28 (13.33)	82 (39.04)	26 (12.38)

Source: Analysis of primary data collected by author.

Additionally, Table 2.5 also represents unfavorable opinions from respondents concerning the teaching methodology used in online classes by colleges (32.38% of respondents are neutral, 24.76% of respondents are dissatisfied and 3.33% of respondents are strongly dissatisfied) and for engagement during online classes provided by various colleges (15.23% of respondents are neutral, 36.66% of respondents are dissatisfied and 9.04% of respondents are strongly dissatisfied).

2.4.2 Influence of Online Classes during the COVID-19 Period on Mental Stress of College Students, Problems Encountered and Experience of Online Learning

Some factors that are identified in this study of hurdles faced by college students during online classes during the pandemic to college students of Gorakhpur city are analyzed in Table 2.6. Table 2.7 depicts the experience by college students of sudden and new online learning during an unanticipated pandemic period. Finally, evidence about the level of mental stress and favorable mode of study among college students during a pandemic is represented in Tables 2.8 and 2.9.

The results obtained from Table 2.6 conclude that major problems faced by the majority of college students while attending online classes are management of time, with a response rate of 75.21% of respondents, and weak internet connection, with a response rate of 69.51%.

Other factors which also create problems but which do not influence critically but have moderate effects while attending online class are an unfavourable study environment, with a response rate of 56.20%, and incompatibility of device used to attend online classes, with a response rate of 29.51%. An

TABLE 2.6
Problems Encountered by Students at the Time of Online Classes during the Pandemic

Problems in Online Classes	Frequency	Percentage Out of Total *N*
Electricity disruptions	59	28.10
Weak internet connection	146	69.51
Incompatibility of device	62	29.51
Management of time	158	75.21
Lack of engagement	32	15.21
Unfavorable study environment	118	56.20

Source: Analysis of primary data collected by author.

TABLE 2.7
Experience of Online Learning during the Pandemic

Experience	Frequency	Percentage Out of Total *N*
Effective	64	30.47
Moderately effective	98	46.67
Ineffective	48	22.86

Source: Analysis of primary data collected by author.

TABLE 2.8
Mental Stress during the Pandemic

Level of Mental Stress	Frequency	Percentage Out of Total N
None	38	18.10
Mild	101	48.10
Modest	42	20
Severe	29	13.80

Source: Analysis of primary data collected by author.

TABLE 2.9
Favorable Mode of Study among College Students during the Pandemic

Favorable Mode	Frequency	Percentage Out of Total N
Offline (face-to-face)	112	53.33
Online	31	14.77
Blended	67	31.90

Source: Analysis of primary data collected by author.

interview of eight respondents was also conducted to understand in detail about influence of problems encountered by college students during online classes and its impact on the mental health of a college student. The respondents of interview stated that despite the problems students were facing to attend online classes during the whole pandemic due to management of time. These methods of teaching and learning were new for all the college students and the problem of weak internet connections some were not able to attend the online unit test and final exams. Some students also secured fewer marks than expected as they have performed good in offline exams. This made them feel demoralized towards their studies as their parents had lost their jobs due to extensive lockdown, so most of the students were not in a condition to afford a new and better devices to attend online classes.

The factors which cause the least effects on college students are electricity disruptions, which were reported by 28.10% of respondents, and lack of engagement during online classes, reported by 15.21% of respondents.

According to Table 2.7, the majority of respondents stated that they think online learning is partially effective for them despite the presence of many problems in the online education system, with a response rate of 46.67% from respondents. According to the responses, around one-third of college students (30.47%) have experienced that online classes are an effective method of teaching during the pandemic, and 22.86% of respondents believed that online classes were not an effective method of teaching.

Furthermore, the experience of college students during online classes concerning their opinion, experience of online learning and attitudes of different college students encountered during the pandemic, all these factors indicate increasing mental stress among college students. According to data represented in Table 2.8, the level of mental stress among college students in Gorakhpur city, nearly half of respondents experienced mild symptoms of mental stress (48.10%), and 20% of respondents experienced a modest level of mental stress due to online classes methodology adopted in an emergency due to the pandemic (COVID-19). The results indicated an alarming situation that 13.80% of respondents have experienced a severe level of mental stress.

Finally, Table 2.9 depicts the data related to the favourable mode of study among college students during the pandemic. The offline method, which involves face-to-face interaction among students and teachers, is the most popular method for teaching and learning, with more than half the response rate of 53.33%. After the offline method of teaching, the next most preferred method is through blended mode, which includes elements of both offline teaching and online teaching method with a response rate of 31.90%. Only a small number of respondents preferred the online mode of study, with a response rate of 14.77%.

To sum up, the evidence obtained from the online questionnaire and findings of the interview show the most preferred application for online classes among college students was Google Meet. The most popular device among college students used for online classes is smartphones, which are used for online learning with a broadband connection which may be attributed to the low cost of the device with maximum efficiency. Furthermore, the satisfaction level from online classes of students also depends on many factors such as management of time, weak internet connection, an unfavourable environment of study and incompatibility of devices used to attend online classes. Finally, this study investigated that a huge percentage of college students have faced mild to a modest level of mental stress due to online classes, and the most preferred mode of the study reported by college students was the offline, face-to-face method.

2.5 DISCUSSION

2.5.1 Execution Procedure of Online Education

The results indicated that the majority of college students of Gorakhpur city utilize the Google Meet application as a medium to attend online classes, various factors connected with the findings such as the efficiency of cost features offered, which are compared by the college students according to their capacities and so on. Because of the unexpected occurrence of COVID-19 transforming into a pandemic, all the colleges adopted online methods of education due to various restrictions imposed by the Indian government such as lockdown, which created an urgent need to use online teaching methods as the only option (Lancet, 2020). The online applications which are not in common and frequent use are YouTube and Facebook but these applications cannot be used primarily as a medium for conducting online education. These applications can be used as an informal method to impart online education (Moghavvemi et al., 2018). Nonetheless, the findings of many research studies revealed that these social media platforms also act as a medium of distraction as a majority of college students used these platforms for unproductive purposes instead of educational activities and videos (Siebers et al., 2021).

Smartphones are the most common devices used by college students because India falls under the developing country category and the majority of the population belongs to rural areas and simultaneously the majority of people belong to smaller income earning groups (Behrman & Deolalikar, 1987). Smartphones are cheaper than any other devices, such as desktops and laptops, but they are also not efficient in providing the best output of video streaming during online classes. Some devices are not even compatible to attend online classes and to attend online classes more effectively. Factors which play a major role are the huge quantity of mobile data and proper and continuous electricity supply. The inadequacy of these factors may hinder the effectiveness of online education as parents do not have proper earning source due to stringent lockdown imposed by the Indian government (El Mansour & Mupinga, 2007).

The findings of the research revealed that the most preferred type of internet connection is broadband connection instead of mobile data due to the low cost and high internet speed to participate in online classes.

2.5.2 Opinions of College Students and Level of Satisfaction

There is a high correlation between the effectiveness and success of systems used in online education. The results indicated the satisfaction level and opinion of college students concerning various aspects of online education. The various factors which are responsible to attend the online classes effectively are fast internet speed, student's technical efficiency, training for effective online learning and teaching, teaching methodologies, engagement at the time of online classes and a favourable study environment for both teachers and students. These are some of the important factors which will help in smooth functioning of teaching and learning (Lancet, 2020).

The results of this research revealed that most of the college students are happy with the speed of internet connections, electricity supply and internet speed. Although college students were not enough satisfied with the teaching methodology adopted by different teachers, engagement during online classes and compatibility of devices utilized by college students to attend the online classes. The unfavourable response can be attributed to a dearth of training for both students and teachers, and educational institutions were also closed due to lockdown to halt the spread of the virus.

2.5.3 Mental Status

The experience of students depends on various factors such as physical and mental health, other financial reasons and so on, irrespective of the mode of teaching. If the college students are happy with the mode of teaching and prolong engagement in online classes then there will be fewer chances of any mental stress among them, the new online education system provides the student with changes and more freedom during the process of learning (Barr, 2014). According to findings of this research based on college students of Gorakhpur city revealed that the most of the college students prefer offline (face-to-face) teaching and learning methods as an effective method of learning even after spending a long time with the online education system. The results of this research correspond to the findings revealed in this study which concluded that most the college students preferred offline method of teaching and learning over online teaching methodology. These findings question the adoption of online teaching methods on an emergency basis at the time of the pandemic.

Findings also revealed that more than two-thirds of the college students experienced mild to modest levels of mental stress due to this forcefully applied online education method (Vahia et al., 2020).

A major problem was the digital divide, many students do not even have a good smartphone to attend their classes effectively. Lack of experience and training on both teachers and students' sides made it more unpopular among college students. This problem can be mitigated in the short term if educational institutes get some funds to make the required electronic devices more easily accessible among college students. To enhance the engagement level among college students, teachers should be given proper training for online teaching methods. In the long term, separate funds from the budget may be allocated to strengthen online teaching methodologies.

2.5.4 Plan of Action to Keep Good Mental Health during Pandemic (COVID-19)

Many problems have been aggravated by this pandemic such as cases of domestic violence. The number of suicides, mental stress, depression and anxiety are rising in different Indian states (Anurudran et al., 2020). The pandemic has also highlighted some psychological issues such as sleep disorders, thoughts of suicide, anxiety and fear of being infected among the entire population due to this pandemic.

It is the need of the present time for the government to take the required steps to counter problems related to mental stress, which can be done through an online therapy session. The governmental and non-governmental organizations both should arrange online counselling facilities to help people dealing with mental stress. There should be a scheduled online counselling session every month to tackle mental stress other than online classes in every university. All the educational institutions should formulate a pre-defined plan to conduct online classes with an assignment with proper guidelines to eliminate any uncertainty which can cause any kind of mental stress among college students. Every educational institute should hire a psychologist to solve the respective problem of students. Government should allocate funds in the long run to establish a psychological counselling centre on every university campus and also add subjects related to mental stress. Educational institutes should work with the government to create a dedicated application for college students seeking the help of any professional psychiatrist. Government should organize frequent educational campaigns regarding mental health in all the colleges.

2.5.5 Limitation of the Research Study

This research study is not free from various limitations, which must be taken into account while examining the data. First, this study is based on a sample size of a small number of respondents, the period for data collection was also 15 days during the pandemic. Second, the sampling method used was based on a purposive sampling of non–probability-based sampling method to select the sample unit (participants), which creates a problem of generalization of findings on the whole population. Third, through Google Forms an online questionnaire was prepared was distributed and interviews were also conducted through virtual mode, so the responses may include some respondents' biases. Finally, analysis of data might be done with more advanced statistical tools to provide better results and better interpretations.

2.6 CONCLUSION AND FUTURE SCOPE

A novel virus has been transformed into a global pandemic, which has influenced the entire educational sector badly. This virus is also responsible for the death of many peoples who were infected with this virus all around the world (Spitzer, 2020). Measures adopted to fight this virus include social distancing, which was the only method to halt the extensive spread of this novel virus (Clemens et al., 2020). India has a high population density, which makes it impossible to contain the spread of the coronavirus (Alfano & Ercolano, 2020). The Indian government have imposed a lockdown to stop the spread of the COVID-19 virus. All kinds of activities, whether related to the economic aspect or social aspect and the educational sector, were shut down and only emergency services were allowed to operate. All the universities have taken steps to encourage online education, which revealed a digital divide among students to access quality education in Gorakhpur city of Uttar Pradesh state (India), this transition from offline (face-to-face) method of education to a completely new online method of education with an emergent implementation without any pre-planning. The findings of this research indicated a disappointing image of the urgent application of online education methods and which contributed to mental stress among college students due to the digital divide created by this virus. This study also throws light on methods and devices used to attend the online classes taken by their teachers and also measured their opinions encountered during online education and their satisfaction level concerning different factors. This study also analysed the scope of online learning among college students. This study is helpful to understand comprehensively about perception, efficacy and problems of online education methods to prevent mental stress among college students. Online education has got a push with this pandemic but still, the mental health issue of students is not given priority by the government, but it is the need of time to give this problem the due importance to consider the better implementation of the online education system. This study will provide a foundation to further studies to investigate more intensively into mental health issues of college students of the entire universities of Gorakhpur city.

This study provides a strong foundation for future research related to it as it gives a detailed comprehensive view of the status of psychological stress levels among college students due to a sudden digital divide created because of COVID-19. This study adopted a smaller sample size of only 210 college students, which may not represent a holistic picture of the whole population. Future researches can incorporate a larger sample size to make the findings more realistic and practical. In the near future, study will be extended to take data from other cities to get more reliable findings as this study only includes data of students living in Gorakhpur district of Uttar Pradesh state.

REFERENCES

Aboagye, E., Yawson, J. A., & Appiah, K. N. (2021). COVID-19 and E-learning: The challenges of students in tertiary institutions. *Social Education Research*, 1–8.

Adedoyin, O. B., & Soykan, E. (2020). COVID-19 pandemic and online learning: The challenges and opportunities. *Interactive Learning Environments*, 1–13.

Adnan, M., & Anwar, K. (2020). Online learning amid the COVID-19 pandemic: Students' perspectives. *Online Submission*, *2*(1), 45–51.

Alam, A. (2020). *Challenges and possibilities of online education during Covid-19.*

Alfano, V., & Ercolano, S. (2020). The efficacy of lockdown against COVID-19: A cross-country panel analysis. *Applied Health Economics and Health Policy*, *18*, 509–517.

Alradhawi, M., Shubber, N., Sheppard, J., & Ali, Y. (2020). Effects of the COVID-19 pandemic on mental well-being amongst individuals in society-A letter to the editor on "The socio-economic implications of the coronavirus and COVID-19 pandemic: A review". *International Journal of Surgery (London, England)*, *78*, 147.

Alvarez Jr, A. V. (2021). Rethinking the digital divide in the time of crisis. *Globus Journal of Progressive Education*, *11*(1), 26–28.

Amerio, A., Brambilla, A., Morganti, A., Aguglia, A., Bianchi, D., Santi, F., . . . Capolongo, S. (2020). COVID-19 lockdown: Housing built environment's effects on mental health. *International Journal of Environmental Research and Public Health*, *17*(16), 5973.

Anurudran, A., Yared, L., Comrie, C., Harrison, K., & Burke, T. (2020). Domestic violence amid COVID-19. *International Journal of Gynecology & Obstetrics*, *150*(2), 255–256.

Asgari, S., Trajkovic, J., Rahmani, M., Zhang, W., Lo, R. C., & Sciortino, A. (2021). An observational study of engineering online education during the COVID-19 pandemic. *PLoS One*, *16*(4), e0250041.

Azubuike, O. B., Adegboye, O., & Quadri, H. (2021). Who gets to learn in a pandemic? Exploring the digital divide in remote learning during the COVID-19 pandemic in Nigeria. *International Journal of Educational Research Open*, *2*, 100022.

Barr, B. (2014). Identifying and addressing the mental health needs of online students in higher education. *Online Journal of Distance Learning Administration*, *17*(2).

Batubara, B. M. (2021). The problems of the world of education in the middle of the COVID-19 pandemic. *Budapest International Research and Critics Institute (BIRCI-Journal): Humanities and Social Sciences*, *4*(1), 450–457.

Behrman, J. R., & Deolalikar, A. B. (1987). Will developing country nutrition improve with income? A case study for rural South India. *Journal of political Economy*, *95*(3), 492–507.

Butnaru, G. I., Niţă, V., Anichiti, A., & Brînză, G. (2021). The effectiveness of online education during COVID 19 pandemic—a comparative analysis between the perceptions of academic students and high school students from Romania. *Sustainability*, *13*(9), 5311.

Campion, J., Javed, A., Sartorius, N., & Marmot, M. (2020). Addressing the public mental health challenge of COVID-19. *The Lancet Psychiatry*, *7*(8), 657–659.

Chakraborty, P., Mittal, P., Gupta, M. S., Yadav, S., & Arora, A. (2021). Opinion of students on online education during the COVID-19 pandemic. *Human Behavior and Emerging Technologies*, *3*(3), 357–365.

Clemens, V., Deschamps, P., Fegert, J. M., Anagnostopoulos, D., Bailey, S., Doyle, M., . . . Visnapuu-Bernadt, P. (2020). Potential effects of "social" distancing measures and school lockdown on child and adolescent mental health. *European Child & Adolescent Psychiatry*, *29*, 739–742.

Cullen, W., Gulati, G., & Kelly, B. D. (2020). Mental health in the COVID-19 pandemic. *QJM: An International Journal of Medicine*, *113*(5), 311–312.

Daniel, J. (2020). Education and the COVID-19 pandemic. *Prospects*, *49*(1), 91–96.

Doyumgaç, I., Tanhan, A., & Kiymaz, M. S. (2021). Understanding the most important facilitators and barriers for online education during COVID-19 through online photovoice methodology. *International Journal of Higher Education*, *10*(1), 166–190.

El Mansour, B., & Mupinga, D. M. (2007). Students' positive and negative experiences in hybrid and online classes. *College Student Journal*, *41*(1), 242.

Giorgi, G., Lecca, L. I., Alessio, F., Finstad, G. L., Bondanini, G., Lulli, L. G., . . . Mucci, N. (2020). COVID-19-related mental health effects in the workplace: A narrative review. *International Journal of Environmental Research and Public Health*, *17*(21), 7857.

Gualano, M. R., Lo Moro, G., Voglino, G., Bert, F., & Siliquini, R. (2020). Effects of COVID-19 lockdown on mental health and sleep disturbances in Italy. *International Journal of Environmental Research and Public Health*, *17*(13), 4779.

Ha, N. H., Nayyar, A., Nguyen, D. M., & Liu, C. A. (2019). Enhancing students' soft skills by implementing CDIO-based integration teaching mode. In *The 15th international CDIO conference* (p. 569).

Iqbal, S. Z., Li, B., Onigu-Otito, E., Naqvi, M. F., & Shah, A. A. (2020). The long-term mental health effects of COVID-19. *Psychiatric Annals*, *50*(12), 522–525.

Kontoangelos, K., Economou, M., & Papageorgiou, C. (2020). Mental health effects of COVID-19 pandemic: A review of clinical and psychological traits. *Psychiatry Investigation*, *17*(6), 491.

Kumar, A., Krishnamurthi, R., Bhatia, S., Kaushik, K., Ahuja, N. J., Nayyar, A., & Masud, M. (2021). Blended learning tools and practices: A comprehensive analysis. *IEEE Access*, *9*, 85151–85197.

Lai, J., & Widmar, N. O. (2021). Revisiting the digital divide in the COVID-19 era. *Applied Economic Perspectives and Policy*, *43*(1), 458–464.

Lancet, T. (2020). India under COVID-19 lockdown. *Lancet (London, England)*, *395*(10233), 1315.

Lee, J. (2020). Mental health effects of school closures during COVID-19. *The Lancet Child & Adolescent Health*, *4*(6), 421.

Liu, J. J., Bao, Y., Huang, X., Shi, J., & Lu, L. (2020). Mental health considerations for children quarantined because of COVID-19. *The Lancet Child & Adolescent Health*, *4*(5), 347–349.

McKibbin, W., & Fernando, R. (2020). The economic impact of COVID-19. *Economics in the Time of COVID-19*, *45*(10.1162).

Moghavvemi, S., Sulaiman, A., Jaafar, N. I., & Kasem, N. (2018). Social media as a complementary learning tool for teaching and learning: The case of YouTube. *The International Journal of Management Education*, *16*(1), 37–42.

Mukhopadhyay, M., Pal, S., Nayyar, A., Pramanik, P. K. D., Dasgupta, N., & Choudhury, P. (2020, February). Facial emotion detection to assess learner's state of mind in an online learning system. In *Proceedings of the 2020 5th international conference on intelligent information technology* (pp. 107–115).

Muthuprasad, T., Aiswarya, S., Aditya, K. S., & Jha, G. K. (2021). Students' perception and preference for online education in India during COVID-19 pandemic. *Social Sciences & Humanities Open*, *3*(1), 100101.

Pokhrel, S., & Chhetri, R. (2021). A literature review on impact of COVID-19 pandemic on teaching and learning. *Higher Education for the Future*, *8*(1), 133–141.

Pragholapati, A. (2020). *COVID-19 impact on students*.

Qazi, A., Naseer, K., Qazi, J., AlSalman, H., Naseem, U., Yang, S., . . . Gumaei, A. (2020). Conventional to online education during COVID-19 pandemic: Do develop and underdeveloped nations cope alike. *Children and Youth Services Review*, *119*, 105582.

Ramsetty, A., & Adams, C. (2020). Impact of the digital divide in the age of COVID-19. *Journal of the American Medical Informatics Association*, *27*(7), 1147–1148.

Siebers, T., Beyens, I., Pouwels, J. L., & Valkenburg, P. M. (2021). Social media and distraction: An experience sampling study among adolescents. *Media Psychology*, 1–25.

Slade, T., Grove, R., & Burgess, P. (2011). Kessler psychological distress scale: Normative data from the 2007 Australian national survey of mental health and wellbeing. *Australian & New Zealand Journal of Psychiatry*, *45*(4), 308–316.

Son, C., Hegde, S., Smith, A., Wang, X., & Sasangohar, F. (2020). Effects of COVID-19 on college students' mental health in the United States: Interview survey study. *Journal of Medical Internet Research*, *22*(9), e21279.

Sostero, M., Milasi, S., Hurley, J., Fernandez-Macias, E., & Bisello, M. (2020). *Telework ability and the COVID-19 crisis: A new digital divide?* (No. 2020/05). JRC Working Papers Series on Labour, Education and Technology.

Spitzer, M. (2020). Masked education? The benefits and burdens of wearing face masks in schools during the current Corona pandemic. *Trends in Neuroscience and Education*, *20*, 100138.

Tarkar, P. (2020). Impact of COVID-19 pandemic on education system. *International Journal of Advanced Science and Technology*, *29*(9s), 3812–3814.

Teymori, A. N., & Fardin, M. A. (2020). COVID-19 and educational challenges: A review of the benefits of online education. *Annals of Military and Health Sciences Research*, *18*(3).

Thakur, A. (2020). Mental health in high school students at the time of COVID-19: A student's perspective. *Journal of the American Academy of Child and Adolescent Psychiatry*, *59*(12), 1309.

Vahia, I. V., Jeste, D. V., & Reynolds, C. F. (2020). Older adults and the mental health effects of COVID-19. *Jama*, *324*(22), 2253–2254.

Vargo, D., Zhu, L., Benwell, B., & Yan, Z. (2021). Digital technology use during COVID-19 pandemic: A rapid review. *Human Behavior and Emerging Technologies*, *3*(1), 13–24.

Velavan, T. P., & Meyer, C. G. (2020). The COVID-19 epidemic. *Tropical Medicine & International Health*, *25*(3), 278.

Xie, X., Siau, K., & Nah, F. F. H. (2020). COVID-19 pandemic–online education in the new normal and the next normal. *Journal of Information Technology Case and Application Research*, *22*(3), 175–187.

3 Investigation of Students' Intention and Related Determinants for E-Learning Continuance in Education after COVID-19

Diksha Khera

3.1 INTRODUCTION

E-learning means imparting learning by the medium of information or digital technologies. In other terms, students and teachers use digital technologies, tools, devices and internet facilities for imparting learning, communication, developing study materials, completing their study tasks and program management (Fry 2001; Means et al. 2009). In education, digital technologies use is not a new phenomenon. For decades, educational institutions are managing their distance learning programs and online learning programs with the help of technologies. E-learning has numbers of benefits like easy to use, information quality, service quality, user-friendly, dynamic course content, various learning style accommodation access to educational programs, improving educational effectiveness, cost-effectiveness, usefulness, flexibility, interactivity and so on (Al-Rahmi et al. 2019; Dumford and Miller 2018; Leszczyński et al. 2018; Panigrahi et al., 2018; Smedley 2010). In the research field also, digital technologies provide a great help to researchers by various platforms and software applications for literature review, mass data collection and data analysis. It is also believed that CDIO-based technical teaching mode can improve the students' soft skills (Ha et al. 2019). The educational institutions are offering various opportunities for online learning and numbers of participating students in online learning are increasing day by day (Alqurashi 2019; Lim and Richardson 2021). Moreover, the continuous technological innovations and internet facilities' accessibility are also motivating users to adopt e-learning in education (Tang and Byrne 2007). Even the advent of Covid-19 pandemic has pressured educational institutions to use digital technologies in learning activities for sustainable education because Covid-19 has forced to maintain social distancing and closed all educational institutions, offices and businesses (Adedoyin and Soykan 2020; Baber 2020; Iivari et al., 2020; Xhelili et al. 2021). According to World Economic Forum (2020), "billions of students across 186 countries are now out of classrooms and learning from home through the suggested online medium by their educational institution due to the pandemic". However, in terms of digital infrastructure and competence skills, neither universities nor students were prepared for the stringent change forced by Covid-19 but during pandemic students and teachers were engaged in numbers of digital applications such as Zoom, Google classroom, BigBlueButton and others for learning education. Raza et al. (2021) also investigated the significant direct impact of social isolation and moderating role of corona fear on the relationship between behavioral intention and usage behavior for learning management system among students. It has also believed that educational institutions would continue blended learning in their curriculum after pandemic when the situation improved. According to Kumar et al. (2021), "Blended learning is hybrid of traditional face-to-face classroom and e-learning experience".

 DOI: 10.1201/9781003425779-3

On the contrary, students and teachers are spending more time with phones and computers for education during this pandemic, which is further creating stress, boredom, weak eyesight problem, social isolation and various other psychological and physical problems among them (Çevik and Bakioğlu 2021; Moawad 2020; Raza et al. 2021). Also, in some studies, there is evidence that online learning reduces the progress of content delivery and learner engagement and students cannot successfully study in the online environment (Alshamrani 2019; Baber 2020; Boyd 2004; Zacharis 2011). The unexpected interruption of family members and pets during online learning in home also impacted the participants' attention (Manfuso 2020). Many students don't have proper facilities and resources to use technologies in education (Adedoyin and Soykan 2020). Due to changes in emotions and behavior of learner, online learning still lacks the success and popularity of efficient pedagogy method (Mukhopadhyay et al. 2020). Moreover, the deficiency of digital competence to use e-learning technologies in students and teachers also deviate them from e-learning (Bennett et al., 2008). In online learning, supervision and control of learning activities of students are also not effective (Arkorful and Abaidoo 2015). Therefore, digital technologies have numbers of advantages and disadvantages.

Now the question arises, whether the educational institutions will continue the e-learning in education after pandemic when almost institutions have opened. The answer of this question only depends on the continuance intentions of students, teachers and institutions for using digital technologies in education. However, continuance intentions are affected from digital technology use's benefits and challenges and users' limitations, experience and satisfaction which they have felt from use of technologies (Alqurashi 2019; Jiang et al. 2021; Joksimović et al. 2015; Joo et al., 2011; Kuo et al. 2014; Lim and Richardson 2021; Yang et al. 2016). So, the future of this new-age learning pedagogy after the end of pandemic only depends on continued usage intentions of students, teachers and institutions for e-learning in education (Jiang et al. 2021; Lim and Richardson 2021). However, a vast literature is available on technology usage intention and adoption before and during Covid-19 period, but very little is available on continuance intention and usage of technology and its significant determinants (Barnes 2011; Bhattacherjee et al., 2008; Daghan and Akkoyunlu 2016; Jasperson et al., 2005; Terzis et al., 2013; Thong et al., 2006). Furthermore, in some previous studies, continuance was evaluated as the extension of adoption process (Jasperson et al. 2005; Karahanna et al., 1999; Venkatesh and Davis 2000) but these were criticized by Bhattacherjee (2001) on basis of short-term usage. Apart from this, no study executed till now has investigated the continuance usage intention for online learning in higher education after Covid-19 when almost educational institutions have opened. Therefore, investigation of long-term e-learning continuance intention of users after pandemic and its determinants should be considered significant for further research. Thus, the present study has made a step forward in this direction because its objective is to assess the long-term continuance intention and its significant determinants for e-learning in education after the end of the Covid-19 pandemic. However, by focusing on limitations of research, researchers only focused on intentions of students and taken responses from those who were studying in higher educational institutions (enrolled in public and private universities) of Punjab and Haryana states of Indian economy. In this research, a complex relationships pattern was assessed between continuance intention and its determinants by integration of four important theories such as Technology Continuance Theory (TCT), Information System Success (ISS) model, Unified Theory of Acceptance And Use of Technology (UTAUT) and Core Construct of Task-technology-Fit (TTF) model. This integration will cover the previous research gaps and better assess the long-term technology acceptance's benefits and challenges with students' attitude, satisfaction and long-term continuance intentions towards e-learning. The analysis of students' continuance intention and its significant determinants will provide stakeholders with vital information to set up the strategic plans for increasing the effectiveness of digital technologies and secure their future. This study would also be beneficial for educational administrators to improve the experience of students with online learning environment in a better context.

3.1.1 Organization of the Chapter

The rest of the chapter is organized as follows. Section 3.2 discusses literature review mentioning regarding e-learning continuance intention, technology continuance theory (TCT), information system success model (ISSM), task-technology-fit (TFT) and unified theory of acceptance and use of technology (UTAUT). Section 3.3 elaborates research methodology. Data analysis and interpretation is highlighted in Section 3.4. Section 3.5 stresses discussion on results. And, finally section 3.6 concludes the chapter with limitations and recommendations.

3.2 LITERATURE REVIEW

3.2.1 E-Learning Continuance Intention

According to Fry (2001), "E-learning is the use of internet and some other important technologies to develop materials for educational purposes, instructional delivery and management of program". It is also known as web-based, network-based, internet-based, computer-aided, mobile-based learning, virtual learning or online learning (Kesim 2011). Symeonides and Childs (2015) stated that "in online learning and distance education, interaction and communication patterns are different from face-to-face learning as students and teachers communicate with each other by using synchronous and asynchronous communication tools". Also, online learning adds more flexibility in learning process (Baber 2020). However, digitalization is not a simple procedure; it has complex contents such as its management, infrastructure availability, digital competence, feelings of fear and social isolation, access to digital resources and so forth (Agnoletto and Queiroz 2020). Moreover, to ensure the effective online learning it is necessary that students spend enough time on participation and interaction with teachers and other students (Cheng et al. 2011), and teachers also have adequate digital competence skills (Agnoletto and Queiroz 2020; Bennett et al., 2008). You and Kang (2014) also emphasized that non-allocation of adequate time in online learning environment generally becomes the reason for unsuccessful online learners.

Obviously, digital transformation in education is not a new phenomenon, it presents since many years through mode of distance education or online programs (Adedoyin and Soykan 2020; Bhattacherjee 2001; Daghan and Akkoyunlu 2016). In previous literature, evidence is available which show that in technology acceptance or adoption, a vast majority of factors such as users' self-efficacy belief (Demiralay and Karadeniz 2010; Venkatesh and Davis 2000), hedonic motivation and cost-effectiveness (Venkatesh et al., 2012), habit (Limayem and Cheung 2008), perceived usefulness and perceived ease of use (Davis 1989), attitude (Gan et al., 2017), and enough time and effort (Hrastinski 2009) are important. Furthermore, the rapid advancement in technological innovations and internet's accessibility have also increased the rate of technologies adoption in learning process in education sector (Perienen 2020; Tang and Byrne 2007). Educational institutions are also offering various opportunities for online learning, and the number of students participating in online learning are increasing day by day (Alqurashi 2019; Lim and Richardson 2021). Also, the use of mobile and other electronic devices as study aids is motivating students towards e-learning and improving their grades, learning efficiency and confidence and also reducing their education costs (Boticki et al. 2015; Reychav et al., 2015). O'Bannon and Thomas (2015) emphasized in their study that teachers perceived various mobile phones' functions and features such as access to the internet, use of educational apps, clickers' capabilities and others are useful in the classroom.

Even the global shutdown of several activities including education due to fear of contact with Covid-19 also forced the educational institutions to transform their traditional physical classroom learning in virtual learning (Çevik and Bakioğlu 2021; Chayomchai et al. 2020). Online learning was the only alternative of physical classroom during the pandemic (Iivari et al., 2020; Xhelili et al. 2021). Mulenga and Marbán (2020) also found Covid-19 had played a mediating role in making people use digital devices and e-learning activities more effectively. They stated Covid-19 forced lecturers to learn digital skills and deliver the contents by e-learning mode. Moreover, several other researchers also conducted research studies on intention and adoption of e-learning during Covid-19 (Baber 2020; Iwai 2020; Jiang et al. 2021; Mulenga and Marbán 2020; Singh et al., 2020). However, the above stated studies were mainly focused on short-term e-learning adoption during Covid-19, but after pandemic when almost all educational institutions have opened, the investigation of long-term e-learning continuance usage intention and its significant determinants is also very important for improving the effectiveness of online learning programs and securing their future. This study would fill the shortcomings in existing literature through identification of students' long term e-learning continuance intention in education and its impacting determinants.

In existing literature, a very few studies are available on technology continuance usage and intention (Chang 2013; Daghan and Akkoyunlu 2016; Jasperson et al., 2005; Karahanna et al., 1999). Chang (2013) explored the determinants of e-learning systems continuance intention in academic libraries by using responses of undergraduate and graduate students and stated that web quality (information quality, system quality and service quality) positively influences perceived values and satisfaction and further, perceived values and satisfaction determine continuance intention.

Daghan and Akkoyunlu (2016) also focused on investigating determinants of continuance usage intention towards online learning environment and revealed an "online continuance usage intention model" by integration of TCT, ISSM, cognitive model and ECM. The findings indicated that confirmation and satisfaction impacted continuance intention, while confirmation and satisfaction explained by information quality, system quality and service quality. Moreover, satisfaction was also impacted by confirmation, utilitarian value, outcome expectations and perceived value.

In study of Jin et al. (2007), "satisfaction" and "information usefulness" were found as main contributors in continuance usage of virtual communities. Limayem and Cheung (2008) stated that habit played an important role in continuance use of digital learning technologies.

Also, Cheung and Limayem (2005) tested moderating role of habit on relationship of continuance intention and use for information system and found that "moderating role of habit increases over time, while impact of continuance intention on continuance usage weakens over time". Attitude is also found as most influential predictor of adoption and continuance intentions (Gan et al., 2017; Singh et al., 2020). In study of Cheung and Lee (2007), self-efficacy and satisfaction also significantly explained continuance intention for distributing knowledge in virtual platform community.

Moreover, continuance intention is significant determinant of continuance behavior (Al-Debei et al., 2013). Bhattacherjee et al. (2008) also extended the "IT continuance model" by linking continuance intention to continuance behavior and integrating impact of two perceived behavioral dimensions such as "self-efficacy" and "facilitating conditions" on intention and behavior in model. The results supported the strong and significant impact of continuance intention on continuance behavior for IT system. Additionally, continuance intention had significantly explained by self-efficacy, whereas continuance behavior explained by facilitating conditions.

Hsu and Chiu (2004) also attempted to examine electronic service continuance by decomposing the TPB as this theory only suggest the determinant of adoption but not post-adoption. Authors decomposed the component of "perceived behavior control" in "self-efficacy" and "perceived controllability", component of "subjective norms" in "social influence" and "interpersonal influence", "attitude" component in "perceived usefulness", "perceived playfulness", "and perceived risk". The results suggested "continuance intention is determined by internet self-efficacy and satisfaction, whereas, satisfaction is jointly determined by perceived usefulness, perceived playfulness and interpersonal influence".

Barnes (2011) examined the continuance use intention in the virtual world and suggested that continuance intention driven by habit had explained by perceived usefulness and enjoyment or hedonic goals. However, frequency of prior use had not any significant impact on habit.

Moreover, (Chen et al., 2012) "integrated fairness theory and ISSM to construct a model for investigating the motivation behind learner's intention to continue the web-based learning usage. The model hypothesized that system usage, three dimensions of quality (system quality, service quality and information quality) and three dimensions of fairness (procedural, distributive and interactional) affect learner's satisfaction. Authors also assumed that satisfaction and dimensions of fairness will influence the learner's intention to continue web-based learning. The results indicated that information quality, system quality, system usage, distributive fairness and interactional fairness exhibit the positive significant effects on satisfaction. Also, procedural fairness and satisfaction play a significant role in influencing learner's intention to continue web-based-learning.

In addition, (Chen et al., 2012) "investigated what social factors, social norm, image, critical mass and electronic word-of-mouth, exert influence on continuance intention to use Web 2.0 (includes applications such as YouTube, blogs, Plurk, Google, and Twitter). The casual model of satisfaction and continuance intention as a function of proposed social factors indicated that satisfaction significantly affects electronic word-of-mouth, which further significantly influences continuance intention. In addition, subjective norm, image and critical mass all have a significant impact on satisfaction, which in turn has an indirect significant influence on electronic word-of-mouth. Finally, all social factors found to have direct significant influence on continuance intention.

Balaban et al. (2013) had also developed the electronic portfolio system success model and further emphasized that system's "satisfaction and intention to use and continue are effected from information quality, system quality and service quality".

By extending the expectation-confirmation model, Susanto et al. (2016) also investigated factors influencing the continuance intention among customers for smartphone banking services. The results indicated that confirmation of expectations after post-adoption significantly influences perceived security, perceived usefulness, trust and satisfaction. In addition, perceived usefulness influences trust, satisfaction and continuance intention. Finally, both satisfaction and self-efficacy influence continuance intention.

By integrating technology acceptance model and task-technology-fit model, Wu and Chen (2017) also investigated continuance intention to use massive open online courses (MOOCs). Their results also revealed that perceived usefulness and attitude are very critical to continuance intention to use MOOC. In addition, perceived usefulness is significant mediator for effects of perceived ease of use, task-technology-fit, reputation, social influence and social recognition on continuance intention. The findings also indicated that in predicting continuance intention, perceived ease of use, task-technology-fit, reputation, social influence and social recognition also play an important role.

Aminu (2018) also examined the factors influencing students' continuance intention towards using MOOC among universities students based on expectation-confirmation model and technology acceptance model. The findings indicated that expectation-confirmation had significant effect on perceived usefulness, perceived ease of use and satisfaction for MOOC. Furthermore, perceived ease of use, perceived usefulness and satisfaction had also significantly affected the continuance intention for using MOOC.

Daneji et al. (2019) also examined the impacts of perceived usefulness, confirmation and satisfaction on continuance intention in using massive open online courses by using expectation-confirmation model. Their findings also indicated that confirmation had significantly impacted on perceived usefulness and satisfaction and further, perceived usefulness and satisfaction impacted continuance intention.

Khayer and Bao (2019) investigated the continuance intention for using Alipay by integrating context-awareness and technology continuance theory. The results revealed that confirmation and perceived usefulness significantly influenced the continuance intention through satisfaction. Also, perceived usefulness, satisfaction, context and ubiquity have significant impact on continuance intention through attitude.

Taghizadeh et al. (2021) also identified the factors influencing continuance usage intention for online learning during pandemic and also examined the relationship between satisfaction and continuance usage intention. For research purpose, three important theories such as diffusion of innovation theory, expectation confirmation theory and Unified theory of acceptance and use of technology were integrated. Furthermore, the moderating role of self-quarantine during pandemic on relationship between satisfaction and continuance intention and direct effect of self-quarantine on continuance intention were tested. The findings indicated that satisfaction significantly impacted on continuance intention and direct and moderating role of self-quarantine was also significant.

Also, Salim et al. (2021) examined the significant impact of smart city services channel characteristics (perceived benefits, perceived ease of use, perceived complexities, perceived capabilities, perceived dependency, perceived securities and perceived trustworthiness) and personal characteristics (innovativeness and control seeking behavior) in compare of other technology-based characteristics, on satisfaction and continuance intention to use smart city services channel.

In light of existing literature on continuance intention, some frequently used theories and models such as ISSM (DeLone and McLean 2003), TCT (Liao et al., 2009), UTAUT (Venkatesh et al., 2012) and TTF model (Gan et al., 2017) had integrated in this study to fill the research gaps and better explain students' e-learning continuance intention and its significant determinants.

3.2.2 Technology Continuance Theory (TCT)

This is the latest integrated theory created in literature of information technology "by combining technology acceptance model (TAM), expectation confirmation model and cognitive model to determine the long-term usage of technological innovation". It was developed by Liao et al. (2009). It brought six variables of above three models in one integrated model to explain information technology long-term usage intention. These were "confirmation, satisfaction, perceived usefulness, perceived ease of use, attitude and information system usage continuance intention".

Confirmation: Perception regarding harmony between users' expectations regarding technology usage and technology's actual performance.

Satisfaction: Judgment made for technology based on technology's performance.

Perceived usefulness: Perception regarding what the users will gain by using technology.

Perceived ease of use: Perception regarding what the users will get ease by using technology.

Attitude: General evaluation made for technology.

Information system usage continuance intention: "Intention of users regarding continuance usage of information system".

TAM explains the "significant positive impacts of perceived technology acceptance benefits such as usefulness and ease of use on attitude towards technology". Also, the expectation confirmation model considers confirmation of expectations in regards of technology usage as the powerful determinant for satisfaction from technology usage (Aminu 2018; Daneji et al., 2009), while the cognitive model states that confirmation behavior "affects satisfaction and satisfaction predicts long-term usage intention" (Salim et al. 2021). However, cognitive model also includes attitude and states that both attitude and satisfaction affect long term usage intention. This cognitive model also considers the significant impact of satisfaction on attitude. In light of technology continuance theory, same relationships were assumed among aforesaid six variables in present study. Also, researcher-assumed attitude plays a significant mediation role in between satisfaction and continuance usage intention.

H1: Confirmation significantly affects satisfaction of students from e-learning.
H2: Satisfaction significantly affects attitude of students for e-learning.
H3: Perceived values significantly affect attitude of students for e-learning.
H4: Satisfaction significantly affects continuance usage intention of students for e-learning in higher education.
H5: Attitude significantly affects continuance usage intention of students for e-learning in higher education.
H6: Attitude plays a significant mediation role in between satisfaction and continuance usage intention.

3.2.3 Information System Success Model (ISSM)

This model was first introduced in 1992 and again revised by DeLone and McLean in 2003. It explains that success of information system affected by its information quality, service quality and system quality. These qualities further effect satisfaction and satisfaction effect on continuance intention (Daǧhan and Akkoyunlu 2016). In existing literature, this model was integrated with different theories and models to explain technology continuance usage intention in context of education (Alsabawy et al., 2013; Balaban et al., 2013; Daghan and Akkoyunlu 2016; Li et al. 2012). Alzahrani and Seth (2021) also investigated the factors influencing students' satisfaction with continuous use of learning management system during Covid-19 pandemic by integrating social cognitive theory, expectation confirmation theory and information system success model. The results stated that service quality didn't influence satisfaction but both information quality and self-efficacy impacted satisfaction. In addition, findings revealed that neither self-efficacy nor satisfaction impacted expectation, although prior experience and social influence did. Moreover, IT infrastructure services also plays a significant role in success of e-learning system via significant effect on perceived usefulness and user satisfaction (Alsabawy et al., 2013). In light of previous literature, it was assumed that web quality reflected by information quality, service quality and system quality significantly effects on students' satisfaction and attitude for e-learning. It was also assumed that satisfaction plays a significant mediation role in between web quality and attitude.

H7: Web quality significantly affects satisfaction of students from e-learning.
H8: Web quality significantly affects attitude of students for e-learning.
H9: Satisfaction plays a significant mediation role in between Web quality and attitude.

3.2.4 Task-Technology-Fit (TTF)

The task-technology-fit model states that an individual will adopt technology only when technology characteristics fit with his task characteristics (Goodhue and Thompson 1995; Zhou et al., 2010). Even if the perceived technology is useful but technology characteristics do not properly match with his task characteristics or cannot improve his task performance, then he will not adopt technology (Goodhue and Thompson 1995; Junglas et al., 2008; Zhou et al., 2010). Also, a good TTF would develop the positive feelings among individuals towards technology and promote the technology adoption (Lin and Huang 2008; Lu and Yang 2014; McGill and Klobas 2009). Good TTF can also improve the attitude and satisfaction of individuals from technology usage and may continue the technology usage (Gan et al., 2017). In light of previous studies, following hypotheses were also put forward:

H10: Task-technology-fit significantly affects satisfaction of students from e-learning.
H11: Task-technology-fit significantly affects attitude of students for e-learning.
H12: Satisfaction plays a significant mediation role in between task-technology-fit and attitude.

3.2.5 Unified Theory of Acceptance and Use of Technology (UTAUT)

Venkatesh et al. (2003) UTAUT includes four important explanatory constructs such as performance expectancy, effort expectancy, social influence and facilitating conditions that influence technology acceptance and long-term usage. In 2012, Venkatesh et al. (2012), extended this theory by including three more constructs such as hedonic motivation, price value (cost) and habit. In present study, four main constructs of UTAUT in our integrated model such as facilitating conditions, hedonic motivation, habit and cost effectiveness (price value) were adapted.

Facilitating conditions: Facilitating conditions refers to "users' perceptions for resources and support available for performing a particular behavior" (Venkatesh et al. 2003).

Hedonic motivation: Venkatesh et al. (2012) defined hedonic motivation as "fun or pleasure derived from use of technology"

Habit: Habit has defined as "extent to which people tend to perform behavior automatically because of learning" (Limayem et al. 2007).

Cost effectiveness: Bartley and Golek (2004) defined cost effectiveness of online learning as "cost and time incurred in travelling and traditional method of education saved from online learning".

Hedonic motivation (or enjoyment) is an important determinant in technology acceptance, usage and continuance intention (El-Masri and Tarhini 2017; Van Der Heijden 2004; Holbrook and Hirschman 1982; Hsu and Chiu 2004; Kang and Lee 2010). Habit is another main predictor of technology usage (Davis and Venkatesh 2004; Kim and Malhotra 2005; Limayem and Hirt 2003). Also, online collaboration is highly cost-effective compared to traditional methods, as it reduces cost of office overheads and allows employees work from home or other locations (El-Gohary 2012; Gilmore et al., 2007). Costs can dominate the adoption and continuance usage of technology decisions (Chan et al. 2008; Coulter and Coulter 2007; El-Masri and Tarhini 2017; Rahman et al., 2020). Facilitating conditions can also change the decision of technology acceptance and continuance usage (El-Masri and Tarhini 2017; Maillet et al., 2015; Venkatesh et al. 2003). In regards of the aforesaid technology use facilitators, it was assumed that significant moderating role of these technology use facilitators in relationship of attitude and e-learning continuance usage intention. It was assumed if users have positive attitude towards e-learning but they don't have enough facilitating support or e-learning is not cost-effective or they are not habitual for e-learning or not enjoying e-learning as compared to face-to-face learning then it can weakens the relationship between attitude and e-learning continuance intention.

H13: Technology use facilitators play a moderating role in relationship of attitude and e-learning continuance usage intention.

3.3 RESEARCH METHODOLOGY

The exploratory research design was formulated in present study with the aim of investigating the students' continuance intention for e-learning in education and its determinants. Due to the Covid-19 situation, an online survey was conducted by using structured questionnaire and convenience sampling. The structured questionnaire in Google Forms was sent to 500 students studying in higher educational institutions (enrolled in public and private universities) of Haryana and Punjab states of India by WhatsApp, Facebook and email. Out of 500 questionnaires, 260 were returned and 13 were discarded due to outliers and incomplete responses. Finally 247 were left for data analysis.

The formulated integrated theoretical model to investigate the students' continuance intention and its determinants has shown in Figure 3.1. Constructs and their respective items in formulated model have shown in Table 3.1.

These items were asked from respondents by using a 5-point Likert scale rated from strongly disagree (1) to strongly agree (5). The demographic profile of respondents has been shown in Table 3.2. The overall measurement fitness, reliability and validity of integrated theoretical model were ensured by confirmatory factor analysis (CFA).

However, at the time of first order CFA process, discriminated validity between some constructs were violated. Due to this, second order CFA process was run according to the direction of exploratory factor analysis (EFA) to attain the satisfactory discriminate validity between constructs. The results of second order CFA (shown in Table 3.3) confirmed the satisfactory overall fitness, reliability and validity of integrated model. In CFA analysis, if chi-square/df is less than 5, goodness fit indices (CFI, IFI, TLI etc.) are greater than 0.80 and badness fit indices (RMR and RMSEA) are less than 0.10 then fitness of measurement model is confirmed (Tsai and Ghoshal 1998). The Cronbach's internal consistency alpha, composite reliability (CR), average variance explained (AVE), maximum shared variance (MSV) and average shared variance (ASV), all had confirmed the reliability and validity of model. In order to confirm convergent validity and internal consistency of constructs, Cronbach's alpha and CR values of all constructs should be greater than 0.70 (Churchill 1979), AVE should be greater than 0.50 (Hair et al. 2010) and CR should also be higher than AVE (Hair et al. 2010).

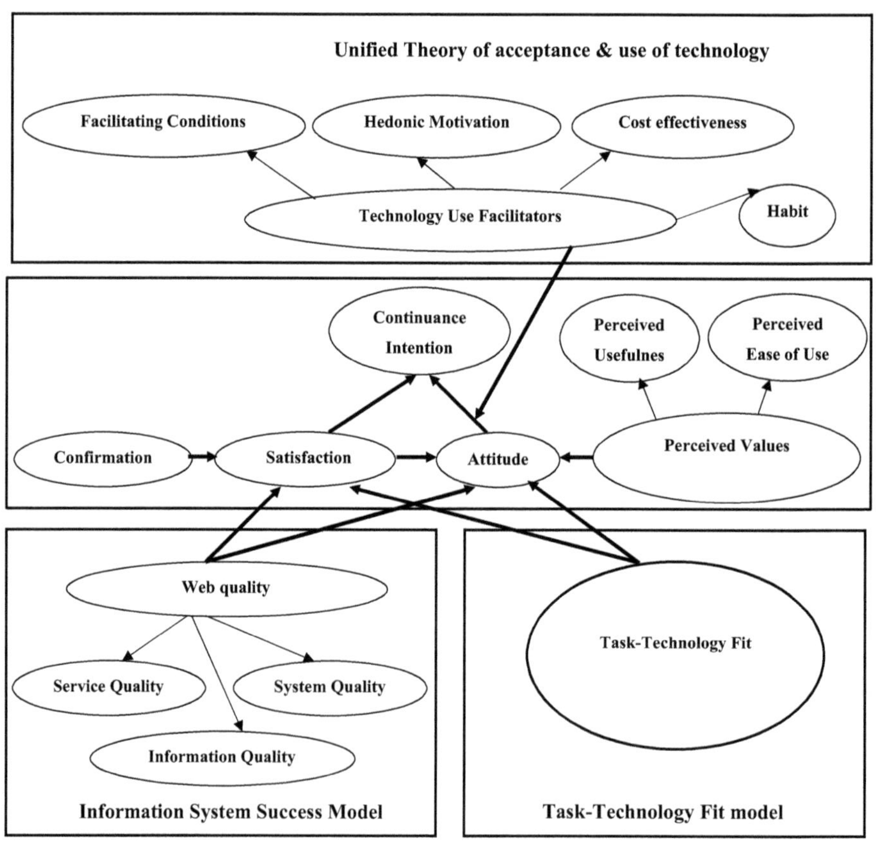

FIGURE 3.1 Theoretical Model.

Source: Authors.

TABLE 3.1
Constructs and Items

Construct	Coding	Item	Reference
Task-technology-fit (TTF)	TTF1	E-learning is enough to help me use the study contents.	(Gan et al., 2017; Lin and Huang 2008)
	TTF2	In general, e-learning fully meets my study needs.	
	TTF3	E-learning made the study tasks easy.	
	TTF4	E-learning best fit the study tasks.	
Information quality (IQL)	IQL1	E-learning provides relevant information for my homework.	(Dalhan and Akkoyunlu 2016)
	IQL2	E-learning presents the information in an appropriate format.	
	IQL3	The information content on the e-learning platforms is good.	
	IQL4	The information from e-learning is up-to-date enough for my study purposes.	
	IQL5	The reliability of output information from e-learning is high.	
	IQL6	E-learning provides the information I need in time.	
Service quality (SQL)	SQL1	Overall, e-learning has excellent service quality.	(Dalhan and Akkoyunlu 2016)
	SQL2	E-learning gives fast service to users.	
	SQL3	The operation hours of the e-learning platforms are convenient to its users.	
System quality	SYQL1	Steps to complete a task on the e-learning platforms follow a logical sequence.	(Dalhan and Akkoyunlu 2016)
	SYQL2	Performing an operation on e-learning platforms always leads to a predicted result.	
	SYQL3	The arrangement of information on the e-learning platforms screens is clear.	
	SYQL4	E-learning platforms have natural and predictable screen changes.	
	SYQL5	E-learning platforms respond quickly during the busiest hours of the day.	
Perceived usefulness	PU1	I find e-learning is quite useful for attending lectures.	(Davis 1989; Singh et al., 2020)
	PU2	It is a fast and easy medium to get connected with teachers.	
	PU3	Using e-learning leads to effective communication with teachers.	
	PU4	It is easy to pass useful information using e-learning.	
	PU5	Through e-learning, it is easy to understand the subject taught.	
	PU6	The use of e-learning would enhance my effectiveness in learning.	
	PU7	Using e-learning would improve my course performance.	
	PU8	Using e-learning would increase my productivity in coursework.	
	PU9	I find e-learning to be useful.	
	PU10	Using e-learning would make it easier to do my study	
Perceived ease of use	PEU1	I find e-learning is easy to use	(Davis 1989; Singh et al., 2020)
	PEU2	My interaction with e-learning platforms is clear and understandable.	
	PEU3	It would be easy for me to find information on learning platforms.	

(Continued)

TABLE 3.1 *(Continued)*
Constructs and Items

Construct	Coding	Item	Reference
	PEU4	E-learning platform features are quite flexible.	
Facilitating conditions	FC1	I have the necessary resources to use e-learning.	(Venkatesh et al., 2012)
	FC2	I have the necessary knowledge to use e-learning.	
	FC3	E-learning is compatible with other teaching-learning methods that I use.	
	FC4	I can get help from others when I have difficulties in using e-learning.	
Cost-effectiveness	CE1	I find e-learning is affordable.	(Singh et al., 2020)
	CE2	E-learning suits my need of low-cost education.	
	CE3	I get value for money by using e-learning for education.	
	CE4	I get the value of efforts and time by using e-learning for education.	
Hedonic motivation	HM1	E-learning is fun.	(Venkatesh et al., 2012)
	HM2	E-learning is enjoyable.	
	HM3	E-learning is entertaining.	
Habit	HT1	The use of e-learning has become a habit for me.	(Venkatesh et al., 2012)
	HT2	I am addicted to using e-learning.	
	HT3	I must use e-learning.	
	HT4	Using e-learning has become natural to me.	
Confirmation	CF1	My experience of using e-learning is better than I expected.	(Daɫhan and Akkoyunlu 2016)
	CF2	The service level provided by e-learning is better than I expected.	
	CF3	Overall, most of my expectations from using e-learning are confirmed.	
Satisfaction	SF1	I am satisfied with the performance of e-learning.	(Daɫhan and Akkoyunlu 2016)
	SF2	I am pleased with the experience of e-learning.	
	SF3	The decision to use e-learning was a wise one.	
Attitude	Att1	To continue the use of e-learning in education would be a good idea.	(Khayer and Bao 2019)
	Att2	I like the idea of continuing the use of e-learning for education.	
	Att3	Continuous use of e-learning in education would be a pleasant experience.	
	Att4	I believe it would be a wise idea to continue the use of e-learning for my coursework.	
Continuance usage intention (CI)	CI1	I intend to continue the use of e-learning in the future.	(Daɫhan and Akkoyunlu 2016)
	CI2	I will continue the use of e-learning in the future.	
	CI3	I will regularly use e-learning in the future.	

TABLE 3.2
Demographic Profile of Respondents

Variable	Category	Frequency	Percentage
Gender	Male	89	36%
	Female	158	64%
	Total	247	100%
Study course	Graduate	91	36.8%
	Post-graduate	59	23.9%
	PhD	86	34.8%
	Post-doctorate	11	4.5%
	Total	247	100%
University	Public	137	55.5%
	Private	110	44.5%
	Total	247	100%
State	Haryana	142	57.5%
	Punjab	105	42.5%
	Total	247	100%
Own computer	Yes	163	66%
	No	84	34%
	Total	247	100%

Source: Field survey

Furthermore, for discriminant validity, AVE values should be higher than both MSV and ASV values of respective constructs (Fornell and Larcker 1981). After getting fit, reliable and valid measurement integrated model, the mean value of items retained in continuance intentions construct was computed to determine the level of intentions of students for continue the use of e-learning in education. Lastly, to identify the determinants for continuance intentions the structural relationships between the constructs of integrated model were tested according to formulated research hypotheses by using structural equation modeling (SEM) technique.

3.4 DATA ANALYSIS AND INTERPRETATION

As seen in Table 3.2, 89 (36%) of 247 respondents were male and 158 (64%) were female. Also, 91 (36.8%) were studying in graduate course, 59 (23.9%) were in post-graduate course, 86 (34.8%) were PhD students and 11 (4.5%) students were in post-doctorate course.

Furthermore, 137 (55.5%) students were from public university and 110 (44.5%) were in private university. Out of 247 students, 142 (57.5%) were from Haryana state and 105 (42.5%) were from Punjab state of India. In regards of owning a computer, 163 (66%) students were who have their personal computer; however, 84 (34%) students didn't have their personal computers.

Moreover, Figure 3.2 shows the second order measurement model of all latent variables with significant standardized factor loadings of all items. The values obtained from second order CFA for model fitness were as follows: chi-square/df =2.139, p-value = 0.000, RMR = 0.080, CFI = 0.884, IFI = 0.885, TLI = 0.878, RMSEA = 0.068.

The standardized factor loadings of all items were significant ($p < 0.05$) and also higher than 0.5; CR and AVE values of all constructs were greater than 0.7 and 0.5, respectively; and CR values were also higher than AVE values (shown in Table 3.3). The AVE values of all constructs were also higher than ASV and MSV values (shown in Table 3.3). The Cronbach's alpha values

TABLE 3.3
Results of Confirmatory Factor Analysis

First Order Construct	Second Order Construct	Item	Standardized Factor Loadings	Alpha	CR	AVE	MSV	ASV
Information quality (IQL)	Web quality (WQ)	IQL	0.985***					
System quality (SYQL)		SYQL	0.899***	00.975	00.970	00.916	00.764	00.492
Service quality (SQL)		SQL	0.984***					
Perceived usefulness (PU)	Perceived values (PV)	PU	0.982***	00.973	00.977	00.955	00.764	00.504
Perceived ease of use (PEU)		PEU	0.972***					
Cost effectiveness (CE)	Technology use Facilitators (TUF)	CE	0.905***					
Habit (HT)		HT	0.950***					
Facilitating conditions (FC)		FC	0.919***	00.953	00.958	00.851	00.676	00.469
Hedonic motivation (HM)		HM	0.916***					
Task-technology-fit (TTF)		TTF1	0.857***					
		TTF2	0.926***					
		TTF3	0.909***	00.935	00.936	00.786	00.621	00.419
		TTF4	0.852***	00.904	00.904	00.702	00.635	00.457
Attitude (Att)		Att1	0.791***					
		Att2	0.840***					
		Att3	0.903***					
		Att4	0.812***					
Confirmation (CF)		CF1	0.759***					
		CF2	0.784***	00.862	00.881	00.714	00.307	00.171
		CF3	0.976***					
Satisfaction (SF)		SF1	0.814***					
		SF2	0.687***	00.784	00.786	00.552	00.288	00.202
		SF3	0.723***					
Continuation intention (CI)		CI1	0.978***					
		CI2	0.812***	00.945	00.950	00.865	00.438	00.305
		CI3	0.990***					

*** $p < 0.001$.

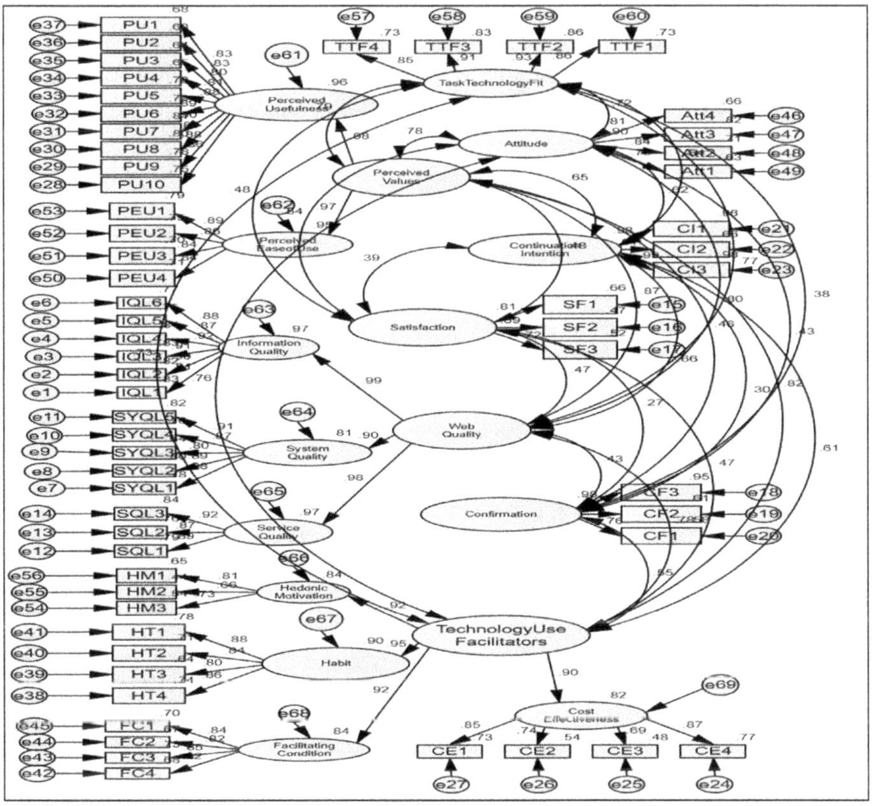

FIGURE 3.2 Measurement Model.

of all constructs were also higher than 0.7. Thus, overall integrated theoretical model was found as fit, reliable and valid.

After finding reliable and valid model, the levels of e-learning continuance intention and its determinants among students were found by computing mean values for the items retained in respective latent variables. Table 3.4 shows that mean values of all latent variables were higher than 3 except mean values of technology use facilitators and attitude. It reveals that respondents are intended to continue the e-learning in their education, as they are satisfied with different web qualities, services and benefits provided by digital technologies in completing their different study tasks. Their expectations with digital technologies are also confirmed and they perceived e-learning's acceptance in higher education is valuable for their study. However, results also indicated that students don't have enough facilitators such as internet facilities, fun, cost-effectiveness, habitual tendency and so forth in using digital technologies for their education. It may also be possible that due to insufficient technology use facilitators, students' attitude for using e-learning technologies in education is negative.

Furthermore, in order to identify the determinants for e-learning continuance intention of students, the structural relationships among dimensions of four important proposed theories were evaluated by considering the coefficient of determination (R^2) and significance of path coefficients of each hypothesis. Figure 3.3 shows the structural relationships which were evaluated in present study.

Table 3.5 and Figure 3.3 indicated that three exogenous variables such as web quality, task-technology-fit and confirmation explained 20% of total variance of satisfaction endogenous variable. However, it was found that web quality and task-technology-fit had positively and significantly

TABLE 3.4
Level of E-Learning Continuance Intention and Its Impacting Factors

Latent Variable	*N*	Mean	SD
Technology use facilitators	247	2.6681	0.75888
Web quality	247	3.2075	1.07542
Perceived values	247	3.3015	1.03381
Task-technology-fit	247	3.2709	1.05586
Attitude	247	2.8806	0.94556
Continuation intention	247	3.1311	1.20682
Confirmation	247	3.2797	1.23012
Satisfaction	247	3.5012	0.91980

TABLE 3.5
Coefficient of Determination

Outcome Variables	R^2
Satisfaction	0.20
Attitude	0.58
Continuance Intention	0.29

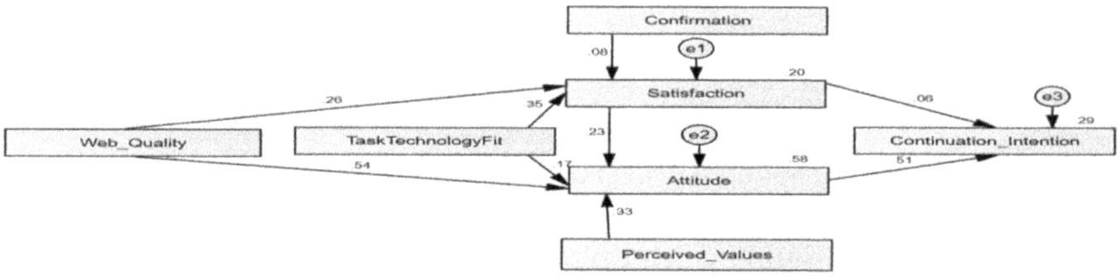

FIGURE 3.3 Structural Model.

impacted on satisfaction but confirmation didn't significantly impact on satisfaction. The results also indicated that 58% of total variance of attitude endogenous variable was explained by four exogenous variables such as web quality, task-technology-fit, satisfaction and perceived values. In explanation of 58% of variance of attitude, all exogenous variables such as web quality, task-technology-fit, satisfaction and perceived values had significantly and positively contributed. Lastly, results revealed that satisfaction and attitude had explained 29% of total variance of continuance intention, however, attitude had significantly impacted on continuance intention but satisfaction didn't impact on continuance intention.

In present study, the mediation role of satisfaction between the relationship of web quality and attitude and between the relationship of task-technology-fit and attitude was also analyzed. Also, the mediation role of attitude between satisfaction and continuance intention was analyzed. Mediation is defined as indirect effect of predictor variable on endogenous variable through the medium of another variable (Shrout and Bolger 2002). The mediating variable which affects the relational power and direction of predictive variable on dependent variable (Baron and Kenny 1986). According to Baron and Kenny (1986), if any predictor variable significantly effects on dependent variable directly and indirectly and relational power of direct effect of predictor variable on dependent variable changed in presence of another variable, then there is mediating role of this another variable between the relation of predictor and dependent variables. Moreover, if direct relation between predictor and dependent variables in presence of mediator becomes insignificant then this mediating variable plays a full mediation role between predictor and dependent variables. Also, if strength of direct relation between predictor and dependent variables in presence of mediator reduces then partial mediation role is played by mediating variable between predictor and dependent variables.

Table 3.7 shows that satisfaction played a partial mediation role between web quality and attitude, as direct effect of web quality on attitude in presence of satisfaction reduced but it was still significant. Moreover, satisfaction played a full mediation role between task-technology-fit and attitude, as direct effect of task-technology-fit on attitude in presence of satisfaction became insignificant. Similarly, attitude also played a full mediation role between satisfaction and continuance intention, as direct effect of satisfaction on continuance intention in presence of attitude became insignificant.

In addition, moderating effect or interaction effect of technology use facilitators in relationship of attitude and continuance intention was also evaluated. Moderation is defined as when strength and direction of relationship of two variables are affected by another variable (Morgan-Lopez and Mackinnon 2006). Moderation effect or interaction effect means when product ($X \times W$) of predictor variable (X) and third variable (W) significantly increases the coefficient of determination (R^2) of dependent variable. Table 3.8 and Figure 3.4 show that technology use facilitators didn't have any significant moderation effect on relationship of attitude and continuance intention, as R^2 was not

TABLE 3.6
Path Analysis Results

Relationship	Standardized Regression Weights	*p*	CR	Hypothesis
CF → SF	0.081	0.156	1.419	H1: Not accepted
SF → Att	0.229	***	4.993	H2: Accepted
PV → Att	0.335	***	8.096	H3: Accepted
SF → CI	0.062	0.295	1.046	H4: Not accepted
Att → CI	0.505	***	8.474	H5: Accepted
WQ → SF	0.263	***	4.607	H7: Accepted
WQ → Att	0.544	***	12.629	H8: Accepted
TTF → SF	0.347	***	6.068	H10: Accepted
TTF → Att	0.165	***	3.735	H11: Accepted

*** $p < 0.001$.

TABLE 3.7
Mediation Analysis Results

Relationship	Non-Mediated Model		Mediated Model				Results
	Direct Effect		Direct Effect		Indirect Effect		
	β	*p*	β	*p*	β	*p*	
WQ → SF → Att	.0.581	.0.002	.0.541	.0.001	.0.067	.0.006	H9: Partial Mediation
TTF → SF → Att	.0.235	0.015	.0.165	.0.062	.0.080	.0.007	H12: Full Mediation
SF → Att → CI	.0.401	0.001	.0.062	.0.370	.0.116	.0.001	H6: Full Mediation

TABLE 3.8
Moderation Analysis Results

Relationship	Non-Moderated Model $R^2 = 0.448$	Moderated Model $R^2 = 0.449$	Result
	Standardized Regression Weights	Standardized Regression Weights	
Att → CI	0.391***		
TUF → CI	0.311***		
Att → CI		0.394***	
TUF → CI		0.290***	
Att X TUF → CI		–0.043	H13: No Moderation

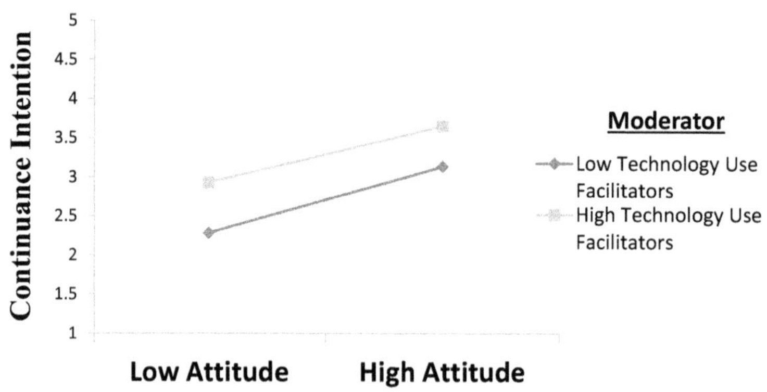

FIGURE 3.4 Moderation analysis of technology use facilitators on link between attitude and continuance intention.

significantly increased and interaction effect of attitude and technology use facilitators on continuance intention was also insignificant.

3.5 DISCUSSION

A main objective of this research was investigation of students' e-learning continuance usage intention and its determinants after the end of Covid-19 pandemic. For solving the proposed research problem, 247 students studying in higher education institutions of Punjab and Haryana states of Indian economy had participated. During analysis it was observed that that on average students are agree to continue the e-learning usage in their education after pandemic, as mean value of continuance intention was greater than 3. Furthermore, their expectations with digital technologies have also confirmed and they are satisfied with information technologies' performance and benefits in their study. They also agreed on the facts that information quality, system quality and service quality of digital technologies are good enough and technologies are fit with their study tasks. They stated that continuance usage of e-learning in education may also provide various perceived benefits such as easy to use, user-friendly, fast communication with teachers, easy to pass information, more subject contents, learning effectiveness, flexibility and course performance improvement and so on.

However, they also exhibited negative attitude to continue e-learning in education and they didn't feel any fun, habit or motivation for e-learning. It may be possible that physical interaction during classrooms with their friends and teachers is enjoyable and motivational for students.

They also considered that the virtual learning is not cost-effective for them, as they would need to own a personal computer and permanent internet facilities for effective learning. They stated that they and their teachers don't have sufficient resources and knowledge to effectively utilize the e-learning technologies in education. In study of Raza et al. (2021), students were also not satisfied with online learning due to poor internet connectivity. Moreover, virtual learning had increased psychological stress, weak eyesight problem, social isolation and other psychological and physical problems due to more time spending with phones and computers for education and other purposes.

As another main focus of this study was to identify which determinants are significantly impacting on students' continuance intention. It was found that web quality which reflects the information quality, system quality and service quality of digital technologies, significantly and positively effects on students' satisfaction with digital technologies. These results were similar to study of Daghan and Akkoyunlu (2016). In addition, task-technology-fit also significantly and positively affects the satisfaction but confirmation didn't affect satisfaction. Results also revealed that in explanation of attitude's variance, web quality, task-technology-fit, perceived values (usefulness and easy to use) and satisfaction contribute the significant and positive role. Our research findings of effects of web quality on satisfaction and attitude supported information system success model of DeLone and McLean (2003). Also, similar findings of positive effects of task-technology-fit and perceived values on attitude were found in studies of Davis 1989; Gan et al., 2017; Singh et al., 2020. The significant positive relationship of task-technology-fit and satisfaction also supported the study of Cheng (2020). Moreover, on continuance intention, attitude significantly and positively impacts but satisfaction didn't impact in our study. The significant effect of attitude on continuance intention supported the findings of Cheng 2020 and Gan et al., 2017. At the time of mediation analysis, it was found that satisfaction plays a partial mediation role in between web quality and attitude but plays a full mediation role in between task-technology-fit and attitude. Lastly, attitude also plays a full mediation role between satisfaction and continuance intention. However, findings didn't support the moderating role of technology use facilitators in relationship of attitude and continuance intention.

3.6 CONCLUSION, LIMITATIONS AND RECOMMENDATIONS

In the present study, the investigation of students' continuance usage intention for e-learning in education after the end of Covid 19 pandemic has mainly focused as it is significant to study whether institutions would continue online learning when situation improved after Covid-19. As we all know, in pandemic time, all educational institutions in whole world were forced to adopt e-learning for sustainable education because with advent of Covid-19 all educational institutions, business places and offices were closed to prevent the spread of Corona virus (Çevik and Bakioğlu 2021; Mulenga and Marbán 2020). However, some institutions are still closed due to the fear of virus. The immense use of digital technologies in education during Covid-19 period has significantly transformed the physical classroom learning in virtual learning (Ribeiro 2020). However, the growth and future of information technologies, especially in education sector after the end Covid-19 period, depend on continuance intentions of students, teachers and institutions for e-learning in education. Therefore, researcher attempted to investigate students' continuance intention and its determinants for e-learning in education. Due to the limitations of research, researcher has only focused on students who were studying in higher education institutions (enrolled in public and private universities) of Punjab and Haryana states of India. For investigating students' continuance usage intentions for e-learning, an integrated theoretical model was framed by clubbing four important theories in our research design such as TCT, ISSM, TTF and UTAUT. These four theories actually based the students' continuance usage intentions on their expectation-confirmation, satisfaction, attitude, technology's perceived benefits and challenges and their limitations which they felt by use of digital technologies in their education.

The findings indicated that students intend to continue the e-learning usage in education because they perceived technology is useful in their education and completing their study tasks. They are satisfied with different web-qualities and their expectations with technology services have also confirmed. Although their attitude towards e-learning is not favorable and their limitations such as internet access, digital competence, price value, enjoyment, social isolation and so on are also deviating them from long-term continuance usage of e-learning.

From the findings, researcher has suggested that if information technologies providers, policymakers and educational institutions wish to continue the e-learning usage in education for the future of digital technologies then they have to do efforts to maintain the students' satisfaction and make their attitude positive by improving digital technologies' quality, service, perceived values and task-technology-fit benefits in education. However, information technologies providers also need to do efforts to make the e-learning fun, motivational and cost-effective. Educational institutions and policymakers should provide necessary resources and knowledge to students and teachers for using digital technologies in education. Policymakers may contribute in success of information technologies by providing necessary funds in financial year plans and can fulfill the dream of digital India. With these efforts, students' continuance intention will improve and digital technologies providers can also ensure the future of digital technologies, especially in education sector. Lastly, this study has claimed that only virtual learning could not be better than physical classroom learning for overall personality development of students but blended learning could improve the students' study performance and personality development. Blended learning will involve the online experiences and benefits with face-to-face learning advantages. Therefore, the educational institutions should use the blended learning to make their students more innovative and effective.

However, this study also has some limitations. First, in this research, students were taken only from higher educational institutions (enrolled in private and public universities) of Punjab and Haryana states. The use of large sample and inclusion of students as well as teachers from different schools, colleges and Indian states for the future studies may increase the generalization of this study. Second, questionnaire method and quantitative data analysis tools were used. It was also recommended future researchers for using qualitative data collection and analysis tools. Third, future studies may be executed by including other impacting factors of continuance intention which were not focused in this study. Fourth, this study was executed by an online medium which had prevented the homogenous distribution of some sample variables such as gender, university, state and so on. In future studies, integration of online and offline data collection mediums can increase the homogeneity of sample distribution. Finally, this research can be conducted in international countries also and comparison may be made. Within scope of this study, it was assumed that stress, eyesight problems and other psychological and physical factors didn't affect students' continuance usage intention for e-learning.

REFERENCES

Adedoyin, Olasile Babatunde, and Emrah Soykan. 2020. "Covid-19 Pandemic and Online Learning: The Challenges and Opportunities." *Interactive Learning Environments*:1–13. doi: 10.1080/10494820.2020.1813180.

Agnoletto, R., and V. Queiroz. 2020. "COVID-19 and the Challenges in Education. Ce." *Bulletin* 5(2):1–22.

Alqurashi, Emtinan. 2019. "Predicting Student Satisfaction and Perceived Learning Within Online Learning Environments." *Distance Education* 40(1):133–148. doi: 10.1080/01587919.2018.1553562.

Al-Debei, Mutaz M., Enas Al-Lozi, and Anastasia Papazafeiropoulou. 2013. "Why People Keep Coming Back to Facebook: Explaining and Predicting Continuance Participation from an Extended Theory of Planned Behaviour Perspective." *Decision Support Systems* 55(1):43–54.

Al-Rahmi, Waleed Mugahed, Noraffandy Yahaya, Ahmed A. Aldraiweesh, Mahdi M. Alamri, Nada Ali Aljarboa, Uthman Alturki, and Abdulmajeed A. Aljeraiwi. 2019. "Integrating Technology Acceptance Model with Innovation Diffusion Theory: An Empirical Investigation on Students' Intention to Use E-Learning Systems." *IEEE Access* 7:26797–26809. doi: 10.1109/ACCESS.2019.2899368.

Alsabawy, Ahmed Younis, Aileen Cater-Steel, and Jeffrey Soar. 2013a. "IT Infrastructure Services as a Requirement for E-Learning System Success." *Computers & Education* 69:431–451.
Alshamrani, M. S. 2019. *An Investigation of the Advantages and Disadvantages of Online Education*. Auckland University of Technology.
Alzahrani, Latifa, and Kavita Panwar Seth. 2021. "Factors Influencing Students' Satisfaction with Continuous Use of Learning Management Systems During the COVID-19 Pandemic: An Empirical Study." *Education and Information Technologies* 26(6):6787–6805. doi: 10.1007/s10639-021-10492-5.
Aminu, Daneji Aisha. 2018. *Predictive Model of Students' Continuance Intention in Massive Open Online Course among University Students*. Universiti Putra Malaysia.
Arkorful, Valentina, and Nelly Abaidoo. 2015. "The Role of E-Learning, Advantages and Disadvantages of Its Adoption in Higher Education." *International Journal of Instructional Technology and Distance Learning* 12(1):29–42.
Baber, Hasnan. 2020. "Determinants of Students' Perceived Learning Outcome and Satisfaction in Online Learning During the Pandemic of COVID19." *Journal of Education and E-Learning Research* 7(3):285–292. doi: 10.20448/JOURNAL.509.2020.73.285.292.
Balaban, Igor, Enrique Mu, and Blazenka Divjak. 2013. "Development of an Electronic Portfolio System Success Model: An Information Systems Approach." *Computers & Education* 60(1):396–411.
Barnes, Stuart J. 2011. "Understanding Use Continuance in Virtual Worlds: Empirical Test of a Research Model." *Information and Management* 48(8):313–319. doi: 10.1016/j.im.2011.08.004.
Baron, Reuben M., and David A. Kenny. 1986. "The Moderator-Mediator Variable Distinction in Social Psychological Research. Conceptual, Strategic, and Statistical Considerations." *Journal of Personality and Social Psychology* 51(6):1173–1182. doi: 10.1037/0022-3514.51.6.1173.
Bartley, Sharon Jeffcoat, and Jennifer H. Golek. 2004. "Evaluating the Cost Effectiveness of Online and Face-to-Face Instruction." *Journal of Educational Technology & Society* 7(4):167–175.
Bennett, Sue, Karl Maton, and Lisa Kervin. 2008. "The 'Digital Natives' Debate: A Critical Review of the Evidence." *British Journal of Educational Technology* 39(5):775–786. doi: 10.1111/j.1467-8535.2007.00793.x.
Bhattacherjee, Anol. 2001. "Understandinignformatiosnystems Continuancea: An Expectation-Confirmatiom Model." *MIS Quarterly*, 25(3):351–370.
Bhattacherjee, Anol, Johan Perols, and Clive Sanford. 2008. "Information Technology Continuance: A Theoretic Extension and Empirical Test." *Journal of Computer Information Systems* 49(1):17–26.
Boticki, Ivica, Jelena Baksa, Peter Seow, and Chee-Kit Looi. 2015. "Usage of a Mobile Social Learning Platform with Virtual Badges in a Primary School." *Computers & Education* 86:120–136.
Boyd, D. 2004. "The Characteristics of Successful Online Students." *New Horizons in Adult Education and Human Resource Development* 18(2):31–39.
Çevik, Mustafa, and Büşra Bakioğlu. 2021. "Investigating Students' E-Learning Attitudes in Times of Crisis (COVID-19 Pandemic)." *Education and Information Technologies* 27:65–87. doi: 10.1007/s10639-021-10591-3.
Chan, Kwok Yue, Min Gong, Yan Xu, and James Y. L. Thong. 2008. "Examining User Acceptance of SMS: An Empirical Study in China and Hong Kong." Pp. 3–7 in *12th Pacific Asia Conference on Information System, Suzhou, China*.
Chang, Chiao Chen. 2013. "Exploring the Determinants of E-Learning Systems Continuance Intention in Academic Libraries." *Library Management* 34(1/2):40–55. doi: 10.1108/01435121311298261.
Chayomchai, Ampol, Wilaiwan Phonsiri, Arnon Junjit, Rujirek Boongapim, and Ubonwan Suwannapusit. 2020. "Factors Affecting Acceptance and Use of Online Technology in Thai People During COVID-19 Quarantine Time." *Management Science Letters* 10(13):3009–3016. doi: 10.5267/j.msl.2020.5.024.
Chen, Shih Chih, David C. Yen, and Mark I. Hwang. 2012. "Factors Influencing the Continuance Intention to the Usage of Web 2.0: An Empirical Study." *Computers in Human Behavior* 28(3):933–941. doi: 10.1016/j.chb.2011.12.014.
Cheng, Cho Kin, Dwayne E. Paré, Lisa Marie Collimore, and Steve Joordens. 2011. "Assessing the Effectiveness of a Voluntary Online Discussion Forum on Improving Students' Course Performance." *Computers and Education* 56(1):253–261. doi: 10.1016/j.compedu.2010.07.024.
Cheng, Yung Ming. 2020. "Quality Antecedents and Performance Outcome of Cloud Based Hospital Information System Continuance Intention." *Journal of Enterprise Information Management* 33(3):654–683. doi: 10.1108/JEIM-04-2019-0107.
Cheung, Christy M. K., and Matthew K. O. Lee. 2007. "What Drives Members to Continue Sharing Knowledge in a Virtual Professional Community? The Role of Knowledge Self-Efficacy and Satisfaction." *KSEM* 4798 LNAI:472–84. doi: 10.1007/978-3-540-76719-0_46.

Cheung, Christy M. K., and Moez Limayem. 2005. "The Role of Habit in Information Systems Continuance: Examining the Evolving Relationship Between Intention and Usage." Pp. 471–82 in *26th International Conference on Information Systems 2005 Proceedings 39*. Association for Information Systems AIS Electronic Library (AISeL).

Churchill, Gilbert A. 1979. "A Paradigm for Developing Better Measures of Marketing Constructs." *Journal of Marketing Research* 16(1):64–73.

Coulter, Keith S., and Robin A. Coulter. 2007. "Distortion of Price Discount Perceptions Through the Left-Digit Effect." *Journal of Consumer Research* 34(2):162–173. doi: 10.1007/s11002-015-9387-5.

Daghan, Gökhan, and Buket Akkoyunlu. 2016. "Modeling the Continuance Usage Intention of Online Learning Environments." *Computers in Human Behavior* 60:198–211. doi: 10.1016/j.chb.2016.02.066.

Daneji, Aisha Aminu, Ahmad Fauzi Mohd Ayub, and Mas Nida Md Khambari. 2019. "The Effects of Perceived Usefulness, Confirmation and Satisfaction on Continuance Intention in Using Massive Open Online Course (MOOC)." *Knowledge Management and E-Learning* 11(2):201–214. doi: 10.34105/j.kmel.2019.11.010.

Dağhan, Gökhan, and Buket Akkoyunlu. 2016. "Modeling the Continuance Usage Intention of Online Learning Environments." *Computers in Human Behavior* 60:198–211. doi: 10.1016/j.chb.2016.02.066.

Davis, Fred D. 1989. "Perceived Usefulness, Perceived Ease of Use, and User Acceptance of Information Technology." *MIS Quarterly* 13(3):319–339. doi: 10.2307/249008.

Davis, Fred D., and Viswanath Venkatesh. 2004. "Toward Preprototype User Acceptance Testing of New Information Systems: Implications for Software Project Management." *IEEE Transactions on Engineering Management* 51(1):31–46. doi: 10.1109/TEM.2003.822468.

DeLone, William H., and Ephraim R. McLean. 2003. "The DeLone and McLean Model of Information Systems Success: A Ten-Year Update." *Journal of Management Information Systems* 19(4):9–30.

Demiralay, Raziye, and Sirin Karadeniz. 2010. "The Effect of Use of Information and Communication Technologies on Elementary Student Teachers' Perceived Information Literacy Self-Efficacy." *Educational Sciences: Theory and Practice* 10(2):841–851.

Dumford, Amber D., and Angie L. Miller. 2018. "Online Learning in Higher Education: Exploring Advantages and Disadvantages for Engagement." *Journal of Computing in Higher Education* 30(3):452–465.

El-Gohary, Hatem. 2012. "Factors Affecting E-Marketing Adoption and Implementation in Tourism Firms: An Empirical Investigation of Egyptian Small Tourism Organisations." *Tourism Management* 33(5):1256–1269.

El-Masri, Mazen, and Ali Tarhini. 2017. "Factors Affecting the Adoption of E-Learning Systems in Qatar and USA: Extending the Unified Theory of Acceptance and Use of Technology 2 (UTAUT2)." *Educational Technology Research and Development* 65(3):743–763. doi: 10.1007/s11423-016-9508-8.

Fornell, Claes, and David F. Larcker. 1981. "Evaluating Structural Equation Models with Unobservable Variables and Measurement Error." *Journal of Marketing Research* 18(1):39–50.

Fry, Kate. 2001. "E-Learning Markets and Providers: Some Issues and Prospects." *Education + Training* 43(4/5):233–239. doi: 10.1108/EUM0000000005484.

Gan, Chunmei, Hongxiu Li, and Yong Liu. 2017. "Understanding Mobile Learning Adoption in Higher Education An Empirical Investigation in the Context of the Mobile Library." *Electronic Library* 35(5):846–860. doi: 10.1108/EL-04-2016-0093.

Gilmore, Audrey, Damian Gallagher, and Scott Henry. 2007. "E-marketing and SMEs: Operational Lessons for the Future." *European Business Review* 19(3):234–247.

Goodhue, Dale L., and Ronald L. Thompson. 1995. "Task-Technology Fit and Individual Performance." *MIS Quarterly: Management Information Systems* 19(2):213–233. doi: 10.2307/249689.

Ha, N. H., A. Nayyar, D. M. Nguyen, and C. A. Liu. 2019. "Enhancing Students' Soft Skills by Implementing CDIO-Based Integration Teaching Mode." P. 569 in *15th International CDIO Conference*.

Hair, Joseph F., Rolph E. Anderson, Barry J. Babin, and Wiiliam C. Black. 2010. *Multivariate Data Analysis: A Global Perspective*. 7th ed. Prentice Hall, Upper Saddle River, NJ.

Holbrook, Morris B., and Elizabeth C. Hirschman. 1982. "The Experiential Aspects of Consumption: Consumer Fantasies, Feelings, and Fun." *Journal of Consumer Research* 9(2):132. doi: 10.1086/208906.

Hrastinski, Stefan. 2009. "A Theory of Online Learning as Online Participation." *Computers & Education* 52(1):78–82.

Hsu, Meng Hsiang, and Chao Min Chiu. 2004. "Predicting Electronic Service Continuance with a Decomposed Theory of Planned Behaviour." *Behaviour and Information Technology* 23(5):359–373. doi: 10.1080/01449290410001669969.

Iivari, Netta, Sumita Sharma, and Leena Ventä-Olkkonen. 2020. "Digital Transformation of Everyday Life—How COVID-19 Pandemic Transformed the Basic Education of the Young Generation and Why Information Management Research Should Care?" *International Journal of Information Management* 55(June):102183. doi: 10.1016/j.ijinfomgt.2020.102183.

Iwai, Y. 2020. "Online Learning During the COVID-19 Pandemic: What Do We Gain and What Do We Lose When Classrooms Go Virtual?" *Scientific American*. Retrieved (https://blogs.scientificamerican.com/observations/online-learning-during-the-covid-19-pandemic/).

Jasperson, Jon, Pamela E. Carter, and Robert W. Zmud. 2005. "A Comprehensive Conceptualization of Post-Adoptive Behaviors Associated with Information Technology Enabled Work Systems." *MIS Quarterly: Management Information Systems* 29(3):525–557. doi: 10.2307/25148694.

Jiang, Haozhe, A. Y. M. Atiqui Islam, Xiaoqing Gu, and Jonathan Michael Spector. 2021. "Online Learning Satisfaction in Higher Education During the COVID-19 Pandemic: A Regional Comparison Between Eastern and Western Chinese Universities." *Education and Information Technologies* 26(6):6747–6769. doi: 10.1007/s10639-021-10519-x.

Jin, Xiaoling, Christy M. K. Cheung, Matthew K. O. Lee, and Huapin Chen. 2007. "Understanding the Sustainability of Virtual Communities in China." Pp. 310–21 in *European Conference on Information Systems (ECIS) 2007 Proceedings*.

Joksimović, S., D. Gašević, V. Kovanović, B. E. Riecke, and M. Hatala. 2015. "Social Presence in Online Discussions as a Process Predictor of Academic Performance." *Journal of Computer Assisted Learning* 31(6):638–654. doi: 10.1111/jcal.12107.

Joo, Young Ju, Kyu Yon Lim, and Eun Kyung Kim. 2011. "Online University Students' Satisfaction and Persistence: Examining Perceived Level of Presence, Usefulness and Ease of Use as Predictors in a Structural Model." *Computers and Education* 57(2):1654–1664. doi: 10.1016/j.compedu.2011.02.008.

Junglas, Iris, Chon Abraham, and Richard T. Watson. 2008. "Task-Technology Fit for Mobile Locatable Information Systems." *Decision Support Systems* 45(4):1046–1057.

Kang, Young Sik, and Heeseok Lee. 2010. "Understanding the Role of an IT Artifact in Online Service Continuance: An Extended Perspective of User Satisfaction." *Computers in Human Behavior* 26(3):353–364. doi: 10.1016/j.chb.2009.11.006.

Karahanna, E., D. W. Straub, and N. L. Chervany. 1999. "Information Technology Adoption across Time: A Cross-Sectional Comparison of Pre-Adoption and Post-Adoption Beliefs." *MIS Quarterly* 23(2):183–213.

Kesim, E. 2011. "Uzaktan Eğitimde Meydana Gelen Değerler Dizisi (Paradigma) Değişimlerinin e-Öğrenme Ekonomisi Alanına Yansımaları." *Türkiye'de E-Öğrenme Gelişmeler ve Uygulamalar (2. Bs.)*:2–19.

Khayer, Abul, and Yukun Bao. 2019. "The Continuance Usage Intention of Alipay: Integrating Context-Awareness and Technology Continuance Theory (TCT)." *Bottom Line* 32(3):211–229. doi: 10.1108/BL-07-2019-0097.

Kim, Sung S., and Naresh K. Malhotra. 2005. "A Longitudinal Model of Continued IS Use: An Integrative View of Four Mechanisms Underlying Postadoption Phenomena." *Management Science* 51(5):741–755. doi: 10.1287/mnsc.1040.0326.

Kumar, Adarsh, Rajalakshmi Krishnamurthi, Surbhi Bhatia, Keshav Kaushik, Neelu Jyothi Ahuja, Anand Nayyar, and Mehedi Masud. 2021. "Blended Learning Tools and Practices: A Comprehensive Analysis." *IEEE Access* 9:85151–85197. doi: 10.1109/ACCESS.2021.3085844.

Kuo, Yu-Chun, Andrew E. Walker, Kerstin E. E. Schroder, and Brian R. Belland. 2014. "Interaction, Internet Self-Efficacy, and Self-Regulated Learning as Predictors of Student Satisfaction in Online Education Courses." *The Internet and Higher Education* 20:35–50.

Leszczyński, Piotr, Anna Charuta, Beata Łaziuk, Robert Gałązkowski, Arkadiusz Wejnarski, Magdalena Roszak, and Barbara Kolodziejczak. 2018. "Multimedia and Interactivity in Distance Learning of Resuscitation Guidelines: A Randomised Controlled Trial." *Interactive Learning Environments* 26(2):151–162. doi: 10.1080/10494820.2017.1337035.

Li, Yan, Yanqing Duan, Zetian Fu, and Philip Alford. 2012. "An Empirical Study on Behavioural Intention to Reuse E-Learning Systems in Rural China." *British Journal of Educational Technology* 43(6):933–948. doi: 10.1111/j.1467-8535.2011.01261.x.

Liao, Chechen, Prashant Palvia, and Jain Liang Chen. 2009. "Information Technology Adoption Behavior Life Cycle: Toward a Technology Continuance Theory (TCT)." *International Journal of Information Management* 29(4):309–320.

Lim, Jieun, and Jennifer C. Richardson. 2021. "Predictive Effects of Undergraduate Students' Perceptions of Social, Cognitive, and Teaching Presence on Affective Learning Outcomes According to Disciplines." *Computers and Education* 161(1). doi: 10.1016/j.compedu.2020.104063.

Limayem, Moez, and Christy M. K. Cheung. 2008. "Understanding Information Systems Continuance: The Case of Internet-Based Learning Technologies." *Information & Management* 45(4):227–232.

Limayem, Moez, and Sabine Gabriele Hirt. 2003. "Force of Habit and Information Systems Usage: Theory and Initial Validation." *Journal of the Association for Information Systems* 4(1):65–97. doi: 10.17705/1jais.00030.

Limayem, Moez, Sabine Gabriele Hirt, Christy M. K. Cheung, and Sabine Gabriele Hirt. 2007. "How Habit Limits the Predictive Power of Intention: The Case of Information Systems Continuance." *MIS Quarterly* 31(4):705–737.

Lin, Tung-Ching, and Chien Chih Huang. 2008. "Understanding Knowledge Management System Usage Antecedents: An Integration of Social Cognitive Theory and Task Technology Fit." *Information and Management* 45(6):410–417. doi: 10.1016/j.im.2008.06.004.

Lu, Hsi-Peng, and Yi-Wen Yang. 2014. "Toward an Understanding of the Behavioral Intention to Use a Social Networking Site: An Extension of Task-Technology Fit to Social-Technology Fit." *Computers in Human Behavior* 34:323–332.

Maillet, Éric, Luc Mathieu, and Claude Sicotte. 2015. "Modeling Factors Explaining the Acceptance, Actual Use and Satisfaction of Nurses Using an Electronic Patient Record in Acute Care Settings: An Extension of the UTAUT." *International Journal of Medical Informatics* 84(1):36–47. doi: 10.1016/j.ijmedinf.2014.09.004.

Manfuso, L. G. 2020. "How the Remote Learning Pivot Could Shape Higher Ed IT." *EdTech Magazine*.

McGill, Tanya J., and Jane E. Klobas. 2009. "A Task–Technology Fit View of Learning Management System Impact." *Computers & Education* 52(2):496–508.

Means, Barbara, Yukie Toyama, Robert Murphy, Marianne Bakia, and Karla Jones. 2009. Project report: Center for Learning Technology. *Association for Learning and Technology*, UK. Available at: https://repository.alt.ac.uk/629/1/US_DepEdu_Final_report_2009.pdf.

Moawad, Ruba Abdelmatloub. 2020. "Online Learning During the COVID-19 Pandemic and Academic Stress in University Students." *Revista Românească Pentru Educaţie Multidimensională* 12(1 Sup2):100–107.

Morgan-Lopez, Antonio A., and David P. Mackinnon. 2006. "Demonstration and Evaluation of a Method for Assessing Mediated Moderation." *Behavior Research Methods* 38(1):77–87. doi: 10.1177/009524438501700109.

Mukhopadhyay, Moutan, Saurabh Pal, Anand Nayyar, Pijush Kanti Dutta Pramanik, Niloy Dasgupta, and Prasenjit Choudhury. 2020. "Facial Emotion Detection to Assess Learner's State of Mind in an Online Learning System." Pp. 107–15 in *ACM International Conference Proceeding Series*.

Mulenga, Eddie M., and José M. Marbán. 2020. "Is Covid-19 the Gateway for Digital Learning in Mathematics Education?" *Contemporary Educational Technology* 12(2):1–11. doi: 10.30935/cedtech/7949.

O'Bannon, Blanche W., and Kevin M. Thomas. 2015. "Mobile Phones in the Classroom: Preservice Teachers Answer the Call." *Computers & Education* 85:110–122.

Panigrahi, Ritanjali, Praveen Ranjan Srivastava, and Dheeraj Sharma. 2018. "Online Learning: Adoption, Continuance, and Learning Outcome—A Review of Literature." *International Journal of Information Management* 43:1–14.

Perienen, A. 2020. "A Teacher's Perspective." *Eurasia Journal of Mathematics, Science and Technology Education* 16(6).

Rahman, Syed Abidur, Mirza Mohammad Didarul Alam, and Seyedeh Khadijeh Taghizadeh. 2020. "Do Mobile Financial Services Ensure the Subjective Well-Being of Micro-Entrepreneurs? An Investigation Applying UTAUT2 Model." *Information Technology for Development* 26(2):421–444. doi: 10.1080/02681102.2019.1643278.

Raza, Syed A., Wasim Qazi, Komal Akram Khan, and Javeria Salam. 2021. "Social Isolation and Acceptance of the Learning Management System (LMS) in the Time of COVID-19 Pandemic: An Expansion of the UTAUT Model." *Journal of Educational Computing Research* 59(2):183–208. doi: 10.1177/0735633120960421.

Reychav, Iris, Mary Dunaway, and Michiko Kobayashi. 2015. "Understanding Mobile Technology-Fit Behaviors Outside the Classroom." *Computers & Education* 87:142–150.

Ribeiro, Ricky. 2020. "How University Faculty Embraced the Remote Learning Shift." *EdTech Magazine*.

Salim, Taghreed Abu, May El Barachi, Okey Peter Onyia, and Sujith Samuel Mathew. 2021. "Effects of Smart City Service Channel- and User-Characteristics on User Satisfaction and Continuance Intention." *Information Technology and People* 34(1):147–177. doi: 10.1108/ITP-06-2019-0300.

Shrout, Patrick E., and Niall Bolger. 2002. "Mediation in Experimental and Nonexperimental Studies: New Procedures and Recommendations." *Psychological Methods* 7(4):422–445.

Singh, Archana, Sarika Sharma, and Manisha Paliwal. 2020. "Adoption Intention and Effectiveness of Digital Collaboration Platforms for Online Learning: The Indian Students' Perspective." *Interactive Technology and Smart Education*. doi: 10.1108/ITSE-05-2020-0070.
Smedley, Jo. 2010. "Modelling the Impact of Knowledge Management Using Technology." *OR Insight* 23(4):233–250. doi: 10.1057/ori.2010.11.
Susanto, Aries, Younghoon Chang, and Youngwook Ha. 2016. "Determinants of Continuance Intention to Use the Smartphone Banking Services: An Extension to the Expectation-Confirmation Model." *Industrial Management and Data Systems* 116(3):508–525. doi: 10.1108/IMDS-05-2015-0195.
Symeonides, Roberta, and Carrie Childs. 2015. "The Personal Experience of Online Learning: An Interpretative Phenomenological Analysis." *Computers in Human Behavior* 51:539–545. doi: 10.1016/j.chb.2015.05.015.
Taghizadeh, Seyedeh Khadijeh, Syed Abidur Rahman, Davoud Nikbin, Mirza Mohammad Didarul Alam, Lidia Alexa, Choo Ling Suan, and Shirin Taghizadeh. 2021. "Factors Influencing Students' Continuance Usage Intention with Online Learning During the Pandemic: A Cross-Country Analysis." *Behaviour and Information Technology*:1–20. doi: 10.1080/0144929X.2021.1912181.
Tang, Michael, and Roxanne Byrne. 2007. "Regular Versus Online Versus Blended: A Qualitative Description of the Advantages of the Electronic Modes and a Quantitative Evaluation." *International Journal on E-Learning* 6(2):257–266.
Terzis, Vasileios, Christos N. Moridis, and Anastasios A. Economides. 2013. "Continuance Acceptance of Computer Based Assessment Through the Integration of User's Expectations and Perceptions." *Computers & Education* 62:50–61.
Thong, James Y. L., Se Joon Hong, and Kar Yan Tam. 2006. "The Effects of Post-Adoption Beliefs on the Expectation-Confirmation Model for Information Technology Continuance." *International Journal of Human Computer Studies* 64(9):799–810. doi: 10.1016/j.ijhcs.2006.05.001.
Tsai, Wenpin, and Sumantra Ghoshal. 1998. "Social Capital and Value Creation: The Role of Intrafirm Networks." *The Academy of Management Journal* 41(4):464–476. doi: 10.11634/216796061706277.
Van Der Heijden, Hans. 2004. "User Acceptance of Hedonic Information Systems." *MIS Quarterly* 28(4):695–704.
Venkatesh, Viswanath, and Fred D. Davis. 2000. "A Theoretical Extension of the Technology Acceptance Model: Four Longitudinal Field Studies." *Management Science* 46(2):186–204.
Venkatesh, Viswanath, M. G. Morris, G. B. Davis, and F. D. Davis. 2003. "User Acceptance of Information Technology: Toward a Unified View." *MIS Quarterly* 27(3):425–478.
Venkatesh, Viswanath, James Y. L. Thong, and Xin Xu. 2012. "Consumer Acceptance and Use of Information Technology: Extending the Unified Theory of Acceptance and Use of Technology." *MIS Quarterly* 36(1):157–178.
World Economic Forum. 2020. The Global Competitiveness Report 2020.
Wu, Bing, and Xiaohui Chen. 2017. "Continuance Intention to Use MOOCs: Integrating the Technology Acceptance Model (TAM) and Task Technology Fit (TTF) Model." *Computers in Human Behavior* 67:221–232. doi: 10.1016/j.chb.2016.10.028.
Xhelili, P., E. Ibrahimi, E. Rruci, and K. Sheme. 2021. "Adaptation and Perception of Online Learning During COVID-19 Pandemic by Albanian University Students." *International Journal on Studies in Education* 3(2).
Yang, Jie Chi, Benazir Quadir, Nian Shing Chen, and Qiang Miao. 2016. "Effects of Online Presence on Learning Performance in a Blog-Based Online Course." *Internet and Higher Education* 30:11–20. doi: 10.1016/j.iheduc.2016.04.002.
You, J. W., and M. Kang. 2014. "The Role of Academic Emotions in the Relationship Between Perceived Academic Control and Self-Regulated Learning in Online Learning." *Computers & Education* 77:125e133.
Zacharis, Nick Z. 2011. "The Effect of Learning Style on Preference for Web-Based Courses and Learning Outcomes." *British Journal of Educational Technology* 42(5):790–800. doi: 10.1111/j.1467-8535.2010.01104.x.
Zhou, Tao, Yaobin Lu, and Bin Wang. 2010. "Integrating TTF and UTAUT to Explain Mobile Banking User Adoption." *Computers in Human Behavior* 26(4):760–767.

4 Education 4.0 and Web 3.0 Technologies Application for Enhancement of Distance Learning Management Systems in the Post–COVID-19 Era

Aditya Kumar Gupta, Vivek Aggarwal, Vinita Sharma, and Mohd Naved

4.1 INTRODUCTION

The concept of e-learning has made the teaching and learning omnipresent with wide applications of numerous digital tools. The e-learning model which was earlier focused to limited audience of distance education programs and executive programs during COVID-19 had become a mainstream education tool for all the traditional models of teaching and learning process. It had enhanced the pedagogies, engagement, learning and skills development of the students. The e-content created, usage of LMS platform for interaction, storage, and conduction, wide application of interactive platform in form of quizzes, discussion forum, polls, live session, recording of session and so on have provided multifaceted teaching and learning, this could be achieved due to application of numerous Web 3.0 technologies for building a robust platform for e-learning in distance or remote learning (Kasim & Khalid, 2016).

Currently in India as per data around 2.5 million students are pursuing various certificates, diplomas, degrees and doctoral courses. The Indira Gandhi National Open University (IGNOU) – The People's University, has wide reach into remote parts of India, Africa and other developing nations. The present increasing population of distance learners has been catered by application of Web 3.0 technologies, to make teaching and learning student centric (Acikgul & Firat, 2021). Real-time and active collaboration between students and faculty, which were lacking earlier, is now possible due to newer technologies that have involved stakeholder engagement in all processes of distance learning.

4.1.1 Background

Using multiple learning apps is a quick and low-cost approach to provide digital possibilities to students. This point is also supported by theory of connectivism which emphasizes the role of technology in teaching, learning and training. Connectivism works on the "node-to-link" concept which can be correlated with the usage of social media for learner-to-educator and learner-to-learner interaction and collaboration where learner and educator are acting as nodes and social media connections act as the links. Connectivism is considered promoted when multiple students make connections among themselves and their instructor to gain knowledge and other learning resources in convenient and meaningful ways.

DOI: 10.1201/9781003425779-4

4.1.2 Scope

This chapter discusses Web 1.0, 2.0, and 3.0 terms used to refer to the three versions of the Web. After describing the differences between educational technology and information systems, this chapter also describes compatibility between various Web generations and e-learning generations. The subject of whether a new learning theory is needed for e-Learning 3.0 is being debated by education academics and so a preliminary attempt is made to address this. COVID-19 pandemic has a significant effect on education. The argument in this chapter is built on the basic ideas of the connectivism theory of learning, which is then examined to see if it may help explain the recent shift in technology. According to UNESCO, nationwide lockdown and school closures affected around 88% of the world's student population. E-learning becomes a ray of hope in this situation and distance learning institutions becomes first mover in adopting this (Mathivanan et al., 2021).

4.1.3 Objectives of the Chapter

The following are the objectives of the chapter:

- To evaluate the various versions of Web technology;
- To reflect the application of Web 3.0 technologies in Education 4.0;
- To elaborate the enhancement of distance learning (e-learning) post-COVID-19 due integration of Web 3.0 technologies;
- And, to investigate the critical factors of Web technologies for enhancement e-learning in Education 4.0 for developing skills stakeholders.

4.1.4 Organization of the Chapter

The rest of the chapter is organized as: Section 4.2 highlights the impact of COVID-19 over education. Section 4.3 traces the evolution of Web technologies from era of Web 1.0 to Web 3.0. Characteristics and technologies associated with Web 3.0 are discussed in detail. Developments in Industry 4.0 impact all industries including education. Section 4.4 describes the evolution of Education 4.0, the impact of Education 4.0 in e-learning enhancement and advancements in e-learning with the help of education. Section 4.5 elaborates the concept of e-learning and also highlights e-learning evolution, framework, advantages and critical success factors of Web technologies for E-learning. Section 4.6 discusses the critical success factors of Web technologies for e-learning. Section 4.7 explains influence of Web 3.0 on e-learning. Section 4.8 discusses the challenges in implementation of technologies in e-learning. And, finally section 4.9 concludes the chapter with future scope.

4.2 IMPACT OF COVID-19 OVER EDUCATION

Over 1.5 billion children were absent from school as of March 29, 2020, as a result of school closures in response to COVID-19. Over 181 countries have undertaken national closures, affecting roughly 88% of the world's student population, according to UNESCO. The UNESCO response to school closures around the world encouraged everyone not only to respond to the immediate COVID-19 requirements, but also to take this opportunity to lay the groundwork for the future.

One would expect that as schools send kids back home in a bid to flatten the COVID-19 infection curve, online learning and material delivery would be a simple flip. In actuality, the epidemic highlights unequal access to the technologies and practices required for success as an online learner or as an educator suddenly tasked with delivering content remotely. Despite what appears to be a substantial build out of e-learning curriculum at many colleges, it remains a minority of course offerings (Yeung & Yau, 2022).

4.3 WEB EVOLUTION (1.0 TO 3.0)

Despite being a relatively new communication channel, the Web has seen multiple generations with fairly short duration. The Web's evolution has been fueled by the rapid advancement of technology (Nazmi Dincer, 2020). The Web provides a speedy dissemination medium for information and knowledge, permitting businesses to not only enhance their efficiency but also offer new products and services to their clients. Furthermore, consumers have an excellent avenue through which to contact with firms, express their thoughts about products and services, and interact with other consumers. To completely comprehend Web 3.0, it is necessary to first comprehend the versions that came before it. Figure 4.1 highlights the evolution of Web 1.0 to 3.0.

4.3.1 Web 1.0 (Read-Only Web)

In 1990–1991, the World Wide Web was made available to the general public. In the early days of the public internet, the World Wide Web served as a resource for people to look for and find information. Web 1.0 existed between 1990 and 2000. It is also known as Syntactic Web or Read-Only Web which provided content to users only to read, without giving any opportunity to reply or communicate with anyone. This was also the time period in which the first shopping carts appeared. In 1994 Amazon was founded, followed by eBay in 1995. The websites created in this era were totally static (Nazmi Dincer, 2020). But, since this was a new experiment to the world, users were excited using static websites.

4.3.2 Web 2.0 Read-Write (Social Web)

Web 2.0, started in the year 2000 and is still going on. It is also known as the Social Web. This Web encouraged interaction among users. In this era, any user can produce content, which can be shared across websites. Various social media websites like Facebook, YouTube, and Twitter are well known applications of Web 2.0. Web technologies such as HTML5, CSS3, and JavaScript frameworks enable various entrepreneurs to invent new concepts, allowing users to add value to this Social Web. Producers only need to create a means to enable and engage them (Kim, 2021).

The basic issue with Web 2.0 is ownership. The social media companies own your stuff, not you. They control who can see your stuff, how you manage it, and even whether it is accessible at all. What's more, this ownership is frequently maintained by algorithms and automation that are prone to error and bias, rather than by a staff of content specialists and evaluators. There have been

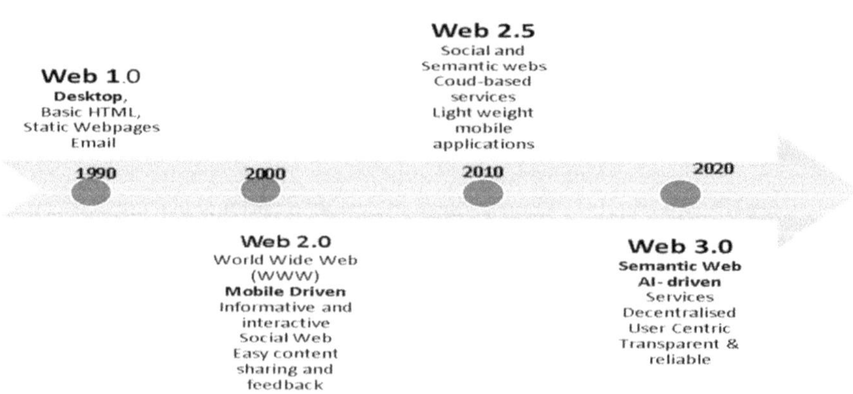

FIGURE 4.1 Evolution of the Web.

Source: Adapted from Vivek Madurai, 2018.

high-profile incidents of censorship by internet business executives, such as Twitter's ban on Donald Trump while he was president of the United States (Alexandre et al., 2021). However, rather than political vendetta, most genuine censoring or predictive engagement with content is driven by code (Lazer et al., 2018).

4.3.3 Web 2.5 Social and Semantic Web (Cloud Based)

Web 2.5 can be called the mix of the Social and Semantic Webs. The notion of Web 2.5 was developed to meet the practical and real progression that witnessed in the period 2010–2020 between Web 2.0 and 3.0. On our road to Online 3.0, several players, including Amazon, Google, Salesforce and so forth provided cloud-based service models which allowed creation of various apps (Ryan & Casidy, 2018). Apps are lightweight applications which enabled mobility as users were able to access content through various devices including cell phones. Such Apps allowed their users to connect them on any device, at any time, and from any location. This is also known as Read-Write Web.

Advancement of mobile technology happened in Web 2.5 which was a revolution in itself as it played a substantial role in engaging a bigger audience through mobile apps. A large number of apps were introduced by businesses in the mobile market to build their presence by addressing mobile consumers. Specific technologies like progressive web apps (PWA) and accelerated mobile pages (AMP) were introduced during this time period.

4.3.4 Web 3.0 (Semantic Web)

Web 3.0 started in the year 2010 and is going on today. This is also known as Semantic Web or Read-Write-Execute Web. It provides users ownership by allowing their data to travel with them between blockchains secured and verified sites. "Web 3.0 is a combination of tools that uses markup data, crowd-sourced material, data mining, and machine learning to improve the intelligence, underlying frameworks, and architecture of the Web in order for machines to comprehend and interpret what humans want—contextual, relevant answers" (Davis & Singh, 2015). Augmented and virtual reality, virtual worlds (e.g., Metaverse), crypto currency, NFTs, machine learning, AI, intelligent teaching bots, and big data might all be developed on this blockchain (Kagermann, 2015). Today, with the help of artificial intelligence and machine learning, computers are able to analyze information with better efficiency than humans. Computers are also able to develop and distribute meaningful content according to a user's specific needs. Apple's Siri, Google's Cloud API, and Wolfram Alpha can be considered as one of the best applications of this era.

4.3.4.1 Web 3.0 Characteristics

According to Tim Berners-Lee, a co-creator of the World Wide Web, the Semantic Web is an expansion of the current Web that can be understood by machines. It made it possible for the most recent features of the Web to be implemented (Shadbolt et al., 2006). Semantic Web had created an environment in which software agents may readily carry out complex activities for users by traversing Web pages and also, helpful in effective utilization of wide range of data and services. It symbolizes the transition from a centralized network of documents to a distributed knowledge network (Patel-Schneider & Horrocks, 2007).

4.3.4.2 Web 3.0 Tools

- *3D web*: A computer-based virtual 3D environment that people may occupy and interact by using avatars (Bower et al., 2017). The characteristics like fast internet, faster processing, superior displays, 3D gaming technology (Ha et al., 2019), and digital reality technologies have created 3D experience of Web browsing (Silva et al., 2008).

- *3D global applications*:
  - Google Earth
  - Virtual Earth
- *3D virtual worlds and avatars*: Combination of 3D gaming, reality and simulation in which users interact via transportable avatars (Lal, 2011).
- *3D wikis*: A virtual 3D encyclopedia. This type of technology can be found in various applications such as Copernicus-3D (Lal, 2011).
- *Online 3D virtual labs*: A powerful platform for planning and implementing collaborative tasks, such as declaring exam results and exchanging media material (Jankowski & Kruk, 2008).
- *3D virtual shopping malls*: Online 3D retail malls in which users can virtually navigate in apparel stores, pharmacies, banks, shoe stores, and bookstores, among many other places. Playing as a result, it is a new engaging and pleasurable manner of buying while sitting at home (Russell, 2013).
- *Social web*: A network of multiple websites which helps connect people in online mode. It is a social system in the sense that it is a medium for computer-mediated thinking, communication, and collaboration. On a system scale, humans jointly construct an emergent informational structure. Web 3.0 technology developments have elevated the social computing to a higher level known as Socio-Semantic Web. It helped humans in creating all kind of knowledge. It may be a document or data model, media services, or software behaviors (Dominic et al., 2014; Ostrowski, 2013; Kapur et al., 2015).
- *Intelligent web*: Artificial intelligence is the one of the pillars for Web 3.0. When looking for information, the technology understands what the learner needs and accordingly provides information, which meets the user's requirements. Semantic search engine acts smartly and looks for the information logically (Dineva, 2022). Corporate knowledge workers require information defined by its meaning rather than text strings. They also require information that is pertinent to their interests and current situation (Mishra et al., 2021). They must locate not only papers but also sections and information entities within documents.

  To accomplish this, the Web's content must be altered using semantic technologies. According to (Wheeler, 2009), Web 3.0 "not only fosters more richly collaborative learning, but it also enables learners to get closer to 'anytime anywhere' learning and will bring intelligent solutions to web searching."
- *Media centric*: The Semantic Web allows users to find similar and related images and sound too (Lal, 2011). The search application of Web 3.0 helps to identify linked similar media things based on their characteristics. Search engines accept a media file as input and search for required media objects depending on its properties (Silva et al., 2008). Other media objects, such as audio and video, can also be searched for by the learner.

4.3.4.3 Web 3.0 Technologies

The Semantic Web mixed with modern technology enables data modeling and the recording of data linkages for machine learning. With the knowledge model, along with intelligence, technologies reach to the next level (Davis, 2022).

Majorly the existing Web is transformed into connected applications which create a reliable logical network of data (Feigenbaum et al., 2007). The solution or applications which were beyond imagination are possible today due to Semantic Web technologies. The combination of semantic concepts and new technology allows for the modeling of data and the recording of data linkages for machine learning. By adding intelligence, and enabling knowledge, semantic technologies have created innovations (Davis, 2022).

Data integration, which involves the combining of data maintained in various formats across several sources, gives specialized capabilities of searching the content. The convergence of these new semantic technologies has resulted in the development of intelligent software agents that supports in knowledge sharing throughout the Web (Ana-Maria, 2013).

The following are some of the major expansions that have changed the mode of exchanging information in the era of Web 3.0:

- *Artificial intelligence*: It refers to self-learning programming that can learn and relearn automatically including the tasks such as tracking user general actions or activities, searching for required results etc. (Sharma, 2019b).
- *Personalization*: Customers are able to choose their preferences and interests, and those get personalized and provide information matching to their search criteria. Customer's profile is important which may be used as a virtual avatar of the owner. The information provided to the owner matches with his/her interests online (Krishnan et al., 2022).
- *Internet of things*: This technology refers to the connection of the gadgets to the internet at common place. Sensors are attached to such gadgets like devices used in office, home, cars, and so forth. It enhances the ability of the customer to be able to monitor data of all the connected devices in a network through internet, from any geographical location (Sharma, 2020).
- *Virtualization*: By using smart gadgets users may enter into any other location virtually, within a few seconds. With the help of 3D objects, search results search results can be obtained. Smart glasses, which combine the virtual and physical levels, may be considered as an example here.
- *Decentralized computing*: Computer power is distributed among several servers. Blockchain technologies, in which information is dispersed over numerous devices, are one example of this. This implies that data can be stored very securely and is not reliant on a single source.
- *Smart agents*: Smart agents are also known as software or personal or educational agents. These are self-contained objects that can execute specified activities can interact with multiple environments simultaneously to complete the owners' tasks (Banerjee et al., 2015). These are created to manage the increased volume of information proactively to search the required information on behalf of the customer (Maes, 1994). If required, the data or information is filtered and only appropriate information is provided to the user. These can be used for emailing, meeting scheduling, and so on (Hussain, 2012; Lashkari et al., 1994; Rhodes, 1996). For e-learning, the intelligent agents can be classified into three types: digital teaching assistants, digital tutors, and digital secretaries.
- *Semantic markup*: A document that explains the Web page with the help of words defined in ontology, allowing computers to understand the content of the Web page (Ostrowski, 2013).

4.3.4.4 Web 3.0 Terminologies

To get a fundamental grasp of the Semantic Web, one must first become acquainted with the following terminology:

1. **URI**: Uniform resource identifiers which are used to identify resources (Shadbolt et al., 2006).
2. **Metadata**: This is a structured approach for describing data so that it may be easily found. It is often known as data about data (Doubt, 2013).
3. **RDF**: Resource description framework a Semantic Web's data models.
4. **RDFS**: This is an abbreviation for resource description framework schema. It increases the power to express domain language and object structures (Brickley & Guha, 2004).
5. **XML**: An abbreviation for extensible markup language. With the help of this, the data can be exchanged among various platforms and applications (Doubt, 2013).
6. **RIF**: This is an abbreviation for rules interchange format. It exchanges rules between various systems.

7. **SPARQL**: This is an abbreviation for RDF's query language.
8. **Ontologies**: It is a public blockchain which Semantic Web infrastructure for data solutions (Acikgul & Firat, 2021).
9. **OWL**: This is language which is necessary to use for generation of ontologies.

4.3.4.5 Relationship between Web Evolution and E-Learning Evolution

E-learning has evolved from Web 1.0 to Web 3.0. Web 1.0 and Web 2.0 focus only on reading and writing of the content rather reflecting or engaging in active learning. The major issue with Web 1.0 based e-learning is to guide students through information access, whereas Web 2.0–based e-learning has given various tools and applications for interaction and sharing through writing. Web 3.0 technologies have created a 3D virtual learning ecosystem for real-time learning which has been enhanced by semantic capabilities. The usage of Web 3.0 technologies for e-learning has eased the acceptance by digital natives. The learning of technical skills is the reason of constant transformation of ways of understanding, building and disseminating knowledge, which also changes the ways of education thoroughly. Due to Web 3.0 technologies, a new mode of education has been evolved, known as Education 4.0.

4.4 EDUCATION 4.0

Educational theorists use the phrase "Education 4.0" to describe the different ways to physically and indirectly incorporate cyber technology into learning. Learning in the age of Education 3.0 was based on principles from cognitive science, neurology, and instructional design. Developments in Industry 4.0 impact all industries including education. Education 4.0 is a phenomenon that evolves to meet the demands of the fourth industrial revolution and is an improvement over Education 3.0. In Industrial Era 4.0, the advancement of technology presents new obstacles, especially in education. There are many ways in which humans and machines might work together to solve issues and create new paths for creation. Currently, digital technology is employed in the teaching and learning process (Davis & Singh, 2015). To stay up with the influx of knowledge and technological advancements, it is also necessary to enhance teacher competence (Kagermann, 2015).

Teachers as learning leaders must be adaptable and willing to change in order to meet the challenges of the industrial age 4.0 (Burritt & Christ, 2016; Sharma & Manocha, 2021). It is the responsibility of teachers to mold their pupils' characters and act as role models for them in terms of fostering their enthusiasm, inventiveness, and social empathy. For students to be successful in industrial era 4.0, they need to be able to think critically, solve problems, be creative, come up with new ideas, communicate, and work together. The growth of this technology necessitates the diversification of human resource capabilities in order to satisfy future industry demands.

4.4.1 Education 4.0 and Students

In the era of Education 4.0, students need to have proficiency in locating, managing, and communicating information via technology (Hussin, 2018). Students in Education 4.0 must develop the skills of innovative thinking and creative action (Greenstein, 2012). As per World Economic Forum (2016) students must possess the following skills in the future, solving complex problems, working with others, managing people, using critical thinking, negotiating, quality control, customer service, making sound judgments, engaging in active learning, and being creative (Soffel, 2016).

4.4.2 Education 4.0 and Educators

The government is striving to boost human resource quality. To deal with the problems of the Education 4.0 era, teachers need to be able to improve their knowledge, quality, and professional skills, as well as change the way they teach. This development in human resources is aimed at addressing future industrial needs. In the framework of increasing human capital, the educator plays a role in the development of student skills. Technology can't replace the role of the instructor, even in the age of Education 4.0 (Hussin, 2018).

Teachers are responsible not only for teaching their students what they need to know, but also for building their character, ethics, and morals. In addition to what which has already been said, the author thinks that teachers in the Education 4.0 era must have the following attitudes and skills (Sharma, 2019a):

1. **Friendly towards technology**: The world is always evolving to a greater level, with technology advancements marking one of these shifts. No one will be able to stop technological progress, so teachers must be willing learn and utilize new technologies if they don't want to be left behind. Technological progress shouldn't be seen as a threat, but rather as a chance to improve and work with other people.
2. **Collaboration (partnership):** Without cooperation or collaboration with others, it will be difficult to obtain the best possible outcomes. Therefore, instructors must have a great desire to collaborate with and/or learn from others. This mindset is required both today and in the future.
3. **Imaginative and daring creativity:** Creativity produces a structure, technique, or method for solving issues and meeting demands. Teachers must demonstrate this inventiveness and work more efficiently to incorporate it in daily routine.
4. **Maintain a sense of humor:** A humorous educator is often the instructor that students remember the most. Laughter and humor can be crucial life skills for fostering relationships and de-stressing. This will reduce people's anger and frustration and allow them to view life from a different perspective.
5. **Holistic teaching:** Individual and group learning are recognized in numerous learning and learning theories. And, recently, holistic learning styles have been on the rise, which insists that educators must obtain each student personal as well family information and how they learn. This helps in providing holistic or wholesome learning and helps in solving the personal and family problems of students.

It is up to students to connect, create, and generate knowledge and innovation in Education 4.0 (Brown-Martin, 2022). Educators and industries in Education 4.0 are focusing on digital economy, artificial intelligence, robots, and data in order to change the educational landscape around the world (Rachmadtullah et al., 2020). In order to meet the challenges of Education 4.0, educators must alter their viewpoints and instructional methods (Roro et al., 2021). If a teacher doesn't have the right qualifications and required certifications that prove their skill and quality, they won't be able to do their job of teaching well.

As soon as possible, teachers need to adapt to this new reality. To put it another way, in addition to teaching, teachers are also responsible for supervising their pupils. Students will take their cues from the teacher's example when it comes to teaching and learning. Teachers must make learning fun, interesting, innovative, and adaptive for their students (Leen et al., 2014). As a facilitator, inspiration, and motivational force, a teacher also cultivates students' imaginations, creativity, and moral character. Teachers are also socially sensitive to the needs of the children they teach. The educator's role cannot be replaced by technology. Preparation is required for the new era of learning, which began in the fall of 2017. Professors can only help students improve their own skills if they have mastered their own.

Students' mental health needs must also be addressed by teachers. Needs for competence, autonomy, relatedness, and sustained learning are among these students' psychological requirements (Chou, 2018). Because of this, no amount of modern technology can ever replace the role of a teacher. There are several reasons for this. The first is that technology itself cannot serve as a catalyst for any of these things. Teachers, on the other hand, are under constant pressure to expand their knowledge base (Gupta et al., 2022).

4.4.3 Education 4.0 and E-Learning Enhancement

Education 4.0 focuses on student-centric learning with an emphasis on a more active role of students and instructors in the classroom discussion, interaction, and analysis of the courses. Education 4.0 has shifted "pedagogy" and "andragogy" towards the new ways of classroom delivery which combined form of heutagogy (student-centered self-directed learning), "peeragogy" (peer-based learning, where learners learn and teach each other), and "cybergogy" (a virtual learning environment for cognitive, emotional, and social learning) (Chan et al., 2019; Mukhopadhyay et al., 2020). The combination of these three "gogies" has promoted constructivists, collaborative and reflective approaches in learning resulted in the lifelong learning experiences which are outcomes of real-life situations. Transversal competencies are achievable with present e-learning Web 3.0 technologies enabling student to have skills as per present market demands. Disciplinary competencies are equally developed in e-learners due to integration of Web 3.0 technologies during process of teaching. The usage of IOT devices in face-to-face and hybrid models is applicable for all e-learners. The invention of digitalization, virtualization, and interaction through synchronous and asynchronous activities has created flexible digital models to entice experiential learning capabilities. Education 4.0 core competencies is training and development of the students for emerging technologies, innovative pedagogies, ICT implementation in teaching and learning and ecosystem for e-learners (Aggarwal et al., 2022).

4.4.4 Advancements in E-Learning with Education 4.0

1. **Widespread learning**: Learning has been possible everywhere with help cloud-based storage, self-paced learning and active learning with usage of the flipped classroom.
2. **Individualized learning**: The individualized learning has boosted the confidence and skill development for slow learners and students with disabilities using various customized applications.
3. **Wide choices for learning**: Students have a basket of courses and selection of course as per interests. Flipped classroom and blended learning (Bower et al., 2017; Kumar et al., 2021) have given more scope for creativity in teaching and learning process.
4. **Enhanced peer learning**: Project-based, experience-based, and case-based teaching methods have become more relevant in e-learning which enhanced peer learning by discussion and reflection with abilities of breakout rooms.
5. **Student centric learning for distance learners**: Student feedback tools for curriculum development, learning skills mapping due to new age quizzes, easy writing, content writing and automation in the process has enriched the student centric learning for distance learners.

These new age trends of Education 4.0 have promoted the active learning making a student driven classroom session leading to skill development as per Industry 4.0 demand. The wide application of various features of LMS, MS Teams, Google Meet, Webex, and so on has been utilized to full potential by majority of the higher education institutions for to have enhanced the learning for distance learners (Bagustari & Santoso, 2019). The student can complete the all-academic tasks such group discussions, quizzes, projects, assignments preparations and uploading, and communications with parents, lecturers, and institutional stakeholders using these tools.

4.5 E-LEARNING DEFINITION

"E-learning" is used to describe the usage of electronic equipment's and electronic media in learning, most notably mobile technologies. The terms "remote learning" or "distance learning" are also used to describe e-learning. Due to the constraints of time, geography, and money, e-learning has traditionally been used as a substitute for face-to-face learning. Learning material in the form of text, audio, and video is delivered via electronic media. Websites, chats, video conferencing, and other similar technologies are all viable options. In developing countries like India, e-learning is a combination of online and face-to-face instruction.

E-learning has three basic characteristics: (1) comprises a network that provides continuous knowledge updating, storage, and dissemination; (2) delivers text messages to users using standard computer technology; and (3) is a training tool that can be used in conjunction with traditional educational techniques (Czerniewicz & Brown, 2009).

According to Rosenberg and others (Brettel et al., 2018), e-learning is internet-based education. Rosenberg defines e-learning as the provision of a sequence of knowledge-and skill-enhancing solutions and resources over the internet. As per Fernando Alonso, learning management systems (LMS) or e-learning platforms are software systems designed to deliver a virtual education and/or online training environment.

4.5.1 E-Learning Environment

Learning-learning environment is influx of network technology in learning environment; an e-learning environment appears. It is gaining popularity as a novel form of learning environment. The e-learning environment should comprise the following function modules for providing complete education:

1. Independent learning tools module
2. Collaborative learning platform modules
3. FAQ module
4. Resource management module
5. E-learning evaluation module.

4.5.2 Developing E-Learning Framework

Internet technology is leveraged in e-learning to generate, enrich, deliver, and facilitate learning at any time and place (Abdon et al., 2007). Steps included in development of E-learning framework include the following.

4.5.2.1 Requirements Analysis or Needs Assessment

First, it must be assessed if e-learning is needed and relevant in educational institutions. To address this question, you need a requirements analysis, not just estimates or suggestions. After a requirements analysis determines e-learning is needed, do a feasibility study that comprises numerous evaluation components, such as technical issues (is it technically viable), internet network and its accompanying infrastructure, usable e-learning platforms, human resources, and knowledge. Prepare educational institutions' human resources to administer e-learning. Aspects of the community's response or views regarding e-learning for education, especially parents, must be considered because parents and the community are vital to educational institutions.

4.5.2.2 The Assemblage of Instructional Designs

At this point, the instructor is responsible for developing lesson plans and tools, including objectives, teaching materials, and teaching media (audio and visual) and also determines which e-learning platform to be utilized to support the student's education.

4.5.2.3 E-Learning's Use and Development Phase

Once all the learning resources are ready, the instructor uses e-learning to facilitate learning. In their virtual classroom, teachers can submit files, reading materials, learning resources, audio or video, assignments, and more. Students have unrestricted access to materials, learning tools, and teachers and classmates. Continuous development is part of the implementation of e-learning to make learning more diversified, innovative, and non-repetitive.

4.5.2.4 Evaluation

In this case, the instructor tested and evaluated e-learning for supporting current teaching system both before and after it was introduced as a software solution. Also, the instructor is expected to decide what the next step should be based on how the learning process is described.

4.5.3 E-Learning Evolution

E-learning parallels the growth of the IT industry. This began when the public, especially academics, acknowledged computers, which were then used and developed for educational purposes to improve efficacy and efficiency. E-learning is the product of ICT innovation in education. E-learning is one of these integrated solutions that offer learners ease, comfort, efficiency, and learning effectiveness. The University of Illinois at Urbana-Champaign established e-learning utilizing a CAI system and PLATO. Since then, e-learning has changed significantly. In 1994, computer-based training evolved into more appealing form, with the use of animation in developing educational materials (Hennessy et al., 2007).

LMS (learning management system) development began in 1997. Since this year, internet technology has been used in education, although the process is still young. Web-based e-learning apps emerged in 1999 and LMS has evolved into a Web-based e-learning platform. Video streaming, multimedia, and interactive displays in conventional and small data formats are also being added along with contents from informational websites, journals, and newspapers. In 2000, several businesses adopted e-learning to teach employees. E-learning tools have proliferated. From 2010 to the present, social media has become popular and influenced e-learning since it brings innovation and a more engaging learning environment. YouTube, Twitter, Instagram, Facebook, Skype, and Hangout are some of the popular social networking tools (Chung et al., 2020). E-learning was originally designed to address the issues of time and space constraints in education by enabling distance learning. In developing nations like India also e-learning is primarily used to enhance remote learning. But now, e-learning has begun to supplement traditional face-to-face teaching, especially in higher education and secondary schools. The e-learning evolution has gone into the following phases.

4.5.3.1 E-Learning 1.0

The major change brought about by the internet was the ease with which people could access information. As part of e-Learning 1.0, learning management systems (also known as LMS) were developed to make it easier for students to stay on top of their classes and their workloads. The concept of "learning objects" was developed and put to use in the development of these systems, and it is a more traditional approach to education than a hierarchical one that relies on one-way communication (Oztok et al., 2013). In this direct-transfer paradigm, the instructor serves as the media-rich content distributor and communicates with students through a variety of methods.

4.5.3.2 E-Learning 2.0

Teaching and learning with the use of Web 2.0 technology has been dubbed "e-Learning 2.0" (Hussain, 2012). Using wikis, blogs, podcasts, and other social Web technologies, Web 2.0 has altered the classroom in terms of how it is not only socially but collaboratively built. Dynamic content generation, which may include reflection and conversation, requires collaboration and engagement while using these tools. It's important to note that this is a method of learning in which information is shared in both directions, allowing for the social construction of new knowledge.

4.5.3.3 E-Learning 3.0

Researchers in the field of education now freely use the phrase "e-Learning 3.0" in a variety of blogs and forums. (Moore, 2010; Rubens et al., 2014; Wheeler, 2009). Cloud computing and the availability of new technologies like collaborative intelligent filtering, expanded and dependable data storage capacity, higher screen resolutions, multi-gesture devices, and 3D touch user interfaces are moving us into the next generation of e-Learning. In the third generation of e-Learning, mobile devices will allow students and teachers to access learning resources at any time and from any location. According to technology experts (Wheeler, 2009), e-Learning 3.0 systems can be built using AI and data mining, which can sift and sort vast amounts of data in order to provide the student with a greater grasp of the learning process itself (Rubens et al., 2014).

According to education researchers, virtual 3D worlds, such as Second Life and the creation of personal avatars in them, are expected to promote the fundamental idea of "anytime, anywhere, and anybody." Personal learning environments (PLEs) are a hot topic in the research community now that Web 2.0 and Web 3.0 technologies are well established (PLEs are also referred to as mashups) (Ebner et al., 2011). Personalization is viewed as the best way to deal with today's knowledge-based society's multitude of information. (Ebner et al., 2011, p. 22). Despite the fact that e-Learning 3.0 systems are not widely used commercially, researchers are developing functioning prototypes or proof-of-concepts. Online service Twine was one of the earliest to employ Semantic Web technology to automatically and intelligently organize material based on the interests of its users (Spivack, 2010). The Adaptive Hypermedia Knowledge Management E-Learning Platform (AHKME) is a good example of a Web 3.0 e-learning system (Rego et al., 2010).

4.5.3.4 Advantages of E-Learning

Denan et al. (2020) identified advantages of internet-based e-learning listed as follows:

1. Professors and students can now connect more readily via the internet, regardless of time, distance, or physical place, with the help of e-learning tools.
2. Teachers and students can both access teaching materials or learning instructions on the internet. This lets them test understanding and mastery of the topic or teaching materials.
3. In addition, students can access instructional materials at any time and from anywhere on their mobile devices, PCs, and laptops, making it easier for them to go back and review the information.
4. Teachers and students in large numbers can engage in online discussion, allowing for an easier and more extensive contribution of insight and information.
5. Passive students become more engaged.
6. It is less expensive in terms of time, place, and cost.

4.6 CRITICAL SUCCESS FACTORS OF WEB TECHNOLOGIES FOR E-LEARNING

There are numerous domains to examine when studying the aspects that form the successful implementation of the latest online technologies in the context of e-Learning which has crucial success factors. These elements can be classified into eight distinct categories:

1. Teacher's approach towards and control of the technology
2. Training style of the teacher
3. Technical competency and learning attitude of student
4. Interactive collaboration approach of student
5. Course structure and the quality of content provided for E-learning
6. Internet access and Wi-Fi campus provided by the institution to students and faculty
7. Robust structure of information technology provided by the institution
8. Institutional support of e-learning activities

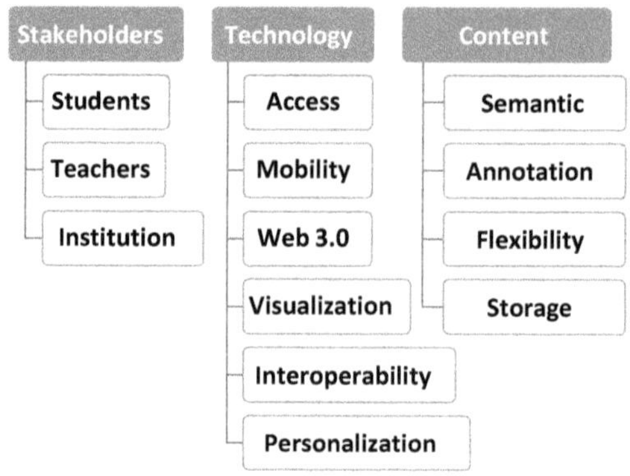

FIGURE 4.2 Critical success factors for e-learning.

As shown in the figure 4.2 for a better understanding, critical success factors can be discussed under the below classification.

4.6.1 Technology

To maximize access to Web technology to promote e-learning, it is critical to ensure the availability of hardware equipment, such as computers; to assure its reliability, to facilitate a fast internet connection, and to have user-friendly interfaces and applications. Because e-learning is intended to be pervasive, mobility is an important consideration (Gupta & Ramchandani, 2019). Mobile technology will encourage cooperation and make learning available at all times. Smart mobile technology enables extensive access to materials, facilitates the omnipresence of e-learning, and is one of its primary drivers. Mobile intelligent technologies improve content access everywhere and at any time (Twine Szymkowiak et al., 2021). The inclusion of visualization as a vital success criterion is due to the sensory experience that Web technologies provide to e-Learning via a number of media, including graphics, animation, and video. Video games, high-powered graphics, virtual reality, immersive Web for authenticity, augmented reality, and 3D and virtual 3D worlds are examples of visualization tools (Dominic et al., 2014).

The use of Web 3.0 to education necessitates a thorough understanding of both its advantages and disadvantages. Web 3.0 pioneered the new notion of e-learning, and as such, this new form of e-learning aims to maximize the use of its resources. Web 3.0 provides machine understandable material, allowing people and computers to communicate in unprecedented ways, student empowerment, enhanced social engagement, personalization, and intelligent agents. Furthermore, ontologies are at the heart of Web 3.0 because they are at the root of intelligent data processing (Acikgul Firat & Firat, 2021), which reduces information overload and distributes the correct information to the right user. They are reusable and shareable, and they are required for content annotation.

One of the technological hurdles for personalizing e-Learning is interoperability. Knowledge's accessibility and permeability are enabled through semantic coding. Content that has been semantically annotated can be reused, shared, and interoperable. Furthermore, the interoperability of Web-based educational systems promotes reusability and cooperation, as well as independence and decentralization (Aggarwal et al., 2022).

Personalization addresses the overabundance of online resources (Hussain, 2012), and it is an essential component of the design and development of advanced learning systems (Huk, 2021). Furthermore, providing tailored learning programmed is critical for today's learners. Personalization is based on three key factors: user profile, artificial intelligence, and intelligent e-Learning systems.

4.6.2 Content

Semantics is included in this category because semantically tagged content provides more access to relevant content. Because Web 3.0 requires dealing with a large number of datasets, big data management is critical. Big data approaches can also be useful for retrieving course material. Finding useful material becomes considerably more difficult without a structure. Machine-readable learning material is a more efficient type of information; not only can it be used with software, but it can also be adaptable and sensitive to the unique needs of learners, assisting more advanced search and recommendation of learning materials.

The importance of having a homogeneous language while semantically annotating content is referred to as annotation homogeneity. Because of the lack of homogeneity, different computer agents are unable to grasp and communicate data. Semantic homogeneity avoids the scarcity of consensus ontologies, which impedes the evolution of e-Learning 3.0 and prohibits semantic metadata interchange.

Flexibility and storage are requirements for the dynamic nature of content, which allows users to change it, as well as provide robust storage options. Using cloud computing as a storage option not only simplifies the deposit and retrieval of large amounts of data, but it also aids e-Learning 3.0 in its quest for decentralization from institutional websites. Furthermore, because cloud computing is Web-based, it is always accessible, simplifies system integration, and enables learning systems. It is also necessary to mention learning objects in connection to content. Their reusability and scalability give schools the ability to tailor them to their individual needs. It is critical that learning objects include a description to aid their search in order to maximize their usefulness and make them easily findable. Some learning object repositories already include metadata linked with them for this purpose.

4.6.3 Stakeholders

When it comes to pupils, it is important to look at teamwork, active engagement, and personal and technical skills. E-learning includes group projects and collaborative activities. The student's active participation refers to the requirement for their input, namely in the enrichment of learning materials. Furthermore, the information provided by the students will serve as the foundation for personalizing the system and the material. Personal and technical abilities are essential for students to fully utilize e-Learning 3.0. The learners' inability to participate in e-learning contexts is hampered by a lack of digital literacy.

Teachers may become overwhelmed as the importance of technology in education grows. As educators, they must be well-versed in technology in order to maximize its benefits. Teachers are more motivated to participate in Web 3.0 when they are more comfortable with technology. Their dedication to online learning scenarios is based on their digital skills. In a Web 3.0 future, teachers' job should be of meaning creation as they collaborate with computers to develop information. Teachers are deepening their relationships with their colleagues, and by participating in online forums, they can promote the material they provide.

Finally, the framework's final CSF addresses the role of educational institutions in e-Learning 3.0, noted that the nature of e-Learning 3.0 is antithetical to the institutions' seclusion; yet, they must bear the duty of investing in technology that is accessible to students and ensuring technical support is available. Training for e-learning is also an institutional obligation that applies to both instructors and students. Furthermore, colleges and other educational institutions should embrace the Web 3.0 capability of integrating multiple applications across institutions.

4.7 INFLUENCE OF WEB 3.0 ON E-LEARNING

Web 3.0 and its inferences for e-learning were developed over time. Educators had the opportunity to shape new Web 3.0 technologies by contributing to the definition of that vision (Dineva, 2022).

The student and the 3D tutor are the two main components of Web 3.0. The learner is a person who wishes to gain knowledge about a given subject. The tutor is an intelligent agent who disseminates communal knowledge to the student (Padma & Seshasaayee, 2011).

Impacts of Web 3.0 for supporting education may be discussed in various ways as follows.

4.7.1 The Impact of Web 3.0/Semantic Web–Based Learning for Instructors

The Semantic Web can help instructors with duties such as course preparation, learner support, assessment, record keeping, and document control (Dineva, 2022; Padma & Seshasaayee, 2011). Google Suite, MS Team, and so on can be taken as good examples of such technological tools which may be used extensively by instructors. Other than these, applications like Quizizz, Kahoot, and others can be used for small e-assessments. Web 3.0 has the potential to help instructors by producing reusable learning items and providing quick feedback to a learner at a specific point of the learning process (Evans, 2021).

Machine-readable markup in research articles makes them more accessible to semantic search engines, resulting in more specific responses to user searches (Morris, 2011). According to (Clark et al., 2004), "the increased expressivity of the Semantic Web, along with search and query tools already in development, will allow advances in non-scientific disciplines as well." For example, a group of historians could each annotate the same text to convey their differing perspectives on its comment, thereby forming communities of deconstruction. Data sets (ontologies) from other domains linked, resulting in "a network effect in academic knowledge."

4.7.2 The Impact of Web 3.0/Semantic Web–Based Learning for Learners

Web 3.0 offers personalized learning for learners. Learning modeling uses the learner's background knowledge, skills, aptitudes, motivations, learning and media preferences, mastery of content being taught, and learning progress to tailor the instruction to the learner (Ebner et al., 2011). Personalized learning can match the complexity of the instruction to the learners' needs. Devedzic notes that learner personalization "presents only the information that is really relevant for the learner, in the appropriate manner, and at the appropriate time" (Devedzic, 2004). Smart agents will assist learners in documenting and archiving their learning products, locating resources, and working collaboratively (Koper, 2004).

Traditionally, school stakeholders must communicate with a unified tech company that hosts the application on a server that is virtually managed by a third party to the school. All of the school's assets are managed by a single point of contact. Legally, the data belongs to the school, although sharing is always limited to the features developed on the hosted application. Furthermore, because the gadgets used by faculty and students are not contextual in the genuine sense, the output is generalized and not user specific. As a result, user-specific development of students becomes a challenge. Furthermore, data evidence is not automated, and teachers are required to serve as administrators.

These will change with the introduction of Web 3.0 for education will be a combination of technology and hardware, with gadgets used by faculty and students becoming smarter and powered by artificial intelligence, and semantic architecture being used to communicate information. Every device, whether mobile, tablet, classroom technology, ID card, bus, or fee collection pointer, will operate as knowledge nodes and carry tokens for contribution and collaboration. The contribution to the school data can be either human or machine generated. This will allow the campus to decentralize the data while also ensuring that the data is created as an asset on the university's defined computers. Data access and user-specific token handshake will be a reality with the arrival of 5G. Each node will then be linked to sea of blockchain hosts, which will not only create assets but also make searches much more user specific.

4.7.3 Benefits of Web 3.0 in Distance Learning

The major benefits of Web 3.0 technologies for distance learning include the following:

- Since machines are interconnected and provide access to information to each other, expenses of information exchange reduce.
- Due to technological aid, teachers are able to create more creative and student engaging projects and assignments. Through technology advancements students and teachers may have individual or group discussion at any time irrespective of having any geographical area.
- Due to technology aid, students can get more knowledge in lesser time. But information overload may create a barrier in learning sometimes.
- Within a fraction of a second, search engines provide links to information from multiple sources. Students may compare different links and go for the best one which is suitable.
- Today, the capability of customized search provides relevant information to students in lesser time, reducing annoyance. Lecture notes, materials, videos, blog entries, and so on will be included in search engines.
- Personal learning agents are a great help in searching the relevant information and after that in making a presentable report on that information which reduces the stress for achieving the relevant information.
- For selection of the right kind of institution, Semantic Web can be used to describe the offered courses and degrees so that credits can be transferred easily. Students can collaborate and interact with people who are spread out. Permission is not required to use or reprint educational content.

4.8 CHALLENGES

The web technologies that have been created recently to fulfill the needs of the Semantic Web are still developing. Therefore, the implementation of the technologies and languages represented in the upper tiers of the semantic stack has been postponed. Standard solutions, such as privacy, trust, and proof, continue to be exceptional.

The research on case studies of the implementation process of e-Learning 4.0 from the analysis phase all the way through to the evaluation of the system is severely lacking. Future researchers might find it useful to look into the problems that students and teachers have with e-learning apps, especially those that have to do with the internet of things (IoT).

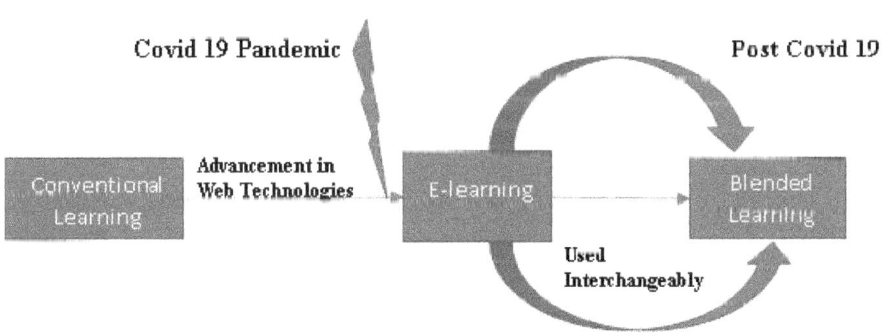

FIGURE 4.3 E-learning in distance education

Source: Mathivanan et al., 2021.

There is a strong relationship between the evolution of the Web and education methodologies. Technological improvements enable new services, sparking new situations in which interaction models for teaching might emerge more proficiently. After Web 3.0, Web 4.0 introduces new options curtailing from more interdependent relationships between human and machine, including sensitive interactions. Despite its importance, this scenario has a long way to go before it can be realized on a broad scale. As a result, the Education 4.0 profile has only just emerged on the real-world stage. With today's cutting-edge technology, Education 3.0 appears to be a viable present situation for teaching, when combined with sustainable learning paradigms. In fact, the story of Industry 4.0 will necessitate the use of at least all of the technology made available by the Web 3.0 domain.

The results show that aspiring teachers in India must acquire skills important for addressing recent developments in information technology and education. The third and fourth industrial revolutions focus on ICT tools. The third industrial revolution utilized ICT for automatic control of production machines, while the fourth industrial revolution is characterized by machine-to-machine communication without human involvement. Designers must specify a pedagogical situation by describing learning tasks, resources, and evaluation modes. Universities design online courses for university and school students on remote learning platforms. Web 4.0 re-humanizes learning and puts humans at the center. It's about supporting and personalizing learning to meet training and learner needs.

4.9 CONCLUSION AND FUTURE SCOPE

E-learning uses the internet to its fullest potential. There is an increase in the use of online learning platforms across all levels of education, including K-12, postsecondary, higher education, test preparation, and self-study. Several niche players operate in the various e-learning segments in India, making the market highly fragmented. Electronic learning is expected to bring about new levels of comfort, efficiency, and effectiveness for students and teachers alike. Information and communication technology (ICT) integration and innovation have produced this outcome.

It is estimated that India's current 370 million internet users will increase to 500 million additional users. For these reasons, India is an enormous market for the e-Learning industry. An increasing number of private colleges offer a variety of undergraduate and graduate e-Learning programs. When it comes to the demand for online higher education, courses like the master of computer applications (MCA) and master of business administration (MBA) programs lead the pack. For health and safety reasons, in-person classes were cancelled during the epidemic. E-learning methods and online classes are becoming more common in educational institutions. Due to the closure of educational institutions the demand for academic books decreased by 40% to 50%. Even among kids and teens, which use their phones and tablets to connect to the internet more and more, there has been a rise in demand for educational content.

The Indian government is eager to implement certain digital reforms that might provide a significant boost to the expansion of the eLearning business. The Ministry of Electronics and Information Technology (MeitY) says on its website that e-Learning is one of the most important ways to learn. Education systems in India have adopted integrated e-learning solutions and developed internet infrastructure. Universities throughout the country are teaming up to offer online courses. International companies that work with local companies to adapt their products to the local market help the industry grow.

With high internet penetration in rural areas continually increasing, the number of online courses and online students will rapidly increase. By 2022, it is anticipated that the global e-Learning market will have expanded to more than USD 243 billion. In India, e-Learning is considered a possible game-changer in the next few years due to the expansion of the online education market and its ability to increase employment opportunities quantitatively. It is intended to close the demand-supply imbalance in the Indian industry. There is an extensive range of technologies involved in the education methodology to improve the quality of teaching and learning in higher education. Extremely influential tools for the future education are as shown in Figure 4.4.

FIGURE 4.4 Future tools of education.

After Web 3.0, the new web is Web 4.0, which began development in 2020 and is under progression based on different models, technologies, and social ties. Because it is formed of various dimensions, Web 4.0 concepts are yet to explore more. Web 4.0 education is supposed to more student-centric rather than faculty-centric. With new technical developments it is possible to innovate and improve education for creative institutions and instructors.

REFERENCES

Abdon, B. R., Ninomiya, S., & Raab, R. T. (2007). eLearning in higher education makes its debut in Cambodia: Implications of the provincial business education project. *International Review of Research in Open and Distance Learning*, *8*(2), 1–14.

Acikgul Firat, E., & Firat, S. (2021). Web 3.0 in learning environments: A systematic review. *Turkish Online Journal of Distance Education*, *22*(1). https://doi.org/10.17718/TOJDE.849898.

Aggarwal, V., Dash, S., Yadav, P. D., & Gupta, A. K. (2022). Role of ICT enabled cloud learning management system tools in fostering entrepreneurship amongst youth. 2022 2nd International Conference on Innovative Practices in Technology and Management (ICIPTM), 508–515. https://doi.org/10.1109/ICIPTM54933.2022.9754158.

Alexandre, I., Jai-sung Yoo, J., & Murthy, D. (2021). Make tweets great again: Who are opinion leaders, and what did they tweet about Donald Trump? *Social Science Computer Review*. https://doi.org/10.1177/08944393211008859.

Ana-Maria, C.-N. (2013). Education in web 3.0. *Journal of Advanced Distributed Learning Technology*, *1*(1).

Bagustari, B. A., & Santoso, H. B. (2019). Adaptive user interface of learning management systems for education 4.0: A research perspective. *Journal of Physics: Conference Series*, *1235*(1), 0–8. https://doi.org/10.1088/1742-6596/1235/1/012033.

Banerjee, P. K., Ma, L. C. K., & Shroff, R. H. (2015). E-governance competence: A framework. *Electronic Government*, *11*(3), 171–184. https://doi.org/10.1504/EG.2015.070120.

Bower, M., Lee, M. J. W., & Dalgarno, B. (2017). Collaborative learning across physical and virtual worlds: Factors supporting and constraining learners in a blended reality environment. *British Journal of Educational Technology*, *48*(2). https://doi.org/10.1111/bjet.12435.

Brettel, M., Friederichsen, N., Keller, M., & Rosenberg, M. (2018). How virtualization, decentralization and network building change the manufacturing landscape: An industry 4.0 perspective. *International Journal of Information and Communication Engineering*, *8*(1), 285–299.

Brickley, D., & Guha, R. V. (2004). *RDF Vocabulary Description Language 1.0: RDF Schema, W3C Recommendation 10 February 2004*. W3C, World Wide Web Consortium, Wakefield.

Brown-Martin, G. (2022). Education and the Fourth Industrial Revolution. In *Medium*. https://medium.com/regenerative-global/education-and-the-fourth-industrial-revolution-cd6bcd7256a3.

Burritt, R., & Christ, K. (2016). Industry 4.0 and environmental accounting: A new revolution? *Asian Journal of Sustainability and Social Responsibility*, *1*(1). https://doi.org/10.1186/s41180-016–0007-y.

Chan, C. G., Embi, M. A. B., & Hashim, H. (2019). Primary school teachers' readiness towards heutagogy and peeragogy. *Asian Education Studies*, *4*(1). https://doi.org/10.20849/aes.v4i1.602.

Chou, P. N. (2018). Smart technology for sustainable curriculum: Using drone to support young students' learning. *Sustainability (Switzerland)*, *10*(10). https://doi.org/10.3390/su10103819.

Chung, E., Subramaniam, G., & Dass, L. C. (2020). Online learning readiness among university students in Malaysia amidst Covid-19. *Asian Journal of University Education*, *16*(2). https://doi.org/10.24191/AJUE.V16I2.10294.

Clark, K., Parsia, B., & Hendler, J. (2004). Will the semantic web change education? *Journal of Interactive Media in Education*, *2004*(1). https://doi.org/10.5334/2004-3-clark.

Czerniewicz, L., & Brown, C. (2009). A study of the relationship between institutional policy, organisational culture and e-Learning use in four South African universities. *Computers and Education*, *53*(1). https://doi.org/10.1016/j.compedu.2009.01.006.

Davis, K., & Singh, S. (2015). Digital badges in afterschool learning: Documenting the perspectives and experiences of students and educators. *Computers and Education*, *88*. https://doi.org/10.1016/j.compedu.2015.04.011.

Davis, M. (2022). Semantic social computing. In *Semantic Wave 2007*. Network Centric Operations Industry Consortium. http://colab.cim3.net/file/work/SICoP/2007-09-20/MDavis09202007.pdf.

Denan, Z., Munir, Z. A., Razak, R. A., Kamaruddin, K., & Sundram, V. P. K. (2020). Adoption of technology on e-Learning effectiveness. *Bulletin of Electrical Engineering and Informatics*, *9*(3), 1121–1126. https://doi.org/10.11591/eei.v9i3.1717.

Devedzic, V. (2004). Education and the semantic web. *International Journal of Artificial Intelligence in Education*, *14*(2).

Dineva, S. (2022). Intelligent e-Learning with new web technologies. *SSRN Electronic Journal*, *7*(1). https://doi.org/10.2139/ssrn.3983423.

Dominic, M., Francis, S., & Pilomenraj, A. (2014). e-Learning in Web 3.0. *International Journal of Modern Education and Computer Science*, *6*(2). https://doi.org/10.5815/ijmecs.2014.02.02.

Doubt, I. F. I. N. (2013). Id31_Keywords.Pdf.

Ebner, M., Schön, S., Taraghi, B., Drachsler, H., & Tsang, P. (2011). First steps towards an integrated personal learning environment at the university level. *Communications in Computer and Information Science*, *177 CCIS*. https://doi.org/10.1007/978-3-642-22383-9_3.

Evans, S. (2021). How web 3.0 will impact higher education. 1–6. https://digitalcommunications.wp.st-andrews.ac.uk/2021/03/11/how-web-3–0-will-impact-higher-education/.

Feigenbaum, L., Herman, I., Hongsermeier, T., Neumann, E., & Stephens, S. (2007). The semantic web in action. *Scientific American*, *297*(6). https://doi.org/10.1038/scientificamerican1207-90.

Greenstein, L. (2012). Assessing 21st century skills: A guide to evaluating mastery and authentic learning. Assessing 21st Century Skills: A Guide to Evaluating Mastery and Authentic Learning, c.

Gupta, A. K., & Ramchandani, S. (2019). Feasibility of digital applications for toilet locating and monitoring services in urban area. *Jaipuria International Journal of Management Research*, *5*(1). https://doi.org/10.22552/jijmr/2019/v5/i1/182300.

Gupta, A. K., Aggarwal, V., Yadav, P. D., Naved, M., Dash, S., & Chandwani, T. (2022). Effectiveness of technological based classroom engagement. In *2022 3rd International Conference on Intelligent Engineering and Management (ICIEM)* (pp. 887–893). London. doi: 10.1109/ICIEM54221.2022.9853199.

Ha, N., Nayyar, A., Nguyen, D., & Liu, C. (2019). Enhancing students' soft skills by implementing CDIO based integration teaching mode. In *Proceedings of the 15th International CDIO Conference*. http://cdio.org/files/document/file/136.pdf.

Hennessy, S., Wishart, J., Whitelock, D., Deaney, R., Brawn, R., Velle, L., McFarlane, A., Ruthven, K., & Winterbottom, M. (2007). Pedagogical approaches for technology-integrated science teaching. *Computers and Education*, *48*(1). https://doi.org/10.1016/j.compedu.2006.02.004.

Huk, T. (2021). From education 1.0 to education 4.0—challenges for the contemporary school. *New Educational Review*, *66*. https://doi.org/10.15804/tner.2021.66.4.03.

Hussain, F. (2012). E-learning 3.0 = e-Learning 2.0 + WEB 3.0? IADIS International Conference on Cognition and Exploratory Learning in Digital Age, CELDA 2012, Celda, 11–18. https://doi.org/10.9790/7388-0333947.

Hussin, A. A. (2018). Education 4.0 made simple: Ideas for teaching. *International Journal of Education and Literacy Studies*, *6*(3), 92–98.

Jankowski, J., & Kruk, S. R. (2008). 2Lip: The step towards the web3D. In *Proceeding of the 17th International Conference on World Wide Web 2008*, WWW'08. https://doi.org/10.1145/1367497.1367694.

Kagermann, H. (2015). Change through digitization—value creation in the age of industry 4.0. In *Management of Permanent Change*. https://doi.org/10.1007/978-3-658-05014-6_2.

Kapur, P. K., Gupta, A. K., & Sachdeva, N. (2015). Measuring brand health. In *2015 4th International Conference on Reliability, Infocom Technologies and Optimization (ICRITO)* (Trends and Future Directions) (pp. 1–6). IEEE. doi: 10.1109/ICRITO.2015.7359353.

Kasim, N. N. M., & Khalid, F. (2016). Choosing the right learning management system (LMS) for the higher education institution context: A systematic review. *International Journal of Emerging Technologies in Learning*, *11*(6), 55–61.

Kim, G. H. (2021). How will blockchain technology affect the future of the internet? *Lecture Notes in Electrical Engineering*, *715*. https://doi.org/10.1007/978-981-15-9343-7_40.

Koper, R. (2004). Use of the semantic web to solve some basic problems in education: Increase flexible, distributed lifelong learning; decrease teacher's workload. *Journal of Interactive Media in Education*, *2004*(1). https://doi.org/10.5334/2004-6-koper.

Krishnan, C., Gupta, A., Gupta, A., & Singh, G. (2022). Impact of artificial intelligence based chatbots on customer engagement and business growth. In Hong, T. P., Serrano-Estrada, L., Saxena, A., & Biswas, A. (eds.), *Deep Learning for Social Media Data Analytics. Studies in Big Data* (vol. 113). Springer, Cham. https://doi.org/10.1007/978-3-031-10869-3_11.

Kumar, A., Krishnamurthi, R., Bhatia, S., Kaushik, K., Ahuja, N. J., Nayyar, A., & Masud, M. (2021). Blended learning tools and practices: A comprehensive analysis. In *IEEE Access*, *9*. https://doi.org/10.1109/ACCESS.2021.3085844.

Lal, M. (2011). LACLO 3—Web 3.0 in education & research. *International Journal of Information Technology*, *3*(2).

Lashkari, Y., Metral, M., & Maes, P. (1994). Collaborative interface agents. In *Proceedings of the National Conference on Artificial Intelligence*, 1. IEEE.

Lazer, D. M. J., Baum, M. A., Benkler, Y., Berinsky, A. J., Greenhill, K. M., Menczer, F., Metzger, M. J., Nyhan, B., Pennycook, G., Rothschild, D., Schudson, M., Sloman, S. A., Sunstein, C. R., Thorson, E. A., Watts, D. J., & Zittrain, J. L. (2018). The science of fake news. *Science*, *359*(6380). https://doi.org/10.1126/science.aao2998.

Leen, C. C., Hong, H., Kwan, F. N. H., & Ying, T. W. (2014). Creative and critical thinking in Singapore schools. In *Office of Education Research, National Institute Education* (vol. 2, issue 2). Nanyang Technological University, Singapore. ISBN: 978-981-09-2387-7.

Maes, P. (1994). Agents that Reduce work and information overload. *Communications of the ACM*, *37*(7). https://doi.org/10.1145/176789.176792.

Mathivanan, S. K., Jayagopal, P., Ahmed, S., Manivannan, S. S., Kumar, P. J., Raja, K. T., Dharinya, S. S., & Prasad, R. G. (2021). Adoption of e-Learning during lockdown in India. *International Journal of Systems Assurance Engineering and Management*. https://doi.org/10.1007/s13198-021-01072-4.

Mishra, A. K., Sinha, A. K., Khasnis, A., & Vadlamani, S. T. (2021). Exploring firm-level innovation and productivity in India. *International Journal of Innovation Science*. https://doi.org/10.1108/IJIS-10-2020-0179.

Moore, D. (2010). Web 2.0. http://darcymoore.net/.

Morris, R. D. (2011). Web 3.0: Implications for online learning. *TechTrends*, *55*(1). https://doi.org/10.1007/s11528-011-0469-9.

Mukhopadhyay, M., Pal, S., Nayyar, A., Pramanik, P. K. D., Dasgupta, N., & Choudhury, P. (2020). Facial emotion detection to assess learner's state of mind in an online learning system. *ACM International Conference Proceeding Series*. https://doi.org/10.1145/3385209.3385231.

Nazmi Dincer. (2020). Evolution of web from 1.0 to 5.0. *Myeltcafe*, 1–9. http://myeltcafe.com/teach/evolution-of-web-from-1-0-to-5–0/.

Ostrowski, D. A. (2013). Semantic computing in social media. *International Journal of Semantic Computing*, *7*(3). https://doi.org/10.1142/S1793351X13500062.
Oztok, M., Zingaro, D., Brett, C., & Hewitt, J. (2013). Exploring asynchronous and synchronous tool use in online courses. *Computers and Education*, *60*(1). https://doi.org/10.1016/j.compedu.2012.08.007.
Padma, S., & Seshasaayee, A. (2011). Personalized web based collaborative learning in web 3.0: A technical analysis. *Communications in Computer and Information Science*, *204 CCIS*. https://doi.org/10.1007/978-3-642-24043-0_17.
Patel-Schneider, P. F., & Horrocks, I. (2007). A comparison of two modelling paradigms in the semantic web. *Web Semantics*, *5*(4). https://doi.org/10.1016/j.websem.2007.09.004.
Rachmadtullah, R., Yustitia, V., Setiawan, B., Fanny, A. M., Pramulia, P., Susiloningsih, W., Rosidah, C. T., Prastyo, D., & Ardhian, T. (2020). The challenge of elementary school teachers to encounter superior generation in the 4.0 industrial revolution: Study literature. *International Journal of Scientific and Technology Research*, *9*(4).
Rego, H., Moreira, T., Morales, E., & Garcia, F. J. (2010). Metadata and knowledge management driven web-based learning information system towards web/e-Learning 3.0. *International Journal of Emerging Technologies in Learning*, *5*(2). https://doi.org/10.3991/ijet.v5i2.1222.
Rhodes, B. (1996). Remembrance agent: A continuously running automated information retrieval system. In *The Proceedings of the First International Conference on the Practical Application of Intelligent Agents and Multi Agent Technology*.
Roro, R., Dewi, V. K., Muslimat, A., Danang Yuangga, K., Sunarsi, D., Khoiri, A., Suryadi, S., Solahudin, M., & Iswadi, U. (2021). e-Learning as education media innovation in the industrial revolution and education 4.0 era. *Journal of Contemporary Issues in Business and Government*, *27*(1).
Rubens, N., Kaplan, D., & Okamoto, T. (2014). E-learning 3.0: Anyone, anywhere, anytime, and AI. *Lecture Notes in Computer Science (Including Subseries Lecture Notes in Artificial Intelligence and Lecture Notes in Bioinformatics)*, *7697 LNCS*. https://doi.org/10.1007/978-3-662-43454-3_18.
Russell, D. R. (2013). Looking beyond the interface: Activity theory and distributed learning. In *Distributed Learning: Social and Cultural Approaches to Practice*. https://doi.org/10.4324/9780203464076-25.
Ryan, J., & Casidy, R. (2018). The role of brand reputation in organic food consumption: A behavioral reasoning perspective. *Journal of Retailing and Consumer Services*, *41*(January), 239–247. https://doi.org/10.1016/j.jretconser.2018.01.002.
Shadbolt, N., Hall, W., & Berners-Lee, T. (2006). The semantic web revisited. In *IEEE Intelligent Systems* (Vol. 21, Issue 3). https://doi.org/10.1109/MIS.2006.62.
Sharma, P. (2019a). Digital revolution of education 4.0. *International Journal of Engineering and Advanced Technology*, *9*(2), 3558–3564. https://doi.org/10.35940/ijeat.a1293.129219.
Sharma, V. (2019b). Impact of industry 4.0 over crowdsourcing in Indian circumstances. *CYBERNOMICS*, *1*(2), 3–10.
Sharma, V. (2020). IoT for crowd sensing and crowd sourcing. In Mansaf Alam, Kashish Ara Shakil, Samiya Khan, (eds.), *Internet of Things (IoT)* (pp. 285–300). Springer, Cham.
Sharma, V., & Manocha, T. (2021). Technological influences over factors for sustainability of smart cities. *Global Journal of Enterprise Information System*, *13*(1), 26–41.
Silva, J. M., Mahfujur Rahman, A. S. M., & El Saddik, A. (2008). Web 3.0: A vision for bridging the gap between real and virtual. In *MM'08—Proceedings of the 2008 ACM International Conference on Multimedia, with Co-Located Symposium and Workshops*. https://doi.org/10.1145/1462039.1462042.
Soffel, J. (2016). *What Are the 21st-Century Skills Every Student Needs?* World Economic Forum, Geneva.
Spivack, N. (2010). Twine. *On March*, *22*, 2012. www.novaspivack.com/?s=.
Twine Szymkowiak, A., Melović, B., Dabić, M., Jeganathan, K., & Kundi, G. S. (2021). Information technology and Gen Z: The role of teachers, the internet, and technology in the education of young people. *Technology in Society*, *65*(January). https://doi.org/10.1016/j.techsoc.2021.101565.
Wheeler, S. (2009). e-Learning 3.0, learning with e's. Retrieved March 21, 2012. http://stevewheeler.blogspot.com/2009/04/learning-30.html#!/2009/04/learning-30.html.
Yeung, M. W. L., & Yau, A. H. Y. (2022). A thematic analysis of higher education students' perceptions of online learning in Hong Kong under COVID-19: Challenges, strategies and support. *Education and Information Technologies*, *27*(1). https://doi.org/10.1007/s10639-021-10656-3.

5 Undergraduate Perception towards E-Learning during the Pandemic

Evidence from State Universities in Sri Lanka

E.W. Biyiri, J.A.P.M. Jayasinghe, and S.N.S. Dahanayake

5.1 INTRODUCTION

During the Covid-19 pandemic, educational institutions, predominantly universities worldwide, implemented e-learning, which entails students participating in online learning activities incorporating digital technology. Lockdowns and isolation necessitated a myriad of adjustments from conventional to e-learning. These adjustments to e-learning were immediately embraced as a preventative strategy against the pandemic spreading (Almetwazi et al., 2020). At this juncture, the impact of information communication technology and its involvement in education cannot be underestimated. Edem Adzovie and Jibril (2022) defined e-learning as "any form of teaching and learning that is done with the assistance of an electronic device such as mobile phone, personal computer over an internet platform." According to Bhuvaneswari and Dharanipriya (2020), e-learning is "the use of information and communication technologies (ICT) in education which continues to evolve to meet the needs and demands of the students." E-learning integrates technology and web services to provide a two-way forum for interaction and conversation among teachers and students, fosters social learning through peer discussions among students, and offers a constructivist experience for learners with constant and prompt teacher feedback (Layali & Al-Shlowiy, 2020). Computer-assisted learning, web-based training, virtual classrooms, and digital collaboration are just a few examples of e-learning applications and processes (Kashive et al., 2020).

As stated earlier, the Covid-19 epidemic awakened the educational sector's eyes to online education due to its speedy transmission and severity. Therefore, the teaching and learning process were switched to e-learning mode (Kumar et al., 2021). Recognizing the significance of online education in such a global epidemic circumstance, academics have subsequently increased their attention to e-learning investigations, particularly in understanding the students' e-learning perspectives. However, prior to the Covid-19 outbreak, many universities and colleges relied on information and communication technology to provide educational materials and learning assistance; therefore, neither e-learning nor remote learning was a revolutionary strategy (Sharma et al., 2019; Johnson et al., 2021). Besides, it is believed that e-learning might have a substantial positive influence on academic achievement, educational quality, and levels of student involvement (Shen and Ho, 2020). Consequently, its prominence derives from various advantages, including no time limitations or speed; students take charge of the learning process, encouraging learner autonomy; students are exposed to a variety of learning resources that promote a student-centered, self-directed, collaborative, and dynamic learning process (Kashive et al., 2020; Layali & Al-Shlowiy, 2020; Reddy et al., 2020).

DOI: 10.1201/9781003425779-5

The importance of social presence, defined as "an individual's perception of the quantity and quality of interpersonal communication in an online learning environment" (Reio & Crim, 2013), in affecting a student's satisfaction with technology-based interaction and communication in e-learning has been recognized by prior studies (Alsadoon, 2018). This has consistently been recognized as the most critical factor in increasing student satisfaction, commitment, online collaboration, learning, and prospective participation in e-learning (Reio & Crim, 2013). Collaborative learning correspondingly can assist students in developing their higher-level cognitive abilities, communication and interpersonal skills, and self-management, along with many other qualities. The importance of professional practice of team environment and collaboration in education has been noted in previous research (Ha et al., 2019). The excellent moral experience will significantly be strengthened by student-teacher practice, co-teaching experience, and co-teaching interactions (Umar & Ko, 2022). Once teachers and students collaborate, they gain more information and aptitudes, generating constructive responses (Chen et al., 2015). Moreover, the student's engagement in the e-learning process is essential for developing a positive e-learning experience, particularly with the assistance of their teacher as well as colleagues, who help them get interested in e-learning (Alyahya et al., 2022). Student participation and collaboration, constant student encouragement, accessibility of information and resources, monitoring of performance and feedback, learning exercises and assessments, and personal reflection are the aspects to consider in determining a positive e-learning experience for students (Elshaer & Sobaih, 2022). On the other hand, learner satisfaction, defined as "an aggregate of feelings or emotional responses to distinct factors while interacting with an e-learning system" (Goh & Chen, 2008), will be increased through e-learning due to the use of numerous teaching materials which might not be available to many students, offering the learning process with a realistic environment wherein students feels comfortable without intervention from others, enabling students to share their opinion (Bahati et al., 2019).

Despite the numerous benefits of e-learning, there are drawbacks that higher education institutions must overcome, such as poor internet solutions, a lack of students' computer literacy, a lack of students' efficiency in using technology for learning, and the possibility of miscommunications between students and teachers (Layali & Al-Shlowiy, 2020; Mousavi et al., 2020). Since e-learning is intimately connected to technology, and the students must employ these technologies in the classroom, their knowledge and proficiency in using them are essential (Sakarji et al., 2019). Despite the popularity and numerous advantages, using online learning system is still challenging in terms of its learner-friendliness (Mukhopadhyay et al., 2020). Therefore, to succeed in the e-learning process, students' perceptions and attitudes must be comprehended (Kashive et al., 2020). The prior study findings revealed that the students are more inclined to adopt e-learning if they perceive it as advantageous to their learning process (Sakarji et al., 2019). However, most of the research on the e-learning perspective has been undertaken in developed countries, retaining an uncertainty on the topic in developing countries (Pham et al., 2019) due to the dearth of literature and limited investigations, leaving knowledge and an empirical gap. Therefore, this research aims to examine the undergraduates' perception of e-learning concerning the key aspects of social presence, collaborative learning, online learning experience, and e-learning satisfaction. In line with the aim, this chapter provides insights into the e-learning experience of undergraduates during the Covid-19 pandemic, covering the aspects of undergraduates' learning preferences, reasons for such learning preferences, and their e-learning satisfaction. Social presence, collaborative learning, and online learning experience were considered determinants of e-learning perceptions. The undergraduates of Sri Lankan state universities, representing all the academic years irrespective of their major study disciplines, were considered in the data collection process, which was conducted for three months from January to April 2022.

5.1.1 Objectives of the Chapter

The objectives of the chapter are:

1. To examine how undergraduates perceive e-learning in relation to social presence, collaborative learning, online learning experience, and satisfaction;

2. To investigate undergraduates' preferences for e-learning and face-to-face learning;
3. And, to determine the reasons underlying undergraduates' learning preferences.

5.1.2 Organization of the Chapter

The rest of the chapter is organized as: Section 5.2 highlights the background of the study. Section 5.3 entails literature review, covering aspects of e-learning during Covid-19, social presence, collaborative learning, and student satisfaction towards e-learning and online learning experience. Section 5.4 discusses methodology. Section 5.5 elaborates results and discussion. And, finally section 5.6 concludes the chapter with recommendations.

5.2 BACKGROUND

Sri Lanka, one of the countries severely affected by this epidemic, has also taken the initiative to transform from face-to-face learning to e-learning as a preventative measure to successfully address educational issues amid the health crisis (Hayashi et al., 2020). This transformation to e-learning in Sri Lankan universities was unexpected and rapid during the crisis, as it was in many other developing countries worldwide. Thus both teachers and students hardly had any preparation time for such a revolutionary method of education (Hayashi et al., 2020). However, to mitigate the pandemic's negative consequences on education, Sri Lankan higher education institutions sought strategic alternatives by employing Moodle-based learning management systems (LMS). Besides, the Lanka Education and Research Network (LEARN) was constantly networked to university web servers and used for e-learning education using the Zoom platform during the epidemic in Sri Lanka (Kumarasinghe & Sriyalatha, 2021). These initiatives enabled most public universities to offer accessible e-learning facilities to their undergraduates. For students' convenience, lesson materials and recordings, reading materials, and video sessions were published via learning management systems and Google Classrooms. Social media platforms like WhatsApp, Facebook, and YouTube were also utilized in certain situations to distribute learning resources and conduct online classes (Priyadarshana et al., 2021). This transformation to e-learning has also been aided by training programs offered by individual universities to equip their academics and other staff (Hettiarachchi et al., 2021).

Despite the positive consequences, due to a lack of suitable infrastructure and adequate access to e-learning, this sudden transformation was challenging for both students and teachers (Hayashi et al., 2020; Rasmitadila et al., 2020, Dissanayake et al., 2021). Students and teachers face numerous challenges due to the immediate transformation of e-learning, which depends on various electronic technologies and networks, including web-based learning, learning management systems, and other software applications. According to Hayashi et al. (2020), decreased student-teacher interaction, interruption of self-improvement activities, and inadequate assessment of teaching and learning gaps were exposed as hindrances. The outcomes of Banu and Kirshanthini (2021) had also disclosed that internet coverage issues in terms of internet speed, difficulties with network access and downloading resources, complications in online exams, problems with practical sessions; economic issues such as poor living and working conditions, and low-income level to facilitate the children for e-learning equipment and other necessities; lack of e-learning resources; struggle with home responsibilities; and emotional disturbances such as frustration, boredom, anxiety, stress, illness, laziness, insecurity, and lethargy were common. Supporting this, Santhirakumar et al. (2022) reported that lack of competency in smartphone usage, unreliable networks, and frequent power outages were significant among the technical issues, despite the fact that there were several economic problems.

Lakmal et al. (2021) discovered comparable findings such as insufficient computer equipment, insufficient internet access, unsuitable technology for specific courses, regular blackouts, reluctance to technological advancements, and poor abilities in e-learning pedagogy as challenges faced due to this unexpected transformation. E-learning is inevitably challenging, especially in developing countries like Sri Lanka; thus, a comprehensive study must be undertaken to understand undergraduates' perceptions, particularly the social presence, collaborative learning, online learning experience, and e-learning satisfaction.

5.3 LITERATURE REVIEW

5.3.1 E-learning during Covid-19

Because of the rapidly accelerating development and expansion of e-learning, as well as the numerous benefits it provides, many educational institutions all over the world have adopted e-learning systems. Bervell and Umar (2020) indicated that the field of higher education had made significant progress toward the implementation of e-learning in the last decade. It is a significant concept in higher education, and research on it, done in a methodical way, has the potential to lead to improved academic outcomes for students, as well as advancements in best practices for online instruction and increased student enrollment in continuing education (Cole et al., 2014). E-learning refers to the process of acquiring formal education through the utilization of various online resources. E-learning relies heavily on the utilization of computer technology and the internet, in contrast to traditional classroom instruction, which may take place anywhere (including outside of traditional classrooms; Sternad Zabukovsek et al., 2022).

Contextually, Edem Adzovie and Jibril (2022) defined learning as "any kind of instruction and education that is carried out with the help of a digital device, such as a mobile phone or personal computer, in conjunction with the use of the internet as the medium." When it comes to meeting the requirements and wants of today's students, "the use of information and communication technologies (ICT) in education" best describes "e-learning" (Bhuvaneswari & Dharanipriya, 2020). With the help of web services and technology, e-learning creates a two-way conversation between educators and their students, encourages collaborative learning through student-to-student discussions, and provides a constructivist environment in which students are provided with immediate and consistent feedback on their progress (Layali & Al-Shlowiy, 2020). E-learning encompasses a wide range of applications and procedures, some of the most well-known of which include computer-assisted learning, web-based training, virtual classrooms, and digital collaboration (Kashive et al., 2020).

As a result of the current scenario of the Covid-19 epidemic, the closure of schools created a barrier to students' education, therefore the use of information technology in the classroom has increased rapidly (Khan et al., 2021). When the Covid-19 virus was discovered, traditional methods of teaching were substituted with e-learning since social gatherings at educational institutions are thought to be a chance for the virus to spread. Thus, the educators now have the ability to incorporate IT solutions for teaching as well as assessment for the completion of students' course work. The efforts of various stakeholders such as students, instructors, and administrators of educational institutions, are on in order to make the most effective use of technology and to streamline the learning process (Henderson et al., 2020). Due to the inherent isolation afforded by remote learning, it is the most effective strategy for preventing the transmission of infectious illnesses. Thus, e-learning is the greatest alternative to prevent the spread of illnesses (Lizcano et al., 2019).

Numerous users of e-learning platforms have concluded that online education is the best way to ensure that students have quick and easy access to lecturers and course materials as e-learning is easily administered (Mukhtar et al., 2020). To add to its benefits, it helped lessen the workload and cut down on the expenses of travel and accommodation for classroom-based education. The time and energy spent on administration, course planning, lecture recording, and administrational activities such as attendance tracking are greatly reduced for e-learning (Maatuk et al., 2022). The efficacy of learning has been evaluated by using certain design aspects, such as cognitive, instructional, and social representation in the e-learning network. According to experts, e-learning is a gateway to development and progress for developing nations (Sternad Zabukovsek et al., 2022).

E-learning is also seen to have the potential to have a significant beneficial impact on academic performance, educational caliber, and the degree to which students actively participate in their education (Shen & Ho, 2020). As a result, its popularity stems from a number of benefits, such as the lack of pace or time constraints; learner autonomy is encouraged; students are exposed to a range of learning tools that support a student-centered, self-directed, collaborative, and dynamic learning process (Kashive et al., 2020; Layali & Al-Shlowiy, 2020; Sharma et al., 2019).

5.3.2 Social Presence

From its inception as a field of study, research on social presence has a lengthy and fruitful pedigree. Short and Williams (1976) argued that social presence is a crucial component of the communication medium. According to this early viewpoint, computer-mediated communication "filters out" crucial audible and visual signals that are present in face-to-face conversation, making it less intimate and unable to promote high levels of social presence. This view asserts that traditional face-to-face classrooms lack the underlying social presence that online learning settings do (Andel et al., 2020). Social presence is one of the tenets of the Community of Inquiry Framework, and it refers to the degree to which students "feel genuine" enough to engage in meaningful conversation with and learn from their online peers (Stewart, 2021). The term "social presence" refers to "one's level of attention to and respect for other people in social situations." (Tung & Deng, 2007).

Recent meta-analytic evidence from Richardson et al. (2017) showed that students who attended classes online report higher levels of happiness and a sense that they are learning more when they encounter a better sense of social presence in their virtual classrooms. Other studies have demonstrated that having a social presence increases a person's desire to participate in future online classes (Andel et al., 2020). The aforementioned research emphasized the need for instructors to have an understanding of how to make the most of the opportunities presented by the social presence in an online classroom setting. As a consequence of this, a number of studies have studied different methods in which social presence perceptions might be increased within the setting of online learning. There is a widespread agreement among researchers who have studied online education that social presence, often known as the capacity to see other people in a mediated setting, is an essential component of successful online education (Richardson et al., 2017).

5.3.3 Collaborative Learning

Students have the potential to develop their higher-level cognitive abilities, spoken communication skills, and self management abilities by engaging in collaborative learning activities (Sternad Zabukovsek et al., 2022). According to Prince (2004), active learning may be accomplished most effectively through the use of collaborative learning. The goal of the instructional strategy known as collaborative learning is to improve learner performance and to make learning more accessible to students. Students improve their capacity to think critically as a result of this (Garrison et al., 2001). Students engage in collaborative learning when they participate and interact with one another in a group setting, where they are responsible for managing their relationships and generating material (Lee, 2014). Students must work in groups in order to reap the benefits of collaborative learning, which necessitates that they work with their peers and be open to learning from them. It has been proposed that schools create more opportunities for students to work together on projects in order to improve students' cognitive performance, as well as their social interactions and metacognition (Kumar, 2017). Students serve as learning resources for one another in an interactive learning environment by engaging in activities such as talking to one another, observing the work of others, exchanging ideas, and coming to agreement as a group (Laza et al., 2022).

Prior research has established the significance of interpersonal dynamics in online learning communities (Molinillo et al., 2018), collaborative learning's effect on student satisfaction (Othman, 2017), and the effects of social media use on academic performance (Al-Rahmi et al., 2018). The following are some of the contributions that this study has made to the existing body of research on educational practices and methods. The findings of this research will add to the existing body of knowledge regarding the ways in which social factors (such as interaction, social presence, and the use of social media) affect collaborative learning and student engagement, which in turn improves their learning performance, as was established by earlier research (Akyildiz & Argan, 2012; Nemetz et al., 2012).

Collaborative learning that takes place online is more productive than learning that takes place in person (Al-Rahmi et al., 2018). In addition, the results demonstrate that active collaborative learning has a strong and positive relationship to the level of involvement shown by the students. Students are more likely to communicate with one another and remain engaged in online learning environments because group conversations are easier to organize and participate in (Gopinathan et al., 2022).

5.3.4 Student Satisfaction with E-Learning

Learner satisfaction is defined as "an aggregate of feelings or emotional responses to distinct factors while interacting with an e-learning system" (Martin & Bolliger, 2018). Learner satisfaction will be increased through the use of e-learning due to the use of numerous teaching materials that might not be available to many students. Offering the learning process with a realistic environment, wherein student feels comfortable without intervention from others, will enable students to share their opinion.

The concept of online learning satisfaction is broad and varied, including factors such as communication, student involvement in online discussions, workload, technological assistance, instructor pedagogical abilities, and feedback (Elshami et al., 2021). The research takes each of these aspects into consideration. The social cognitive theory, the interaction equivalence theorem, and the social integration theory are the three hypotheses that underpin the satisfaction associated with online learning. Students advance their education through making connections with one another, taking part in activities, and receiving feedback in a social setting. A student's enjoyment of a class can be affected by their interactions with both their other classmates and their teachers, as well as by the material that is being taught (Elshami et al., 2021).

Student engagement in extracurricular activities and academic achievement has been shown in an increasing body of research to have a favorable correlation with students' overall sense of well-being. The cost-effectiveness of an institution, the satisfaction of its students and professors, and the efficacy with which they learn are all aspects that contribute to defining the overall quality of an educational experience (Delfino, 2019). Previous research concluded that there was no significant difference between face-to-face learning and well-designed online learning. Nevertheless, other studies have found that participants were happier with face-to-face teaching than with online learning (Paul & Jefferson, 2019). The more conventional manner of studying in a classroom has been supplemented with the more modern method of learning online. The swift transition away from traditional classroom settings and toward online education was precipitated by Covid-19. A small number of scholars conducted surveys prior to Covid-19 to determine how satisfied students and teachers were with online education.

5.3.5 Online Learning Experience

Since the Covid-19 pandemic, significant changes have been made to the way education is provided across the world. Many educational institutions, like colleges and schools, have shifted to providing all of their courses and educational programs through electronic and online modes. The educational system was changing at a considerably higher rate. In order to keep up, teachers had to rely solely on online platforms to administer all of their classes, tests, and other instructional necessities (Mishra et al., 2020).

There were many difficulties for teachers, students, and their families during the Covid-19 epidemic. Thus, the education needed to continue uninterrupted, hence a rapid shift to distant online learning was implemented. The online courses were the opportunity to participate in real-time discussions with other students using recorded lectures, online chats, and presentations (Shawaqfeh et al., 2020).

The studies that had been done on the topic of students' experiences with online learning during the Covid-19 epidemic had shown a few major difficulties, including problems with internet connections and IT equipment (Bączek et al., 2021; Niemi & Kousa, 2020; Agung et al., 2020; Basuony et al., 2020), lack of opportunities for collaborative learning (Bączek et al., 2021; Yates et al., 2020), lack of motivation for learning (Basuony et al., 2020; Niemi & Kousa, 2020; Yates et al., 2020), and increased learning burdens (Niemi & Kousa, 2020).

Maintaining consistent connectivity to the internet is an essential component of the educational experience for today's students. According to Berge (2005), students' success in online courses may depend on factors such as students' technological preparedness and teachers' pedagogical stance. According to Cavanaugh et al. (2009), having access to a computer, whether a desktop or a laptop, is a critical aspect of students' capacity to adjust to online learning. In addition, students who are not proficient in the usage of electronic gadgets could struggle with the online learning environment. Therefore, Cavanaugh et al. (2009) argued that students need to have good digital literacy to learn and communicate with others.

Participation and collaboration on the part of students, consistent encouragement of students, accessibility of information and resources, performance monitoring and feedback, learning exercises and assessments, and personal reflection are the aspects that should be considered when determining whether or not students will have a positive experience with e-learning (González-Zamar et al., 2022).

5.4 METHODOLOGY

This study explores undergraduates' perceptions towards e-learning during the pandemic. In order to achieve the objective, this study utilized both qualitative and quantitative data.

5.4.1 Model

This study mainly focuses on the undergraduates' perceptions towards e-learning in terms of social presence, collaborative learning, online learning experience, and satisfaction. The variables for the study are derived from the existing literature. Figure 5.1 depicts the model developed based on the main objective. Furthermore, this study attempts to examine the undergraduates' learning preferences and the reasons for their choice of learning. Figure 5.2 depicts the model used to achieve this objective.

5.4.2 Study Population and Sample

The population of this study consisted of all the undergraduates of the state universities in Sri Lanka. A structured questionnaire was utilized to collect the primary data for the study, which is distributed through online channels. The convenient sampling technique was adopted for the study and 1012 responses were received for the final analysis.

5.4.3 Instrument

The questionnaire's instruments were derived from existing measurements (Khagi et al., 2021). The first part of the questionnaire included questions on the demographic information of students. The second part of the questionnaire consists of the instruments created for social presence, collaborative learning, online learning experience, and satisfaction. The third part of the questionnaire consists of a question to inquire about the learning preference of the undergraduates and an open-ended question to inquire about the reasons for their preferences. For the measurement, a 5-point Likert scale ranging from 1 as strongly disagree to 5 as strongly agree is used.

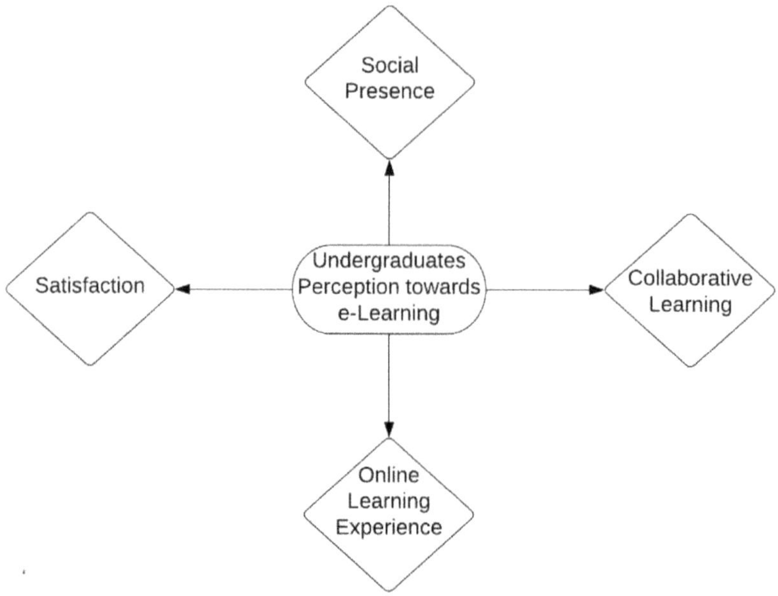

FIGURE 5.1 Purposed model illustrating undergraduates' perception towards e-learning.

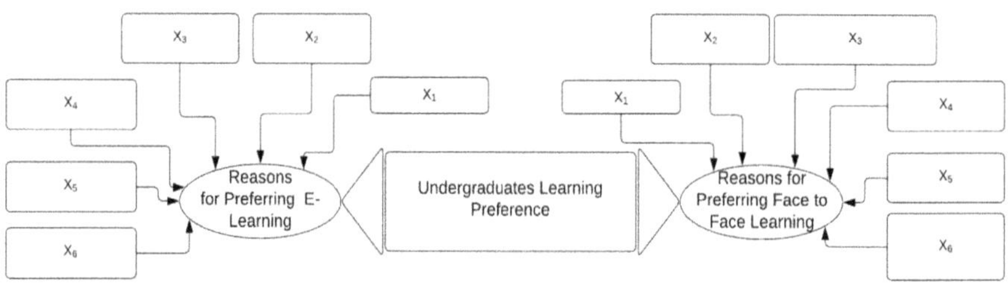

FIGURE 5.2 Purposed model illustrating undergraduates' learning preference.

5.4.4 Data Analysis

Descriptive analysis was employed to analyze the undergraduates' perception towards E-learning. The responses related to the learning preferences of the undergraduates were analyzed through content analysis using the NVivo 12 Plus software.

5.5 RESULTS AND DISCUSSION

This section describes the results of the current study based on the objectives of the study. Accordingly, the respondents' demographic profile, undergraduates' perception towards E-learning, undergraduates' learning preference, and reasons for their preference are described.

5.5.1 Respondents Profile

The questionnaire was distributed online among the undergraduates of state universities in Sri Lanka. The responses were received from 1012 undergraduates of eight state universities. The

TABLE 5.1
Demographic Profile of the Respondents

Variable	Frequency	Percentage
Gender		
Male	221	22%
Female	791	78%
Year of the study		
First year	586	58%
Second year	154	15%
Third year	180	18%
Fourth year	92	9%
Course pursuing		
Arts	394	39%
Commerce	21	2%
Science	62	6%
Management	316	31%
Tourism	71	7%
Technology	97	10%
Engineering	13	1%
Other	38	4%
Experience in e-learning		
Yes	1012	100%
No	0	0%
Devices used		
Desktop	6	1%
Laptop	270	27%
Laptop/smartphone	263	26%
Smartphone	458	45%
Tablet	15	1%
Tools used		
Zoom	768	76%
Google Classroom	96	9%
WhatsApp and YouTube	145	14%
Other	3	0%

Source: Survey data, 2022.

respondents' profile is depicted in Table 5.1 such as gender, year of study, course pursuing, experience of e-learning, the devices used for e-learning, and the tools used for e-learning. According to the results, the majority of the respondents are female undergraduates, which is a percentage of 78%. The remaining 22% of the respondents are male.

The majority of the respondents (58%) study in the first year, while 15% of respondents study in the second year, 18% of the respondents study in the third year, and 9% of the respondents study in the final year.

The respondents are following different subject areas such as 39% of the respondents from the arts stream, 31% of the respondents follow management-related degree programs, 10% of the respondents are from the technology discipline, 7% of the respondents follow tourism-related degree programs, 6% of the respondents are from the science stream, and 1% of the respondents are from an engineering discipline.

All the respondents have experience with e-learning. The majority of the students use a smartphone (45%) for their learning process; 27% of the respondents use a laptop; 26% of the respondents use a laptop or a smartphone; and 1% of the respondents use a desktop or a tablet for their learning process.

According to the results, most universities in Sri Lanka use the Zoom application for the teaching and learning process during the pandemic. The Sri Lankan government has given the facility to use the platform to continue higher education during the pandemic. Accordingly, 76% of the respondents use the Zoom application, 14% of the respondents use WhatsApp and YouTube, and 9% of the respondents use Google Classroom.

5.5.2 Undergraduates' Perception towards E-Learning

A descriptive analysis was employed to ascertain the perception of undergraduates towards e-learning during the pandemic concerning the social presence, collaborative learning, online learning experience, and e-learning satisfaction. The findings are presented in Table 5.2.

The mean value of each item is considered to interpret the undergraduates' perception towards e-learning. According to the analysis, the results show that the undergraduates have more negative perceptions towards online learning experiences. Further, undergraduates hold moderate

TABLE 5.2
Undergraduates' Perception towards E-Learning

Item	*N*	Mean	SD
Social presence		3.10	1.024
1. I felt comfortable introducing myself in online classes	1012	3.10	1.142
2. I felt comfortable participating in online classes	1012	3.01	1.207
3. I felt that my opinion was also accepted in the discussion	1012	3.20	1.068
Collaborative learning		**3.04**	**0.927**
1. I felt that I am a part of the learning process in my class	1012	3.14	1.087
2. I actively exchanged ideas in my online classes	1012	3.03	1.085
3. I was able to develop problem-solving skills	1012	3.04	1.095
4. Group discussion in my online class was not time-consuming	1012	2.98	1.045
Satisfaction		**2.98**	**1.016**
1. I was able to learn happily in the online class	1012	2.79	1.191
2. I was stimulated to do additional reading on the topic discussed in the online class	1012	3.02	1.111
3. Discussion assisted me in understanding others' opinions	1012	3.09	1.097
4. The online classes were a useful learning experience	1012	3.13	1.164
5. I am satisfied with my learning	1012	2.98	1.170
6. Overall, online classes met my learning expectations	1012	2.93	1.154
Online learning experience		**2.98**	**1.016**
1. I put a good effort to learn online in order to participate in the class	1012	3.23	1.152
2. Taking online classes is a pleasant way to communicate with others	1012	2.92	1.109
3. I could easily express myself in online classes	1012	2.98	1.121
4. Online learning environments are better than face-to-face learning environments	1012	2.53	1.208
5. The interruptions during online classes were unimportant due to my positive e-learning experience	1012	2.84	1.099

Source: Survey data, 2022.

perceptions towards social presence and collaborative learning in an e-learning environment. The results further indicate that the undergraduates are less satisfied with e-learning during the pandemic.

The results of the current study show that the mean value for the items of social presence ranges from 3.01 to 3.02, indicating that the undergraduates moderately agreed that e-learning creates a platform for social presence. Prior studies have recognized the importance of social presence in affecting a student's satisfaction with technology-based interaction and communication in e-learning (Alsadoon, 2018). This has consistently been recognized as the most critical factor in increasing student satisfaction, commitment, online collaboration, learning, and prospective participation in e-learning (Reio & Crim, 2013). However, the current study shows that Sri Lankan undergraduates hold moderate positive perceptions in terms of social presence.

The results of the current study suggest that the undergraduates in Sri Lanka hold moderate positive perceptions concerning collaborative learning, as the mean values for the items are between 2.9 and 3.01. Collaborative learning involves two or more students learning or attempting to learn something together while sharing resources, knowledge, and experience. According to Gokhale (1995), learners are able to reach higher levels of knowledge and remember information longer when they work in a group.

It is crucial for the student to be involved in the e-learning process in order to have a positive e-learning experience, especially with the help of their teacher and other colleagues who encourage their interest in e-learning (Alyahya et al., 2022). According to previous studies, different type of interaction is essential in boosting student satisfaction in distance learning environments (Bray et al., 2008; Burnett, 2001; Moore & Kearsley, 1996; Northrup et al., 2002). Therefore, it is important to include collaborative learning activities in the online class.

The mean values for the items related to undergraduates' satisfaction with e-learning range from 2.79 to 3.09. Overall results show that the undergraduates in Sri Lanka are not that satisfied with e-learning as the mean value is 2.98. The literature suggests that many factors determine the undergraduates' satisfaction with e-learning education. However, the technology infrastructure and internet quality play a major role in determining the success of e-learning and student satisfaction (Piccoli et al., 2001; Webster & Hackley 1997). Therefore, higher education institutions must overcome the drawbacks of e-learning such as technological limitations, poor network connections, lack of students' computer literacy, students' ability in using technology for learning and miscommunications between students and teachers miscommunications between students and teachers (Layali & Al Shlowiy, 2020; Mousavi et al., 2020).

The current study results further indicate that the undergraduates in Sri Lanka have a negative perception of the online learning experience as the mean values for the items of the variable range from 2.53 to 3.23. The reason behind the negative perception towards e-learning could be the sudden transition of teaching and learning as both teachers and students have a lack of prior online learning experience.

The results of the descriptive analysis are summarized in Figure 5.3, which depicts that the undergraduates are holding more negative perceptions towards online learning experiences. Further, undergraduates hold moderate perceptions towards social presence and collaborative learning. The results indicate that the undergraduates are less satisfied with e-learning during the pandemic.

5.5.3 Undergraduates' Learning Preference

The current study inquired about the undergraduates' learning preferences. The results are shown in Table 5.3. According to the results, the majority of the undergraduate (73.3%) prefer to have traditional face-to-face classes and 26.7% of the respondents prefer to have e-learning. The results of the previous analyses show that the undergraduates hold more negative perceptions towards e-learning and the results of the study preference are also in line with the previous results indicating that the

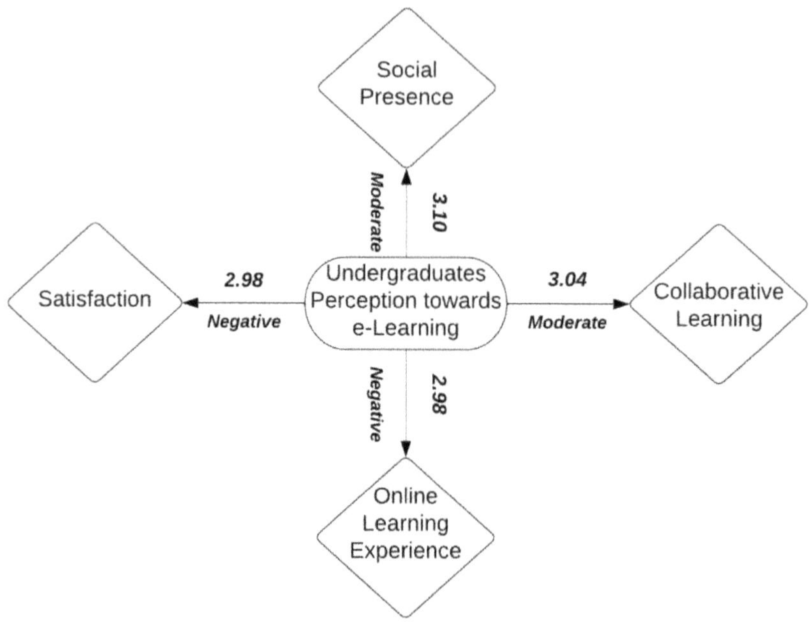

FIGURE 5.3 Undergraduates' perception towards e-learning.

TABLE 5.3
Undergraduates' Learning Preference

Variable	Frequency	Percentage
Face-to-face learning	742	73.3%
E-learning	270	26.7%
Total	1012	

Source: Survey Data, 2022.

majority of the respondents prefer to have face-to-face learning. The following section describes the reasons for undergraduates' mode of learning preference.

5.5.4 Reasons for Preferring Face-to-Face Learning

As mentioned in the previous section, the majority of the undergraduates prefer face-to-face learning and the respondents mentioned their reasons for preferring face-to-face learning. The results indicate that the responders prefer face-to-face learning for various reasons. According to Figure 5.4, it is clear that the majority of the undergraduates prefer face-to-face learning due to the good interaction with other students, which is a percentage of 18.43%. Further, 16% of references include that the undergraduates prefer face-to-face learning since they do not need technical devices or network coverage for learning. Moreover, 12.3% of the references indicate that undergraduates prefer face-to-face learning due to the good interaction with the teacher. Additionally, 11.8% of references indicate that the undergraduates can focus more on learning during face-to-face learning, 11.3% of references mentioned the easiness of grabbing the content, 11% of the references mentioned that the face-to-face learning is convenient, 8.0% of references mentioned that the

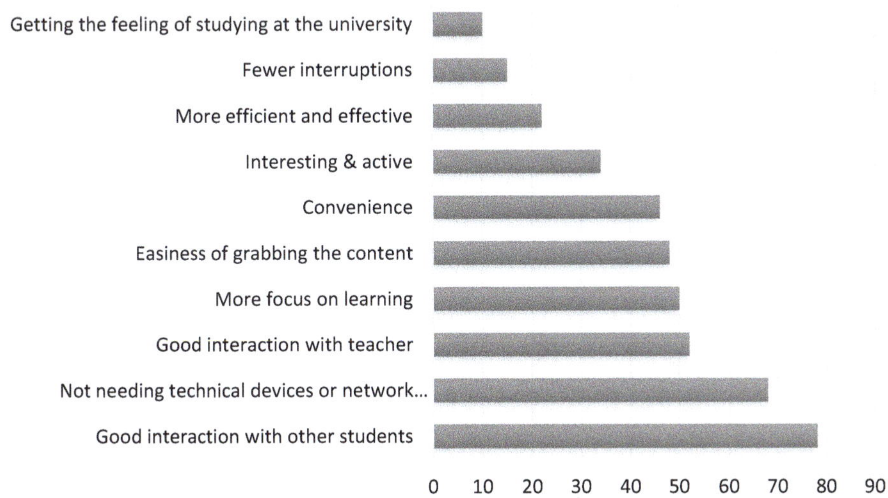

FIGURE 5.4 Reasons for preferring face-to-face learning.

Source: Survey data, 2022.

face-to-face learning interesting and active, 5.2% of references indicate that the face-to-face learning is more effective and efficient, 3.5% of references mentioned that there are fewer interruptions during face-to-face learning, and 2.3% of references include that the undergraduates prefer face-to-face learning since it will generate the feeling of studying at the university.

5.5.5 Reasons for Preferring E-Learning

About 26.7% of undergraduates prefer e-learning, and the authors explored why this is so. The results of the analysis are depicted in Figure 5.5.

According to the results, the majority of the undergraduate prefer e-learning due to the ease of time management; 25% of the references include that it is easy to manage time with e-learning compared to face-to-face learning. Further 24.8% of references mentioned that undergraduates prefer e-learning due to the convenience. Additionally, 14.6% of references indicate that e-learning is more cost-effective than face-to-face learning, especially for students, who have the opportunity of saving money on transport, food and accommodation costs. There are 10.16% of references who stated that the availability of the recorded lessons is another reason for preferring e-learning.

Moreover, 9.6% of references include that the undergraduates prefer e-learning since it is safe to attend classes from home, especially during the time of the pandemic. Additionally, 5.6% of references mention that undergraduates prefer e-learning since online classes are accessible from anywhere and students should not be present at the university. Plus, 2.8% of references include freedom of e-learning, 2.25% of references include that the e-learning is effective, 2.25% of references mention that e-learning improves IT knowledge, and 1.7% references include that e-learning is flexible.

According to the results, the undergraduates of Sri Lanka prefer e-learning due to the easiness of time management, convenience, availability of the recorded lessons, cost-effectiveness, accessibility from anywhere, improving IT knowledge, freedom, and flexibility. The previous studies also confirm similar findings with regard to the students' preference for e-learning. According to the study conducted by Agarwal and Kaushik (2020), the respondents claim that online sessions broke monotonous routines, were a good utilization of time, and the material was easy to access. The study conducted by Muthuprasad et al. (2021) found that students prefer recorded classes and opined that the flexibility and convenience of online classes make it an attractive option. According

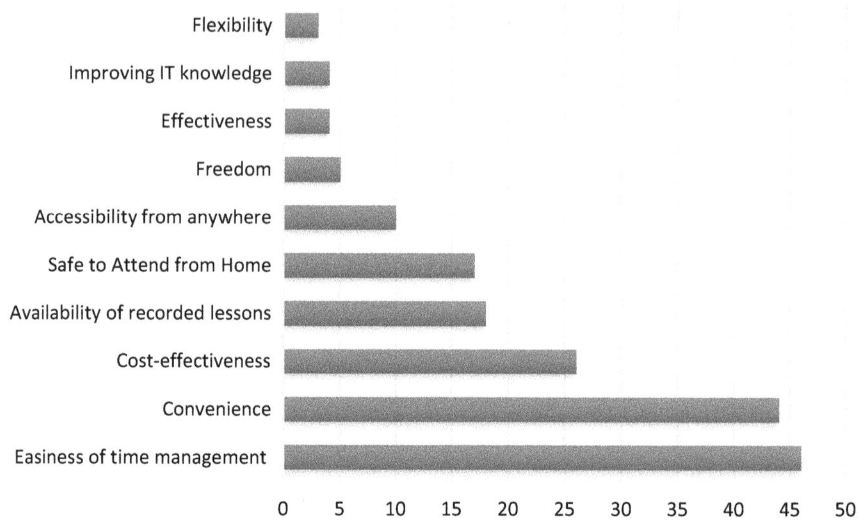

FIGURE 5.5 Reasons for preferring e-learning.

Source: Survey data, 2022.

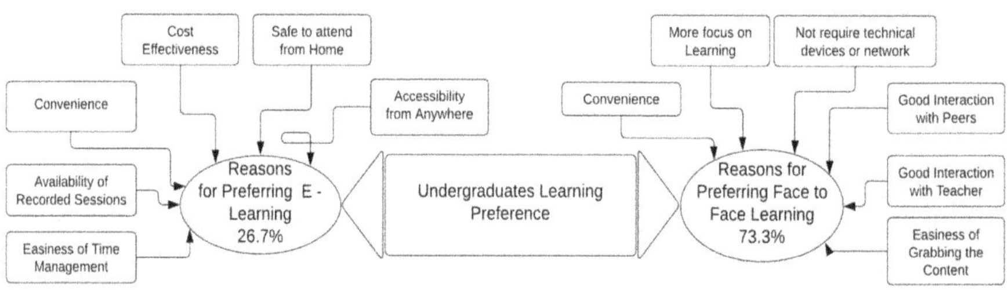

FIGURE 5.6 Undergraduates' preference for learning.

to Almahasees et al. (2021), the students claim that self-learning, low costs, convenience, and flexibility are the main advantages of e-learning. Based on these results, the authors developed the following model (Figure 5.6) to present the findings of the qualitative data analysis.

5.6 CONCLUSION AND RECOMMENDATIONS

Over the previous few decades, there has been an ongoing controversy on e-learning; however, significant attention and extensive adoption occurred during the global Covid-19 pandemic. This unexpected scenario has disclosed numerous shortcomings in educational establishments, including universities. However, new avenues for reframing and establishing a more dynamic and comprehensive educational system have emerged. Accordingly, the current study explored the undergraduates' perception towards e-learning in terms of social presence, collaborative learning, online learning experience, and satisfaction with e-learning. Further, it is aimed to explore undergraduates' preferences for e-learning and face-to-face learning and the reasons for their particular preferences.

The results indicate that undergraduates moderately agreed that e-learning creates a platform for social presence, and the respondents hold more negative perceptions pertaining to social interaction.

Further, the undergraduates hold moderate positive perceptions concerning collaborative learning. Overall results show that the undergraduates in Sri Lanka are not that satisfied with e-learning and the undergraduates in Sri Lanka negatively perceive the online learning experience.

The majority of the undergraduates prefer face-to-face learning. Notably, the undergraduates hold more negative perceptions towards e-learning. The main reason for the negative perception of e-learning can be identified through the content analysis of their learning preference. Accordingly, it was found that the undergraduates prefer face-to-face learning mostly since they can well interact with other students and technological infrastructure or network connection is not compulsory for face-to-face teaching and learning process. Thus, it can be assumed that the undergraduates are dissatisfied with e-learning due to the poor network coverage and the lack of technical devices. Based on the results, it is recommended for the government and private network facilities providers to establish good network facilities covering Sri Lanka. Further, the Sri Lankan government has introduced a loan facility with state banks for undergraduates to buy a laptop for their studies, which is commendable considering the requirements of continuing education during the pandemic through e-mode.

Moreover, it is recommended to higher educational institutes to provide training programs to university teachers on online teaching methods. Additionally, the educators must include methods to create the online classroom more interactive and collaborative, which will lead to enhance the undergraduates' satisfaction towards e-learning and create a good learning experience.

REFERENCES

Agarwal, S., & Kaushik, J. S. (2020). Student's perception of online learning during COVID pandemic. *The Indian Journal of Pediatrics*, *87*(7), 554. https://doi.org/10.1007/s12098-020-03327-7.

Agung, A. S. N., Surtikanti, M. W., & Quinones, C. A. (2020). Students' perception of online learning during COVID-19 pandemic: A case study on the English students of STKIP Pamane Talino. *SOSHUM: Jurnal Sosial Dan Humaniora*, *10*(2), 225–235.

Akyildiz, M., & Argan, M. (2012). Using online social networking: Students' purposes of Facebook usage at the University of Turkey. *Journal of Technology Research*, *3*(September 2010), 1–11. http://search.proquest.com/docview/1022983264?accountid=12253.

Almahasees, Z., Mohsen, K., & Amin, M. O. (2021). Faculty's and students' perceptions of online learning during COVID-19. *Frontiers in Education*, *6*, 638470. https://doi.org/10.3389/feduc.2021.638470.

Almetwazi, M., Alzoman, N., Al-Massarani, S., & Alshamsan, A. (2020). COVID-19 impact on pharmacy education in Saudi Arabia: Challenges and opportunities. *Saudi Pharmaceutical Journal*, *28*(11), 1431–1434. https://doi.org/10.1016/j.jsps.2020.09.008.

Al-Rahmi, W. M., Alias, N., Othman, M. S., Marin, V. I., & Tur, G. (2018). A model of factors affecting learning performance through the use of social media in Malaysian higher education. *Computers & Education*, *121*, 59–72. https://doi.org/10.1016/J.COMPEDU.2018.02.010.

Alsadoon, E. (2018). The impact of social presence on learners' satisfaction in mobile learning. *Turkish Online Journal of Educational Technology-TOJET*, *17*(1), 226–233.

Alyahya, M. A., Elshaer, I. A., Abunasser, F., Hassan, O. H. M., & Sobaih, A. E. E. (2022). e-Learning experience in higher education amid COVID-19: Does gender really matter in a gender-segregated culture? *Sustainability*, *14*(6), 3298. https://doi.org/10.3390/su14063298.

Andel, S. A., de Vreede, T., Spector, P. E., Padmanabhan, B., Singh, V. K., & Vreede, G. J. de. (2020). Do social features help in video-centric online learning platforms? A social presence perspective. *Computers in Human Behavior*, *113*(April), 106505. https://doi.org/10.1016/j.chb.2020.106505.

Bączek, M., Zagańczyk-Bączek, M., Szpringer, M., Jaroszyński, A., & Wożakowska-Kapłon, B. (2021). Students' perception of online learning during the COVID-19 pandemic: A survey study of Polish medical students. *Medicine*, *100*(7), e24821. https://doi.org/10.1097/MD.0000000000024821.

Bahati, B., Fors, U., Hansen, P., Nouri, J., & Mukama, E. (2019). Measuring learner satisfaction with formative e-assessment strategies. *International Journal of Emerging Technologies in Learning (iJET)*, *14*(07), 61. https://doi.org/10.3991/ijet.v14i07.9120.

Banu, M. N. N, & Kirshanthini, D. (2021). Challenges faced by school student through e-Learning during the covid-19 period: CP/N/Elton hall Tamil Vidyalaya in Lindula, school-centered study (Grade 11). *Indiana Journal of Humanities and Social Sciences*, *2*(6), 11–15.

Basuony, M. A. K., EmadEldeen, R., Farghaly, M., El-Bassiouny, N., & Mohamed, E. K. A. (2020). The factors affecting student satisfaction with online education during the COVID-19 pandemic: An empirical study of an emerging Muslim country. *Journal of Islamic Marketing*. https://doi.org/10.1108/JIMA-09-2020-0301.

Berge, Z. L. (2005). *Virtual schools: Planning for success*. Teachers College Press, Columbia University.

Bervell, B., & Umar, I. N. (2020). Blended learning or face-to-face? Does Tutor anxiety prevent the adoption of learning management systems for distance education in Ghana? *Open Learning*, *35*(2), 159–177. https://doi.org/10.1080/02680513.2018.1548964.

Bhuvaneswari, S. S. B., & Dharanipriya, A. (2020). Attitude of UG students towards e-Learning. *International Journal of Humanities and Social Sciences*, *9*(2), 35–40.

Bray, E., Aoki, K., & Dlugosh, L. (2008). Predictors of learning satisfaction in Japanese online distance learners. *International Review of Research in Open & Distance Learning*, *9*(3), 1–24.

Burnett, K. (2001). Interaction and student retention, success and satisfaction in web-based learning. Retrieved from ERIC database.

Cavanaugh, C. S., Barbour, M. K., & Clark, T. (2009). Research and practice in K-12 online learning: A review of open access literature. *International Review of Research in Open and Distance Learning*, *10*(1). https://doi.org/10.19173/irrodl.v10i1.607.

Chen, P., Hernandez, A., & Dong, J. (2015). Impact of collaborative project-based learning on self-efficacy of urban minority students in engineering. *Journal of Urban Learning, Teaching, and Research*, *11*, 26–39.

Clark, R. C., & Mayer, R. E. (2016). *E-learning and the science of instruction: Proven guidelines for consumers and designers of multimedia learning*. John Wiley & Sons.

Cole, M. T., Shelley, D. J., & Swartz, L. B. (2014). Online instruction, e-Learning, and student satisfaction: A three year study. *International Review of Research in Open and Distance Learning*, *15*(6), 111–131. https://doi.org/10.19173/irrodl.v15i6.1748.

Delfino, A. P. (2019). Student engagement and academic performance of students of partido state university. *Asian Journal of University Education*, *15*(1), 22–41. https://doi.org/10.24191/ajue.v15i3.05.

Dissanayake, D. M. M. I., Biyiri, E. W., & Wickramasinghe, D. M. J. (2021). Online teaching and learning during the Covid 19 outbreak: The case of tourism and hospitality management undergraduates in state universities in Sri Lanka. In K. Yatigammana, D. Pathiranage, & M. De Pasqual (eds.), *Online education in Sri Lanka: Lessons learnt during the Covid 19 pandemic* (pp. 78–89). National E-Learning Resource Centre, University of Kelaniya.

Edem Adzovie, D., & Jibril, A. B. (2022). Assessment of the effects of Covid-19 pandemic on the prospects of e-Learning in higher learning institutions: The mediating role of academic innovativeness and technological growth. *Cogent Education*, *9*(1). https://doi.org/10.1080/2331186x.2022.2041222.

Elshaer, I. A., & Sobaih, A. E. E. (2022). FLOWER: An approach for enhancing e-Learning experience amid COVID-19. *International Journal of Environmental Research and Public Health*, *19*(7), 3823. https://doi.org/10.3390/ijerph19073823.

Elshami, W., Taha, M. H., Abuzaid, M., Saravanan, C., Al Kawas, S., & Abdalla, M. E. (2021). Satisfaction with online learning in the new normal: Perspective of students and faculty at medical and health sciences colleges. *Medical Education Online*, *26*(1). https://doi.org/10.1080/10872981.2021.1920090.

Garrison, D. R., Anderson, T., & Archer, W. (2001). Critical thinking, cognitive presence, and computer conferencing in distance education. *International Journal of Phytoremediation*, *21*(1), 7–23. https://doi.org/10.1080/08923640109527071.

Goh, T. T., & Chen, N. S. (2008). Evaluating learner satisfaction in a multiplatform e-Learning system. In *Handbook of research on user interface design and evaluation for mobile technology* (pp. 1079–1099). IGI Global.

Gokhale, A. A. (1995). Collaborative learning enhances critical thinking. *Journal of Technology Education*, *7*(1). https://doi.org/10.21061/jte.v7i1.a.2.

González-Zamar, M.-D., Vázquez-Cano, E., López Meneses, E., Elshaer, I. A., & Elnasr Sobaih, A. E. (2022). *Citation: Elshaer, I FLOWER: An approach for enhancing e-Learning experience amid COVID-19*. https://doi.org/10.3390/ijerph19073823.

Gopinathan, S., Kaur, A. H., Veeraya, S., & Raman, M. (2022). The role of digital collaboration in student engagement towards enhancing student participation during COVID-19. *Sustainability*, *14*(11), 6844. https://doi.org/10.3390/su14116844.

Ha, N. H., Nayyar, A., Nguyen, D. M., & Liu, C. A. (2019). Enhancing students' soft skills by implementing CDIO-based integration teaching mode. In *The 15th international CDIO conference* (p. 569). Aarhus University, Denmark.

Hayashi, R., Garcia, M., Maddawin, A., & Hewagamage, K. (2020). Online learning in Sri Lanka's higher education institutions during the CO VID-19 pandemic. *ADB Briefs*. https://doi.org/10.22617/brf200260-2.

Henderson, D., Woodcock, H., Mehta, J., Khan, N., Shivji, V., Richardson, C., Aya, H., Ziser, S., Pollara, G., & Burns, A. (2020). Keep calm and carry on learning: Using microsoft teams to deliver a medical education programme during the COVID-19 pandemic. *Future Healthcare Journal*, *7*(3), e67–e70. https://doi.org/10.7861/fhj.2020-0071.

Hettiarachchi, S., Damayanthi, B., Heenkenda, S., Dissanayake, D., Ranagalage, M., & Ananda, L. (2021). Student satisfaction with online learning during the COVID-19 pandemic: A study at state universities in Sri Lanka. *Sustainability*, *13*(21), 11749. https://doi.org/10.3390/su132111749.

Johnson, J. B., Reddy, P., Chand, R., & Naiker, M. (2021). Attitudes and awareness of regional pacific Island students towards e-Learning. *International Journal of Educational Technology in Higher Education*, *18*(1). https://doi.org/10.1186/s41239-021-00248-z.

Kashive, N., Powale, L., & Kashive, K. (2020). Understanding user perception toward artificial intelligence (AI) enabled e-Learning. *The International Journal of Information and Learning Technology*, *38*(1), 1–19. https://doi.org/10.1108/ijilt-05-2020-0090.

Khagi, R. B., Panthee, B., Pun, K. M., & Shrestha, S. (2021). Perception of nursing students towards online learning during COVID-19 pandemic. *Journal of Patan Academy of Health Sciences*, *8*(2), 47–55. https://doi.org/10.3126/jpahs.v8i2.31432.

Khan, M. A., Vivek, N. M. K., Khojah, M., & Tahir, M. (2021). Students' perception towards e-Learning during covid-19 pandemic in India: An empirical study. *Sustainability (Switzerland)*, *13*(1), 1–14. https://doi.org/10.3390/su13010057.

Kumar, A., Krishnamurthi, R., Bhatia, S., Kaushik, K., Ahuja, N. J., Nayyar, A., & Masud, M. (2021). Blended learning tools and practices: A comprehensive analysis. *IEEE Access*, *9*, 85151–85197.

Kumar, R. (2017). The effect of collaborative learning on enhancing student achievement a meta-analysis. *Advanced Drug Delivery Reviews*, *135*(January 2006), 989–1011. https://doi.org/10.1016/j.addr.2018.07.012%0Awww.capsulae.com/media/Microencapsulation.

Kumarasinghe, P. J., & Sriyalatha, M. A. K. (2021). Undergraduate student's perspectives on e-Learning during COVID 19 outbreak in Sri Lankan Universities. *International Journal of Engineering and Management Research*, *11*(5), 64–72. https://doi.org/10.31033/ijemr.11.5.8.

Lakmal, K., Khashunika, J., & Yatigammana, M. (2021). Challenges and opportunities in online education in Sri Lanka during the covid-19 pandemic: Evidence from University of Kelaniya. *International Journal of Educational Research & Social Sciences*, 2(4), 832–849. https://doi.org/10.51601/ijersc.v2i4.143.

Layali, K., & Al-Shlowiy, A. (2020). Students perceptions of e-Learning for ESL/EFL in Saudi universities at time of coronavirus: A literature review. *Indonesian EFL Journal*, *6*(2), 97. https://doi.org/10.25134/ieflj.v6i2.3378.

Laza, L., Ecoy, A., & Teric, M. D. (2022). Increasing academic achievement in solving surface area and volume in geometry through collaborative learning. *SSRN Electronic Journal*. https://doi.org/10.2139/SSRN.4097595.

Lee, S. M. (2014). The relationships between higher order thinking skills, cognitive density, and social presence in online learning. *The Internet and Higher Education*, *21*, 41–52. https://doi.org/10.1016/J.IHEDUC.2013.12.002.

Lizcano, D., Lara, J. A., White, B., & Aljawarneh, S. (2019). Blockchain-based approach to create a model of trust in open and ubiquitous higher education. *Journal of Computing in Higher Education*, *32*(1), 109–134. https://doi.org/10.1007/S12528-019-09209-Y.

Maatuk, A. M., Elberkawi, E. K., Aljawarneh, S., Rashaideh, H., & Alharbi, H. (2022). The COVID-19 pandemic and E-learning: Challenges and opportunities from the perspective of students and instructors. *Journal of Computing in Higher Education*, *34*, 21–38. https://doi.org/10.1007/s12528-021-09274-2.

Martin, F., & Bolliger, D. U. (2018). Engagement matters: Student perceptions on the importance of engagement strategies in the online learning environment. *Online Learning Journal*, *22*(1), 205–222. https://doi.org/10.24059/olj.v22i1.1092.

Mishra, L., Gupta, T., & Shree, A. (2020, September). Online teaching-learning in higher education during lockdown period of COVID 19 pandemic. *International Journal of Educational Research Open*, *1*, 100012. https://doi.org/10.1016/j.ijedro.2020.100012.

Molinillo, S., Aguilar-Illescas, R., Anaya-Sánchez, R., & Vallespín-Arán, M. (2018). Exploring the impacts of interactions, social presence and emotional engagement on active collaborative learning in a social web-based environment. *Computers & Education*, *123*, 41–52. https://doi.org/10.1016/J.COMPEDU.2018.04.012.

Moore, M., & Kearsley, G. (1996). *Distance education: A systems view*. Wadsworth.

Mousavi, A., Mohammadi, A., Mojtahedzadeh, R., Shirazi, M., & Rashidi, H. (2020). e-Learning educational atmosphere measure (EEAM): A new instrument for assessing e-students' perception of educational environment. *Research in Learning Technology*, *28*. https://doi.org/10.25304/rlt.v28.2308.

Mukhopadhyay, M., Pal, S., Nayyar, A., Pramanik, P. K. D., Dasgupta, N., & Choudhury, P. (2020, February). Facial emotion detection to assess Learner's State of mind in an online learning system. In *5th International Conference on Intelligent Information Technology (ICIIT 2020)* (pp. 107–115). Association for Computing Machinery. https://doi.org/10.1145/3385209.3385231

Mukhtar, K., Javed, K., Arooj, M., & Sethi, A. (2020). Advantages, limitations and recommendations for online learning during COVID-19 pandemic era. *Pakistan Journal of Medical Sciences*, *36*(COVID19-S4), S27–S31. https://doi.org/10.12669/PJMS.36.COVID19-S4.2785.

Muthuprasad, T., Aiswarya, S., Aditya, K., & Jha, G. K. (2021). Students' perception and preference for online education in India during COVID -19 pandemic. *Social Sciences & Humanities Open*, *3*(1), 100101. https://doi.org/10.1016/j.ssaho.2020.100101.

Nemetz, P., Aiken, K. D., Cooney, V., & Pascal, V. (2012). Should faculty use social networks to engage with students? *Journal for Advancement of Marketing Education*, *20*(1), 19–28.

Niemi, H. M., & Kousa, P. (2020). A case study of students' and teachers' perceptions in a Finnish high school during the COVID pandemic. *International Journal of Technology in Education and Science*, *4*(4), 352–369. https://doi.org/10.46328/ijtes.v4i4.167.

Northrup, P., Lee, R., & Burgess, V. (2002). Learner perceptions of online interaction. In *ED-MEDIA 2002 world conference on educational multimedia, hypermedia & telecommunications.*

Othman, M. S. (2017, August). Evaluating student's satisfaction of using social media through. *International Journal of Advances in Engineering & Technology*, 12.

Paul, J., & Jefferson, F. (2019). A comparative analysis of student performance in an online vs. face-to-face environmental science course from 2009 to 2016. *Frontiers in Computer Science*, *1*, 7. https://doi.org/10.3389/FCOMP.2019.00007/BIBTEX.

Pham, L., Limbu, Y. B., Bui, T. K., Nguyen, H. T., & Pham, H. T. (2019). Does e-Learning service quality influence e-Learning student satisfaction and loyalty? Evidence from Vietnam. *International Journal of Educational Technology in Higher Education*, *16*(1). https://doi.org/10.1186/s41239-019-0136-3.

Piccoli, G., Ahmad, R., & Ives, B. (2001). Web-based virtual learning environments: A research framework and a preliminary assessment of effectiveness in basic IT skills training. *MIS Quarterly*, *25*(4), 401. https://doi.org/10.2307/3250989.

Prince, M. (2004). Does active learning work? A review of the research. *Journal of Engineering Education*, *93*(3), 223–231. https://doi.org/10.1002/j.2168-9830.2004.tb00809.x.

Priyadarshana, A. J. M., Abeyrathna, G., & Edirisinghe, E. A. N. J. (2021). Tertiary level students' perception of online learning during the COVID-19 pandemic (evidence from students residing in Kegalle District, Sri Lanka). *Journal of Academic Session-Advanced Technological Institute, Kegalle*, *1*(1), 65–79.

Rasmitadila, R., Aliyyah, R. R., Rachmadtullah, R., Samsudin, A., Syaodih, E., Nurtanto, M., & Tambunan, A. R. S. (2020). The perceptions of primary school teachers of online learning during the COVID-19 pandemic period: A case study in Indonesia. *Journal of Ethnic and Cultural Studies*, *7*(2), 90. https://doi.org/10.29333/ejecs/388.

Reddy, P., Sharma, B., & Chandra, S. (2020). Student readiness and perception of tablet learning in higher education in the pacific – A case study of Fiji and Tuvalu. *Journal of Cases on Information Technology*, *22*(2), 52–69. https://doi.org/10.4018/jcit.2020040104.

Reio, T. G., & Crim, S. J. (2013). Social presence and student satisfaction as predictors of online enrollment intent. *American Journal of Distance Education*, *27*(2), 122–133. https://doi.org/10.1080/08923647.2013.775801.

Richardson, J. C., Maeda, Y., Lv, J., & Caskurlu, S. (2017). Social presence in relation to students' satisfaction and learning in the online environment: A meta-analysis. *Computers in Human Behavior*, *71*, 402–417. https://doi.org/10.1016/J.CHB.2017.02.001.

Sakarji, S. R., Mohd Nor, K., Mohd Razali, M., Talib, N., Ahmad, N., & Wan Mohamad Saferdin, W. A. A. (2019). Investigating students acceptance of e-Learning using technology acceptance model among diploma in office management and technology students at Uitm Melaka. *Journal of Information System and Technology Management*, 13–26. https://doi.org/10.35631/jistm.413002.

Santhirakumar, S., Narmilan, A., Jayapraba, S., & Ketheeswaran, K. (2022). The impact of Covid-19 outbreak on school e-learning system. *Isagoge-Journal of Humanities and Social Sciences*, *2*(1), 16–33.

Sharma, B., Nand, R., Naseem, M., & Reddy, E. V. (2019). Effectiveness of online presence in a blended higher learning environment in the Pacific. *Studies in Higher Education*, *45*(8), 1547–1565. https://doi.org/10.1080/03075079.2019.1602756.

Shawaqfeh, M. S., Al Bekairy, A. M., Al-Azayzih, A., Alkatheri, A. A., Qandil, A. M., Obaidat, A. A., Al Harbi, S., & Muflih, S. M. (2020). Pharmacy students perceptions of their distance online learning experience during the COVID-19 pandemic: A cross-sectional survey study. *Journal of Medical Education and Curricular Development*, *7*, 238212052096303. https://doi.org/10.1177/2382120520963039.

Shen, C. W., & Ho, J. T. (2020). Technology-enhanced learning in higher education: A bibliometric analysis with latent semantic approach. *Computers in Human Behavior*, *104*, 106177. https://doi.org/10.1016/j.chb.2019.106177.

Short, J., & Williams, E. B. C. (1976). *The social psychology of telecommunications*. Wiley.

Sternad Zabukovsek, S., Zimmermannová, J., Umar, M., & Ko, I. (2022). *e-Learning: Direct effect of student learning effectiveness and engagement through project-based learning, team cohesion, and flipped learning during the COVID-19 pandemic*. https://doi.org/10.3390/su14031724.

Stewart, M. K. (2021). Social presence in online writing instruction: Distinguishing between presence, comfort, attitudes, and learning. *Computers and Composition*, *62*, 102669. https://doi.org/10.1016/j.compcom.2021.102669.

Tung, F. W., & Deng, Y. S. (2007). Increasing social presence of social actors in e-Learning environments: Effects of dynamic and static emoticons on children. *Displays*, *28*(4–5), 174–180. https://doi.org/10.1016/j.displa.2007.06.005.

Umar, M., & Ko, I. (2022). e-Learning: Direct effect of student learning effectiveness and engagement through project-based learning, team cohesion, and flipped learning during the COVID-19 pandemic. *Sustainability*, *14*(3), 1724. https://doi.org/10.3390/su14031724.

Webster, J., & Hackley, P. (1997). Teaching effectiveness in technology-mediated distance learning. *Academy of Management Journal*, *40*(6), 1282–1309. https://doi.org/10.2307/257034.

Yates, A., Starkey, L., Egerton, B., & Flueggen, F. (2020). High school students' experience of online learning during Covid-19: The influence of technology and pedagogy. Technology. *Pedagogy and Education*, *9*, 1–15. https://doi.org/10.1080/1475939X.2020.1854337.

6 Online Teaching Sustainability and Strategies during the COVID-19 Epidemic

Gbemisola Janet Ajamu, Joseph Bamidele Awotunde, Taibat Bolanle Jimoh, Emmanuel Abidemi Adeniyi, Kazeem Moses Abiodun, Idowu Dauda Oladipo, and Muyideen Abdulraheem

6.1 INTRODUCTION

The coronavirus (COVID-19) outbreak has forced educational institutions to suspend learning to curb the spread of the virus. An epidemic of this nature will have a negative impact on the educational system of any nation in one way or another, thus students' right to education is threatened at times of crisis like this. Education is undergoing technological change, demographic instability, globalization, and better quality of life. Historically, higher education has been viewed as a prerequisite for a skilled "elite," and a political aspiration has been set in different nations (including Nigeria) to become the norm for far broader sections of the populace as a whole. When learners are "all" and learning is "all the time," distance and online learning and study have a vast potential to conquer, but there are still many obstacles and challenges.

Massive outbreaks of epidemics disease, natural catastrophe, or severe air pollution have occurred across the globe, impacting not just the wellbeing of humans but also the education sector. SARS, for example, reached many countries around the world at the end of 2002. Across some regions of China, face-to-face education has been banned to control the virus. Additionally, in 2009, many people around the world were affected by the outbreak of H1N1 flu, triggering school closures in several countries and regions, including Bulgaria, China, France, Italy, Japan, New Zealand, Serbia, South Africa, Thailand, the United Kingdom and the United States [1]. At the end of 2019, as COVID-19 is spreading rapidly globally, leading to the death of more than 3000 people, this force various nations to introduce multiple measures to control this virus, including closing schools [2]. UNESCO reported that, as of 12 March, 46 countries on five continents had announced the closing of schools to contain COVID-19. In particular, 26 countries have fully closed schools across the world, disrupting the learning experience of nearly 376.9 million children and young people who would usually attend schools. A further 20 countries partly shut down schools (localized school closures) to avoid or contain COVID-19 spread. If these 20 countries also order national school closures, 500 million children and young people are still threatened with not attending their schools [2].

Taking care of the infected people and communities has been the target in this unusual period of COVID-19 outbreak. The emergence of the coronavirus epidemic which causes acute respiratory distress syndrome, results in the disruption of the educational system. Hence, it requires immediate and intense attention from educators [3]. The urgent attention to focus intensely on preparing future students has never been as demanding as compared to this period of global emergency. The intense effects of the outbreak of COVID-19 will forever change the way future learners will be educated. This pandemic poses both logistical and practical concerns and challenges to the safety and well-being of learners. Knowing fully well that the potential spread of the deadly disease is

DOI: 10.1201/9781003425779-6

possible in the process of learning. Since the outbreak of this disease (COVID-19), the most efficient preventive measure is social distancing, pending the time of developing vaccine and treatment or both [3–5].

During COVID-19's outbreak, school closures in many countries worldwide left more than 376.9 million learners exempt from the learning process. New methods, such as online learning, were then used to keep learning undisturbed. However, according to the literature and international experts, several challenges have been reported during the application of online learning globally. For instance, (1) internet access may be poor if there are thousands of learners studying at the same time; (2) because there are hundreds of materials available online, some instructors may find it challenging to discover the most suitable internet resources for their educational circumstances; (3) some teachers and students lack the digital abilities needed to teach and learn online; (4) many students lack crucial learning abilities like adaptability, independent research, self-control, and drive, which are necessary elements for successful online learning; and (5) some teachers rely solely on direct instruction, oblivious to crucial aspects of online learning such as collaboration.

By way of explaining further, students are precluded from gathering together for class learning, either in small groups or small halls [3]. Since the advent of COVID-19, social separation has proven to be the most effective prophylactic method pending the creation of a vaccine, therapy, or both [3–5]. This, by definition, prevents students from congregating in classrooms, lecture halls, or small-group spaces [3]. Various schools have been "flipping" individual-based instructions for asynchronous learning "anywhere/anytime" in recent years. Many schools have already begun to "flip" the classroom to give personalized learning for virtual classrooms "anytime/anywhere" in the last few years. Students, on the other hand, continue to congregate for laboratory sessions, small-group interactions, simulations, and technology sessions, such as learning science practical's and emerging technologies [6, 7].

An attempt to move or shift all existing courses or subjects online within a space of little time will be a disruptive one. To create a complete online course, you'll need an elaborate lesson plan design, teaching resources such as video and audio content, and a technical support team [8]. On the other hand, with COVID-19 emergence, most members of the school are facing difficult challenges in the following areas: lack of online teaching experience, early and untimely preparation, and lack of educational technology support teams.

In recent years there has been a gradual increase in online learning developments most especially during the COVID-19 pandemic. But there are very few cases where they have brought about significant changes in terms of stability and quality. This is rather striking, given that the expectations towards the educational use of ICT were being hyped on the wave of the more general diffusion of the technological state of the art in society. It is a common opinion that one of the most obvious reasons for this sort of "lull" (especially in sub-Saharan Africa) is the persistent lack of culture in organizations and institutions in the use of online teaching and learning as ordinary educational practice, which would not only meet the need to reduce training costs, but also the demands for new and improved innovative processes in teaching. To date, the sustainable implementation of teaching/learning processes supported by online teaching-learning remains an open question. That is why, in recent years, experts in the area have begun to initiate a lively and complex debate on what factors may be for and against the sustainability of online learning. However, there appears to be some convergence in the argument that, to be sustainable, online learning should:

- Give specific added value to schooling by adding virtual environments and interactivity;
- Endorse collective research and shared participation capable of promoting a new society;
- Propose a use of the technology able to support specific teaching methodologies effectively for specific disciplinary contexts;
- Pay attention to how to develop teaching materials so that they are easily reusable in different situations to cut time and costs;
- Take initiatives aimed specifically at online sustainability, that is, initiatives capable of creating the necessary conditions for frequent use of online learning approaches.

The chapter describes online teaching sustainability in higher institutions and several online learning strategies that were implemented during the COVID-19 outbreak. Such approaches are described in three dimensions: (1) learning content (2) support learners, and (3) learning activities. Therefore, in this chapter, the significance of the adoption of online teaching and learning technology in this lockdown period is discussed.

6.1.1 Objectives of the Chapter

The objectives of the chapter are as follows:

1. To discuss the online teaching sustainability specially in higher institution during COVID-19 pandemic;
2. To explore online learning strategies that can be employed during the pandemic outbreak;
3. To understand the significance of online learning during COVID-19 outbreak;
4. And, to discuss COVID-19's potential consequences for the education sector as instructional methodologies.

6.1.2 Organization of the Chapter

The remainder of the chapter is organized as follows. Section 5.2 discuss higher education for sustainability. Section 5.3 highlights the importance of online teaching and learning technology adoption during COVID-19. Section 5.4 discusses instructional strategies and potential implications for COVID-19. Section 5.5 stresses an information and communication technology (ICT)-based approach to assist education and teaching in a pandemic. Section 5.6 provides a case study in Nigeria discussing the condition of education in the pandemic. Section 5.7 elaborates discussions and findings. And, finally section 5.8 concludes the chapter with future scope.

6.2 REVIEW OF HIGHER EDUCATION FOR SUSTAINABILITY

Education is both an individual target and a way of addressing certain features of sustainable development. UN Sustainable Development Goal (SDG) 4 encourages better education and pursues to "guarantee equivalent and available excellence edification and to inspire opportunities for lifelong erudition for everybody" [9]. The SDG is concerned with enhancing access to information and gender parity, and ensuring that quality education is available at all levels to provide awareness and skills for a prosperous future. Higher education (HE) is famous for playing a leading role in promoting sustainable development (SD) [10, 11]. Nonetheless, this possible mechanism needs guidance in a sense in which universities and colleges are generally viewed as adding to the environmental crisis. Sustainability questions current paradigms and systems, as well as prevailing activities in HE; universities, and colleges, are faced with this fact as they try to contribute meaningfully to sustainability.

HE history shows that both universities and colleges were at the forefront of developing and deconstructing paradigms. They led social reform by scientific breakthroughs but also through training scholars, politicians, and potential leaders [10, 12, 13]. It is, therefore, time for the international community to acknowledge the profound importance of higher education in achieving all 17 SDG aimed at reducing hunger, saving the earth, fostering gender equality, preserving and supporting communities and cultural awareness, and ensuring the wellbeing of everyone and universities to support the world.

During an age of globalization, universities and colleges still have an impact through their multinational sourcing and offshore collaborations, as well as through educating national and international students [14–16]; they should not be underestimated for their possible impact not only on economic growth and poverty alleviation but also on health and community building. The future leaders, decision makers, students, and practitioners of the world are partially created and influenced by their educational institutions—one of the most important ways that could elicit social transformation and enhance the development of innovative ideas and patterns [17–20]. Worldwide, intergovernmental personnel, governments, business, and educational institutions have indicated that university students through their individual and expert activities have the awareness, morals, and abilities they need to accord to an ecologically friendly community [17, 18].

The UN describes SD as an "invention that accommodates the current requirements beyond undermining approaching generations' competency to fulfil their requirements" [21]. As such, SD tackles not only environmental concerns but also fiscal, social and cultural problems [22, 23]. Considering the intensified requirement concentrated towards the communities and surroundings attributable among other reasons, to intensify people's relocation, intensify development and modernization, and the continuing degradation of non-sustainable capital, it is apparent that worldwide activity is required to build an extra maintainable future [24–26]. Despite its primary position as a source of awareness, HE will help as an effective device to aid generate an extra prosperous future [27–30]. Therefore, in recent years, the idea of "education for SD" has been one of the main policy programs seeking to tackle many of the human development concerns.

Indeed, the role of HE in developing a prosperous future is likely to yield better significance as the environment persists to evolve into been more globalized and symbiotic [31, 32]. According to UNESCO, education sustainable development (ESD) "enables individuals to improve their mode of thought and to strive for a better future." It consequently entails providing entree to decently valued edification at each phase of life. More precisely, by incorporating environmental problems into all areas of education, study, and operation, it means educating students on the need for sustainable growth [33–36]. This includes reconstructing the edification structure at every stage to aid public reason and respond in directions that promote a further prosperous world (e.g., environmental citizenship, conservation, climate change, sustainability, clean energy, and social responsibility) [37, 38]. In application, this refers to preparing learners with the awareness, expertise, approaches, and standards needed to build a prosperous future [39].

To this end, students will develop analytical and innovative thinking abilities, partake in true interdisciplinary erudition experiences and build a belief philosophy that stresses accountability for themselves, others, and the world. SD curriculum and the UN SDGs also go hand in hand [40]. Also, more and more universities offer degree and certificate programs in SD. We are facing immense global challenges in the modern period (e.g., the immigrant predicament, worldwide weather alteration, widespread lack, and analphabetism), and these issues were probably better solved by universal schooling and international cooperation [41, 42]. Higher edification has not solitary a function to perform in the field but as well as the potential to perform a principal function. By the aimed the year of 2030, the UN has positioned 17 objectives, wide as well as symbiotic, through its SDG initiative, which are required to build a prosperous future on our planet [29, 43, 44].

The central role of HE as an information resource extends through all thinking realms. HE thus has a special function to execute in assisting SDGs in their attainments. Further precisely, SDG 4 acts primarily with edification and its objectives of "ensuring comprehensive and equal excellence education and fostering opportunities for permanent erudition for everyone" [45]. Travel and online learning play a significant role in doing this. As it is, persons are prepared with the required information and potentials to tackle a prosperous future through high-quality education and lifelong learning, edification turns out to be crucial in accomplishing every of the SDGs, particularly online teaching. Furthermore, advanced edification establishments will partake in the UN higher education sustainability initiative programme and the UN educational institution offers several instances of sustainability in practice.

HEIs have a vital responsibility to perform in their strategic strategies and activities in promoting and guiding sustainable growth creativities. Solitary of the main issues been discussed: what will members in educational institutions, lecturers, staff, and learners do to promote sustainable change through their declarations in established strategy, mission and standards, planned strategies, and corporate philosophy? Inclusion is widely described by UNESCO as "a method of focusing on and reacting to the variety of requirements of every adolescent, juvenile and grownups by the inclusion in schooling, philosophies, and societies and by minimizing and removing forbiddance in and out of edification." Equity is loosely demarcated as the concept of justice that entitles each person to equal opportunities for entree to and involvement in edification. Equity also requires comprehending the developmental demands of students to reduce barriers to academic achievement.

The HEs will contribute effectively to SD growth and deployment in the following ways. HE is the learning atmosphere for all educational practitioners; delivering ESD awareness to all stakeholders is of utmost importance; members of higher education institutions are in a critical role to contribute to an inclusive and environmentally sustainable future by placing SD as a core academic and organizational focus; universities and higher education networks can perform research and offer recommendations and guidance on improving regional education structures as well as capacity building issues for sustainable growth across sectors; and HEI will provide expertise and assistance to local ESD initiatives. They will blend the local expertise and understanding with higher-level information. Using evidence-based data, as well as problem-based science analysis, HEI will improve the interaction between study results and decision-making. Universities and HEI also have a central role to play in all priority focus areas of the ESD global action programme.

6.3 IMPORTANCE OF ONLINE TEACHING AND LEARNING TECHNOLOGY ADOPTION DURING COVID-19

Technology has and still has a significant part to play in the growth and expansion of online learning. Consequently, the use of online resources has increased at many educational institutions [46]. In the last decade, numerous initiatives have tried to incorporate new internet technologies into higher education learning and teaching system. In many schools and institutions, online learning is becoming a significant long-term strategy [46]. Given the speedy development of online learning and its significance for secondary and post-secondary education, government and educational policymaking must provide quality online programs, especially during the COVID-19 outbreak. The introduction of an online course is a motivator to students, as it enhances their exposure to higher degree graduation rates as well as improve and attract non-traditional students to online learning. In academia, the internet has found a place, particularly in teaching programs. During the COVID-19 epidemic, fully online programs offered students an advantage in isolation, allowing them to meet pre-service and in-service instructors who would otherwise not be able to take part in courses [47].

Online education is a hot subject of great concern nowadays in different countries. Nations around the world have made numerous successful attempts at online education in the age of mobile internet, but online education is more of a complement to school education, and large-scale regular online education lacks instances. The initiative "School's Out, But Class's On," initiated by the Chinese government during the COVID-19 epidemic, has created a large-scale, everyday online application for education. How to avoid learning interrupted as COVID-19 continues to spread in many world countries has become a big challenge for the global educational community. During the COVID-19 outbreak, educational policymakers around the world looked for a way to launch the initiative "Disrupted Classes, Undisrupted Learning," which will provide flexible online learning for millions of students from home.

This online learning platform may include a range of locations with synchronous services that provide audio and video technology and live instruction. They can also use platform technology to deliver asynchronous services, such as learning management system (LMS), Blackboard, ANGEL, or WebCT [48]. Today due to the coronavirus outbreak, there is a peculiar issue facing the global education community. Learners at all locations need to learn new skills, be literate, and consider ever-changing dynamics [49]. The problem seems to be to balance the need for intensive and personal contact with the reality of minimal financial resources, to learn practical knowledge. Online education was seen as a way of providing continuous learning to those who are geographically separated from conventional institutions over time or have responsibilities that hinder their ability to attend daily courses or other extraordinary difficulties.

Online education has been around for a long time, in various ways. Conventional distance learning environments were based on passive media communication (paper, audio, and video broadcast) [49]. Now, coronavirus has made advances in network and networking technology which have allowed large numbers of individuals the opportunity to deliver online courses. With improvements in network communications and the resulting enhanced online learning paradigm, individuals expect interactivity and classroom-based education similar to "traditional."

Moreover, computers and smartphones linked to the internet allow users to interact with each other across the globe. Indeed, computer-based learning researchers has established three forms of interactivity that help to learn in online courses: interaction with the material, learners' ability to access, control, synthesize, and communicate material information; interaction with instructors; learners' ability to connect with and receive input from their instructors; and interactivity. Hence, online interactions with teachers will be similarly important [50]. This has led some researchers to conclude that asynchronous media, as they promote fewer effective forms of communication, are less able to reflect participants' "social presence" in online classes [50, 51].

Asynchronous dialogue offers participants a chance to focus on the work of their peers when developing their own, and on their writing before publishing them. Within an online course, this helps to build a certain consciousness among students and a practice of reflection [51, 52]. Conversations between students in the online forum seem clearly to matter. Nevertheless, Rourke et al. [53] described the evolution of social presence, the perceived contact with others, as one of the key components of online learning groups' growth. Another compelling case for more study is how social identity grows in online discourse.

Online learning offers knowledge and social networking through virtual communities that are both advanced and widely focused. Virtual learning can never substitute face-to-face discussions to create and maintain primary community relationships, due to its decreased social presence. You can make friends online—very real, personal friends—but that is less likely. There is no chance that in the future, emoticons will be the only smiles and hugs and kisses children receive from their parents. On the other hand, studying and teaching online can provide emotional support, companionship, and a sense of belonging when real hugs are unlikely [54, 55]. For example, some couples use email to interact while one or both of them are traveling, parents exchange emails with their college children, and there are broad and active parenting skills newsgroups in which parents share their problems and knowledge and support each other during parenting crises [56]. These new forms of online links are genuine and hardly second-rate. Witness marriage cases between former online pen pals or the digital classmates who are hugging each other on graduation day. Today, the internet is used in the same way as letters, and later the telephone was used to preserve conventional group relationships.

As a result of COVID-19, governments and educational authorities all around the world have quickly shifted the whole teaching methods to virtual communities, including content from elementary, secondary, and even higher education. The formats are organized online in various ways like virtual team settings, and virtual sessions that can take place online or be deferred in some situations. Examinations have also been moved to an online format. Updating content material may be a benefit of the online format, and virtual activities appear to be functional, but the effects of these modifications will need to be evaluated in the future. Isolation, increasing use of email, and difficulties creating barriers between work and home come from the transfer from the job or school setting to home, which can have an impact on schools, students, and support workers.

6.3.1 Online Learning Sustainability

Promoting ESD will become even more relevant in the future [57–59]. Promoting flexible online education will in specific be the main international aspects of ESD at the school level. In addition to qualitative education, virtual education can contribute to the social experience of the student and their family, and can also certainly put learners to the forefront in remote areas. Virtual and interactive learning is becoming a significant alternative to traditional schooling because of the ability to gain the right to access education for everyone [60]. This style of learning varies from traditional learning as students cannot communicate make eye contact with their teachers and peers [61].

Such terms are frequently adjusted by remote education, e-learning, or digital training in research, but scholars accept that there is a distinction in each of the concepts based on the nature of their teaching environment [62, 63]. Three key motivating factors that impact these components are information technology, business requirements, educational brokers, and institutions [60]. Also, the most significant of the powers is IT since it is the means to improve the learning experience. Indeed, either involved in solely online schools, mixed classes, or on-campus classes, in a virtual community, many participants more than ever are studying; specifically, distance learners [64]. The rapid growth of aspects of information technology (IT) and the increasing information and communications technology resources are two of the most significant considerations that have driven the advancement of remote and virtual learning [58–60, 63].

Also, remote and virtual classroom tools have been identified as vehicles for traversing the landscape of schooling. This is critical since users can access study tools on any platform that exists in the public domain without any of the arbitrary constraints placed by patent providers and copyright companies on open content [60, 65]. Throughout this sense, the information community has grown, demanding the consistent reconstruction of its knowledge base and promoting the research theory [65, 66]. Within such an environment, trained individuals are required for a wider variety of cognitive careers than those in "normal" society [67].

The prevalence of laws, tablets and laptops, social networking sites, virtual learning environments (VLE), online evaluation and response activities, lecture capture, and e-portfolios further intensified the use of online learning in education. HE organizations need to build ethical mechanisms to direct university workers in understanding successful policies and regulations that leverage on their ability to use new technology more specifically and responsibly.

Responding to criteria that are essential in ensuring more effective online education progress, Salmon [68] (2005) argued that technologies should:

1. Be located at the organizational macro-scale (thus providing defined management that offers a top-down approach);
2. Have sufficient monetary assistance (further than the project execution process so that the various stakeholders feel empowered);
3. Comply with organizational ambitions for educational institutions (impact on learning and awareness of relevance among students);
4. Have legal frameworks promoting broad acceptance (technological and pedagogical assistance accessible when necessary).

The discussion on sustainable has been established in two particular guidance in the education sector, with a strong difference:

1. Sustainable development and global warming training, which contribute to environmental management as a research subject through (a) education delivery and (b) syllabus development as evidence of assessable skills and qualities;
2. Sustainability of learning and teaching strategies and activities [69], aimed at cultivating the concept of positive transformation and encouraging clear productivity [69, 70]. Online teaching and learning will consider all these paths.

Remote and online education have already raised several sustainability concerns. Computerization of documentation and materials greatly eliminates the need for printing test reports, tests, task training materials and manuals, scholarly articles, study material, and seminars [70]. It is easily demonstrated in repositories where paper digitization and the idea of the "Green Libraries" are prominent [71–73].

In 2015, a resolution with emerging world sustainable development goals to be adopted by 2030 was accepted by the United Nations [74]. Task four sets out some daunting guidelines on education and HE under this strategy, amongst them:

1. Ensuring fair access to accessible and reliable basic, vocational, and higher education for both genders;
2. Developing and enhancing student, incapacity- and gender-sensitive education system and provide comfortable, peaceful, equitable, and efficacious academic learning for everyone;
3. Increasing the availability of trained teachers significantly through the global collaboration for teacher preparation in developing countries, in particular, least advanced nations and small island developing countries.

Indirectly, the resolution of the United Nations appears to indicate that virtual education and hybrid learning are a method of advancing for reacting to the unique issue raised by the resolution. They can be proactive in overcoming these encounters, leading HE to extend its supply and connect with other investors who are usually inaccessible in the conventional teaching and learning process.

Highlighting learning activities and virtual education with the issues to be tackled in the future. Sustainability will go beyond the advantages of learning and teaching, and provide funding for further advancement to tackle these possible issues. If online learning has the attributes necessary to incorporate successfully and reliably into the broader institutional setting, then they are more viable and creative [75]. Technology and sustainability also are connected, and digital training becomes less creative if it is not sustainable, and therefore needs to be incorporated into the policies and needs of the institution [75]. It facilitates broader awareness for all investors and a stronger sense of relevancy. In short, given the broader organization, online learning technologies must be applied if they are to contribute to the current demands and be adaptable to unforeseen issues. That needs institutional strategy formulation that systematically supports online training initiatives [76].

6.4 INSTRUCTIONAL STRATEGIES AND POTENTIAL IMPLICATIONS FOR COVID-19

The move towards online learning becomes so imperative during the COVID-19 outbreak among the bodies making educational policy and the governments globally [77]. The adoption of the latest technology is necessitated by its capability and convincing evidence to offer more cost-effective programs to more students that meet the needs of modern-day learners [78, 79]. With the possibility of this achievement, online learning is also visualized as a tool capable of improving student learning, even though it is not seen as a deliberately planned event but as a consequence. The three vital elements for planning instructional strategies for online learning are the learning content, the learning activities, and the learning supports (Figure 6.1). Despite that the listed elements reflect separate stakeholders, they lay more emphasis on the activities on each process of learning. These elements offer a strong framework for designing instructional materials and emphasize the significance of planning precise roles for the learners, the tutor, and the technology in the learning environment.

6.4.1 Course Content

Most teachers see choosing and developing technology-based flexible content as the most significant step to creating an online learning environment. The reflection of this can be seen in the results of the materials focusing majorly on content. Sometimes it is estimated that the online tutors

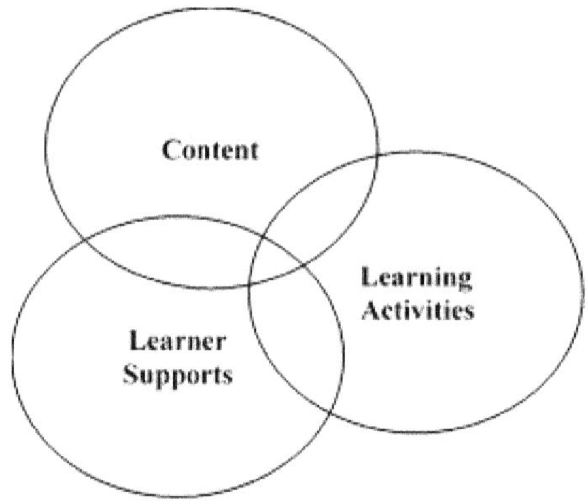

FIGURE 6.1 The critical design elements for instructional strategies for online learning.

spend 90% of their planning and development on content creating and online learning materials. Modern thinking proposes that creating content should take a far lesser role in the design processes. Teachers should split down the teaching contents into many sections and utilize a modular teaching strategy to get students to focus more on the online study. Teachers, on the other hand, break down the instructional content into smaller modules, each lasting about 40–45 minutes, while focusing on attaining a clear knowledge structure in the curriculum.

6.4.2 Learning Activities

The second important element in the earlier discussed design framework is learning activities. Learning activities in technologically based environments play an important role in predicting learning outcomes [80]. Learning activities determine how learners will connect with the course resources and the level of knowledge that would be constructed. To add more, contemporary thinking proposed that the learning activities must be engaging and active [81]. There is a need to stimulate collaborative and cooperative activities among the cohort and by doing so, reflection and articulation opportunities must be provided. The activities have to offer the function and the context for learners to handle the content and information [82]. The creation of instructive features for constructive learning in an online setting suggests the need for instructional approaches to design [83], which in turn advances the learning outcomes through learning processes and strategies that employ different modes of communication.

6.4.3 Learning Supports

An online learning environment has usually been regarded as flexible, and it requires learning supports to be designed as an essential part of the learning processes. The necessity of this support is to guide the learners and also to ensure a feedback mechanism that will be sensitive and responsive to individual needs [84]. Support to learners in the distance education contexts is a term that always embraces wide mechanisms such as the library support and counselling and academic support [85]. Learning support in this chapter is narrowly used and restricted to aspects of online learning environments alone. Strong frameworks have been developed by numbers of writers to describe the ideal form of supports needed for the online learning platform and the strong argument was made for an involved and active tutor. The learning activity is said to be a deliberate process that focuses on the use of provided technologies as a way to achieve an enhanced learning process. Each of the elements for instructional strategies can be deliberately manipulated to influence earning results and plays a significant role in achieving qualitative learning. When compared to traditional in-class lectures, teachers have less control over online education, and many students are more likely to "skip classes" [86]. As a result, students play a big role in the evolution of online teaching and its learning efficiency. On this point, professors should employ a variety of strategies to moderately change students' homework and reading requirements in order to increase students' willingness to learn outside of the classroom. Hence, instructors should employ a variety of techniques to modestly change students' homework and reading requirements in order to improve students' active learning outside of class. Based on the above on online teaching, these instructional strategies would aid in improving student participation and attentiveness in order to facilitate a seamless transition to online learning during the COVID-19 outbreak.

6.5 INFORMATION AND COMMUNICATION TECHNOLOGY (ICT)-BASED APPROACH TO ASSIST EDUCATION AND TEACHING DURING A PANDEMIC

During pandemics, such as the present one, when the COVID-19 outbreak has infected the entire world, online teaching can be used. As illustrated by its significance during the COVID-19 pandemic, online education enables unparalleled opportunities for education. This educational paradigm has the opportunity to enhance to democratization and the development of the education sector [87], by the fact that in order to get meaningful results in online courses, learners must participate actively [88], Simulation, research, and role play can all help students–teachers–colleagues–digital course materials interact, which can be accomplished through research and simulation [89], all participants being invited to participate in open conversations [90], and student-centered learning [91]. The ICT, the teacher, and the student's experience with ICT are all factors that contribute to the success of the online learning process. Even though the teacher plays a critical role in online education [92], other factors influencing the educational process include the amount of time required for study and student discipline [93]. Integrating video recordings and live classes with more online interaction can help lessen the impact of unpredictable networks and boost student active involvement [94].

The use of social networking platforms to boost collaborative learning activities is considered an effective way for students to feel more in charge of their education [95] and encourages the pupil to talk to their colleagues about their difficulties. Other research looked at how collaborative learning might help students and educators save time when exchanging emails, saving, reviewing, and editing documents, as well as other activities that increase efficiency [96]. On the other hand, social media plays an essential role in ICT-based learning and social separation during pandemics. Students' grasp of complex subjects will be considerably improved by using social media and sharing varied information on the same channels [97] and make it possible for people to submit and share their thoughts. Furthermore, teleconferencing software such as Zoom and Google Teams have become the primary method to perform online classes. Furthermore, conversing is an effective way to alleviate some of the challenges that students may encounter when learning a given topic. This is owing to the fact that these conversations are saved, and students can read and study them whenever they choose [98].

Because of the COVID-19 pandemic, ICT-based learning has become the only way to learn, and ICT technologies and methodologies are used in online learning [99]. Various governments in poor nations have committed in online learning facilities in recent years, with some colleges offering lessons online via their university's learning management system (LMS). COVID-19 has wreaked havoc on our health care system [100, 101], economy, and educational system [102, 103]. It is vital to note that the acceptance and application of ICT in education is more successful in advanced nations, therefore the issues that educational institutions or policymakers face in developed countries are not like those in developing countries. This study is significant because it investigates the genuine challenges associated with ICT-based learning systems in developing nations following the complete transformation of learning to be online.

Faced with COVID-19, the education system's shared vision realized that throughout the epidemic, instructors and learners are motivated to modify interactive learning technologies to meet contemporary educational needs. Everyone was friendly and knew how to use social media applications, whether it was teachers or students. Applications such as WhatsApp, Facebook, Twitter, and Instagram have made it easier to use online instructional platforms. The use of various applications like Cisco, Webex, Google Meet, Zoom, and LMS among others are very useful in online learning and teaching during the COVID-19 pandemic. There are also some great educational programs available, like Office 365, Google Classroom, and a far more user-friendly teleconference application that may be freely downloaded and is simple to use [97]. As a result, it appears that there is no need to fret about getting emerging innovations all of a sudden, as certain applications are already implanted in our HEIs. The majority of stakeholders had smartphones, with only a small percentage having computers, which are required resources for implementing interactive learning. Various universities in developed countries features an ICT center and an LMS that aids in the flawless management of online teaching and learning styles.

The Indian government began seriously considering this issue, prioritizing ICT and the use of digital learning as part of the mandatory teaching and learning process at the tertiary level. Furthermore, it is evident in the preparation of a newly drafted education policy for 2019, which has been hailed as a responsible and smart technologies efficient action during this epidemic. SWAYAM (Study Webs of Active-Learning for Young Aspiring Minds) is a government-sponsored scheme or massive open online course (MOOC) infrastructure that offers online classes in various quadrants [104]. SWAYAM PRABHA is a network of 32 DTH channels dedicated to broadcasting high-quality educational programming seven days a week. The MHRD inaugurated the Annual Refresher Programme in Teaching (ARPIT) on November 13, 2018, as an online training program using the SWAYAM platform [104].

6.5.1 Types of Online Learning

In this section, we discuss types of online learning.

6.5.1.1 Asynchronous Online Courses

These types of courses do not run in real time. Coursework and duties are assigned to students with a deadline for finishing course work and exams. People frequently interact on discussion forums, blogs, and wikis. As a result, no classes are held. This type of online learning settings aid students with restricted timetables or demanding workloads [105].

6.5.1.2 Synchronous Online Courses

Concurrent online contact between the lecturer and all enrolled students is required in these types of courses. Participants communicate via text, video, or audio chat, comparable to a webinar in certain ways. This learning platforms enable students from all around the world to participate in a course in real time [106].

6.5.1.3 Hybrid Courses

Hybrid or blended courses are learning environments that allow students to interact in person as well as online [107]. This type of online classes meets in person many times throughout the semester and allow for computer-based collaboration in between those sessions. One of the most important aspects of a mixed course is that online resources are not used to replace in-person class time; rather, they are meant to supplement and expand on the concepts presented in class. Although the terms "blended" and "hybrid learning" are sometimes used interchangeably, there is a distinction because online features of hybrid courses are intended to replace in-person class time. In a hybrid medium of education, online engagements can be done simultaneously via real-time meeting sessions or intermittently, with students interacting at distinct intervals.

The distinctions between traditional face-to-face communication and synchronous communication are blurring as access to synchronous communication tools grows, and online education methods (e.g., MOOCs) have overlapped, allowing new synchronous hybrid or combined methods to emerge [108]. Different models of synchro modal classes can be devised and executed, according to previous research [109].

6.5.2 Commonly Used Online Learning Applications

The growth of the online education has tremendously increase even before the COVID-19 pandemic; thus, online application development and implementation has shown promising opportunities in education during pandemic. By 2025, the online education market was predicted to be worth $350 billion [110]. Students have progressed past binge-watching Netflix or Disney+. Although the school year has begun, several countries have chosen to use a remote learning option and others are slightly open, while 33 nations' schools remain closed. There appears to be sufficient room for the new online learning applications and courses. The followings are some of the commonly used online platforms.

6.5.2.1 Learning Management Systems (LMS) and Student Management Systems (SMS)

SMS is data management software for students, staff, alumni, and donors. Curriculums, timetables, and communication are also important. Another name for these applications is student information systems (SIS). SMS provides instant access to student information, facilitates online payments, and improves contact with school officials. During the COVID-19 pandemic, successful development and usage of LMSs has become a vital problem for many higher education institutions. Despite the fact that university LMSs include a lot of functionality, the effectiveness of those approaches is inextricably linked to a thorough grasp of the problems, and the elements that influence how the systems are used by their users. In Afghanistan universities, for instance, a LMS system called Higher Education Learning Management System (HELMS) was developed and implemented for teaching and learning during the COVID-19 outbreak by the education ministry [111]. Nigerian universities also employed the use of LMS for the teaching of students during the pandemic outbreak.

LMS have grown in popularity among both educational institutions and students as a software tool for planning, administering, and assessing the entire educational process [112]. Knowledge management systems, course management software, and virtual educational or learning environments are all terms used to describe LMS [113]. Moodle, Sakai, Blackboard, and ATutor are some of the most well-known LMS software systems for online learning. Since the COVID-19 virus became a pandemic in March 2020 [114], a large number of governmental and private institutions worldwide, including schools and universities, have been shuttered. Since the start of the new academic year in 2020, Nigeria's education problem has been worsened by important difficulties in teaching and learning. Ever since the beginning of the school year in September 2020, the Federal Ministry of Education (FME) required public colleges to distribute educational materials via online channels while the country remained quarantined. The most often used online platforms for obtaining instructional information online were Google Classroom, WhatsApp, Facebook, and Telegram [115].

Education can be delivered in a variety of methods, including computer-based training, internet-based education, web-based training, and, more recently, mobile-based training. Electronic learning entails a number of educational activities utilizing electronic instruments in order to transition education from an industrialization to an information and communication technology era. E-learning platforms, often known as LMS, are online web-based or mobile software systems that use the internet to allow lecturers and learners to interact in teaching and learning. LMS allow teachers to control course content and other areas of instruction. Students, on the other hand, can access course materials published by instructors and engage in events such as quizzes, homework, assignments, chats, and forums.

6.5.2.2 Massive Open Online Courses (MOOCs)

The novel COVID-19 wave has altered global dynamics, with the pandemic affecting every industry, particularly educational sectors. As a result, 1.6 billion kids have been affected globally, with 9 out of 10 students suffering as a result of quarantines and school closures. As a result of these repercussions, experts have been reviewing online learning methodologies and technological studies, during the COVID-19 epidemic, offering crucial insight and filling this gap [116]. After the pandemic, Federal Ministry of Education (FMOE) Nigeria established a new approach called "Suspension of Classes and Non-stop Learning" to deal with the crisis by postponing the resumption of both the primary and secondary pupils and students respectively or continuing online learning during the COVID-19 pandemic. For example, since May 2019, 1454 Chinese institutions have employed online tutoring platforms to deal with the pandemic, and 17.75 million students have used online learning facilities [117].

The MOOC is an innovative and cutting-edge online educational system that has been developed in the last decade [118]. This approach altered university and school teaching and learning processes, resulting in a major academic transformation in recent years. The success of MOOCs in higher education eventually demonstrates its motivational power. The MOOC movement attracted universities from all around the world, and various MOOC platforms and initiatives were launched [119]. According to a recent study published by the Ministry of Education in China, colleges have implemented more than 10 MOOC platforms, and more than 3200 MOOCs were launched by over 460 universities and institutions. As a result, this system was used by 55 million students, and more than 6 million students earned MOOC certificates at tertiary institutions [120]. These efforts have demonstrated the tremendous advancements in massive learning via online platforms.

However, a previous study has demonstrated a low rate of recall or usage persistence, and according to [121], only about 5% of MOOCs are completed. Most online courses, according to [122], have a 10% success rate. Similarly, Shao [123] (2018) discovered that MOOC platforms have a 3.7% success rate. In general, the initial engagement of learners is the first step in a MOOC program's effective implementation. Users' continuing engagement is the most important factor in their long-term success. Many students, for example, are driven by the new medium of instruction and ideal MOOC functionalities that enable them to decide to engage and then gain the knowledge they need to increase their motivation and effectiveness. However, individuals eventually stop learning owing to environmental or personal circumstances, resulting in a poor success rate [124].

This learning platform is open to the public and can be used to give education to a huge number of people [125]. MOOCs initially arrived on the higher education horizon in 2008, coinciding with the announcement of George Siemens and Stephen Downes' Connectivism and Connective Knowledge (CCK08) [126]. MOOCs have spread online learning to a wide scale across the globe, providing new potential and problems [127]. MOOCs are a new type of teaching and learning model that leverages the internet to provide course materials to famous universities and organizations all over the world, resulting in a revolution. Teachers are now being motivated to become skilled in e-learning technologies, such as MOOCs, so that science can be utilized and exploited in the teaching and learning activities in the 21st century [128].

6.5.2.3 Video Conferencing

During the 2019 COVID-19 outbreak, the adoption of video conferencing (VC) software increased dramatically [129, 130]. There are an increasing number of pieces in the media about how to look your best when participating in a video conference. To boost your appeal, consider changing the illumination, angling the camera lower, or using the built-in "touch up" software capabilities. VC is distinct in that a livestream is always visible, resulting in an unusual perspective of ourselves, which can sometimes heighten anxieties about facial attractiveness. Because of this new trend, we wondered if people have grown concerns about their face appearance as a result of VC, and whether this could lead to future COVID-19 pandemic-related cosmetic therapies [129].

A synchronous approach for interactive audio, video, and data sharing between two or more groups is VC. It allows instructors and students to communicate in real time via video and voice, as well as share content and send messages [131]. It also enables for rapid feedback and encourages students to work together to learn [132]. Learners and teachers can collaborate in web-based interactions that are not limited to certain technology or software via VC. VC has become one of the most popular technologies for synchronous online teaching as technology progresses [133]. Although it faces technical limitations, it encourages dynamic collaboration endeavours [134].

During the COVID-19 crisis, free VC applications including Zoom, Google Meet, Microsoft Teams, and Skype were actively used, according to the UN Development Programme. Businesses may boost productivity, streamline and speed decision-making, and minimize customer service costs by using VC, and the costs of employee travel interpersonal interactions, exchange, and meeting processes. In education, VC leads to continuous teaching all through the COVID-19 cycle and creates the framework for developing online teaching process in remote learning circumstances [135, 136].

Student satisfaction with VC has been a mixed bag [137]. Dawson [138] discovered that synchronization improves the sense of community in the classroom and, as a result, student happiness. Furthermore, according to a Dogget study, over 90% of students favoured the instructor's usage of VC, as well as their willingness to inquire. Nevertheless, 80% said they would have felt more at ease in a traditional classroom situation, and 57% said VC technologies made it difficult to engage with the presenter [139]. VC was shown to be an excellent method for teaching surgical tutorials to medical students by authors in [140]. Thistlehwaite et al. [141] (2012), on the other hand, contrasted the learning experiences of students who used discussion forums (DF) to students who used both DF and VC (which is anticipated to boost virtual community). During their four-year experience with VC, they discovered that video conferencing was not related with improved student learning. The clarification of the module's goals and tasks were the only deviations [142].

6.6 THE APPLICATION OF ONLINE TEACHING AND LEARNING DURING COVID-19: A CASE STUDY IN NIGERIA

The implementation of the online learning framework in Nigeria and other low- and middle-income countries may face major setbacks because it may generate a digital divide that widens the inequality gap [143–144]. In poorer countries, using this new learning style will be harmful to the poor and oppressed [145]. Nigeria is not excluded in this context due to the educational institutions' lack of readiness to embrace and adapt to the online learning framework. According to Kyari et al. [146] (2018), online preparedness and advancement in Nigeria's higher education institutions (HEIs) are still in the early stages. As a result, there is a pressing need in Nigeria to include information and communication technology (ICT) into educational training. Nigerian universities have been unable to integrate online into their educational curricula due to infrastructural issues and insufficient internet connectivity [147]. The outbreak of the COVID-19 in Nigeria, as well as the unforeseen closure of schools, is a blow for the educational institutions, as educational institutions in Nigeria are yet to find their feet in the adoption of online to complement the traditional teaching method.

Before the COVID-19 pandemic, which impacted all economic sectors globally, the online teaching method is still in its early stage in Nigeria HEIs. According to data, Nigeria has 180 higher education institutions, but just 11 universities, accounting for 7% of the total, have authorized remote learning environments [148]. However, the government, in collaboration with telecommunication network providers, works through the Ministry of Education, and television and radio stations in Nigeria attempted to provide ongoing education for primary and secondary school pupils through these sources. However, there is no immediate gauge of HEI continuity. Most developing countries in Africa face a big issue as educational institutions around the world evolve and the massive change from conventional face-to-face teaching to online or virtual learning. Because their online models were still in the early phases of adoption, they were unable to keep up with such a transition. This is a significant setback, necessitating the identification of the obstacles to online deployment in Nigerian higher education institutions.

The outbreak evidenced the need for online learning and teaching globally, and the developing countries are not left out of the paradigm shift. Hence, the lecturers have adopted the use of various online teaching like WhatsApp, Telegram, Zoom, and Google Meet to teach their students in this challenging period. The use of these technologies facilitates learning in HEIs globally and become normal practice to remove the barriers of face-to-face learning, time, and space in conventional learning platforms [149]. When students utilize their own devices to access the internet, such as laptops and cell phones, they are more engaged in learning processes using online platforms and e-library resources [150].

Few research in Nigeria have looked at student use of online learning. For instance, in the Nigerian context, Agbo et al. [151] (2020) studied students' perspectives and attitudes regarding the utilization of WhatsApp social media groups for computing education. Students in Nigerian HEIs use WhatsApp to communicate, according to the report, and efficiently interact with their instructor and classmates. According to the authors, WhatsApp allows students who are hesitant to seek face-to-face academic assistance from teachers to do so, and peers can communicate with each other over the internet. Oyelere et al. [152] (2016) looked on mobile learning in HEIs in Nigeria. The study discovered that modern technologies can be used in the classroom to promote social and collaborative learning.

Students were anxious to explore social networking sites using portable phones, hence, experimental evidence of the role of social media in mobile learning is provided. The authors did warn, nevertheless, that electronic gadgets utilized in academic settings must be used under restrictive regulations that are conducive to learning. Baro et al. [153] (2015) looked into Library and Information Science students' understanding of and use of Web 2.0 tools at Delta State University, Abraka. Almost all pupils, according to the report, also have WhatsApp activated on their smartphones, and WhatsApp is the most widely used app because it makes it simple for users to receive information and reduces the time it takes to do so. Therefore, the chapter conduct a study to know the online learning platforms used in Nigeria HEIs for teaching and learning during COVID-19 outbreak lockdown.

The followings are the research questions used in this chapter:

RQ1. What online platforms are Nigeria HEIs using in delivering lectures during the lockdown?
RQ2. What are some of the advantages of using online platforms in teaching and learning for students and teachers?
RQ3. What are the problems that students and teachers in Nigerian HEIs face when it comes to online teaching and learning?

6.6.1 Methods and Materials

For this study, a mixed-methods research approach was adopted, with a large survey research dimension. To better understand the research difficulties, this technique concentrated on gathering relevant quantitative and qualitative data [154]. The multiple data collection style is thought to be the best fit for this study since it allows the researchers to collect data from a variety of sources, including lecturers and learners. The survey used online techniques to gather data from Nigerian students in HEIs, and then an interview with instructors to gather information using various online platforms to teach their students during the lockdown period. SurveyMonkey was used to create the anonymous survey, and the link was sent to the students with the help of their lecturers during online teaching. The online questionnaires were separated into many sections; for instance, demographics, the online platform on which students got lectures, the advantages of getting lectures via online platforms, and the problems of using online platforms, as well as their thoughts on the best online platform for receiving lectures.

6.6.1.1 Data Collection

The data collection process of the online questionnaire was followed by a qualitative collection of data [155]. It involved interviewing the volunteer lecturers to learn more about the kind of online platform they employ when delivering lectures due to the worldwide shutdown triggered by the COVID-19 outbreak, the advantages of employing such a technology and its drawbacks. The University of Ilorin, Ilorin, Nigeria, with a total of 350 students' respondents in the study, the Faculty of Information and Communication Sciences (FCIS) comprising five departments were used for the purpose of this study, 70 students in each department. A sampling technique was used to choose the respondents, who were limited to those who enrolled in the online course using a smartphone and received lectures.

6.6.1.2 Data Analysis

Simple percentages were used to assess the descriptive data, and the findings were displayed in tables, while the answers from the interview with the lecturers were noted and added right into the discussion section.

6.6.2 Results

6.6.2.1 Population Distribution of Respondents

The number of respondents from each department from the university is given in Table 6.1. Table 6.1 shows that more men represent 183 respondents with 52%; women represent 167 or 48% of respondents used for the survey.

The online platform used for instruction during this time of widespread lockdown, as reported by lecturers in FCIS at the University of Ilorin in Ilorin, Nigeria, is shown in Table 6.2. The results show that all the departments are using both Zoom and Google Classroom; this was so because the university purchase the product license for each faculty in the university for easy accessibility to the two platforms. The faculty and the departments can now pick the one that is very useful and suitable for their use and class lecture. The Department of Computer Science used additional an social media platform to enhance their teaching with the students, because a lot of students complained that the two platforms provided by the university ate up much data and slowed their devices in many cases.

TABLE 6.1
Respondents' Gender Distribution

S/N	Department	Male	Female
1	Computer Science	43 (61%)	27 (39%)
2	Information and Communication Science	37 (53%)	33 (47%)
3	Telecommunication	51 (73%)	19 (27%)
4	Mass Communication	23 (33%)	47 (67%)
5	Library and Information Science	29 (31%)	41 (59%)
Total		183 (52%)	167 (48%)

TABLE 6.2
Online Platforms Used by Students during COVID-19 Lockdown

S/N	Department	Online Platforms Used for Teaching and Learning
1	Computer Science	Zoom, Google Classroom, WhatsApp, Telegram
2	Information and Communication Science	Zoom, Google Classroom, WhatsApp
3	Telecommunication	Zoom, Google Classroom
4	Mass Communication	Zoom, Google Classroom
5	Library and Information Science	Zoom, Google Classroom

TABLE 6.3
Benefits of Online Teaching and Learning during COVID-19 Pandemic

Statements	Agree	Strongly Agree	Disagree	Strongly Disagree
There are always lecturers present	174 (49.7%)	134 (38.3%)	34 (9.7%)	8 (2.3%)
Possibility to store lectures and files for later usage	213 (60.9%)	64 (18.3%)	57 (16.3%)	16 (4.6%)
Collaborative learning	203 (58.0%)	98 (28.0%)	37 (10.6%)	12 (3.4%)
Anytime, anyplace education	252 (72%)	57 (16.3%)	26 (7.4%)	15 (4.3%)
Sharing educational resources	165 (47.1%)	132 (37.7%)	45 (12.9%)	8 (2.3%)
Opportunity to question a lecturer	235 (67.2%)	74 (21.1%)	27 (7.7%)	14 (4.0%)
Favorable homeschooling	181 (51.7%)	125 (35.7%)	30 (8.6%)	14 (4.0%)

TABLE 6.4
Limitations of Online Teaching and Learning during COVID-19 Outbreak

Statements	Agree	Strongly Agree	Disagree	Strongly Disagree
During the online classes, there were problems with internet accessibility and signal strength	263 (75.1%)	47 (13.4%)	15 (4.3%)	25 (7.2%)
The smartphone is too expensive to get; hence, there was no smartphone to use	245 (70.0%)	52 (14.9%)	37 (10.6%)	16 (4.5%)
The cost of internet data bundles was a barrier to using online platforms	253 (72.3%)	57 (16.3%)	23 (6.6%)	17 (4.8%)
The messages received or materials downloaded are too many for the available memory	239 (68.3%)	86 (24.6%)	17 (4.8%)	8 (2.3%)
Inability to utilize these online applications properly	65 (18.6%)	32 (9.1%)	145 (41.4%)	108 (30.9%)
Associated eye problems and straining eyes	205 (58.6%)	104 (29.7%)	17 (4.9%)	24 (6.8%)
The online teaching and learning are time-consuming	121 (34.6%)	40 (11.4%)	57 (16.3%)	132 (37.7%)

6.6.2.2 Benefits of Online Teaching and Learning

Results in Table 6.3 discovered that the majority (88.0%) of the respondents agree and strongly agree that lecturers are always available is one of the benefits of obtaining lectures through an online platform. The possibility of store lectures and files for later usage was strongly agreed by majority of the respondents; 60.9% and 18.3% agreed with the statement, totalling 88.2%. The collaborative learning question was another advantage of online teaching and learning; 86.0% agree and strongly agree that receiving lectures online support the collaborative learning. Almost all the respondents agree and strongly agree that the online teaching and learning allow learning anytime and anywhere as students and lecturers can join the lecture without any disturbance, with 88.3% agreeing and strongly agreeing to the statement. Additionally, the sharing educational resources was approving, with 84.8% of the respondents indicating that this is one benefit of receiving lectures through online platforms. Nearly all (88.3%) of the respondents concur and strongly concur that attending lectures online offers them the freedom to ask instructors questions. The majority of the respondents agree and strongly agree (87.4%) that taking classes online makes it possible to learn comfortably at home.

6.6.2.3 Limitations of Online Teaching and Learning

Table 6.4 shows the results of the limitation of online teaching and learning of Nigerian students, using University of Ilorin, Nigeria, as a case study. The results revealed that 88.5% agree and strongly agree that during the online classes, there were problems with internet accessibility and signal strength. Almost all the respondents agree and strongly agree (84.9%) that the smartphone is too expensive to obtain; hence no smartphone was available to use during online teaching and learning. The findings revealed that 88.6% strongly agree and agree that the cost of internet data bundles was a barrier to using online platforms for teaching and learning during the COVID-19 outbreak in HEIs in most Nigeria universities. The majority of the respondents strongly agree and agree (92.9%) that the messages received or materials downloaded are too many for the available memory; hence there was not enough space to accommodate all the information. A majority of the respondents (72.3%) does not see the inability to utilize these online applications properly as a problem for online teaching and learning, but some (27.3%) still believe that this can be a challenge in using the online platforms. Most of the respondents strongly agree and agree that the utilization of online platforms have issue with associated eye problems and straining eyes. The results revealed that 46% of the respondents agree and strongly agree that the online teaching and learning is time-consuming, while 54% disagree and strongly disagree with the statement.

6.7 DISCUSSION OF THE FINDINGS

6.7.1 Online Platforms Used in Teaching/Learning

The study as shown in Table 6.3 revealed that out of the five departments, only one department uses another platform apart from Zoom and Google Classroom; this was because both platforms had been paid for by the school, and the school had trained the lecturers on how to use the platform, hence it was very easy to use by both the lecturers and the students of the university. This result is consistent with Maxwell and Hussaini [156] (2020), who conducted research on the use of social media in scientific teaching and learning in colleges of education in Kaduna State, Nigeria, that both inside and outside of the classroom, students have been using social media to communicate with friends, colleagues, and their lecturers for educational purposes. According to Parsons [157] (2000), Zoom's usability and dependability are what have fuelled this phenomenal acceptance, along with openness, and his readiness to share it with the schools in particular. Tim O'Neil, Brandeis University's IT Director, as stated by Earon [158] (2020) (p. 4):

> Especially in comparison to competitor products, Zoom has made it possible to implement online learning programs more efficiently. All online users may more easily integrate content sharing, breakout sessions, and commentary thanks to Zoom's high-quality video capabilities.

6.7.2 Benefits of Online Platforms during COVID-19 Pandemic in Nigerian Universities

According to Table 6.4's results, most interviewees firmly agree that lecturers are available at all times, which enables collaborative learning because it gives users the chance to save lectures and material for later use. Some advantages of attending lectures online include the ability to share learning materials, the freedom to ask the lecturer questions, and comfortable learning environments from home. The findings of available lecturers and learning at any time and anywhere are consistent with earlier research by Gon and Rawekar [159] (2017) that online has been discovered to be a novel and practical medium for teaching-learning interaction, with persistent instructor accessibility and learning whenever, everywhere.

The results on the advantages of attending lectures via online platforms include exchanging learning resources and the opportunity to ask questions of the lecturer, which are consistent with the body of literature as described by the research conducted in [160]. Additionally, it was noted that online teaching and learning encourages communication and interaction between students and instructors. Students recognize Zoom and Google Classroom as some transnational and communication platforms that allow freely expression oneself freely without restriction in environment, thus eliminating the lecture-specific limitations caused by poor collaboration. Additionally, Gon and Rawekar [159] (2017) noted that additional encounters in the kind of questions and answers, exchange of educational materials, as well as various heartfelt expressions of gratitude, congratulations, among others, when compared to traditional courses, were exhibited during lecturing through online teaching and learning. The online learning and teaching provide educational advantages as well, aiding students in effectively learning specific ideas and preparing them for important lectures.

6.7.3 Challenges Related to Online Teaching and Learning

More than half of respondents agreed and strongly agreed with the findings about the difficulties of online learning that receiving online lectures is difficult if one doesn't have a smartphone. Not many students and their parents can actually afford smartphones, so this discovery is not shocking. Some kids might borrow smartphones from their associates or family only to listen to lectures because such phones are costly to purchase. According to Bouhnik and Deshen [161] (2014), the issue that certain students do not have access to the application is only a temporary arrangement given how many students now own smartphones. The vast majority of the faculty and students concur and strongly believe that having so many learning available resources confuses them. This shows that some lecturers send too many learning materials for students to read, which probably tends to confuse them. The overwhelming majority of respondents accept and strongly accept that while they are attending online lectures, having quite so many comments come during the lecture confuses them. Also, the downloading of some of these materials take much of their smartphone memory. The findings revealed that most of the respondents agree and strongly agree that the cost of internet data bundles was a barrier to using online platforms for teaching and learning during COVID-19 outbreak. Though many students disagree and strongly disagree that online teaching and learning consuming time, but some of the students still strongly agree that the online teaching ate a huge amount of their time daily. Almost all the respondents in the faculty agree and strongly agree that the online platforms for teaching and learning causes associated eye problems and strains eyes. Many of the students in the faculty agree and strongly agree that during the online classes, there were problems with internet accessibility and signal issues. Almost all the students disagree and strongly disagree that inability to utilize the online applications properly can hinder the utilization of online platforms. This demonstrates the students' proficiency with the use of online applications. This result is in line with a report by Baro et al. [153] (2015) that found faculty students mostly learned how to use Web 2.0 tools by self-practice.

The survey also identified additional challenges faced by pupils, including limited access to the internet; among other things, no power supply makes it impossible to finish university classes. Respondents in this study stated that, when compared to traditional classroom instruction, online learning is just as successful, despite the opinion of some students that face-to-face engagement with lecturers is necessary for both instructional and intellectual considerations. In light of the fact that online education could result in successful outcomes in Nigeria, hence, the issues and challenges mentioned before will prevent the online classes from being delivered effectively [97]. Therefore, many of these students are unable to use and participate on online teaching and learning due to technological and financial issues, thus, make the effectiveness of in-person instruction exceeds that of online instruction. In order to have an effective and profitable online curriculum, students must also be equipped to handle with the fast-paced nature of online education, but they also need a sound system, a laptop or tablet, and technological knowledge that they may need to enjoy using online lessons [162].

6.8 CONCLUSIONS AND FUTURE SCOPE

It is critical that the government and academic education ministry learn from the COVID-19 situation and adopt a forward-thinking approach. Practical solutions should be applied by taken scholarly approach, and after that, there must be reflection and review. The phrase "make your work count twice" (first the job you're doing and second getting researches published and disseminated, for example by creating a curriculum that you plan to use for a class by publishing it, and the plan for educational scholarship has never been more imperative) has never been more applicable to instructors. Using the resources provided by social media is one way in which students can contribute and have a good impact. And other modalities as mentors to their peers, patients, and communities to help positively change behaviours. Because of the low concentrations of students in online learning, it is necessary to adjust the pace of instruction in order to ensure that instructional content is delivered successfully. Teachers must provide timely feedback to students, including online video tutoring and e-mail motivation after class, according to the principle of sufficient care. Also, the concept of high-quality involvement includes certain steps to enhance the degree and profundity of the participation of students in classes. In spite of the increasing reach of online education, contingency plans must be created in advance to address future issues such as traffic congestion on the online education platform. Furthermore, because this "migration" to online teaching occurs quickly during the COVID-19 outbreak, students' fear must be relieved in a variety of methods so that they may participate fully and successfully in online learning. Students and instructors can assist in documenting and analysing the impact of the current improvements so that new ideas and practices can be learned and applied in the future. This is not only a pivotal moment for many disciplines in primary, secondary, and higher institutional contexts, but it is also an opportunity to contribute to the growth of online education in the context of active curricular innovation and change. Despite the fact that the drive toward distance education is gaining traction across a variety of stakeholders, the desire to make online education both valid and valuable will continue to require greater attention. The advantages of this study are purely theoretical. The practical aspect should be considered for future work; the benefit will provide readers with new and fresh information. Theoretically, researchers will be able to solve numerous obstacles that can be encountered when adopting online learning and teaching methods in the future. Workshops, seminars, or special events involving instructors and other educators to prepare for distance or online learning help alleviate problems that arise while adopting online learning, as do activities such as routine or periodic evaluations between the school and parents.

REFERENCES

[1] Cauchemez, S., Fraser, C., Van Kerkhove, M. D., Donnelly, C. A., Riley, S., Rambaut, A., . . . Ferguson, N. M. (2014). Middle East respiratory syndrome coronavirus: Quantification of the extent of the epidemic, surveillance biases, and transmissibility. The Lancet Infectious Diseases, 14(1), 50–56.

[2] Huang, R. H., Liu, D. J., Tlili, A., Yang, J. F., & Wang, H. H. (2020). Handbook on facilitating flexible learning during educational disruption: The Chinese experience in maintaining undisrupted learning in COVID-19 outbreak (p. 46). Beijing: Smart Learning Institute of Beijing Normal University.

[3] Rose, S. (2020). Medical student education in the time of COVID-19. JAMA, 323(21), 2131–2132.

[4] Awotunde, J. B., Oluwabukonla, S., Chakraborty, C., Bhoi, A. K., & Ajamu, G. J. (2022). Application of artificial intelligence and big data for fighting COVID-19 pandemic. International Series in Operations Research and Management Science, 320, 3–26.

[5] Nicola, M., O'Neill, N., Sohrabi, C., Khan, M., Agha, M., & Agha, R. (2020). Evidence-based management guideline for the COVID-19 pandemic-review article. International Journal of Surgery, 77, 206–216.

[6] Wilson, J. M., & Byron, P. R. (1996). A multimedia model for undergraduate education. Technology in Society, 18(3), 387–401.

[7] Smetana, L. K., & Bell, R. L. (2014). Which setting to choose: Comparison of whole-class vs. small-group computer simulation use. Journal of Science Education and Technology, 23(4), 481–495.

[8] Bao, W. (2020). COVID-19 and online teaching in higher education: A case study of Peking university. Human Behavior and Emerging Technologies, 2(2), 113–115.

[9] Lee, B. X., Kjaerulf, F., Turner, S., Cohen, L., Donnelly, P. D., Muggah, R., . . . Waller, I. (2016). Transforming our world: Implementing the 2030 agenda through sustainable development goal indicators. Journal of Public Health Policy, 37(1), 13–31.

[10] Tilbury, D. (2011). Higher education for sustainability: A global overview of commitment and progress. Higher Education in the World, 4(1), 18–28.
[11] Verhulst, E., & Lambrechts, W. (2015). Fostering the incorporation of sustainable development in higher education. Lessons learned from a change management perspective. Journal of Cleaner Production, 106, 189–204.
[12] Tilbury, D. (2013). Another world is desirable: A global rebooting of higher education for sustainable development. In The sustainable university (pp. 97–112). Oxfordshire: Routledge.
[13] Ashida, A. (2022). The role of higher education in achieving the sustainable development goals. In Sustainable development disciplines for humanity: Breaking down the 5Ps—People, planet, prosperity, peace, and partnerships (pp. 71–84). Singapore: Springer Nature Singapore.
[14] Tang, H. H. H., & Tsui, C. P. G. (2018). Democratizing higher education through internationalization: The case of HKU SPACE. Asian Education and Development Studies, 7(1), 26–41.
[15] Camilleri, M. A. (2019). Higher education marketing: Opportunities and challenges in the digital era. Academia (16–17), 4–28.
[16] Alshuwaikhat, H. M., & Abubakar, I. (2008). An integrated approach to achieving campus sustainability: Assessment of the current campus environmental management practices. Journal of Cleaner Production, 16(16), 1777–1785.
[17] Bekessy, S., Burgman, M., Wright, T., Leal Filho, W., & Smith, M. (2003). Universities and sustainability. Carlton: Tela Series, Australian Conservation Foundation.
[18] Cortese, A. D., & Hattan, A. S. (2010). Research and solutions: Education for sustainability as the mission of higher education. Sustainability: The Journal of Record, 3(1), 48–52.
[19] Lozano, R. (2006). Incorporation and institutionalization of SD into universities: Breaking through barriers to change. Journal of Cleaner Production, 14(9–11), 787–796.
[20] Awotunde, J. B., Ayo, E. F., Ajamu, G. J., Jimoh, T. B., & Ajagbe, S. A. (2023). The influence of industry 4.0 and 5.0 for distance learning education in times of pandemic for a modern society. In Advances in distance learning in times of pandemic (pp. 177–214). UK, Chapman and Hall/CRC.
[21] Tsalis, T. A., Malamateniou, K. E., Koulouriotis, D., & Nikolaou, I. E. (2020). New challenges for corporate sustainability reporting: United Nations' 2030 Agenda for sustainable development and sustainable development goals. Corporate Social Responsibility and Environmental Management, 27(4), 1617–1629.
[22] Loach, K., Rowley, J., & Griffiths, J. (2017). Cultural sustainability as a strategy for the survival of museums and libraries. International Journal of Cultural Policy, 23(2), 186–198.
[23] Di Fabio, A., & Rosen, M. A. (2018). Opening the black box of psychological processes in the science of sustainable development: A new frontier. European Journal of Sustainable Development Research, 2(4), 47.
[24] Olalekan, R. M., Omidiji, A. O., Williams, E. A., Christianah, M. B., & Modupe, O. (2019). The roles of all tiers of government and development partners in the environmental conservation of natural resource: A case study in Nigeria. MOJ Ecology & Environmental Sciences, 4(3), 114–121.
[25] Adedoyin, F. F., Alola, A. A., & Bekun, F. V. (2020). An assessment of environmental sustainability corridor: The role of economic expansion and research and development in EU countries. Science of the Total Environment, 713, 136726.
[26] Awotunde, J. B., Ogundokun, R. O., Ayo, F. E., Ajamu, G. J., Adeniyi, E. A., & Ogundokun, E. O. (2019, September). Social media acceptance and use among university students for learning purposes using UTAUT model. In International conference on information systems architecture and technology (pp. 91–102). Cham: Springer.
[27] Blanco-Portela, N., Benayas, J., Pertierra, L. R., & Lozano, R. (2017). Towards the integration of sustainability in higher education institutions: A review of drivers of and barriers to organisational change and their comparison against those found of companies. Journal of Cleaner Production, 166, 563–578.
[28] Aleixo, A. M., Leal, S., & Azeiteiro, U. M. (2018). Conceptualization of sustainable higher education institutions, roles, barriers, and challenges for sustainability: An exploratory study in Portugal. Journal of Cleaner Production, 172, 1664–1673.
[29] Leal Filho, W., Shiel, C., Paço, A., Mifsud, M., Ávila, L. V., Brandli, L. L., . . . Caeiro, S. (2019). Sustainable development goals and sustainability teaching at universities: Falling behind or getting ahead of the pack? Journal of Cleaner Production, 232, 285–294.
[30] Elrehail, H., Emeagwali, O. L., Alsaad, A., & Alzghoul, A. (2018). The impact of transformational and authentic leadership on innovation in higher education: The contingent role of knowledge sharing. Telematics and Informatics, 35(1), 55–67.

[31] Saeed, K. (2019). Towards sustainable development: Essays on system analysis of national policy. Oxfordshire: Routledge.
[32] McLaughlin, P., Stasinopoulos, P., Shimeta, J., Ryan, R., Currell, M., Allinson, G., ... Maqsood, T. (2020). From small things: Building cross-disciplinary, transformative learning experiences through a global mobility experience for higher education students. In Tertiary education in a time of change (pp. 65–81). Singapore: Springer.
[33] Sinakou, E., Donche, V., Boeve-de Pauw, J., & Van Petegem, P. (2019). Designing powerful learning environments in education for sustainable development: A conceptual framework. Sustainability, 11(21), 5994.
[34] Zamora-Polo, F., & Sánchez-Martín, J. (2019). Teaching for a better world. Sustainability and sustainable development goals in the construction of a change-maker university. Sustainability, 11(15), 4224.
[35] Gatti, L., Ulrich, M., & Seele, P. (2019). Education for sustainable development through business simulation games: An exploratory study of sustainability gamification and its effects on students' learning outcomes. Journal of Cleaner Production, 207, 667–678.
[36] Wilhelm, S., Förster, R., & Zimmermann, A. B. (2019). Implementing competence orientation: Towards constructively aligned education for sustainable development in university-level teaching-and-learning. Sustainability, 11(7), 1891.
[37] Paletta, A., Fava, F., Ubertini, F., Bastioli, C., Gregori, G., La Camera, F., & Douvan, A. R. (2019). Universities, industries, and sustainable development: Outcomes of the 2017 G7 environment ministerial meeting. Sustainable Production and Consumption, 19, 1–10.
[38] Hensley, N. (2020). Educating for sustainable development: Cultivating creativity through mindfulness. Journal of Cleaner Production, 243, 118542.
[39] Maidou, A., Plakitsi, K., & Polatoglou, H. (2019). Knowledge, perceptions, and attitudes on education for sustainable development of pre-service early childhood teachers in Greece. World Journal of Education, 9(5), 1–15.
[40] Kioupi, V., & Voulvoulis, N. (2019). Education for sustainable development: A systemic framework for connecting the SDGs to educational outcomes. Sustainability, 11(21), 6104.
[41] Meehan, C. R., Levy, B. L., & Collet-Gildard, L. (2018). Global climate change in US high school curricula: Portrayals of the causes, consequences, and potential responses. Science Education, 102(3), 498–528.
[42] Laininen, E. (2019). Transforming our worldview towards a sustainable future. In Sustainability, human well-being, and the future of education (pp. 161–200). Cham: Palgrave Macmillan.
[43] Corbett, J., & Mellouli, S. (2017). Winning the SDG battle in cities: How an integrated information ecosystem can contribute to the achievement of the 2030 sustainable development goals. Information Systems Journal, 27(4), 427–461.
[44] Wu, J., Guo, S., Huang, H., Liu, W., & Xiang, Y. (2018). Information and communications technologies for sustainable development goals: State-of-the-art, needs, and perspectives. IEEE Communications Surveys & Tutorials, 20(3), 2389–2406.
[45] Ossiannilsson, E. (2018). Promoting active and meaningful learning for digital learners. In Handbook of research on mobile technology, constructivism, and meaningful learning (pp. 294–315). Hershey, PA: IGI Global.
[46] Kim, K. J., & Bonk, C. J. (2006). The future of online teaching and learning in higher education. Educause Quarterly, 29(4), 22–30.
[47] Yang, M., Mak, P., & Yuan, R. (2021). Feedback experience of online learning during the COVID-19 pandemic: Voices from pre-service English language teachers. The Asia-Pacific Education Researcher, 30(6), 611–620.
[48] Khan, A. R., & Qudrat-Ullah, H. (2021). Learning management systems. In Adoption of LMS in higher educational institutions of the middle east (pp. 13–17). Cham: Springer.
[49] Schrum, L. (2000). Online teaching and learning: Essential conditions for success. In Distance learning technologies: Issues, trends, and opportunities (pp. 91–106). Hershey, PA: IGI Global.
[50] Swan, K. (2002). Building learning communities in online courses: The importance of interaction. Education, Communication & Information, 2(1), 23–49.
[51] Friedman, L. W., & Friedman, H. (2013). Using social media technologies to enhance online learning. Journal of Educators Online, 10(1), 1–22.
[52] Hiltz, S. R. (1994). The virtual classroom: Learning without limits via computer networks. UK: Intellect Books, UK.
[53] Rourke, L., Anderson, T., Garrison, D. R., & Archer, W. (1999). Assessing social presence in asynchronous text-based computer conferencing. The Journal of Distance Education/Revue de l'ducation Distance, 14(2), 50–71.

[54] Wang, Y. C., Kraut, R., & Levine, J. M. (2012, February). To stay or leave? The relationship of emotional and informational support to commitment in online health support groups. In Proceedings of the ACM 2012 conference on computer supported cooperative work (pp. 833–842).
[55] Huang, K. Y., Chengalur-Smith, I., & Ran, W. (2014). Not just for support: Companionship activities in healthcare virtual support communities. Communications of the Association for Information Systems, 34(1), 29.
[56] Bryson, B. A. (2019). Stress, social support, and life satisfaction among adults with rare diseases. Health Psychology, 39(10), 912.
[57] Beynaghi, A., Trencher, G., Moztarzadeh, F., Mozafari, M., Maknoon, R., & Leal Filho, W. (2016). Future sustainability scenarios for universities: Moving beyond the United Nations decade of education for sustainable development. Journal of Cleaner Production, 112, 3464–3478.
[58] Laurie, R., Nonoyama-Tarumi, Y., Mckeown, R., & Hopkins, C. (2016). Contributions of education for sustainable development (ESD) to quality education: A synthesis of research. Journal of Education for Sustainable Development, 10(2), 226–242.
[59] Aksela, M., Wu, X., & Halonen, J. (2016). Relevancy of the massive open online course (MOOC) about sustainable energy for adolescents. Education Sciences, 6(4), 40.
[60] Contreras, L. E. V., Vega, N. E. M., Pulgarin, A. G. H., & Palencia, E. P. (2015). Designing a distance learning sustainability bachelor's degree. Environment, Development, and Sustainability, 17(2), 365–377.
[61] Lei, S. A., & Gupta, R. K. (2010). College distance education courses: Evaluating benefits and costs from institutional, faculty, and students' perspectives. Education, 130(4).
[62] Martin, F., & Bolliger, D. U. (2018). Engagement matters: Student perceptions on the importance of engagement strategies in the online learning environment. Online Learning, 22(1), 205–222.
[63] Freeze, R. D., Alshare, K. A., Lane, P. L., & Wen, H. J. (2019). IS success model in the e-Learning context based on students' perceptions. Journal of Information Systems Education, 21(2), 4.
[64] Edward, C. N., Asirvatham, D., Johar, M., & Md, G. (2018). Effect of blended learning and learners' characteristics on students' competence: An empirical evidence in learning oriental music. Education and Information Technologies, 23(6), 2587–2606.
[65] Miao, F., Mishra, S., Orr, D., & Janssen, B. (2019). Guidelines on the development of open educational resources policies. Paris: UNESCO Publishing.
[66] Tennant, J. P., Waldner, F., Jacques, D. C., Masuzzo, P., Collister, L. B., & Hartgerink, C. H. (2016). The academic, economic, and societal impacts of open access: An evidence-based review. F1000Research, 5.
[67] Thagard, P. (2019). Mind-society: From brains to social sciences and professions (treatise on mind and society). Oxford: Oxford University Press.
[68] Salmon, G. (2005). Flying not flapping: A strategic framework for e-Learning and pedagogical innovation in higher education institutions. ALT-J, 13(3), 201–218.
[69] Stepanyan, K., Littlejohn, A., & Margaryan, A. (2013). Sustainable e-Learning: Toward a coherent body of knowledge. Journal of Educational Technology & Society, 16(2), 91–102.
[70] Casanova, D., & Price, L. (2018). Moving towards sustainable policy and practice–a five-level framework for online learning sustainability. Canadian Journal of Learning and Technology/La revue canadienne de l'apprentissage et de la technologie, 44(3).
[71] Brodie, M. (2012). Building the sustainable library at Macquarie University. Australian Academic & Research Libraries, 43(1), 4–16.
[72] Jankowska, M. A., & Marcum, J. W. (2010). Sustainability challenges for academic libraries: Planning for the future. College & Research Libraries, 71(2), 160–170.
[73] Jayalakshmi, C., & Sarangapani, R. (2019). Impacts and implements of greening the libraries. KLA Journal of Information Science & Technology, 41–46.
[74] Johnston, R. B. (2016). Arsenic and the 2030 agenda for sustainable development. Arsenic Research and Global Sustainability—Proceedings of 6th International Congress on Arsenic in the Environment, 2016, 12–14.
[75] Trentin, G. (2007). A multidimensional approach to e-Learning sustainability. Educational Technology, 36–40.
[76] Liu, Q., Geertshuis, S., & Grainger, R. (2020). Understanding academics' adoption of learning technologies: A systematic review. Computers & Education, 151, 103857.
[77] Pather, N., Blyth, P., Chapman, J. A., Dayal, M. R., Flack, N. A., Fogg, Q. A., Green, R. A., Hulme, A. K., Johnson, I. P., Meyer, A. J., & Morley, J. W. (2020). Forced disruption of anatomy education in Australia and New Zealand: An acute response to the Covid-19 pandemic. Anatomical Sciences Education, 13(3), 284–300.

[78] Oliver, R. (1999). Exploring strategies for online teaching and learning. Distance Education, 20(2), 240–254.
[79] Team, T. C. E. (2020). COVID-19: Navigating uncertainties together. Cell, 181(2), 209.
[80] Lajoie, S. P., Pekrun, R., Azevedo, R., & Leighton, J. P. (2019). Understanding and measuring emotions in technology-rich learning environments. Learning and Instruction, 101272.
[81] Barkley, E. F., & Major, C. H. (2020). Student engagement techniques: A handbook for college faculty. Hoboken, NJ: John Wiley & Sons.
[82] Stahl, B. C. (2019). Teaching ethical reflexivity in information systems: How to equip students to deal with moral and ethical issues of emerging information and communication technologies. Journal of Information Systems Education, 22(3), 8.
[83] Al Mamun, M. A., Lawrie, G., & Wright, T. (2020). Instructional design of scaffolded online learning modules for self-directed and inquiry-based learning environments. Computers & Education, 144, 103695.
[84] Bryant, D. P., Bryant, B. R., & Smith, D. D. (2019). Teaching students with special needs in inclusive classrooms. Los Angeles; London: Sage Publications.
[85] Rumble, G. (2019). The planning and management of distance education. UK: Routledge.
[86] Ha, N. H., Nayyar, A., Nguyen, D. M., & Liu, C. A. (2019). Enhancing students' soft skills by implementing CDIO-based integration teaching mode. In The 15th international CDIO conference (p. 569).
[87] Larreamendy-Joerns, J., & Leinhardt, G. (2006). Going the distance with online education. Review of Educational Research, 76(4), 567–605.
[88] Chang, S. H. H., & Smith, R. A. (2008). Effectiveness of personal interaction in a learner-centered paradigm distance education class based on student satisfaction. Journal of Research on Technology in Education, 40(4), 407–426.
[89] Hrastinski, S., & Watson, J. (2009). Designing and evaluating an online role play in conflict management. Campus-Wide Information Systems, 26(4), 287–297.
[90] Moreno-Ger, P., Burgos, D., Martínez-Ortiz, I., Sierra, J. L., & Fernández-Manjón, B. (2008). Educational game design for online education. Computers in Human Behavior, 24(6), 2530–2540.
[91] Sonwalkar, N. (2007, June). Adaptive individualization: The next generation of online education. In Edmedia+ innovate learning (pp. 3056–3063). Waynesville, NC: Association for the Advancement of Computing in Education (AACE).
[92] Barclay, C., Donalds, C., & Osei-Bryson, K. M. (2018). Investigating critical success factors in online learning environments in higher education systems in the Caribbean. Information Technology for Development, 24(3), 582–611.
[93] Montgomerie, K., Edwards, M., & Thorn, K. (2016). Factors influencing online learning in an organisational context. Journal of Management Development, 35(10), 1313–1322.
[94] Sun, L., Tang, Y., & Zuo, W. (2020). Coronavirus pushes education online. Nature Materials, 19(6), 687–687.
[95] Kurtz, G. (2014). Integrating a Facebook group and a course website: The effect on participation and perceptions on learning. American Journal of Distance Education, 28(4), 253–263.
[96] Huang, Y. M. (2017). Exploring the intention to use cloud services in collaboration contexts among Taiwan's private vocational students. Information Development, 33(1), 29–42.
[97] Ogundokun, R. O., Daniyal, M., Misra, S., & Awotunde, J. B. (2021). Students' perspective on online teaching in higher institutions during COVID-19 pandemic. International Journal of Networking and Virtual Organisations, 25(3–4), 308–332.
[98] Subramani, R. (2015). The academic usage of social networking sites by the university students of Tamil Nadu. Online Journal of Communication and Media Technologies, 5(3), 162.
[99] Al-Ansi, A. M. (2017). Reforming education system in developing countries. International Journal of Education and Research, 5(7), 349–363.
[100] Folorunso, S. O., Awotunde, J. B., Banjo, O. O., Ogundepo, E. A., & Adeboye, N. O. (2021). Comparison of active COVID-19 cases per population using time-series models. International Journal of E-Health and Medical Communications (IJEHMC), 13(2), 1–21.
[101] Folorunso, S. O., Ogundepo, E. A., Awotunde, J. B., Ayo, F. E., Banjo, O. O., & Taiwo, A. I. (2022). A multi-step predictive model for COVID-19 cases in Nigeria using machine learning. International Series in Operations Research and Management Science, 320, 107–136.
[102] Awotunde, J. B., Ogundokun, R. O., Adeniyi, A. E., Abiodun, K. M., & Ajamu, G. J. (2022). Application of mathematical modelling approach in COVID-19 transmission and interventions strategies. Studies in Systems, Decision and Control, 366, 283–314.
[103] Awotunde, J. B., Ogundokun, R. O., Adeniyi, E. A., Misra, S., & Ajamu, G. J. (2022). The adoption and utilization of electronic business in response to the global economy during COVID-19. International Journal of Business Analytics (IJBAN), 9(1), 1–20.

[104] Bhagat, S., & Roshan, R. (2017). SWAYAM: Study webs of active-learning for young aspiring minds making a digital India. International Journal of Advance Engineering and Research Development, 4(9), 96–103.
[105] Reese, S. A. (2015). Online learning environments in higher education: Connectivism vs. dissociation. Education and Information Technologies, 20(3), 579–588.
[106] Wang, Q., Huang, C., & Quek, C. L. (2018). Students' perspectives on the design and implementation of a blended synchronous learning environment. Australasian Journal of Educational Technology, 34(1).
[107] Raes, A., Detienne, L., Windey, I., & Depaepe, F. (2020). A systematic literature review on synchronous hybrid learning: Gaps identified. Learning Environments Research, 23(3), 269–290.
[108] Alexander, M. M., Lynch, J. E., Rabinovich, T., & Knutel, P. G. (2014). Snapshot of a hybrid learning environment. Quarterly Review of Distance Education, 15(1).
[109] Bower, M., Dalgarno, B., Kennedy, G. E., Lee, M. J., & Kenney, J. (2015). Design and implementation factors in blended synchronous learning environments: Outcomes from a cross-case analysis. Computers & Education, 86, 1–17.
[110] Hoq, M. Z. (2020). E-Learning during the period of pandemic (COVID-19) in the kingdom of Saudi Arabia: An empirical study. American Journal of Educational Research, 8(7), 457–464.
[111] Mohammadi, M. K., Mohibbi, A. A., & Hedayati, M. H. (2021). Investigating the challenges and factors influencing the use of the learning management system during the covid-19 pandemic in Afghanistan. Education and Information Technologies, 26(5), 5165–5198.
[112] Holmes, K., & Prieto-Rodriguez, E. (2018). Student and staff perceptions of a learning management system for blended learning in teacher education. Australian Journal of Teacher Education (Online), 43(3), 21–34.
[113] Ahmed, A., & Sutton, M. J. (2017). Gamification, serious games, simulations, and immersive learning environments in knowledge management initiatives. World Journal of Science, Technology and Sustainable Development, 14(2/3), 78–83.
[114] Awotunde, J. B., Jimoh, R. G., Abdulraheem, M., Oladipo, I. D., Folorunso, S. O., & Ajamu, G. J. (2022). IoT-based wearable body sensor network for COVID-19 pandemic. Studies in Systems, Decision and Control, 378, 253–275.
[115] Noori, A. Q., Orfan, S. N., Akramy, S. A., & Hashemi, A. (2022). The use of social media in EFL learning and teaching in higher education of Afghanistan. Cogent Social Sciences, 8(1), 2027613.
[116] Yee, M. L. S., & Abdullah, M. S. (2021). A review of UTAUT and extended model as a conceptual framework in education research. Jurnal Pendidikan Sains Dan Matematik Malaysia, 11, 1–20.
[117] Cao, J., Yang, T., Lai, I. K. W., & Wu, J. (2021). Is online education more welcomed during COVID-19? An empirical study of social impact theory on online tutoring platforms. The International Journal of Electrical Engineering & Education, 0020720920984001.
[118] Huang, J., Dasgupta, A., Ghosh, A., Manning, J., & Sanders, M. (2014, March). Superposter behavior in MOOC forums. In Proceedings of the first ACM conference on learning@ scale conference (pp. 117–126).
[119] Jung, Y., & Lee, J. (2018). Learning engagement and persistence in massive open online courses (MOOCS). Computers & Education, 122, 9–22.
[120] Lu, Y., Wang, B., & Lu, Y. (2019). Understanding key drivers of MOOC satisfaction and continuance intention to use. Journal of Electronic Commerce Research, 20(2).
[121] Breslow, L., Pritchard, D. E., DeBoer, J., Stump, G. S., Ho, A. D., & Seaton, D. T. (2013). Studying learning in the worldwide classroom research into edX's first MOOC. Research & Practice in Assessment, 8, 13–25.
[122] Jordan, K. (2014). Initial trends in enrolment and completion of massive open online courses. International Review of Research in Open and Distributed Learning, 15(1), 133–160.
[123] Shao, Z. (2018). Examining the impact mechanism of social psychological motivations on individuals' continuance intention of MOOCs: The moderating effect of gender. Internet Research, 28(1), 232–250.
[124] Wang, Q., Khan, M. S., & Khan, M. K. (2021). Predicting user perceived satisfaction and reuse intentions toward massive open online courses (MOOCs) in the Covid-19 pandemic: An application of the UTAUT model and quality factors. International Journal of Research in Business and Social Science (2147–4478), 10(2), 1–11.
[125] Rafiq, K. R. M., Hashim, H., Yunus, M. M., & Pazilah, F. N. (2019). Developing a MOOC for communicative English: A battle of instructional designs. International Journal of Innovation, Creativity and Change, 7(7), 29–39.
[126] Emigawaty, E. (2017). Perancangan Arsitektur Dan Purwarupa Model Pembelajaran massive open online course (MOOCS) Di Perguruan Tinggi Menggunakan Layanan Mobile. Data Manajemen dan Teknologi Informasi (DASI), 18(1), 25–30. Universitas Amikom Yogyakarta.

[127] Praherdhiono, H., Adi, E. P., & Prihatmoko, Y. (2018). Konstruksi demokrasi belajar berbasis kehidupan pada implementasi LMS dan MOOC. Edcomtech: Jurnal Kajian Teknologi Pendidikan, 3(1), 21–28. Malang Kode.

[128] Ismail, M. E., Hashim, S., Ismail, I. M., Ismail, A., Razali, N., Daud, K. A. M., & Khairudin, M. (2018). Penggunaan massive open online course (MOOC) dalam kalangan pelajar vokasional [The use of massive open online course (MOOC) among vocational students]. Journal of Nusantara Studies (JONUS), 3(1), 30–41.

[129] Cristel, R. T., Demesh, D., & Dayan, S. H. (2020). Video conferencing impact on facial appearance: Looking beyond the COVID-19 pandemic. Facial Plastic Surgery & Aesthetic Medicine, 22(4), 238–239. Alexandria.

[130] Awotunde, J. B., Jimoh, R. G., Oladipo, I. D., Abdulraheem, M., Jimoh, T. B., & Ajamu, G. J. (2021). Big data and data analytics for an enhanced COVID-19 epidemic management. Studies in Systems, Decision and Control, 358, 11–29.

[131] Ajadi, T. O., Salawu, I. O., & Adeoye, F. A. (2008). E-learning and distance education in Nigeria. Online Submission, 7(4).

[132] Al-Samarraie, H. (2019). A scoping review of videoconferencing systems in higher education: Learning paradigms, opportunities, and challenges. International Review of Research in Open and Distributed Learning, 20(3).

[133] Roth, J. J., Pierce, M., & Brewer, S. (2020). Performance and satisfaction of resident and distance students in videoconference courses. Journal of Criminal Justice Education, 31(2), 296–310.

[134] Reese, R. J., & Chapman, N. (2017). Promoting and evaluating evidence-based telepsychology interventions: Lessons learned from the university of Kentucky telepsychology lab. In Career paths in telemental health (pp. 255–261). Cham: Springer.

[135] Fatani, T. H. (2020). Student satisfaction with videoconferencing teaching quality during the COVID-19 pandemic. BMC Medical Education, 20(1), 1–8.

[136] Sahi, P. K., Mishra, D., & Singh, T. (2020). Medical education amid the COVID-19 pandemic. Indian Pediatrics, 57(7), 652–657.

[137] Kumar, A., Krishnamurthi, R., Bhatia, S., Kaushik, K., Ahuja, N. J., Nayyar, A., & Masud, M. (2021). Blended learning tools and practices: A comprehensive analysis. IEEE Access, 9, 85151–85197.

[138] Dawson, S. (2006). A study of the relationship between student communication interaction and sense of community. The Internet and Higher Education, 9(3), 153–162.

[139] Doggett, D., & Mark, A. (2008). The videoconferencing classroom: What do students think? Journal of Industrial Teacher Education, 44(4), 29.

[140] Smith, A. C., White, M. M., McBride, C. A., Kimble, R. M., Armfield, N. R., Ware, R. S., & Coulthard, M. G. (2012). Multi-site videoconference tutorials for medical students in Australia. ANZ Journal of Surgery, 82(10), 714–719.

[141] Thistlethwaite, J. E., Davies, D., Ekeocha, S., Kidd, J. M., MacDougall, C., Matthews, P., . . . Clay, D. (2012). The effectiveness of case-based learning in health professional education. A BEME systematic review: BEME Guide No. 23. Medical Teacher, 34(6), e421–e444.

[142] Giesbers, B., Rienties, B., Tempelaar, D. T., & Gijselaers, W. (2014). Why increased social presence through web videoconferencing does not automatically lead to improved learning. E-Learning and Digital Media, 11(1), 31–45.

[143] Igbokwe, I. C., Okeke-James, N. J., Akudo, F. U., & Anyanwu, J. A. (2020). Administrative roles in primary schools for curbing COVID-19 pandemic in Nigeria: Henry Fayol's approach. European Scientific Journal, 16(16), 63–72.

[144] Aboagye, E., Yawson, J. A., & Appiah, K. N. (2021). COVID-19 and e-Learning: The challenges of students in tertiary institutions. Social Education Research, 1–8.

[145] Reimers, F. M. (2020). What the covid-19 pandemic will change in education depends on the thoughtfulness of education responses today. Worlds of Education [Online].

[146] Kyari, S. S., Adiuku-Brown, M. E., Abechi, H. P., & Adelakun, R. T. (2018). E-learning in tertiary education in Nigeria: Where do we stand? Europe, 348, 26–4.

[147] Anene, J. N., Imam, H., & Odumuh, T. (2014). Problem and prospect e-Learning in Nigerian universities. International Journal of Technology and Inclusive Education (IJTIE), 3(2), 320–327.

[148] NUC. (2020). National universities commission. www.nuc.edu.ng/.

[149] Henrie, C. R., Halverson, L. R., & Graham, C. R. (2015). Measuring student engagement in technology-mediated learning: A review. Computers & Education, 90, 36–53.

[150] Bawack, R. E., & Kamdjoug, J. R. K. (2020). The role of digital information use on student performance and collaboration in marginal universities. International Journal of Information Management, 54, 102179.

[151] Agbo, F. J., Olawumi, O., Oyelere, S. S., Kolog, E. A., Olaleye, S. A., Agjei, R. O., . . . Olawuni, A. (2020). Social media usage for computing education: The effect of tie strength and group communication on perceived learning outcome. International Journal of Education and Development using Information and Communication Technology, 16(1), 5–26.
[152] Oyelere, S. S., Paliktzoglou, V., & Suhonen, J. (2016). M-learning in Nigerian higher education: An experimental study with Edmodo. International Journal of Social Media and Interactive Learning Environments, 4(1), 43–62.
[153] Baro, E. E., Ikolo, V., & Atanda, L. A. (2015). Awareness and use of Web 2.0 tools by LIS students in Delta State University, Abraka. Global Journal of Academic Librarianship, 4(1), 1–16.
[154] Zhu, M., Sari, A., & Lee, M. M. (2018). A systematic review of research methods and topics of the empirical MOOC literature (2014–2016). The Internet and Higher Education, 37, 31–39.
[155] Braun, V., Clarke, V., Boulton, E., Davey, L., & McEvoy, C. (2021). The online survey as a qualitative research tool. International Journal of Social Research Methodology, 24(6), 641–654.
[156] Maxwell, A. F., & Hussaini, Y. J. (2020). Social media usage in teaching and learning of science in colleges of education in Kaduna State, Nigeria. International Journal of Education and Evaluation, 6, 44–67.
[157] Parsons, J. (2020). Ok. Zoomer: Why zoom is the world's new favorite social network. https://metro. co. uk/2020/03/23/ok-zoomer-zoom-worlds-new-favourite-socialnetwork-12443418/(dan pristupa 10.5.2021).
[158] Earon, S. A. (2020). The value of video communications in education. Zoom website. https://zoom. us/docs/doc/The Value of Video Communications in Education. pdf.
[159] Gon, S., & Rawekar, A. (2017). Effectivity of e-Learning through WhatsApp as a teaching learning tool. MVP Journal of Medical Sciences, 19–25.
[160] Rambe, P., & Chipunza, C. (2013, August). Using mobile devices to leverage student access to collab oratively-generated resources: A case of WhatsApp instant messaging at a South African University. In 2013 international conference on advanced ICT and education (ICAICTE-13) (pp. 314–320). Hong Kong: Atlantis Press.
[161] Bouhnik, D., & Deshen, M. (2014). WhatsApp goes to school: Mobile instant messaging between teachers and students. Journal of Information Technology Education. Research, 13, 217.
[162] Awotunde, J. B., Ogundokun, R. O., Ayo, F. E., Ajamu, G. J., & Ogundokun, O. E. (2021). UTAUT model: Integrating social media for learning purposes among university students in Nigeria. SN Social Sciences, 1(9), 1–27.

7 Inclusiveness and Sustainability of Teaching and Learning Technologies amidst the COVID-19 Pandemic in Higher Education An Indian Perspective

Anil Kumar and Subhanshu Goyal

7.1 INTRODUCTION

India has a glorious history of the teaching-learning process. Early education was delivered through *gurukula* under the supervision of "Guru". The acquisition of knowledge, wisdom and truth was always considered as the ultimate human goal in Indian thought and philosophy. Takshsila (modern-day Pakistan) is considered to be the oldest seat of learning from 8th century BCE. Also, Nalanda University in India is considered as the oldest university in the world. It was the first international residential university in history which flourished under the Gupta dynasty. Teachers and students travelled from various parts of Tibet, Korea, Sri Lanka, China, and Central Asia to study and gain knowledge. It is claimed that the university accommodated over 1500 teachers and scholars, and about 10,000 students, in its flourishing years. The university imparted education in several domains like politics, law, science, philosophy and arts. Hiuen Tsang, a famous Chinese traveller, was also a student at this splendid university. Later on, stupas and temples also held the position as learning centres. The philosophy of learning underwent transformations under Mughal rule, British rule and finally in independent India. The education policy in India after 1947 saw a paradigm shift with the changing need of the global ecosystem. The National Educational Policy (NEP) 2020 by the Government of India is the latest educational policy of the 21st century and focuses on many increasing concerns related to the education system in India (www.education.gov.in). It is based on the principle that education must focus not only on cognitive capabilities but also psychological, social, emotional and economical aspects and development of the human mind. The sudden outbreak of COVID-19 pandemic in the year 2020 has posed the biggest challenge to the teaching-learning process throughout the world and forced educational institutes to change their pedagogical approach from traditional learning methodologies to online and blended modes of learning. Ensuring learning continuity is the priority of all stakeholders during the unusual situation of pandemic. The sustainability and inclusiveness of the teaching and learning process amidst COVID-19 pandemic poses a major challenge throughout the world. The growing concern for technology-enabled education systems across the globe has sparked a new beginning for the innovative solutions for the teaching-learning process. The need for adoption of new technologies has been clearly understood and implementation of a new ecosystem for the education sector is the need of the present society. For instance, University of Delhi (DU), one of India's largest institutions of

DOI: 10.1201/9781003425779-7

higher learning, has created a virtual online platform for teaching. Two major applications, Google Classroom and Google Hangout, have been provided with a university domain to provide learning support. Many video-based collaboration services (e.g., Webex, Zoom, Loom, Skype) are very well integrated with DU email accounts.

7.1.1 Objective of the Chapter

The objective of the chapter is to explore the various applications offered by Ed-Tech companies as an alternative to physical mode of learning during the time of crisis as well as the schemes of the central and state government in India to aid and improve online teaching learning process. The changes in preference for different digital tools during COVID-19 and its usage to sustain the education process are also analysed. This chapter also highlights the benefits offered by web-based learning along with the challenges for inclusiveness of online learning by different colleges and/or universities from an Indian perspective.

7.1.2 Organization of the Chapter

The chapter is organized as follows: Section 7.2 provides a quantitative view of COVID-19 pandemic. The evolutions of web-based learning systems covering various latest digital tools are discussed in section 7.3. In section 7.4, the process of the paradigm shift towards online learning is covered along with different initiatives taken by the Government of India and different states of India. Section 7.5 covers the schemes by the Government of India for inclusion and improvement of higher education focusing on fund management among the higher educational institutions and inclusion of disadvantaged groups of society. Section 7.6 elaborates on the National Education Policy 2020 and its sustainability in technology-driven education systems. In sections 7.7 and 7.8, the major challenges and gains due to web-based learning are discussed. Finally, section 7.9 concludes the chapter with the usage of web-based learning tools in the teaching and learning process, highlighting the scope for integration of modern technologies.

7.2 QUANTITATIVE VIEW OF COVID-19 PANDEMIC

Before assessing the effect of COVID-19 pandemic, it is crucial to analyse the magnitude of this pandemic in quantitative terms across the globe. On 11 March 2020, the World Health Organization (WHO) declared COVID-19 as an international health emergency, which is still considered as a threat to global health. COVID-19 pandemic still claims a large number of lives worldwide. WHO reported more than 50.4 million confirmed cases of COVID-19 cases and over 6.2 million related deaths as of April 20, 2022. WHO Americas and European regions witnessed over 4.7 million deaths (WHO). However, there is no conformity on the exact statistics related to COVID-19 deaths as many countries were not able to provide complete death-related data and therefore the actual number of COVID-19-related deaths may be much more than currently reported.

A UNESCO report figured that more than 1.5 billion students and learners across the world are or have been affected due to closure of school and university in the times of the COVID-19 pandemic (UNESCO). There are reports of discontinuation of formal schooling and increasing drop-outs from schools and colleges due to the closure of institutions during the COVID-19 pandemic. The loss of jobs and financial instability forced many parents to discontinue the education of their children. Therefore, continuity of learning from home is the major challenge for all stakeholders of education. Even though no research provides the insights on the evaluation of impact of pandemic on student dropout rate, a study in this area is anticipated to bring out the authentic data. The robustness of information and communication technology infrastructure and sufficient availability of learning tools, digital learning material in the form of e-books, massive open online courses (MOOCs), digital notes, and so on are of prime importance in such severe crises (Huang

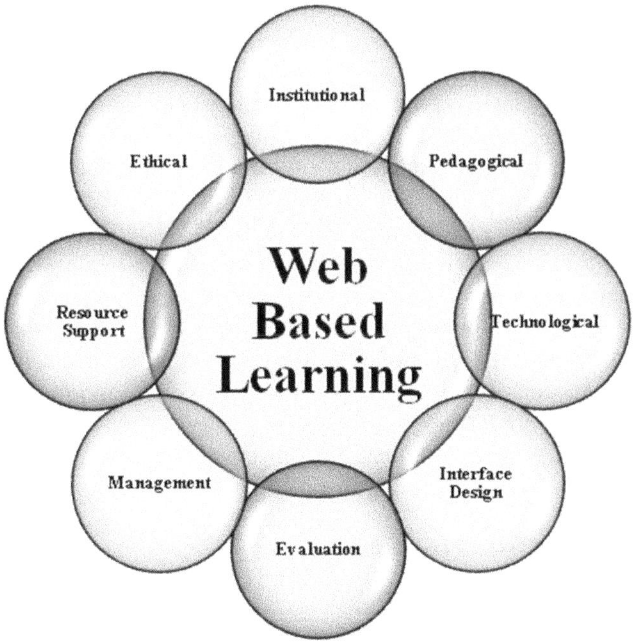

FIGURE 7.1 Framework for web-based learning.

et al., 2020). Amidst COVID-19 crisis, the web-based learning system provides an alternative for dissemination of knowledge throughout the world (Dhawan, 2020). The framework for web-based learning is shown in Figure 7.1.

7.3 EVOLUTION OF WEB-BASED LEARNING SYSTEMS

The term *web-based learning* is used to denote a different variety of learning models (e.g., online learning, digital learning, internet-based learning, blended learning, and mobile learning). Most of the related terms (e.g., open learning, online learning, internet-based learning, blended learning, computer-facilitated learning, mobile learning) have in common the use of computer system connected to the internet and offers the flexibility to learn from anywhere, anytime, with any means, in any rhythm (Cojocariu et al., 2014). The internet penetrates deeply in the social fabric and has been used extensively in all walks of life. As the internet provides mobility and remote access to data and all kinds of interactions among the people, it becomes imperative to use technology for innovative solutions. The education sector has also seen a significant growth in the usage of online digital tools that have evolved over the past two decades. The universities in the United States, the United Kingdom and other European countries took the lead to implement the digital solutions for teaching purposes. In India, Educomp, an Ed-Tech company launched in 1994 which took the lead in the mission of online education. After 2010, various Ed-Tech companies penetrated the Indian market with the purpose to give a new dimension to the education sector. In the year 2019, Byju's, a learning application, emerged as a high valued Ed-Tech startup and consequently, many start-ups became evident to give services parallel to Byju's (www.byjus.com). Li Kang, AI English executive director said, "Online Learning is the future and if there was no virus, that attainment of digital classes would have taken another few years but this has improved the process". Although Indian cities, especially remote areas, are facing the problem of frequent electricity shortages and unstable internet connectivity, still these Ed-Techs are able to realize their gains. The online platforms like

YouTube provide an impetus to the recorded lectures to the general public. Professors, teachers and other stakeholders have the facility to prepare their lectures in the online environment and may be posted to the general public or restricted learners depending on the copyright of the content.

Google Scholar provides a huge repository of research articles, books, and knowledge material to the world. The researchers, students and other learning fraternity may utilize this repository for contributing the enhancement of knowledge in their specific domain. The COVID-19 situation has forced the educational institute to adopt an alternative to physical mode of learning. The shift to online mode became a challenge for all stakeholders to be in sync with all the participants involved in the system. Although open universities that provide a distance mode of learning and degrees were in place, the pandemic situation of COVID-19 forced the use of other alternatives of learning. Some of the best-known digital solutions have been used extensively throughout the world. Table 7.1 witnessed a tremendous change in the usage of different virtual interaction applications like Google Meet, Webex, Zoom, Hangouts, Teams, and Cisco during two different timestamps of the COVID-19 period. The Google Meet application has shown the highest increase in its use for the teaching-learning process, whereas the usage of Zoom, YouTube and Hangouts applications declined for the given period.

7.3.1 Latest Tools by Ed-Tech Companies

The various tools provided by Ed-Tech companies that have flourished and provide digital solutions for online teaching are enlisted as follows.

7.3.1.1 Zoom Classes

Zoom classrooms can be used for the learning process and student academic activities. Different features like digital whiteboard, group chats, content sharing on one-click and more leads to increase in student participation and learning retention. Both attendance and attention can be facilitated with this tool. Students can learn at their own pace by viewing the videos/lectures hosted by teachers.

7.3.1.2 Ekstep

This open learning platform provides equitable access to every learner. The interactive content may be created and published with the help of this collaborative open learning platform. This platform provides educational videos that can be used by students irrespective of temporal or physical limitations. This platform also facilitates the quantification of learning outcomes and open framework to scale up in accordance with the requirement of the user.

TABLE 7.1
Comparison of Virtual Interaction Applications Usage during COVID-19 in India

Virtual Interaction Applications	Survey 1 (Before June 2020)	Survey 2 (Before September 2021)	Variance
Google Meet	17.62	37.14	19.52
Zoom	47.62	18.10	−29.52
Google Classroom	4.76	21.90	17.14
Microsoft Teams	2.38	5.24	2.86
YouTube	14.76	5.71	−9.05
Hangouts	5.24	2.38	−2.86
Webex	2.86	3.81	0.95
Other (WhatsApp, Moodle, etc.)	4.76	5.71	0.95
Survey Responses (*N*=210)			

7.3.1.3 Google Classes

This is the most widely used platform by teachers during the closure of schools and colleges due to COVID-19. It facilitates learning and management of coursework through an easy interface. The ready-to-use options for different student centric activities like creating online classes, preparing and assigning tasks to students, evaluation and grading of students, and providing feedback to students can be done easily.

7.3.1.4 Lark

It provides a centralized solution for student centric activities like scheduling of classes, creation of assignments, preparation of notes, finalization of project reports and much more, which are facilitated in the cloud. Teachers can use this tool to create customized lesson plans which are robust in nature. A verified calendar feature is available in this application that facilitates teachers to synchronize their schedules. There are features to design timetables for their classes as well as facilities for arranging meetings with colleagues. It also supports marking of students and grading of assignments in a real-time environment. Also, students can get valuable feedback from teachers.

7.3.1.5 Ding Talk

This is a free collaborative communication platform that has been considered as a powerful digital learning solution given by UNESCO during the time of the COVID-19 outbreak. Parents, schools and teachers can use this application to facilitate the learning process of learners and simplify the process of social interaction among the users of this application. Free digital tools such as live streaming of data, online grading of students, video conferencing and instant messaging are provided along with this application that helps in the learning process of students remotely.

All these online tools are being recognized, reviewed, accepted and adopted by educators and learners from across the globe that foster an environment of normal and routine pattern of learning in the harsh reality of the COVID-19 crisis. Besides use of technology there is a requirement to understand online etiquette to be followed by students and facilitators (Saxena, 2020). The uses of these technologies provide the possibility of continuing the process of knowledge delivery overcoming the hindrance created by pandemic situations so that health risk could be minimized.

7.4 PARADIGM SHIFT TOWARDS ONLINE LEARNING

The Human Resource Department (HRD) of the Government of India offered various web-based solutions for the teachers and learners to continue their learning process during the lockdown period. The HRD ministry initiates a range of online platforms that accord learning to students across the country.

7.4.1 Government of India Initiatives

The different innovative internet-based platforms have evolved over the last few years. Some of the initiatives of the Government of India are listed below.

7.4.1.1 SWAYAM

The three fundamental principles of Education Policy (i.e., access, equity and quality) were taken care of while initiating the project of SWAYAM by Government of India (India Report–Digital Education). The intention of the project is to outreach the learning resources to all learners, including the marginalized section of society. SWAYAM tries to minimize the digital gap among the various groups of students and bring the underprivileged students to include in the mainstream and become part of the digital revolution. All the courses on this portal are interactive in nature and are available free of cost to any student. These courses are prepared by renowned teachers in the country. More than 1000 teachers specialized in their domain across the country were involved in preparation and finalization of these courses. The courses available on SWAYAM portal follow a four quadrants approach. Firstly, video lectures are available. Secondly, reading material is in text format that can be downloaded/printed and may be used for future reference. Thirdly, assessment is provided through objective tests, quizzes and assignments. Fourthly, a discussion forum for doubt sessions about any concerned topic. The use of multimedia, audio-video techniques and state-of-the-art pedagogy/ technology improves the learning outcomes.

7.4.1.2 e-PG Pathshala

e-PG Pathshala is a project under the National Mission on Education through ICT (NME-ICT), and UGC has been given the responsibility of being implemented across India. It is an access point to all post graduate courses. It provides digital content in 70 subjects across various disciplines of science, arts, social sciences, and mathematical sciences. The e-content is of high quality and curriculum-based, which forms the basis for an excellent education system.

7.4.1.3 Digital Infrastructure for Knowledge Sharing (DIKSHA)

DIKSHA (Digital Infrastructure for Knowledge Sharing) is a national portal for school education, a program of National Council for Education Research and Training (NCERT). DIKSHA was launched on September 5, 2017, and has since been used by 35 states/Uts affecting millions of learners and teachers (www.diksha.gov.in). It envisioned the idea of "One Nation, One Platform". It is a program of the nation, by the nation and for the nation. DIKSHA is developed based on Sunbird, open-source technology licensed by MIT, which provides a digital infrastructure for learning and support multiple languages and solutions and offers over 100 micro services which act as a fundamental building block for the creation of digital platforms related to teaching and learning. It was developed based on the principles of open access, open licensing diversity, open architecture and autonomy. The different states are using this portal in its own way as this portal offers choice and freedom to choose from a variety of learning programs. The capabilities and solutions given by DIKSHA enable the teachers as well as learners to achieve the learning goals in a simple and unified way and support inclusiveness in imparting school education for greater social equality. The equal participation of all stakeholders in the education ecosystem (e.g., educationists, experts, organizations, institutions) paved the way towards achieving the highest goal of education. The different interfaces to access DIKSHA applications are depicted in Figure 7.2.

DIKSHA provides more than 80,000 curriculum-linked and curated content writings in 15 languages. The wide range of learning material includes experiential content, video activities, quizzes, assignments, interactive games, worksheets and lesson plans, all of which are significant to create an engaging learning experience. DIKSHA can be accessed by learners and teachers across the country. It is currently offering more than 18 languages and the various curricula of education boards across India. In the situation of COVID-19 where continuation of regular schooling is not possible, DIKSHA tools and innovative technology enabled interfaces that make it possible to continue education of students from home. Hence involving the use of technology for the improvement of teachers and learners is a stimulating step for a robust and bright education system. The solutions provided on the DIKSHA platform are depicted in Figure 7.3.

7.4.1.4 CBSE Podcast

CBSE started the podcast app 'CBSE-Shiksha Vani', a technology-based application available on Play Store for Android phone users. This application is beneficial to all schools, teachers and students for receiving up-to-date crucial information and directives of higher official bodies related to examinations, admissions and related important events. Easy availability of information related to initiatives and educational tools of government may improve awareness and learning outcomes. This podcast helps in dissemination of information and directives in a uniform manner to all stakeholders.

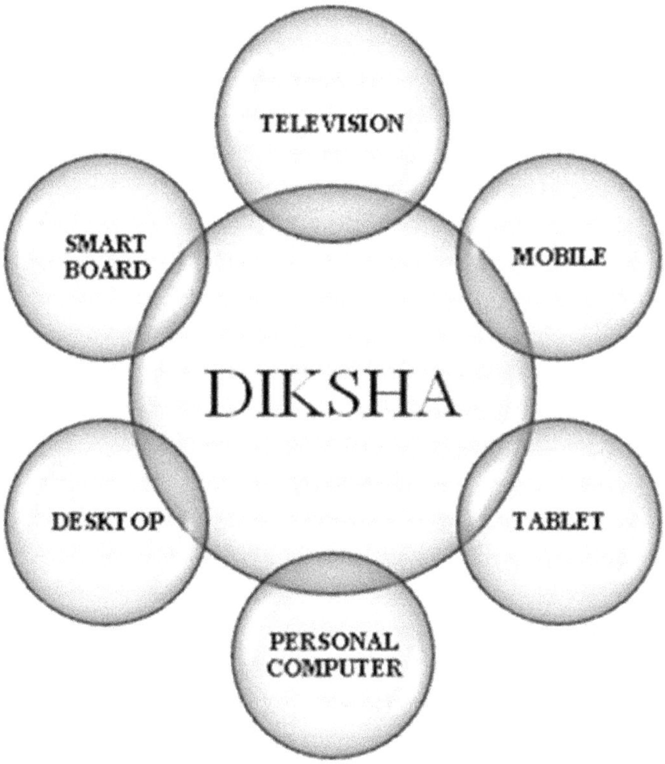

FIGURE 7.2 Diverse interfaces to access DIKSHA.

7.4.1.5 National Digital Library of India

The National Digital Library of India is a technology-driven integrated platform having a collection of contents from different institutes of repute. The content ranges from books, articles and manuscripts to video lectures, theses and more, amounting to more than 60 types of educational material. These materials are available in more than 400 languages. These contents can be accessed free of cost by schools, colleges, universities, teachers, students, lecturers, disabled and disadvantaged pupils, and anybody who has a passion to learn.

7.4.1.6 IIT-PAL

IIT-PAL is a project of the Ministry of Education of Government of India which provides free video lectures especially to classes 11 and 12. The video lectures are prepared by the subject experts and are available in the areas of physics, chemistry, mathematics and biology. The purpose of IIT-PAL is to assist the students in preparation of the competitive examinations held after class 12. These video lectures help the students in classifying the basic concepts and clear and strong understanding of core ideas of the subject and to self-prepare for the exam. The students can quickly access these video lectures on the website of the National Testing Agency. The videos are telecasted on Swayam Prabha DTH Channel.

7.4.1.7 Swayam Prabha DTH Channel

These channels are dedicated towards the telecasting of different academic programmes round the clock through GSAT-15 satellites. A new content of 04 hours daily is telecasted on this channel with the repetition of five more times in a day. This arrangement provides the flexibility of time according

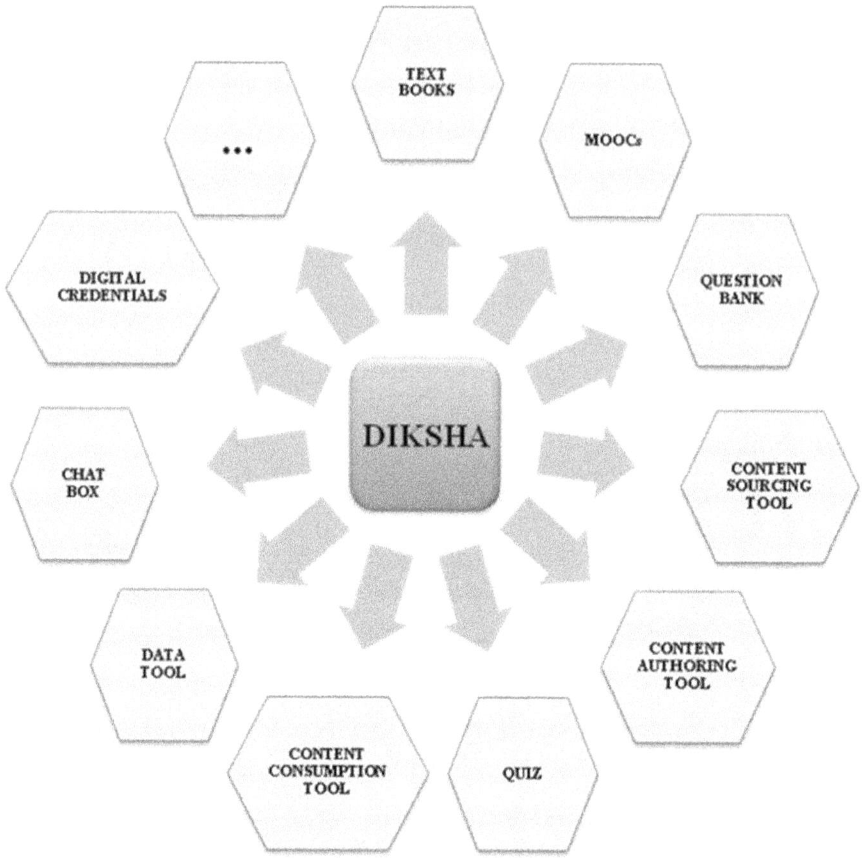

FIGURE 7.3 E-learning solutions on DIKSHA.

to their convenience. The contents are supported by reputed institutions and organizations like IITs, UGC, NPTEL and IGNOU. The portal is maintained by the Information and Library Network Centre (INFILIBNET).

7.4.1.8 e-ShodhSindhu

e-ShodhSindhu has been developed by the Ministry of Education. Government initiatives like UGC Infonet Digital Library Consortium, INDEST-AICTE consortium and NLIST merged together to form e-ShodhSindhu. It is a research-oriented platform which provides access to articles of more than 15,000 core and peer reviewed journals. It provides current as well as the archived data about journals of different disciplines from different publishers and their affiliates including the central universities.

7.4.1.9 Vidwan

Vidwan is the collection of profiles of eminent personalities in the areas of teaching and research in India. This project is developed and maintained by INFILIBNET with the support from the NME-ICT. This portal quickly provides access to subject experts, research scholars, funding agencies and policymakers. It is one access point to the leading experts and knowledge stakeholders. This is significant in selecting the panel of experts for various committees and organizations as well as the task forces of different ministries and governments which may be beneficial to evaluation and monitoring of policies and schemes.

7.4.1.10 UMANG

UMANG (Unified Mobile Application for New Age Governance) is the application to implement mobile governance in a systematic manner. This platform is an initiative by the Ministry of Electronics & Information Technology (MEITY). This platform provides a centralized solution for the implementation of different government services ranging from central government to state government services. This single mobile interface offers quick and easy access to all government services. The services of different governments are categorically shown in this application for better readability. It is based on the principle of One App, One Platform, Many Government Services connected government, efficient governance, and universal access and participation of citizens are some of key benefits of UMANG for citizens as well as government. This application also offers the option of e-PG Pathshala, which is a gateway for books and study material of NCERT. This application can be downloaded free of cost and provides access to more than 10 million electronic forms of books, audios, videos and other materials of different levels of primary and secondary education.

7.4.2 Initiatives of Indian States

The states and union territories of India started several schemes to cater to the needs of students during COVID-19 pandemic. Some schemes related to e-learning are discussed briefly as follows.

7.4.2.1 Delhi

The concept of e-learning is initiated by Delhi Government based on the theme that "Every home is a school and every parent a teacher". The role of parents in the time of COVID-19 has increased manifold. As the physical interaction between teacher and students was completely cut, the only persons with whom students can talk or involve in dialogue were their parents. There are efforts from the government to arrange for live online classes and digital entrepreneurship mindset classes. The online happiness classes were also arranged. The arrangement was also done for training the faculty members like Online Capacity Building Program (OCBP) and the lecture series Learning Never Stops (LNS).

7.4.2.2 Punjab

The government of Punjab initiated a different platform for the e-learning of students. A mobile application "iScuela Learn" was created to make learning fun for students. It focused on essential skills in reading, writing and language development. This application has a record hit of 10,000+ downloads as of January 2021. ICT computer labs, month wise, eBook distribution, YouTube channels (Edusat Punjab), and radio and cable TV channels are some of the efforts to tackle the pandemic situation and maintain the continuity of education for students.

7.4.2.3 Andhra Pradesh

The different e-learning schemes were introduced to provide quality education through the "Abhyasa" app of the education department. The art of learning smart was achieved through e-contents, toll-free audio and video calls for doubt sessions of students, radio and TV lessons, webinars and Facebook live training are other measures taken by the government to fill the academic gap which was created by the pandemic.

7.4.2.4 Bihar

The government of Bihar State started different programs for online learning. Education portal revived to provide digital platform to students. Facebook and WhatsApp learning promoted better reach of education to students. YouTube channels and TV channels dedicated for mobile learning are used to continue learning in crisis. Different applications like "Mera Bharat, Mera Vidyalaya" and "VidyaVahini Bihar" are utilized to disseminate knowledge to learners.

7.4.2.5 Jammu and Kashmir

AI-based educational chatbot, radio and TV classes as well as initiatives by voluntary teachers are some of the noble efforts for the wider availability of information to students. These efforts ensure a minimum environment to sustain learning during the COVID-19 crisis in Jammu and Kashmir.

All the above-mentioned state government schemes are the result of a consistent effort to sustain the continuity of the learning process in a seamless manner.

7.5 SCHEMES OF HIGHER EDUCATION

The higher education of any country is realized through the university and colleges. In India, the Department of Higher Education which falls under the Ministry of Education is responsible for the overall growth of the higher education sector. It also ensures the access of quality education for all kinds of learners. The prime objectives of higher education are to improve the gross enrolment ratio, expand universities to disadvantaged groups, remove regional barriers and improvement of overall infrastructure as well as global participation. The Government has initiated different schemes for inclusion and improvement of higher education.

7.5.1 Rashtriya Uchatter Sikasha Abhiyan (RUSA)

The purpose of this scheme is to provide and manage funds which will cover a total of 316 state public universities and 13,024 colleges. The central government fund will be utilized for developing the state university depending on the nature of state (i.e., general state, special category state or Union territory). Fund management is the priority under this scheme so that funds can be distributed in an optimized manner among different universities and colleges.

7.5.2 Integration of Persons with Disabilities in the Mainstream

The scheme covers around 50 polytechnics in India and provides grant-in-aid so that persons with disabilities can be integrated within the mainstream of higher education.

7.5.3 Pandit Madan Mohan Malviya Mission on Teachers and Training (PMMMNMTT)

The scheme is to enhance the quality of education across schools and colleges. The faculty development programmers (FDPs), short-term courses and conferences are organized to cultivate positive change among teachers and make them aware about new innovations and knowledge in their domain area.

7.6 NATIONAL EDUCATION POLICY 2020 AND SUSTAINABILITY IN TECHNOLOGY-DRIVEN EDUCATION

The National Education Policy of the Government of India is the policy that emphasized the importance of use of technology in teaching-learning process. The policy envisioned the idea of innovative aspects of modern technologies paving the way for robust and reliant framework for teaching environment.

7.6.1 Overview of National Education Policy 2020

The new National Education Policy (NEP-2020) is the policy approved by Government of India on July 29, 2020, and is the replacement of 1986 Education Policy. It provides a completely new vision to the education system encompassing from elementary education to higher education along with vocational education with an expectation to bring significant change in rural and urban India (Govinda, 2020). The NEP prioritizes retaining "core essentials" and focusing on "experiential learning and critical thinking". NEP advocates a four-year multidisciplinary undergraduate program with the option of exit at the end of every year. It includes both professional and vacation domain; after completion of first-year students will be given a certificate. In case of exit from any course after two years, a diploma will be awarded. At the end of third year, a bachelor's degree will be awarded; on completion of four years of courses the student will be awarded a four-year multidisciplinary bachelor's degree. The scheme of NEP tries to create an academic environment that matches with the international standard. The outcome of NEP may be assessed after four years when all the courses will be streamlined. There are lots of issues that are considered while implementing NEP like poor enrolment ratio of students, substandard quality of teachers, lack of motivation among students and growing unemployment due to lack of skills.

7.6.2 Objectives of National Education Policy

The sustainability of the education system is the prime importance for any country. To sustain the new challenges in the 21st century, the Government of India promoted the online mode of learning beside traditional teaching in National Education Policy. Some of the major objectives are as follows.

7.6.2.1 Gross Enrolment Ratio (GER)

The NEP framework is expected to achieve a GER of 50% by 2035. There will be an increase of 35 million new seats to higher education institutes (HEIs). The prime objective is to improve the overall enrolment of students in schools, colleges and universities (Kumar, 2021).

7.6.2.2 Flexible Multidisciplinary Approach

NEP policy suggested the holistic, multidisciplinary and flexible approach towards undergraduate courses with addition of different core courses, skills enhancement courses, general elective courses and interdisciplinary papers. The flexibility for multiple entry and exit points during the four-year undergraduate program enhances the productivity and employability of learners. The students have options to get a certificate, diploma, degree or interdisciplinary degree depending on the completion of the number of years in a particular course. This new approach has the provision for an Academic Bank of Credits (ABC), which is a repository of academic credits earned from different institutes. These credits earned by students can be transferred and counted towards the final degree. Moreover, online courses by different digital portals like SWAYAM and NPTEL have been duly recognized by the government and the credit earned through these online courses can be utilized in the degree program. These kinds of flexible arrangements will set up the excellent multidisciplinary education at par with global standard by fostering the research culture at the early stages of student careers.

7.6.2.3 Improved Institutional Architecture

All the HEIs have the capability to transform into centres of excellence having well-resourced centres and a vibrant multidisciplinary culture. They will act as research- and teaching-intensive institute. The concept of affiliation of college will be eliminated in next 15 years and graded autonomy will be granted to all colleges. This improved architecture of the institute will provide a holistic approach for academic excellence.

7.6.2.4 Promotion of Indian Languages

NEP recommended setting up of Indian Institute of Translation and Interpretations (IITI), a national institute for different languages like Pali, Persian, Prakrit, Sanskrit and all languages department in HEIs. These institutes will ensure the development of all Indian languages and preservation of Indian culture. There will be promotion of local languages as medium of instruction for different courses. The education will be globalized through collaboration of institutes and mobility of students and teachers across these collaborating institutes. Moreover, international universities will be facilitated to open their campuses in India.

7.6.2.5 Professional Education

NEP promotes professional education not only in specific domain-oriented universities and colleges but also in other universities so that a true multidisciplinary approach may be followed in all higher educational institutes.

7.6.2.6 Adult Education

NEP is targeting 100% youth and adult literacy across the country. For this purpose, learning centres can be revived in semi-urban and rural areas and awareness programs can be arranged to achieve total literacy in the country.

7.6.2.7 Improvement for Financing Education

Education is an important investment for development of any nation, and therefore, a significant amount of money is invested in the education sector. The finance in education comes from both government and non-government agencies for maintenance and improvement of educational institutes. NEP proposes enhanced contributions from central and state governments to improve the overall framework of the education system. Therefore, an adequate amount of funds is crucial to improve the quality outcome for a better future.

7.6.2.8 Online and Digital Education

Although a lot of digital tools and techniques for teaching-learning processes have been in place for the last few years, the pandemic situation of COVID-19 created a mixed reaction on the use of digital technologies for imparting knowledge in schools and colleges. Disasters create havoc in the lives of people (Todorova and Bjorn-Andersen, 2011). NEP laid emphasis on use of digital techniques for dissemination of knowledge. The different government schemes had already been initiated for online education. Technical awareness on the usage of different digital tools and their features is a challenge for real implementation of digital and online education in the country. For this, a National Education Technology Forum (NETF) is proposed in NEP for the mobility of ideas on use and implementation of online tools to improve learning and knowledge sharing. The proper integration of technology at all appropriate levels of education is needed for the realization of NEP.

7.6.3 Regulatory Bodies of Higher Education in India

These are significant changes in the administrative policy of higher education. Earlier UGC and AICTE were the statutory bodies for the governance of HEIs like universities and colleges. Higher Education Commission of India (HECI) is a top authority for higher education. HECI will have four independent agencies.

1. The *National Higher Education Regulatory Council* (NHERC) will provide the regulation and design the policy for implementation of quality education and research in HEIs.
2. The *General Education Council* (GEC) will be responsible for setting up standards and proposing ways to improve the quality of HEIs.
3. The *Higher Education Grants Council* (HEGC) will take care of the funds involved in setting up and maintaining HEIs.
4. The *National Accreditation Council* (NAC) will be held responsible for the accreditation of higher educational institutes as the standard norms provided by the statutory bodies. The grading of institutes will be a tedious process that will take care of all parameters required for a good-quality academic institute.

7.6.4 Challenges before National Education Policy

Some of the significant challenges before the implementation of salient features of NEP in higher education are enumerated as follows.

7.6.4.1 Inadequate Financial Support

One of the biggest concerns of higher education is the inadequate fund to the increasing demand of institutions. The Government is not able to meet the expenses of expanding the public education system. This results in mushrooming of private universities and colleges. These private institutions charge exorbitant fees from students, thus limiting the access of education to the elite section of society. This situation adversely impacts the small and rural public institutes. Therefore, keeping a check on the finances of private universities is the need of the hour. Moreover, financial adequacy is required to maintain and flourish the public universities.

7.6.4.2 Enrolment

The gross enrolment ratio (GER) of India was 27% in 2019–2020, which is an improvement from the year 2018–2019, which was 26.3% for the 18- to 23-year age group. This ratio is lower than world average (29.09%) and also lower than developed countries like the United States (60.0%), Germany (70.5%), and the United Kingdom (60.0%) and other emerging countries like Brazil (51.2%) and China (49.1%). Although GER is an indicator of participation of students, another measure (EER) can be used, which is defined as ratio of number of students enrolled in higher education to the number of students who have successfully completed 12th grade in the age group of 18–23 years. This may improve the precision for measuring the access of education. The NEP-2020 is expected to improve the GER up to 50% by the year 2030 in India. Increasing the number of schools and colleges, promoting degrees via distance or online mode along with accessibility and affordability are some of the measures given the government to improve the enrolment ratio. There is a need to improve the GER with emphasis on enrolment of rural population so that the concept of equity can be promoted in the society.

7.6.4.3 Appropriate Accreditation

Students from remote areas are lured into fake universities which do not meet the standards of higher education. The regulatory authorities like UGC and AICTE have a bigger responsibility to monitor and ensure the quality education through proper affiliation and recognition. The fake universities can be blacklisted or the course could be derecognized in case of poor quality of education.

7.6.4.4 Quality

The quality of HEIs is based on different factors like employability of students in terms of skilled manpower in the industry, availability of well qualified teachers, up-to-date syllabuses as per the market trends, adopting the evolving technology and so on. The learning content and depth of the subject are prerequisites for quality education. The intention to increase enrolment ratio without improving the infrastructure also adds to substandard quality. There is a need to improve the quality of education so that developing countries like India can keep up with international standards. Therefore, sustaining the quality of education is an evolving process and skilled manpower is the ultimate product of a good-quality education system.

7.6.4.5 Political Interference

Higher education is a critical issue in India. Although a large chunk of the government budget goes into higher education, still the public institutions are deprived of funds for improving their infrastructure. Political persons have influence on administration of educational institutes which exert their political pressure and therefore, a biased hierarchy of management is promoted leading to degradation of education in HEIs. Reservation in educational institutes is a contested topic. While one set of people consider caste-based reservation a necessity to remove the social disparities, others consider it as an exclusive system for upper-class individuals. A lot of persons affiliated to political parties are inclined towards exerting influence on the overall management of institutions. This situation will add to the degradation in quality of higher education. Moreover, student-level organizations backed up by political powers are involved in the rampant activism in higher institutions. As a result, the overall quality of education declines due to political interference.

Considering the above-mentioned challenges before NEP, it is quite imperative that NEP should be implemented in good spirit. NEP has the capability to transform India into a vibrant knowledge society by providing a holistic and interdisciplinary approach suitable for the 21st century. NEP leverages on progressive technologies and tools to bring out the capabilities of every student and make them future ready citizens.

7.7 MAJOR CHALLENGES AND GAINS DUE TO WEB-BASED LEARNING

In the education sector, the teaching-learning process has witnessed the increased dependency on digital services. This technology enabled teaching is not only considered as an alternative to traditional classroom teaching but also as a weapon to revolutionize distance teaching and providing a platform to bring online and offline teaching modes at the same levels. This created a concept of blended learning. However, no technology comes free of cost. There are always barriers for innovative implementation of technology.

Web-based learning provides a modern solution for ever-increasing and demanding situations in the education system. However, the implementation of web-based learning solutions has to face challenges in implementing real solutions.

Some of the significant challenges are discussed as follows.

7.7.1 Digital Infrastructure

Information and communication technologies facilities like digital devices in the form of desktop, laptops and smartphones are the building blocks to make a robust web-based teaching learning system. Even though digital devices have seen a significant growth in terms of sales, still a large chunk of potential students are deprived of digital gadgets. The availability of digital devices uniformly across all learners is a big challenge to make online learning a promising reality in a country like India. The National Education Policy 2020 recognizes the importance of using the innovative feature of technology while acknowledging its hidden risk and security breaches. NEP is providing a novel framework for a world-class quality education in the country, but implementation of providing an equitable society in terms of digital devices is somewhat nebulous. Providing a robust digital infrastructure is still a major challenge for implementation of web-based learning.

7.7.2 Uninterrupted Internet Connection

One of the foremost challenges for web-based learning is the availability of an uninterrupted internet connection. In a vast country like India the issue of providing net connection in the remotest part of India is really tough considering the current situation of internet usage. In the year 2020, India crossed over 749 million internet users and this figure is expected to reach over 1.5 billion users by 2040. This indicates a big potential market for internet services. Despite the large number of internet users, the internet penetration requires more time to come up equally. There is gender disparity in the access of the internet as the usage of internet is more in case of men as compared to women. Also, there is a gap among young and old adults so internet usage is low among older adults due to lack of internet literacy and psychological fear of using the internet. This situation can be improved by making the citizens more tech-savvy.

7.7.3 Digital Illiteracy and Lack of Motivation among Learners

Although a huge chunk of the population has digital devices still the motivation to utilize the full potential of smart devices is lacking. Most users are limited to selective features of smart devices. The fear of network vulnerability along with lack of right guidance to use app-based systems leads to underutilization of digital devices. Therefore, providing appropriate training of different features and applications at the grassroots level is a prerequisite to bridge the digital divide among the different sections of the society (Nedungadi et al. 2018). Besides the availability of digital devices, another important parameter in online learning is the motivation of the learners. The assessment of the learner's state of mind in an online learning system is important. There are a lot of novel ideas emerging in research to understand the motivation factor of learners, especially face detection and other related technology (Mukhopadhyay et al. 2020).

7.7.4 Lack of Trained Teachers

Teachers are at the center of any learning process system. The same is true for web-based learning systems. The teachers are reluctant to accept the change of methodology for imparting knowledge. However, this psychological barrier to stick to the traditional approach of learning is not going to succeed in the modern technology-driven ecosystem of knowledge sharing. The growing distance between the approach of pedagogical professionals and the students they teach is the harsh reality (Proyer et al. 2022). Training and transforming them into tech-savvy teachers is the biggest challenge while implementing web-based learning systems.

7.7.5 Interaction and Engagement in E-Learning Environment

From a teacher's perspective, interaction and engagement of learners in a web-based environment is a real concern. Also, the students are not prepared regarding the usage of online learning management systems (Parkes et al. 2014). Connecting with the students through a webcam and keeping them motivated throughout the learning session is a challenging task. Even though visual interaction through various audio-video tools helps in increasing the attention of learners, still simulating the feel of physical form of learning is a distant reality and a much more comprehensive approach is required to develop a highly interactive web-based learning model. Appealing and innovative interaction strategies need to be adopted in web-based systems to keep the learners motivated.

7.7.6 Evaluation and Feedback of Learning Process

The evaluation of students or learners and feedback from students are the two final but significant steps in any teaching learning process. There are numerous strategies in web-based learning that can be involved for online feedback, various types of quizzes, mock tests, and time-bound assignments, case studies and project based assessment in online mode. The online approach for all tasks related to assessment and feedback is a mandatory phenomenon to make web-based learning successful and effective for quality education especially in times of crisis like COVID-19 pandemic.

7.7.7 Decline in Soft Skills of Learners

Soft skills, which are the personal attributes of mixing with other people and how to behave in a group, play a significant role in the growth of a career of any learner. With the paradigm shift towards an online environment, there has been a decline in the soft skills of students. The improvement in soft skills of students in an online mode of learning is a big challenge for the educators. The students must be encouraged to apply agile methods to improve soft skills for their holistic development (Ha et al. 2019).

7.7.8 Practical Implementation through Virtual Labs

Web-based models perform less well than expected when it comes to real implementation of concepts throughout all academic disciplines and more specially in pure sciences and technology-oriented subjects. The core concepts can be explained and summarized easily through online techniques but the implementation of these concepts through virtual lab setup is a complex task. Although different free virtual labs like National Science Digital Library: ChemCollective Virtual Labs, PBS: Nova Labs, FlyLab JS, University of Colorado Boulder: Interactive Simulations for Science and Math, Reactor Lab, Line Rider, Chrome Music Lab, Zooniverse and so on have evolved over the past few years, it is too early to comment that the web-based model is fully equipped to face the challenges of lab simulation.

7.7.9 Lack of Comprehensive Educational Suite for the Web-Based Learning Model

A lot of Ed-Tech companies are struggling hard to be service providers for all educational needs of the web-based learning model. Even though Google seems to be ahead of other service providers in terms of different apps for learning, still the stakeholders are devoid of a clear-cut comprehensive suite to handle the overall requirement of this evolving web-based learning model. One-model-fits-all approaches in the real environment are missing. The web-based learning system needs to integrate with other ad hoc pieces of products to make a workable solution for web-based learning models.

7.8 MAJOR GAINS DUE TO WEB-BASED LEARNING

In modern times, technology is driving the world, and the same is true for web-based systems. The survival of the education system depends on the modern use of technical platforms which offer a sustainable and modern approach for the implementation of learning systems in the real world.

Some of the prime advantages of web-based learning are as follows.

7.8.1 Anytime, Anywhere, Anyone Approach

Web-based learning offers a plethora of options to learners through the anytime, anywhere, anyone (AAA) approach. It gives a huge advantage compared to the traditional chalkboard model of learning in terms of temporal, spatial and personal flexibility of knowledge givers and seekers in the whole new system of technology-oriented learning. Provided the different electronic gadgets like desktop, laptops, mobile phones and smartphones with internet connection, anyone can hook on to online learning platforms round the clock at any place and reap the benefits of knowledge dissemination via electronic medium and learn at their own pace. In these environments, students are independent to learn and communicate with instructors and peer students (Singh and Thurman, 2019).

7.8.2 Remove the Psychological Barriers between Tutor and Learner

In actual classroom settings, the majority of students encountered the problem of being bogged down by non-performance (or by lack of self-confidence). This fear of non-performance creates a psychological pressure and may result in poor performance (Bakar et al. 2020). These kinds of scenarios are absent in web-based learning and give an easy feeling to every learner to perform as per their potential.

7.8.3 Continuous Learning in Times of Crisis

There are different kinds of crisis-like situations throughout the world at different times such as human-made disasters and natural disasters. Presently, COVID-19 and its variants are creating havoc in the whole world. The web-enabled learning system provides a relief in these crises and continuity in learning can be maintained.

7.8.4 Objective Evaluation of Learners and Prompt Feedback

It becomes quite easy to evaluate students and assess the performance of students or learners using web-based techniques. The various online platforms have the facility of comprehensive evaluation of students. For instance, platforms like Google Classrooms, Google Forms, Google Hangouts and other related applications are widely used throughout the world by teachers to quickly prepare objective tests or quizzes. These applications can further be used for speedy evaluation and summarizing the results in a consolidated manner. On-the-spot feedback from students can be accessed and assignments can be taken (Basilaia et al. 2020).

7.8.5 Enhancing the International Dimension of Educational Services

Web-based learning systems are influencing users consistently. All the educational set-ups at national and international level are pressing hard to utilize the full potential of technology-based solutions. Web-based learning systems have the potential to break the boundaries among states and nations and promote a global environment. This global reach broadens the imagination of learners and provides an international exposure to all stakeholders.

7.9 CONCLUSION AND FUTURE SCOPE

The technology-driven education system is emerging as an alternative choice to the traditional teaching learning system. However, internet-based technology cannot be a replacement to traditional classroom teaching. There is a long way ahead before realizing the figurative benefits of digital learning. The collaborative initiatives of governments, Ed-Tech companies and various educational groups are required to provide valuable inputs for implementing web-based education at the grassroots level. The recent trends in artificial intelligence, machine learning and cloud computing gives an impetus for the next level of learning system. The internet of things will play a significant role in the delivery of information to the learners. The learners will be identified with their unique identification and customized learning will be in place in near future.

"The key lesson for others may be to embrace e-learning technology before disaster strikes!" (Pietro 2017). Technology gives a vibrant path to the journey of education but a rigorous and effective use of tools and techniques will add new dimensions to interaction between educators and learners. The conclusion is that teachers and learners should continue the use of evolving technology-based learning tools even during the normal course of teaching. Preparing the young generation for future challenges holds the key for effective implementation of a robust and technology centric education system that can sustain even during crisis situations such as COVID 19.

REFERENCES

Bakar, A., Shah, K., and Xu, Q. (2020). The effect of communication barriers on distance learners achievements. Revista Argentina de Clínica Psicológica, 29(5), 248.

Basilaia, G., Dgebuadze, M., Kantaria, M., & Chokhonelidze, G. (2020). Replacing the classic learning form at universities as an immediate response to the COVID-19 virus infection in Georgia. International Journal for Research in Applied Science & Engineering Technology, 8(III).

Cojocariu, V.-M., Lazar, I., Nedeff, V., & Lazar, G. (2014). SWOT analysis of e-Learning educational services from the perspective of their beneficiaries. Procedia-Social and Behavioral Sciences, 116, 1999–2003.

Dhawan, S. (2020). Online learning: A panacea in the time of COVID-19 crisis. Journal of Educational Technology Systems, 49(1), 5–22.

Govinda, R. (2020). NEP 2020: A critical examination. Social Change, 50(4), 603–607. https://doi.org/10.1177/0049085720958804.

Ha, N. H., Nayyar, A., Nguyen, D. M., & Liu, C. A. (2019). Enhancing students' soft skills by implementing CDIO-based integration teaching mode. In The 15th international CDIO conference (p. 569).

Huang, R. H., Liu, D. J., Tlili, A., Yang, J. F., Wang, H. H., Zhang, M., Lu, H., Gao, B., Cai, Z., Liu, M., Cheng, W., Cheng, Q., Yin, X., Zhuang, R., Berrada, K., Burgos, D., Chan, C., Chen, N. S., Cui, W., Hu, X., et al. (2020). Handbook on facilitating flexible learning during educational disruption: The Chinese experience in maintaining undisrupted learning in COVID-19 outbreak. Smart Learning Institute of Beijing Normal University.

Kumar, A. (2021). New education policy (NEP) 2020: A roadmap for India 2.0. In W. B. James, C. Cobanoglu, & M. Cavusoglu (Eds.), Advances in global education and research, 4, 1–8. USF M3 Publishing. www.doi.org/10.5038/9781955833042.

Mukhopadhyay, M., Pal, S., Nayyar, A., Pramanik, P. K. D., Dasgupta, N., & Choudhury, P. (2020, February). Facial emotion detection to assess Learner's State of mind in an online learning system. In Proceedings of the 2020 5th international conference on intelligent information technology (pp. 107–115).

Nedungadi, P. P., Menon, R., Gutjahr, G., Erickson, L., & Raman, R. (2018). Towards an inclusive digital literacy framework for digital India. *Education + Training*, 60(6), 516–528. https://doi.org/10.1108/ET-03-2018-0061.

Parkes, M., Stein, S., & Reading, C. (2014). Student preparedness for university e-Learning environments. The Internet and Higher Education, 25, 1–10. https://doi.org/10.1016/j.iheduc.2014.10.002.

Pietro, G. Di. (2017). The academic impact of natural disasters: Evidence from the L'Aquila earthquake. Education Economics, 26(1), 62–77. https://doi.org/10.1080/09645292.2017.1394984.

Proyer, M., Pellech, C., Obermayr, T., Kremsner, G., & Schmölz, A. (2022). First and foremost, we are teachers, not refugees: Requalification measures for internationally trained teachers affected by forced migration. European Educational Research Journal, 21(2), 278–292. doi:10.1177/1474904121989473.

Saxena, K. (2020). Coronavirus accelerates the pace of digital education in India. EDII Institutional Repository.

Singh, V., & Thurman, A. (2019). How many ways can we define online learning? A systematic literature review of definitions of online learning (1988–2018). American Journal of Distance Education, 33(4), 289–306.

Todorova, N., & Bjorn-Andersen, N. (2011). University learning in times of crisis: The role of IT. Accounting Education, 20(6), 597–599. https://doi.org/10.1080/09639284.2011.632913.

8 Framework to Integrate Education 4.0 to Enhance the E-Learning Model for Industry 4.0 and Society 5.0

Aditya Kumar Gupta, Vivek Aggarwal, Vinita Sharma, and Mohd Naved

8.1 INTRODUCTION

E-learning, or technology-based learning, is a kind of e-learning that is used to describe the digitization of the educational process. In a broader sense, multimedia assistance for educational processes using information and communication technology may be understood as this idea of improving educational quality. This term refers to education that is supported by modern technology and delivered through computer networks, usually the internet. This way, digital information can be sent to everyone in the school or community where it is used (Mital' et al., 2021).

Learning to adapt to an ever-changing, complicated environment requires new educational paradigms, as well as formal and informal strategies for teaching 21st-century skills. Research data from educational institutions should be used to continually update competence models throughout the globe, ensuring that they reflect current trends in the workplace. As a result of the technological revolution in communications, people's behavior has changed. The current and future dynamics of Industry 4.0 create a reality that necessitates modifications in Education 4.0 (Hussain, 2012; Sharma, 2019). The post-pandemic collateral harm of a society in total technological transformation necessitates educational models that include artificial intelligence, data management, omnipresent technology, robotics, and cloud computing.

For all fields of knowledge, it is possible to begin by reconstructing knowledge and the ways in which it might be put to use, not just in doing but also in understanding. It is also important to think about how research findings may be used to improve education in the 21st century. Problem resolution and a focus on social requirements can only be achieved if students are trained in sophisticated reasoning abilities, with scientific and critical thinking as well as the development of healthy habits for mental health and interpersonal interactions. Another educational problem is the employments of disruptive and intelligent technology that help students acquire both soft and hard skills simultaneously (Kirby, 2004).

The history of education from its inception is essential to understand currently adopted Education 4.0. Since antiquity, educational revolutions have taken place, as detailed by Ernst & Young LLP (Hartmann & Bovenschulte, 2013; Huk, 2021). It was during this first educational revolution (Education 1.0) that students were taught in a more casual, church controlled, exclusive manner. As a response to society's goal to make education more accessible and to train as many people as possible, the second educational revolution (Education 2.0) developed sophisticated and formal teaching methodologies for mass education (schools, colleges, universities). Information and communication technologies (ICTs) are increasingly being introduced into the classroom as part of the third educational revolution (Education 3.0).

DOI: 10.1201/9781003425779-8

8.1.1 Scope of the Study

Technology, personalized data, and our increasingly networked society are all a component of Education 4.0, a future vision for education. This educational revolution, which gives students the opportunity to choose and develop their own education, is characterized by its emphasis on dynamic, flexible, and adaptive learning routes. By embracing new technological and pedagogical developments, educational institutions will be better equipped to fulfil the unique needs of each student as part of the Education 4.0 movement (Ha et al., 2019).

Industry 4.0–guided industrial growth has had a direct impact on Education 4.0 development. Education must be linked to Industry 4.0 in order to prepare future generations for the fourth industrial revolution (IR 4.0). Technology advancements such as big data, cloud computing, biometrics, and 3D printing are just some of the innovations that might be included into Education 4.0 (Dominic et al., 2014; Mukhopadhyay et al., 2020). New educational reforms like Education 4.0 attempt to improve the way technology is incorporated into classroom learning in order to make it more relevant to the working world. When these two tendencies come together, a new paradigm known as Education 4.0 is born. Intended to better prepare students for the challenges of IR 4.0, this collection of educational innovations is intended as a guide for educators (Brink, 2021).

Education 4.0, which is the educational manifestation of IR 4.0 and its educational embodiment, required a few elements in order for students to obtain high levels of dexterity while utilizing cutting-edge technological instruments (Kumar et al., 2021; Mital' et al., 2021). Teachers were still unsure of what it meant to create teaching and learning processes in Education 4.0 (Jimoyiannis et al., 2013).

While this was going on, schools were being thrown into a world of digital and technical surroundings they didn't fully understand because of the COVID-19 problem (Brian and Ray, 2020). Two issues arose in higher education: a lack of knowledge of how to help Generation Z students enhance their cognitive talents and the reality that even the most powerful technical tools cannot completely replace a cognitive theory. For the advancement of e-learning models in business and society, this research is providing a framework for integration of Education 4.0. To continue with their courses in 2020, many institutions didn't require much preparation other than acquiring educational platforms, changing curriculum, and educating teachers and students on how to utilize them as a consequence of the educational plans for 2030. But for others, it has been and will continue to be difficult to execute the active learning technique in virtual contexts (Dominic et al., 2014).

8.1.2 Background of the Study

IR 4.0 focuses on the automation of the process, and digitalization and incorporating the information technology in all manufacturing process. IR 4.0 leads to the need for new skills for global graduate to fit into new system of product manufacturing and service creation. The skills which have been emphasized by Industry 4.0 and Society 5.0 are complex problem-solving, critical thinking, creativity, people management, teamwork, emotional intelligence, quick decision-making, service, and cognitive flexibility. Education 4.0 focuses on the active and collaborative learning which results in enhanced reflective decision-making skills of e-learners. Student-centric classes provide an opportunity for students to be active drivers for class discussions. Student achievement was driven by personalized learning embed e-learning and integration of Web 4.0 technologies in the teaching and learning process. This chapter investigates the different facets of Education 4.0 with regard to Industry 4.0 and Society 5.0. This chapter proposes a holistic framework for enhancing e-learners' skills for new emerging Industry 4.0 and Society 5.0.

8.1.3 Objectives of the Study

The literature review reveals research gap for e-learning student in form of academic engagement and social engagement. The chapter explores student perspective to propose a conceptual framework consisting of technological and humanistic factors, for developing a holistic learning and skills needed for the present-day job requirements in e-learning (Gupta & Dey, 2018). The framework has been explored for defining the critical success factors for future schools for formulating a new model of e-learning education for Industry 4.0 and Society 5.0 requirements. The chapter provides factors to overcome challenges in the implementation of e-learning for the policymakers, stakeholders, academic managers, teaching fraternity, industry, and supporting staff to create a conducive environment for students, to perform adaptively in the new technology is driven high skills job requirement by industry.

The objectives of the chapter are as follows:

- To investigate influence of Industry 4.0 on e-learning teaching and learning;
- To explain Education 4.0 for new technology-based e-learning enhancement;
- To integrate Industry 4.0 and Society 5.0 into Education 4.0 for lifelong skills;
- And, to understand the effect of Industry 4.0 and Society 5.0 on online teaching and learning.

8.1.4 Organization of the Chapter

The rest of the chapter is organized as follows: Section 8.2 highlights the concept of Education 4.0 and its links with educational innovation and Industry 4.0. Section 8.3 traces the evolution from Society 1.0 to Society 5.0, describing the role of technology in social development. Section 8.4 describes a theoretical model for online teaching and learning. It also discusses a model for integrated learning for distance education and e-learning. Section 8.5 discusses the effect of Industry 4.0 on online teaching-learning methods. Section 8.6 explains the framework of Education 4.0. Section 8.7 traces the evolution of Industry 1.0 to Industry 4.0, including the benefits of advancements in the success of distance learning. Section 8.8 discusses some of the commonly used learning management systems (LMS) used in technically oriented education. And, finally section 8.9 concludes the chapter with future scope.

8.2 EDUCATION 4.0

Education 4.0 depends on digital strategy, digital security, and a robust foundation for its success (Fukuyama, 2018). For the sake of defining the facilitators of digital revolution in Education 4.0, can be divided them into four broad categories: (1) technology; (2) organizational structures; (3) instruction in digital competence; and (4) students' soft and hard abilities. Education 4.0 relies on learning analytics to forecast students' future performance and keep them improving over time. An educational model that incorporates Industry 4.0's educational components is the first step in creating a more flexible system that includes pedagogical techniques and technology that aids learning (Carayannis & Morawska-Jancelewicz, 2022; Sułkowski et al., 2021).

8.2.1 Education 4.0 to Educational Innovation

IR 4.0 has profound effects on educational innovation. In IR 4.0, the human-machine interface is made broader by artificial intelligence (AI) and digital physical frameworks (Giang et al., 2021). An innovation revolution has resulted in a new educational model for the future, called "Education 4.0." As a consequence of IR 4.0, many human jobs will be taken over by intelligent robots. As a response, education should emphasize skills and knowledge that aren't easily replaced by machines.

In light of the innovative disruption that led to Education 4.0, which stresses educational progress and skill, future learning will be individualized, hyperintelligent, portable, transnational, and virtual (Giang et al., 2021; Sharma, 2019). As technology continues to advance into the 21st century, it is transforming the landscape of education and instructional advances into new types of

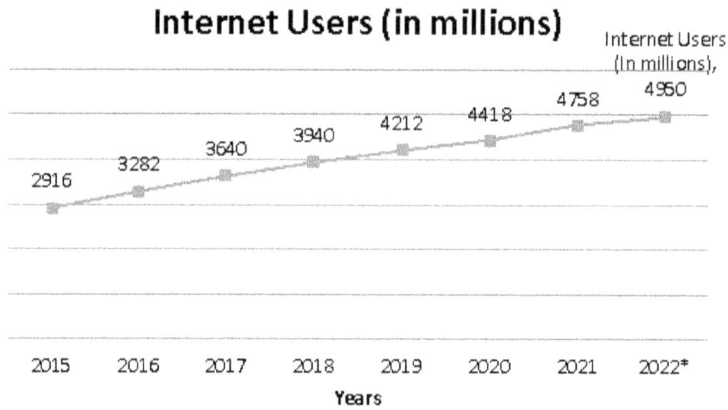

FIGURE 8.1 Internet users in the world.

Source: Bank, 2020; ITU, 2021; Statistica, 2021.

computerized teaching methods. Examples of these new computerized teaching methods include AI, big data, distributed computing, mobile devices, the internet of things (IoT), augmented reality (AR), and virtual reality (VR).

Each industrial revolution has had a profound impact on our lives, career, and relationships. Managers and staff alike must quickly adjust to this ever-shifting environment. There is no avoiding risk and innovation; therefore, they must be prepared and receptive to new ideas and methods. It is impossible to compete in this continually changing world without enough knowledge and the ability to continually adapt (Mohamed Hashim et al., 2022). Managers must lead the company in a way that encourages people to alter their long-term outlooks, ideas, and attitudes. As a strategy, organizations need to know how to use knowledge management (KM) ideas to improve system and process performance.

With the merging of humanities and social sciences, and science and technology, there will be less distinction between these fields. Ipoh, Malaysia, is a restaurant that employs "celebrity robots" instead of waiters and waitresses to serve clients (Shahroom & Hussin, 2018). This demonstrates that the usage of human service is reduced as a result of service automation. Because not everyone has the same level of access to and use of technology, there will always be inequity in society (Abdon et al., 2007). More than 7.5 billion people exist on the planet, yet only 4.95 billion (about 60%) have access to the internet.

8.3 SOCIETY 5.0

A human-centered society is the ultimate goal of Society 5.0. A good quality of life for all citizens is a primary aim of economic growth and community issue resolution (Morawska-Jancelewicz, 2021). Society 5.0 provides the required commodities and services to guarantee that everyone receives what they need, regardless of their location, age, gender, language, or any other barrier. To achieve this aim, it is required to combine cyber and real (physical) data in order to generate high-quality data that can be used to develop novel solutions to society's problems. There are 17 objectives and 169 specific targets and timeframes specified by the UN as part of the Sustainable Development Goals (SDGs) or Sustainable Development Agenda (SDA). The goal of the SDGs is the same as that of Society 5.0 (Rêgo et al., 2021). In order to meet the challenges of the fourth industrial revolution and actualize Society 5.0, it is critical to assess educational preparation (Riviezzo et al., 2020).

The term "Society 5.0" was proposed in the Fifth Science and Technology Basic Plan as a future society that Japan and world should aspire to (Sułkowski et al., 2021). There is a need of Society

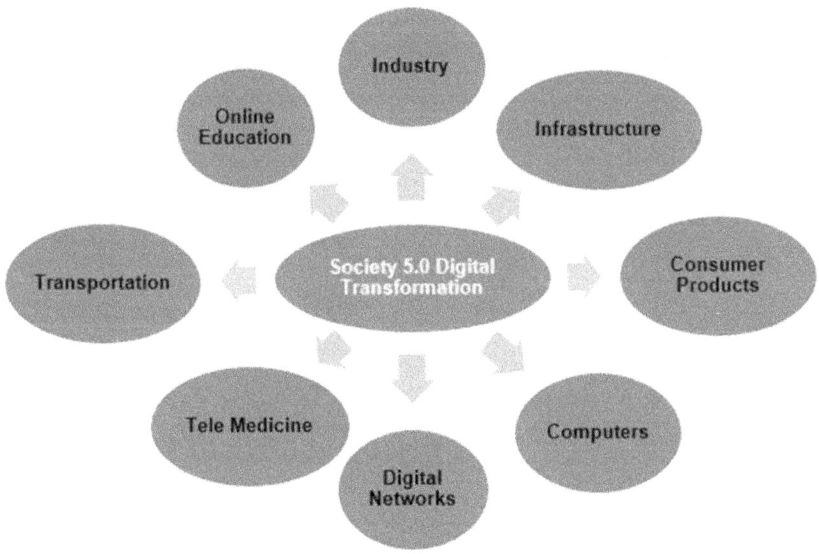

FIGURE 8.2 Digital transformations in Society 5.0.

5.0 as it ensures no human is left behind, as it emphasizes well-being and happiness of humans. It is a human-centric approach which balances the economic advancements with the resolution of social problems that highly integrates cyber space and physical space. The current society which is prevailing is Society 4.0 and is called as informational society and prior to Society 4.0 we have Society 3.0, Society 2.0 and Society 1.0 which are termed the industrial society, farming society, and hunting society, respectively.

8.3.1 Significance of Society 5.0

The convergence of cyberspace and physical space is high in Society 5.0. In the past, people would use the internet to access a cloud service for storing data in cyberspace and search for, retrieve, and analyze information or data. In Society 5.0, a massive amount of data from sensors in physical space is collected and stored in cyberspace. This massive data is evaluated by AI in cyberspace and the results are given back to humans in physical space in various forms (Dineva, 2022; Sharma, 2019). People, things, and systems are all connected in cyberspace In Society 5.0, and ideal solutions obtained by AI transcending human capabilities are sent back into physical space. This method adds value to industry and society in ways that was not before feasible.

In Society 5.0, new value created via innovation will overcome regional, age, gender, and language disparities, allowing for the provision of finely customized products and services to different individual requirements and latent demands. It will be feasible to create a society that can both encourage economic progress and find answers to social problems in this manner.

Society 5.0 achieves advanced convergence between cyberspace and physical space, allowing AI-based on big data and robots to do or assist as an agent in the work and adjustments that humans have previously performed (Krishnan et al., 2022; Gupta & Ramchandani, 2019). This liberates humans from mundane tasks and tasks at which they are not particularly skilled, and it enables the provision of only those products and services that are required for people who require them at the

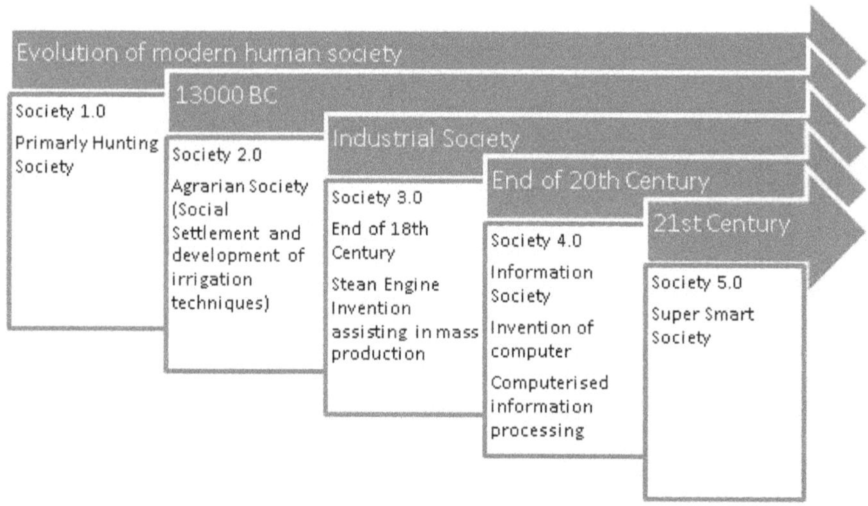

FIGURE 8.3 Evolution of Society 1.0 to Society 5.0.

Source: Chin, 2019.

time they are required, thereby optimizing the entire social and organizational system (Rodríguez-Abitia & Bribiesca-Correa, 2021).

8.3.2 Evolution of Society 1.0 to Society 5.0

There are various phases of civilization that may be traced back to human history. In Society 1.0, individuals hunt and gather to maintain a healthy relationship with the natural world. In addition, agricultural cultivation, better organizational structures, and country development all had a role in the emergence of Society 2.0 (Fukuyama, 2018). As a result, Society 3.0 is a society that encourages industrialization and the mass production of a wide range of goods for human needs. When people see the benefits of interconnecting intangible assets as part of an information network, they begin to envision a "Society 4.0" future. Society 5.0, a continuance of Society 4.0, strives to create a society oriented on human well-being at the moment.

8.4 THEORETICAL MODEL FOR ONLINE TEACHING-LEARNING

It is hard to develop a single philosophy of online education because of these two concepts. For example, despite their growing usage in conventional face-to-face and online learning contexts, blended learning approaches do not readily fit into the distant education paradigm, as one example.

How do you come up with a theory for online education if you know it would be a very difficult endeavor? For as long as anybody can remember, online education has been concerned with offering access to educational experiences and are at least as flexible as campus-built education in terms of time and place.

8.4.1 Anderson's Model

Anderson was able to build a sound theoretical foundation for online education by examining each of these four perspectives (Dziuban et al., 2015). He said that the internet has transformed from a text-based medium to one that accommodates and makes all kinds of content freely available (Anderson, 2009). The internet's connecting capabilities are best suited to human storage and retrieval of

FIGURE 8.4 Anderson's online learning model.

information. Apart from that, as he accurately said, the confluence of four overlapping lenses defines effective learning environments: the focus on community, knowledge, learners, and evaluation.

Anderson assembled these three parts into a model. He emphasized that community/collaborative models and self-paced learning are incompatible (Cifuentes, 2021). Because of the intense interactions between teachers and students, community/collaborative models are difficult to maintain. Self-paced learning models are made so that students can study on their own, so there is less contact between students and teachers.

8.4.2 An Integrated Framework for E-Learning

To be clear, no face-to-face contact is included in the Anderson model of blended learning, which is vital to remember. As a result, the quest for an integrated paradigm for online learning might be seen through the lens of face-to-face education and even hybrid learning. Pedagogy and technology were integrated in one way or another in each of these approaches. This author's blending with pedagogical purpose model was one of the models included in the study. In this model, pedagogical goals and activities guide the methods used by faculty members, including online technology (Anderson, 2009; Dziuban et al., 2015).

The model also shows that a broad variety of pupils could benefit best by combining the goals, activities, and techniques across several modalities. In order to create learning modules, the model consists of six fundamental pedagogical objectives and techniques for attaining them. Additional modules may be included as required and when suitable into the model, which is designed to be adaptable. As a paradigm, pedagogy drives the practices that are most effective for supporting student learning in this model. The modules may or may not be depicted as intersecting or overlapping, depending on the technique used. Consider the possibility of including some reflection into the collaborative action, for example. The collaborative teams' work should be evaluated by requesting that they examine their own work.

FIGURE 8.5 Anderson's blending with pedagogical purpose model.

Source: Picciano, 2009.

8.4.3 Effect of Industry 4.0 over Online Teaching-Learning Methods

Tactics that encourage students to think critically and creatively about what they are doing are called "active learning" strategies. As a consequence of this method's focus on students' skills, the teaching-learning process must follow a complex cognitive taxonomy that stimulates higher-order thinking. Education 4.0, which is the educational manifestation of IR 4.0 and its educational embodiment, required a few elements in order for students to obtain high levels of dexterity while utilizing cutting-edge technological instruments.

To reimagine the teaching-learning process, researchers worked with Generation Z engineering students for three years using the Anderson & Krathwohl Taxonomy of Learning (A&KTL). A few changes were made to the teaching method in 2020 in light of the COVID-19 crises. Andragogic didactics for first- and second-year students helped them develop soft skills, while technology changes for third-year students helped them to develop an awareness of their own metacognitive processes (Caratozzolo et al., 2021). College students and faculty both need to be taught a broad variety of 21st-century abilities (cognitive, social, and emotional competencies), according to a new wave of research.

In today's virtual educational settings, where training, learning, upgrading, and reskilling are all done using digital technology, a new kind of literacy called "digital literacy" is required. According to the Organisation for Economic Co-operation and Development and the World Economic Forum, new cognitive tools are needed to fully develop the soft skills of Generation Z students (Soffel, 2016). Education 4.0 demands that learning content and experiences provide students with high-quality learning skills that include the ability to think critically about information, to propose innovative and creative solutions to complex disruptive problems, and think analytically through non-routine pathways. The skills and abilities required for learning IR 4.0 skills for students may be summarized into four categories: ethical, digital, business, and soft skills (Tsiligiris & Bowyer, 2021). The attempts of developing nations to provide fundamental human needs, such as education, are fraught with difficulties. Examples include a lack of space and facilitators (Kituyi and Kyeyune, 2012), among others. Students are flocking to universities and colleges throughout the country because of changes to the educational system, which have allowed many youngsters of school age to receive free education at all levels except tertiary and university (Kituyi and Kyeyune, 2012). Higher education institutions

(HEIs) have found it very challenging to educate and manage students on the current infrastructure. Distance education has proven to be a viable alternative.

Due to the rise in use of e-learning, teaching in HEIs has become more cost-effective. Classes have utilized slide projectors and television since the 1950s. The University of Illinois in the United States was one of the world's first institutions to offer online courses in 1960. There was no internet at the time, but students began forming a learning network using inter-connected computer terminals. In 1984, Toronto University provided the first online course. In 1986 the Electronic University Network was created using DOS and the Commodore 64. Three years later, the University of Phoenix was the first to offer online bachelor's and master's degrees. This marked the beginning of a revolution whose potential at the time was unknown to the general public, but which would make education more accessible than anyone could have imagined.

For a long time, All India Radio and Doordarshan have televised educational recordings for higher education and school-aged children. Many educational institutions, including the UGC, IGNOU, and NCERT, utilize All India Radio and Doordarshan. However, learners must interact with the broadcasts because they are all recorded (Sarkar, 2020). In 1994, ISRO began offering teleconferencing at IGNOU's headquarters in New Delhi. Using a phone line, one-way video, and two-way audio enabled live learner interaction. Many online courses in India benefited from teleconferencing, including management, computer science, and teacher training. ISRO's teleconferencing service at IGNOU has been used for years by numerous educational institutions, government, and private organizations. In 2000, teleconferencing was added to a Gyandarshan educational channel. It became GD-interactive alongside other channels.

Two-way video communication was required. ISRO, MHRD, and IGNOU launched EDUSAT, a satellite designed by the late President APJ Abdul Kalam, in 2005. Due to insufficient communication technology, EDUSAT was unable to meet the needs as expected. Previously, one-to-many video communication in both directions was difficult. Teachers and students are fortunate to have so many two-way mobile applications now. But, the challenge is to improve the utility of online education, not technology.

A broad variety of stakeholders, including students, teachers, technologists, and policymakers, are affected by the implementation of e-learning in HEIs. Some of the issues that commonly come up throughout the process include costs, quality management, and business culture (The International Encyclopedia of Higher Education Systems and Institutions, 2020). The base of knowledge for basic professional comprehension and the acquisition of new skills for in-depth information acquisition must be maintained by HEIs by rethinking their roles, revising their curricula in response to shifting demands, and providing the services, methods, and services that their customers demand. HEIs in poor nations are falling behind their counterparts in wealthy countries when it comes to taking use of the many advantages that ICTs provide (Aggarwal et al., 2022; Fukuyama, 2018; Ohei & Brink, 2019). These include Moodle, Blackboard, and KEWL (Knowledge Environment for Web-based Learning). Despite the best efforts of universities in developing and underdeveloping India, they are plagued by problems of inefficiency and ineffectiveness. This is due to the tremendous growth in undergraduate enrollment and the shortage of space. Because of chronic issues including rising demand and diminishing investments, brain drain, utilizing working conditions, and restricted access to global knowledge bases, efforts made to solve these difficulties have been unsuccessful (Shirkhani et al., 2016; Gupta & Dey, 2018).

Many e-learning systems lack the adaptability required by instructors to accommodate the needs of a wide range of students in a number of contexts. Because of this, HEIs in underdeveloped countries have yet to maximize the advantages of e-learning platforms. A lack of adequate frameworks, for example, may be to blame for this failure to fully integrate e-learning into educational institutions (Kituyi and Kyeyune, 2012; Mafuna & Wadesango, 2012). Figure 8.7 displays a few of the Industry 4.0--related technologies. ICTs are the backbone of IR 4.0, enabling tomorrow's cutting-edge technology and educational environments (Mourtzis, 2018; Shahroom & Hussin, 2018).

Systems, tools, and virtual learning environments for industrial engineering and management may all benefit from this technical basis (Dalenogare et al., 2018). Recent trends in modernizing the educational environment have concentrated mostly on digitalization of all physical assets and their integration with systems, which is part of the Industry 4.0 idea that has emerged in recent years. There are four fundamental components that form the foundation of the Industry 4.0 idea with the integration of digital technologies (Mital' et al., 2021):

- Receipt and organization of information in the form of a database or spreadsheet;
- Implementation and effective flow management;
- Virtualization of processes and systems;
- Processing and system digitization in real life.

Even while digitalization of educational processes in technical disciplines is a difficult but important process due to the following reasons, it is not an exception. E-learning, or technology-based learning, is a sort of digitization of the educational process. More broadly, this concept may be seen as a sort of ICT-enhanced multimedia support for the educational process, with the ultimate objective of improving the quality and accessibility of education. Computer networks are used by educational institutions and communities that are supported by current technologies and deployed as part of such communities' educational infrastructures as "educational technology." When teaching online, there are two main kinds of teaching methods that may be used:

- *Synchronous teaching*: a virtual classroom where instruction takes place in real time with students and teachers connected to the network at all times.
- *Asynchronous teaching*: through email or online discussion boards, between the instructor and student. It is possible to transfer study materials on a computer and execute a portion of the teaching process while offline.

8.4.3.1 Advantages of E-Learning

The following are some of the primary benefits of using e-learning:

- The ability to use a variety of instructional strategies;
- Personalization of the research to suit the needs of each student;
- Ease of keeping track of things;
- Making sure that computer literacy is increased;
- Increasing the quantity of information to be orientated in on classroom desks;
- Providing more adaptability in the teaching process and a stronger focus on students' individual projects;
- Enabling greater and more rapid access to information;
- Improving quality in extracurricular activities, closer ties with students;
- Establishing external cooperation and direct instructional collaboration with overseas institutions.

8.4.3.2 Disadvantages of E-Learning

The following are some of the primary drawbacks of online education:

- Increasing pressure on the technology;
- It takes a long time to get the materials ready for use;
- A time-consuming task management process;
- The study of books other than computer-presented materials is no longer required.

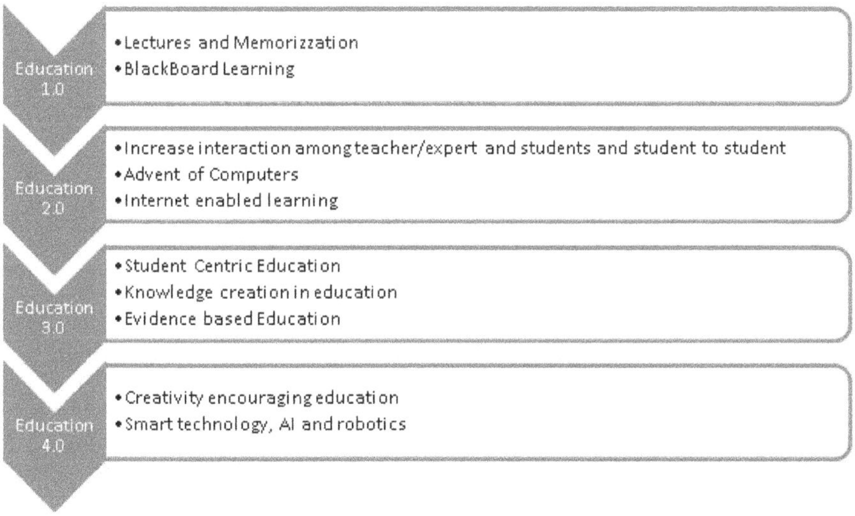

FIGURE 8.6 Education 4.0.

Source: Shahroom & Hussin, 2018.

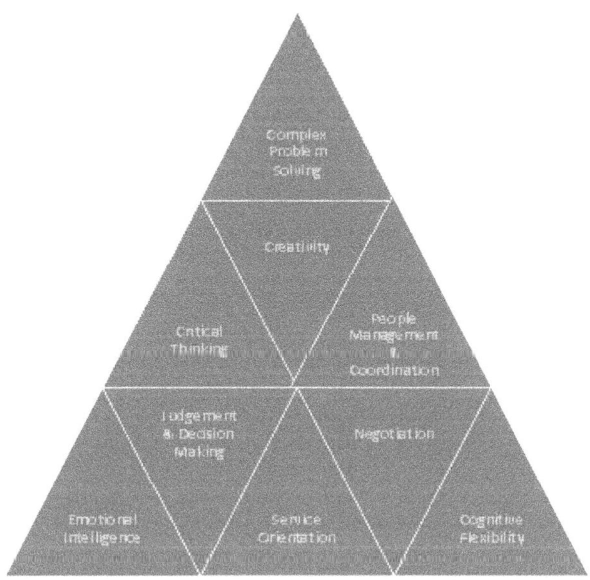

FIGURE 8.7 Education 4.0 skills.

8.5 EDUCATION 4.0 FRAMEWORK

Education 4.0 is a preferred method of education that aligns with IR 4.0. This industrial revolution focuses on smart technology, AI, robotics, the IoT, augmented and virtual reality, robotics, and so forth, all of which now impact our daily lives. For universities to continue producing successful graduates, they must prepare students for a world in which cyber-physical systems are pervasive in all industries. This requires teaching students about this technology as part of the

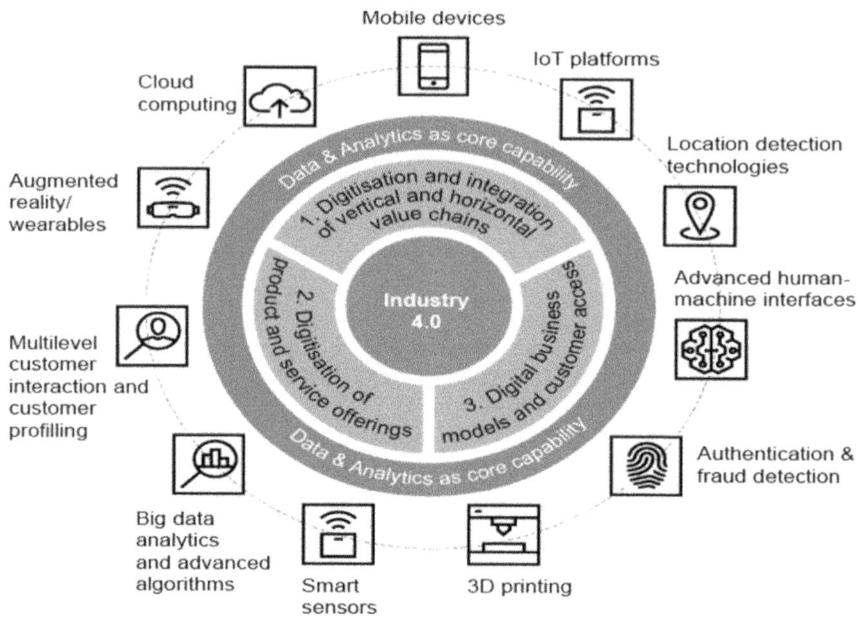

FIGURE 8.8 Industry 4.0 framework.

Source: PricewaterhouseCoopers, 2018.

curriculum, altering the entire approach to learning, and utilizing this technology to enhance the college experience.

When HEIs and classrooms were fully digitalized according to Industry 4.0 principles, a new movement known as Education 4.0 emerged (Thames and Schaefer, 2017). An Education 4.0 framework will assist students gain the required skills and competencies for the new workplace based on IR 4.0 via the development of digital and/or online education. Engineers and managers need access to advanced, lifetime training thanks to the IoT, cloud computing, virtual and augmented reality, big data, and learning analytics. Learning analytics have been demonstrated in a number of studies to immediately provide information on how to enhance classroom teaching (Sahlaoui et al., 2021; Shahroom & Hussin, 2018; Thames and Schaefer, 2017).

Learning analytics may have a positive impact on big, complicated organizations such as colleges and universities. When it comes to educational technology, "Education 4.0" refers to the inclusion of Industry 4.0 processes and technology. The ultimate purpose of utilizing this technology and adopting new methods is to place students at the center of the education process, shifting the focus from teaching to learning.

8.6 EVOLUTION OF INDUSTRY 1.0 TO INDUSTRY 4.0

On the way from Industry 1.0 to Industry 4.0, we'll need a few key technologies, as shown in Figure 8.8 (PricewaterhouseCoopers, 2018). Systems, tools, and virtual learning environments for industrial engineering and management may all benefit from this technical basis.

- Product and manufacturing projects and work plans supported by computerized systems employing computer-aided design and manufacturing (CAD/CAM);
- Integrating engineering and logistics systems in product development and manufacture to enable information exchange systems (Nayyar & Kumar, 2020);

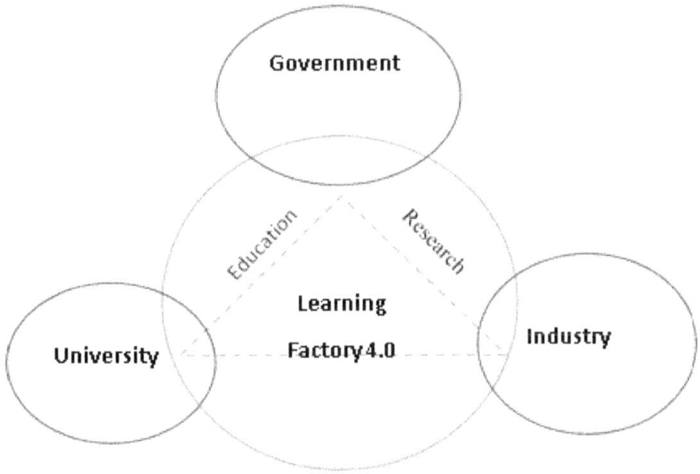

FIGURE 8.9 Learning factory 4.0.

Source: Veza et al., 2015; Vijayan et al., 2019.

- Digital automation infrastructure based on sensors embedded in automated systems for monitoring and data collecting and analysis;
- The term "flexible production lines" refers to the use of digital automation and sensor technology in manufacturing processes (such as radio frequency identification [RFID] in product components and raw materials);
- Finite element methods, computational fluid dynamics, and other methods are used to create virtual models for engineering projects and to commission the design of systems based on models, and the synthesized models mimic the attributes of the real-world models they replicate;
- Big data gathering and analysis that uses predictive analytics, data mining, statistical analysis, and other methods to analyses enormous amounts of data.

8.7 LMS SYSTEMS USED IN TECHNICALLY ORIENTED EDUCATION

Technological advances have changed instructors' educational practices, bringing new perspectives on education. The internet is preferred in education due to its technological advantages and ability to reach a vast population. The school system is undergoing major changes due to technological advances. An LMS enables e-learning management, student monitoring, delivery, learning tracking, testing, communication, registration, and scheduling. Many of the LMS are free (e.g., Moodle, Chamilo, Google Classroom) and others are paid (e.g., Blackboard, Microsoft Teams) (Cavus, 2010). Moodle is a popular and effective open-source LMS. Let's have a quick summary of some of the most often used software solutions (free versions) in the field of technical education, including their basic specs.

8.7.1 Chamilo

This software solution is a freely accessible system that focuses on enhancing global access to education. This software is most frequently utilized in the educational process because it:

- Releases introductory materials on the topic;
- Increases the availability of study materials;

- Provides design and development of interactive learning tools and assessments;
- Generates mutual respect between students and teachers;
- Accumulates homework and projects for the semester.

8.7.2 Google Classroom

Since 2014, Google has offered a free e-learning software solution called Google Classroom. Users that have a Google account may access the system. Teachers may swiftly design and manage specified projects using this program, and the platform delivers standard feedback. E-learning and mobile learning education may be accessed through a web browser as well as a mobile application on the platform. In order to facilitate student-teacher online connectedness, the platform does not allow students or teachers to enter tests or create a discussion forum.

8.7.3 Moodle

Moodle is a set of tools for developing online learning environments and courses. Blue trends and innovative approaches to teaching are at the heart of this continually developing endeavor (Mital' et al., 2021). Blue color is associated with learning situations which are challenging and it's based on primary premise is the belief that students gain the most through classroom interaction, both inside and between the actual study materials. GNU General Public License open-source software is offered free of charge with the system. The system's ability to create courses in almost any way is one of its most valuable features. It may be tailored to suit the preferences of every individual user. Moodle was the preferred learning platform of 245 countries in 2022. Most registrations are in Spain, the United States, Mexico, Germany, Brazil, France, India, Indonesia, Colombia, and Russia (Moodle, 2022). The platform had 327 million users in July 2022. Distance learning will likely become the norm.

8.8 CONCLUSION AND FUTURE SCOPE

Digitalization in education is not the only area to be affected by the fast growth of technology. Industry 4.0 is reshaping the world's living and working standards, and many traditional educational styles and learning methodologies are no longer relevant. Disruption is a must for every revolution. It shatters traditions, habits, relationships, ways of thinking, and, of course, the way we educate. As technology has advanced, societies have experienced significant alterations, resulting in structural changes and a shift away from previous forms of authoritarianism. Pedagogy geared at the working class has been a key part of education policy since the industrial revolution (Geschwind et al., 2019). Research on digital technologies in Education 4.0 and their impact on Society 5.0 and the Economy 5.0 are being evaluated as part of the present study. One of the most important items on the to-do list is to determine the best course of action for future study into how students learn digital technologies and how educational institutions can adapt. In light of the recent advancement of digital technology in a wide range of sectors, academics are looking for new ways to enhance education.

At the beginning of the new century, the term "Education 2.0" was used to describe the use of technology in the educational process. At this point, the instructor was not only committed to teaching but also served as a moderator to encourage student engagement in the classroom and uncover the hidden abilities of their pupils via group projects (Gupta et al. 2022).

Many companies across the world are now creating intelligent instruction design and digital platforms that employ AI to deliver learning, assessment, and feedback to students, discover gaps in knowledge, and divert students to subject adjacencies when necessary. Teaching and learning are about to undergo a paradigm shift. Traditional education has severe holes in its foundation. Here's another wonderful illustration of how our culture is steadily making its way up the Maslow pyramid (Singh et al., 2022).

A timeline used to show how education has evolved through time. The first industrial revolution in England at the end of the 18th century generated a new paradigm of existence, transforming the economic, political, social, cultural, and environmental foundations of nations in a profound way (Hamilton Ortiz et al., 2020). A new educational paradigm was born, one based on the notion of economic growth and geared toward meeting those demands. Educational institutions, in order to keep their brand image intact and evolving, needed to integrate their process with new age technologies for creating a skilled workforce for Industry 4.0 and Society 5.0 (Chin, 2019). Brand building activities to tap students need to rework with the integration of technologies applications for learning and development of the various stakeholders.

REFERENCES

Abdon, B. R., Ninomiya, S., & Raab, R. T. (2007). eLearning in higher education makes its debut in Cambodia: Implications of the provincial business education project. *International Review of Research in Open and Distance Learning, 8*(1), 1–14.

Aggarwal, V., Dash, S., Yadav, P. D., & Gupta, A. K. (2022). Role of ICT enabled cloud learning management system tools in fostering entrepreneurship amongst youth. In *2022 2nd International Conference on Innovative Practices in Technology and Management (ICIPTM)*, 508–515. https://doi.org/10.1109/ICIPTM54933.2022.9754158.

Anderson, T. (2009). The theory and practice of online learning: Towards a theory of online learning. *Electronic Journal of E-Learning, 38*(4).

Bank, W. (2020). *World {Bank}*. data.worldbank.org.

Brian, D., & Ray, P. D. (2020). The rise of online learning during the COVID-19 pandemic I world economic forum. In *World Economic Forum Covid Action Platform* (pp. 1–8). www.weforum.org/agenda/2020/04/coronavirus-education-global-covid19- online-digital-learning/.

Brink, C. (2021). The responsive university and the crisis in South Africa. In *The Responsive University and the Crisis in South Africa*. https://doi.org/10.1163/9789004465619.

Caratozzolo, P., Alvarez-Delgado, A., & Hosseini, S. (2021). Creativity in criticality: Tools for generation Z students in STEM. In *IEEE Global Engineering Education Conference, EDUCON, 2021-April*, 591–598. https://doi.org/10.1109/EDUCON46332.2021.9454110.

Carayannis, E. G., & Morawska-Jancelewicz, J. (2022). The futures of Europe: Society 5.0 and industry 5.0 as driving forces of future universities. *Journal of the Knowledge Economy, 0123456789*. https://doi.org/10.1007/s13132-021-00854-2.

Cavus, N. (2010). The evaluation of Learning Management Systems using an artificial intelligence fuzzy logic algorithm. *Advances in Engineering Software, 41*(2), 248–254.

Chin, E. (2019). Society 5.0: Aiming for a new human-centered society. In *Linkedin.com*. www.linkedin.com/pulse/society-50-aiming-new-human-centered-edward-chin.

Cifuentes, L. (2021). A guide to administering distance learning. In *A Guide to Administering Distance Learning*. https://doi.org/10.1163/9789004471382.

Dalenogare, L. S., Benitez, G. B., Ayala, N. F., & Frank, A. G. (2018). The expected contribution of Industry 4.0 technologies for industrial performance. *International Journal of Production Economics, 204*. https://doi.org/10.1016/j.ijpe.2018.08.019.

Dineva, S. (2022). Intelligent e-Learning with new web technologies. *SSRN Electronic Journal, 7*(1). https://doi.org/10.2139/ssrn.3983423.

Dominic, M., Francis, S., & Pilomenraj, A. (2014). E-Learning in web 3.0. *International Journal of Modern Education and Computer Science, 6*(2). https://doi.org/10.5815/ijmecs.2014.02.02.

Dziuban, C., Moskal, P., Thompson, J., Kramer, L., DeCantis, G., & Hermsdorfer, A. (2015). Student satisfaction with online learning: Is it a psychological contract? *Journal of Asynchronous Learning Network, 19*(2). https://doi.org/10.24059/olj.v19i2.496.

Fukuyama, M. (2018). Society 5.0: Aiming for a new human-centered society. *Japan Spotlight*, August, 5(27), 47–50.

Geschwind, L., Kekäle, J., Pinheiro, R., & Sørensen, M. P. (2019). Responsible universities in context. In *The Responsible University: Exploring the Nordic Context and Beyond*. https://doi.org/10.1007/978-3-030-25646-3_1.

Giang, N. T. H., Hai, P. T. T., Tu, N. T. T., & Tan, P. X. (2021). Exploring the readiness for digital transformation in a higher education institution towards industrial revolution 4.0. *International Journal of Engineering Pedagogy, 11*(2). https://doi.org/10.3991/IJEP.V11I2.17515.

Gupta, A., & Dey, A. (2018). Influence of student engagement on learning gains. *Amity Business Review, 17*(2), 85–86.

Gupta, A. K., Aggarwal, V., Yadav, P. D., Naved, M., Dash, S., & Chandwani, T. (2022). Effectiveness of technological based classroom engagement. In *2022 3rd International Conference on Intelligent Engineering and Management (ICIEM)* (pp. 887–893). IEEE: London. doi: 10.1109/ICIEM54221.2022.9853199.

Gupta, A. K., & Ramchandani, S. (2019). Feasibility of digital applications for toilet locating and monitoring services in urban area. *Jaipuria International Journal of Management Research, 5*(1). https://doi.org/10.22552/jijmr/2019/v5/i1/182300.

Ha, N., Nayyar, A., Nguyen, D., & Liu, C. (2019). Enhancing students' soft skills by implementing CDIO based integration teaching mode. *Proceedings of the 15th International CDIO Conference.*

Hamilton Ortiz, J., Gutierrez Marroquin, W., & Zambrano Cifuentes, L. (2020). Industry 4.0: Current status and future trends. In *Industry 4.0—Current Status and Future Trends.* https://doi.org/10.5772/intechopen.90396.

Hartmann, E. A., & Bovenschulte, M. (2013). Skills needs analysis for "industry 4.0" based on roadmaps for smart systems. *Using Technology Foresights for Identifying Future Skills Needs. Global Workshop Proceedings.*

Huk, T. (2021). From education 1.0 to education 4.0—challenges for the contemporary school. *New Educational Review, 66.* https://doi.org/10.15804/tner.2021.66.4.03.

Hussain, F. (2012). E-learning 3.0 = e-Learning 2.0 + WEB 3.0? *IADIS International Conference on Cognition and Exploratory Learning in Digital Age, CELDA 2012, Celda,* 11–18. https://doi.org/10.9790/7388-0333947.

The International Encyclopedia of Higher Education Systems and Institutions. (2020). *The International Encyclopedia of Higher Education Systems and Institutions.* https://doi.org/10.1007/978-94-017-8905-9.

ITU. (2021). *Statistics.* www.itu.int.

Jimoyiannis, A., Tsiotakis, P., Roussinos, D., & Siorenta, A. (2013). Preparing teachers to integrate web 2.0 in school practice: Toward a framework for pedagogy 2.0. *Australasian Journal of Educational Technology, 29*(2). https://doi.org/10.14742/ajet.157.

Kirby, D. A. (2004). Entrepreneurship education: Can business schools meet the challenge? *Education + Training, 46.* https://doi.org/10.1108/00400910410569632.

Kituyi, G. M., & Kyeyune, R. (2012). An analysis of e-Learning information system adoption in Ugandan universities: Case of Makerere university business school. *Information Technology Research Journal, 2*(1).

Krishnan, C., Gupta, A., Gupta, A., & Singh, G. (2022). Impact of artificial intelligence-based chatbots on customer engagement and business growth. In Hong, T. P., Serrano-Estrada, L., Saxena, A., & Biswas, A. (eds.), *Deep Learning for Social Media Data Analytics. Studies in Big Data* (vol. 113). Cham: Springer. https://doi.org/10.1007/978-3-031-10869-3_11.

Kumar, A., Krishnamurthi, R., Bhatia, S., Kaushik, K., Ahuja, N. J., Nayyar, A., & Masud, M. (2021). Blended learning tools and practices: A comprehensive analysis. *IEEE Access, 9.* https://doi.org/10.1109/ACCESS.2021.3085844.

Mafuna, M., & Wadesango, N. (2012). Students' acceptance and experiences of the new learning management system (LMS) -Wiseup. *Anthropologist, 14*(4), 311–318. https://doi.org/10.1080/09720073.2012.11891252.

Mital', D., Dupláková, D., Duplák, J., Mital'ová, Z., & Radchenko, S. (2021). Implementation of industry 4.0 using e-Learning and m-Learning approaches in technically-oriented education. *TEM Journal, 10*(1). https://doi.org/10.18421/TEM101-46.

Mohamed Hashim, M. A., Tlemsani, I., & Matthews, R. (2022). Higher education strategy in digital transformation. *Education and Information Technologies, 27*(3). https://doi.org/10.1007/s10639-021-10739-1.

Moodle. (2022). *Moodle statistics.* stats.moodle.org.

Morawska-Jancelewicz, J. (2021). The role of universities in social innovation within quadruple/quintuple helix model: Practical implications from polish experience. *Journal of the Knowledge Economy.* https://doi.org/10.1007/s13132-021-00804-y.

Mourtzis, D. (2018). Proceedings of 3rd international conference on the industry 4.0 model for advanced manufacturing. *Lecture Notes in Mechanical Engineering,* 9783319895628.

Mukhopadhyay, M., Pal, S., Nayyar, A., Pramanik, P. K. D., Dasgupta, N., & Choudhury, P. (2020). Facial emotion detection to assess learner's state of mind in an online learning system. *ACM International Conference Proceeding Series.* https://doi.org/10.1145/3385209.3385231.

Nayyar, A., & Kumar, A. (eds.). (2020). *A roadmap to Industry 4.0: Smart Production, Sharp Business and Sustainable Development* (pp. 1–21). Berlin: Springer.

Ohei, K. N., & Brink, R. (2019). Web 3.0 and web 2.0 technologies in higher educational institute: Methodological concept towards a framework development for adoption. *international Journal for Infonomics, 12*(1), 1841–1853. https://doi.org/10.20533/iji.1742.4712.2019.0188.

Picciano, A. G. (2009). Blending with purpose: The multimodal model. *Journal of Asynchronous Learning Network, 13*(1). https://doi.org/10.24059/olj.v13i1.1673.

PricewaterhouseCoopers. (2018). *Industrial manufacturing—{PwC}*. www.pwc.nl.

Rêgo, B. S., Jayantilal, S., Ferreira, J. J., & Carayannis, E. G. (2021). Digital transformation and strategic management: A systematic review of the literature. *Journal of the Knowledge Economy*. https://doi.org/10.1007/s13132-021-00853-3.

Riviezzo, A., Napolitano, M. R., & Fusco, F. (2020). Along the pathway of university missions: A systematic literature review of performance indicators. In Daniel, A. D., Teixeira, A. A. C., & Preto, M. T. (eds.), *Examining the Role of Entrepreneurial Universities in Regional Development* (pp. 24–50). Portugal: Universidade de Lisboa. https://doi.org/10.4018/978-1-7998-0174-0

Rodríguez-Abitia, G., & Bribiesca-Correa, G. (2021). Assessing digital transformation in universities. *Future Internet, 13*(2). https://doi.org/10.3390/fi13020052.

Sahlaoui, H., Alaoui, E. A. A., Nayyar, A., Agoujil, S., & Jaber, M. M. (2021). Predicting and interpreting student performance using ensemble models and shapley additive explanations. *IEEE Access, 9*. https://doi.org/10.1109/ACCESS.2021.3124270.

Sarkar, S. (2020). The history and usefulness of online teaching in India. In *Times of India Blog*. https://timesofindia.indiatimes.com/readersblog/mridul-mazumdar/the-history-and-usefulness-of-online-teaching-in-india-20481/.

Shahroom, A. A., & Hussin, N. (2018). Industrial revolution 4.0 and education. *International Journal of Academic Research in Business and Social Sciences, 8*(9), 314–319. https://doi.org/10.6007/ijarbss/v8-i9/4593.

Sharma, P. (2019). Digital revolution of education 4.0. *International Journal of Engineering and Advanced Technology, 9*(2), 3558–3564. https://doi.org/10.35940/ijeat.a1293.129219.

Shirkhani, Z., Vahedi, M., & Arayesh, M. B. (2016). Identifying barriers of e-Learning implementation by M.Sc. students in agricultural faculty of Islamic Azad University, ILAM branch. *International Journal of Agricultural Management and Development, 6*(3), 353 362. www.ijamad.iaurasht.ac.ir.

Soffel, J. (2016). What are the 21st-century skills every student needs? *World Economic Forum, 10*. https://doi.org/10.21608/jstc.2017.117920.

Statistica. (2021). *Internet users in the {World} 2025*. www.statista.com.

Sułkowski, Ł., Kolasińska-Morawska, K., Seliga, R., & Morawski, P. (2021). Smart learning technologization in the economy 5.0—the polish perspective. *Applied Sciences (Switzerland), 11*(11). https://doi.org/10.3390/app11115261.

Thames, L., & Schaefer, D. (2017). *Cybersecurity for Industry 4.0* (pp. 1–33). Heidelberg: Springer.

Tsiligiris, V., & Bowyer, D. (2021). Exploring the impact of 4IR on skills and personal qualities for future accountants: A proposed conceptual framework for university accounting education. *Accounting Education, 30*(6). https://doi.org/10.1080/09639284.2021.1938616.

Veza, I., Gjeldum, N., & Mladineo, M. (2015). Lean learning factory at FESB—University of Split. *Procedia CIRP, 32*. https://doi.org/10.1016/j.procir.2015.02.223.

Vijayan, K. K., Mork, O. J., & Giske, L. A. L. (2019). Integration of a case study into learning factory for future research. *Procedia Manufacturing, 31*. https://doi.org/10.1016/j.promfg.2019.03.041.

Singh, V. V., Singh, S., Dash, S., & Gupta, A. K. (2022). Estimation of employee engagement in organisations during crisis using machine learning technique. In *2022 3rd International Conference on Computation, Automation and Knowledge Management (ICCAKM)* (pp. 1-6), Dubai, United Arab Emirates. doi: 10.1109/ICCAKM54721.2022.9990181

9 Towards Digital Equity

Reimagining Digital Learning through the Lens of Bloom's Taxonomy

Chanel L. Fort and Samaa Haniya

9.1 INTRODUCTION

The push for online learning in response to COVID-19 has shifted the education system towards the interplay of ubiquitous access to new knowledge and innovative teaching and learning practices. This paradigm shift in the education ecosystem aims to equip learners with high-demand essential skills for the career marketplace, leading to career pathways that more readily access economic mobility. Yet, disparities in this access exist within the education and workforce systems. While impactful for economic gains, the evolution of the digital era limited significant groups of people by the digital divide from taking advantage of such opportunities (Fletcher, 2000; Haniya & Rusch, 2017; Verizon, 2017). The sudden arrival of COVID-19 has even expanded the digital gap causing digital inequities in communities of color, rural communities, and among historically black colleges and universities (HBCUs), especially as these groups sought to transition to the virtual learning and workplace at the start of the pandemic with limited support (Edmond, 2021; Elkholm & Fore, 2021; Sraders & Lambert, 2020; UNICEF 2021).

According to the National Digital Inclusion Alliance (2022), *digital inequity* is a term that implies inadequate access to information technology needed for full active participation in society. It refers to having systemic barriers in accessing digital tools, internet connectivity, online services, digital literacy training, and quality technical support needed to thrive in a digital era. The digital age is characterized by the ubiquity of access to information and communication technologies that shape individuals' lives (Ragnedda, 2018). Having inadequate access to digital technologies limits transformative learning opportunities among groups who need upward economic mobility the most. To overcome these challenges, we must develop digitally inclusive and culturally responsive learning experiences to support all learners. Developing such solutions starts by putting in place practical pedagogical approaches.

Bloom's Taxonomy is one of the distinguished pedagogical approaches with great potential for making learning more equitable, accessible, and transformative for the broadest range of learners. Bloom's Taxonomy has remained fundamental to transforming teaching, learning, and assessment throughout the evolution of the digital era and until now. At its inception, the taxonomy composed an inclusive approach for assessing students' cognitive level of development based on learners' needs using a hierarchical review of learning outcomes (Seaman, 2011; Seddon, 1978). As Bloom furthered his studies in cultural, social, and epistemic dimensions of learning, he introduced mastery learning—a differentiated teaching technique using recursive feedback and enrichment strategies leading towards the mastery of learned concepts (Brandt, 1985; Guskey, 2007). Mastery learning is crucial to any learning environment to achieve educational outcomes for the human good. By integrating Bloom's Taxonomy and mastery learning, we transform learning practices at different levels of development while encouraging higher-order thinking skills among diverse learners to become active knowledge producers (Cope & Kalantzis, 2017). Research suggests that education

 DOI: 10.1201/9781003425779-9

can significantly impact the economy's growth when it involves active civic engagement, knowledge about global change, economics, workplace skills, and the use of digital technologies (Campbell et al., 2021; Ha et al., 2019; Haniya & Rusch, 2017; Kumar et al., 2021). The World Bank estimates that a 10% increase in broadband penetration leads to a 1.2% increase in per capita GDP for developed countries and a range of 0.9% to 1.5% increase for developing countries of the Organisation for Economic Co-operation and Development (The World Bank 2022; Campbell et al., 2021). The future of work considers knowledge as profitable gains and skills as workplace collateral, thereby transitioning career pathways to performance based with high use of technological tools and penetration of digital networks (Brown, 2013; Brown et al., 2013; Campbell et al., 2021). Thus, digital equity is crucial to achieving social good and economic gain for all in a knowledge society.

9.1.1 Organization of the Chapter

The rest of this chapter is divided into the following sections: Section 9.2 discusses the knowledge economy's evolution and explains the digital divide's global implications and its effects on learning. Section 9.3 elaborates on the need for transformative learning to mitigate the problem of the digital divide and digital inequity in marginalized populations. Section 9.4 explains the rise and development of Bloom's Taxonomy's contributions to learning thus far. Section 9.5 explores the taxonomy's benefits for changing the status quo and improving learning in the new knowledge economy and digital society. Section 9.6 outlines the challenges, opposing perspectives, and revisions of Bloom's Taxonomy. Section 9.7 provides more elaboration on a number of case studies to further discuss how Bloom's Taxonomy is helpful to promote digital equity. And, finally section 9.8 presents concluding remarks on the significance of employing Bloom's Taxonomy to improve digital learning in the new knowledge economy.

9.2 EVOLUTION OF THE KNOWLEDGE ECONOMY IN THE INFORMATION AND DIGITAL AGE

Globalization has contributed to the spread of knowledge flow and technological innovations to a great extent. Friedman (2007) calls Globalization 1.0 the first stage of globalization, establishing trading between the Old World and New World. Friedman (2007) explains that during this era, which occurred until about 1800, global integration was the driver where nations competed for horsepower, steam power, and wind power. The countries with the most cost-effective means to deploy this power led the competition for global integration. The second stage of globalization, Globalization 2.0, the era including the Great Depression and World Wars I and II, lasted from around 1800 to 2000. In this era, the competitive force was multinational companies where steamships and railroads in the earliest years of the era, followed by telephones and mainframe computers in the later years, were the drivers for global change and economic expansion (Friedman, 2007). In both stages of Globalization 1.0 and Globalization 2.0, the movement between the individual acquisition of knowledge and technology was more stagnant, and teaching and learning were traditional. During this time, the call for digital equity did not arise as a dominant concern yet.

The advent of technological changes fueled by social and economic pursuits places us in Globalization 3.0, where individuals are the power engines for collaborating and competing globally. Using the personal computer, fiber optic cable, broadband, and workflow software allows individuals to create digital content for sharing, uploading, and communicating across the internet without boundaries (Friedman, 2007). Preceding the digital era of technological integrations in education, economics, healthcare, and the workplace was the information age of the 1990s, when information literacy was the denominate force for learning, communicating, working, and teaching (Jackman, 1999). The information age of the 20th century gave credence to the technological disruptions of the 21st century to facilitate communication and economic growth. Examples include the World Wide Web expansion, the web browser's agility, and enhanced internet usability for digital learning and the workplace.

Friedman (2007) explains that in 1991, Sir Timothy John Berners-Lee, a British computer scientist, conceptualized a tool for accessing documents, images, videos, and information. Berners-Lee's ultimate invention was the World Wide Web—a collaborative means for global connectivity. His vision for global connectivity spawned from his and other colleagues' interests for more easily sharing scientific research. As a result of Berners-Lee's ingenuity, HTML (Hypertext Markup Language), URL (uniform resource locator), and HTTP (HyperText Transfer Protocol) became the new social language by the end of the 20th century. As Globalization 3.0 informs, on August 6, 1991, the world gained on-demand access to the global storage of resources (Friedman, 2007), forever changing business, industry, and education. As Friedman (2007) explained, on-demand access further influenced digitization, placing sourcing and transporting information at the center stage towards the end of the 20th century.

The World Wide Web's inception led scientists and other academic researchers to create user-friendly browsers for sourcing and accessing information and sharing it across the internet to reach the globe. On August 9, 1995, Netscape, a startup company in Mountain View, California, further revolutionized the internet (Friedman, 2007). The then well-known internet computing company espoused digitization by launching its operations, becoming the largest internet service provider, and stimulating the digital era's expansion. Netscape created a user-friendly commercial browser of mixed-modality knowledge representations (Smith & Kennett, 2017), illustrating products and services, business profiles, educational content, and other valuable sources of information intriguing to the World Wide Web and internet users. Their commercial browser was the most popular at the time and more easily accessible for people of all ages. Amid the resounding competition from Microsoft, Netscape was sold to AOL for $10 billion by the end of the 20th century (Friedman, 2007). Still, this transaction and the continued momentum towards increasing access to digitization through internet service providers marked the most significant leap in socialization, making digital access to knowledge a commodity—an economic gain.

The economic gains of knowledge, defined as the knowledge economy, is articulated by Friedman (2007) as Globalization 3.0—a digital society of global access to knowledge, competition, and collaboration. Globalization 3.0 continues transforming digital access to information that individuals and career markets need to bolster economic growth. This social shift towards the economic gains of knowledge prompted conversations on upward social mobility for historically marginalized populations. Brown (2013) and Brown et al. (2013) agreed that social mobility is performance-based access to economic opportunity, forgoing meritocratic practices to employability and promotional development. Like the education for the masses movement of the 1900s (Goldin & Katz, 2008), social mobility has become the moniker for economic achievement in the 21st century.

The knowledge economy's emphasis on global information access, flexibility, agility (Chou, 2019), and expanding use and functionality of the internet and the World Wide Web is impacting digital teaching and learning to a large degree, especially since the experience of the COVID-19 pandemic. In keeping with the rhetoric, the knowledge economy after COVID-19 seeks to illustrate the inequities exposed among communities of color, rural communities, and HBCUs at the start of the COVID-19 pandemic, increasing the digital divide in education.

9.2.1 The Digital Divide

The digital divide is not merely related to the growing gap between privileged and underprivileged members of society in terms of having appropriate access to technology tools, including hardware, software, and affordable internet. Ragnedda (2018) explained the problem of the digital divide goes beyond accessing digital devices to include digital literacy and the effective use of information and communication technologies (ICTs). Such digital exclusion will affect individuals' quality of life to thrive in a knowledge economy and digital world, especially since the US Department of Labor has indicated that 77% of US jobs require computer skills (Verizon, 2021).

The digital divide is also a global phenomenon concerning educators at the international level. During the COVID-19 pandemic, schools and businesses worldwide were forced to close due to social distancing mandates (Centers for Disease Control and Prevention [CDC], 2020). These closures exposed the issue of digital inequities between nations. Nearly 1.6 billion children worldwide were directly affected by school closures (Elkholm & Fore, 2021). Furthermore, 77 million children and young people were without in-person classroom learning for 18 months or even longer (Elkholm & Fore, 2021). The digital inequities were seen not only as learning losses for students but also as missed opportunities for educational practitioners to effectively incorporate digital learning in the classroom with limited resources.

New business startups like Learnable, part of the World Economic Forum's Uplink community, recognized the call to action and the social good of providing ready access to digital learning. Learnable uses machine learning, artificial intelligence, and augmented reality to create content that is easy to share via a mobile application (Edmond, 2021). This digital learning technology was helpful for students with limited access to technologies during the pandemic and remained a solution for students most affected by the digital divide. Another remarkable initiative is the partnership between UNICEF and Ericsson. Together they launched the global Giga initiative, which aims to connect every school in developing countries to the appropriate broadband connection by 2030, especially in regions needing critical infrastructure (The Economist Intelligence Unit, 2021; The World Bank, 2021).

Currently, the workforce and education systems are undergoing transformative changes to overcome the experiences of the digital divide. For example, in America, efforts are now being made to provide funding to deploy infrastructure and digital learning tools (laptops, desktops, smartphones, and others). In the United States, there is an uneven distribution of resources (Verizon, 2021) across its 13,500 school districts (National Center for Education Statistics [NCES], 2022). The uneven distribution of resources leaves numerous schools underfunded and unable to acquire technology upgrades. Historically, the underfunding imposes on learners in rural communities, communities of color, and at HBCUs.

The United Negro College Fund's division of HBCUv, a virtual community for HBCUs, reported that one top research university in the United States receives more federal funding than all 102 HBCUs combined (Richardson, 2022). Yet, HBCUs generate $14.8 billion in economic productivity annually and 134,090 jobs in their local and regional workforces. They are the educational resource for 25% of Black STEM (science, technology, engineering, and math) degree holders, the economic engine for developing employability skills, an underutilized resource for improving STEM workforce challenges, and the alma mater for 50% of Black doctors in the United States (Frederick D. Patterson Research Institute, 2022; Jackson & Rudin, 2019; National Academies of Sciences, Engineering, and Medicine [NASEM], 2019; Richardson, 2022). Verizon Innovative Learning (2017) depicts the existence and frustrations of students and educators experiencing the social dilemma of the digital divide in their 2017 documentary *Without a Net: The Digital Divide in America* (Verizon, 2021). Fletcher (2000) and Haniya and Rusch (2017) agreed that the digital divide is a social concern among communities of color and rural communities in the United States. This technological dilemma impairs student abilities to engage in collaborative mixed-modality learning experiences (ACS, 2013; Fletcher, 2000; Harper et al., 2009; Lewin, 1946).

The concern for digital equity is a global concern. Digital equity advocates in Tanzania explained the county is undergoing a digital transformation by increasing the internet's connection value for its citizens. The transformation involves deploying broadband access, connectivity, and coverage to at least 80% of the market, availability of 3G and 4G devices for connecting to the internet, gaining access to SMS platforms, and implementing e-learning readiness curriculums (African Intellectuals, 2022; Mwananchi, 2022). As with the Americas, a region more developed in technological changes, digital access advocates in Tanzania also claim that overcoming the digital divide and digital inequities is a social and economic good.

Since 2014, Verizon Innovative Learning and other peer corporations have committed more than $2 billion to improve K-12 educational technology and digital accessibility, which was beneficial (Verizon, 2021). Global organizations like the Bill and Melinda Gates Foundation and the Skoll Foundation leverage their economic potential to champion social change and overcome inequities. The Gates Foundation has invested $60.1 billion towards education, poverty, and health since its inception in 2000 (Bill & Melinda Gates Foundation, 2022). The Skoll Foundation has invested approximately $935 million worldwide into solving social issues for populations the technology industry has historically overlooked (Skoll Foundation, 2021).

The education system must continue to receive substantial financial investments to promote a culture of quality access and the effective use and application of e-learning technologies (Fletcher, 2000; Lewin, 1946). In doing so, students can adequately explore mixed-modality learning opportunities without feeling the need for remediation or other psycho-emotional dilemmas associated with limitations in student motivations due to the underinvestment in school systems (Hammond et al., 2021; Harper et al., 2009; Lewin, 1946).

9.2.2 The Digital Learner

To advance education and reach a higher level of digital equity, we first need to understand who the learner is in a knowledge economy and global digital world. Since the early 21st century and moving to the fourth industrial revolution, educating the whole child has been at the forefront of the education system. Social changes and technological advancements have reshaped the learner's characteristics over the years (Chou, 2019; Philbeck & Davis, 2019; Ruyter et al., 2019; Watson, 2020). For example, the third industrial revolution claimed the information age as the age of information literacy—gathering, evaluating, and synthesizing knowledge (Jackman, 1999). During that era, learners were identified as persons who took advantage of digital access to information and pursued the traditional and alternative career pathways of that time. Later, the fourth industrial revolution emerged, involving the intersection of digital, physical, and biological worlds for improving global productivity and transforming individual and organizational teaching and learning (Adhikari, 2020). In this era, the new learner refers to the digital learner influenced by the 21st-century changes of globalization, the knowledge economy, and technological innovations.

Digital learners in the 21st century is intrigued by the multimodal access to new knowledge. They are active members of the knowledge economy and recognize knowledge as capital gains and digital skills as workforce collateral leading to social mobility. Mwananchi Digital (2022) and Shade (2014) explained that digital skills afford equitable access to the digital economy—the internet-based acquisition of goods and services that Ciuriak (2019) identified as the revolutionary innovation for overcoming economic disparities. Where there is digital inclusion, digital learners immerse themselves in technologies. Schools actively interact with technology tools and learning management systems (LMS) such as Blackboard, Canvas, and Moodle. Additionally, learners engage in digital collaborative workspaces (e.g., Google Workspace and Microsoft Teams), digital whiteboards (e.g., MIRO, Mural, and Jamboard), live interactive polling and quizzes (e.g., Poll Everywhere and Slido), animated presentation platforms (e.g., Prezi and Doodle), and video conferencing tools (e.g., Cisco Webex, Zoom, and Google Meet).

Digital learning technologies help learners interact and collaborate in ways traditional teaching has not afforded, thereby creating equitable learning environments. Learning technologies in the classroom shift learning agency by giving learners more responsibility and autonomy. Learners are seen as active knowledge makers (Amina, 2017), digital collaborators, problem-solvers, and co-designers. And teachers are no longer seen as the sole source for information sharing. New learners are also more prone to pursuing industry-based credentials, short-term and long-term certificate programs, undergraduate and graduate degrees, and professional degrees in digital learning communities. They are excited by new modes for learning (e.g., online, distance education, and hybrid) in synchronous and asynchronous learning environments since it allows them to participate in the knowledge economy easily.

Greenstein (2019) and Ross (2017) mentioned that 21st-century learners are supported by additional co-curricular engagement because some are working-class adults, entrepreneurs, single parents, low-income, and first-generation college students who need the extra support to ensure academic success. Greenstein (2019) added that these learners emphasize digital access to structured degree pathways and are people seeking lifestyle flexibility. Since work-life balance is becoming a social norm, new learners have differences in why, how, and when they pursue educational interests. The 21st-century learner has many traditional and virtual options for acquiring knowledge and skills. These learners value "engagement, belonging, confidence, and vision" (Ross, 2017, p. 8). For this reason, education practitioners must reimagine digital learning towards digital equity that meets the needs of digital learners.

9.3 THE NEED FOR TRANSFORMATIVE LEARNING

Understanding the meaning of learning is essential before thinking of any change. Learning as a concept can be defined as the psychological process of transforming knowledge from one cognitive level to another based on one's lived experiences, world views, and lifestyle perspectives (Haythornthwaite & Andrews, 2011). Learning is an interpretive process that stores new information by rationalizing and linking it to existing knowledge (Ross, 2017). Haythornthwaite and Andrews (2011) further explained learning as evolutionary and encapsulated in societal norms, environmental factors, and media sources. Based on the definition of learning, both cognitive and external factors determine our meanings of life and identity, our perspectives on lived experiences, and the conditions of humanity. Haythornthwaite and Andrews' (2011) research shares three fundamental learning components: transformation, framing, and emergence. The three components build upon the definition of learning leading to the emergence of e-learning theory and its practice. As the foundations imply, transformation addresses the cognitive change occurring during the learning process; framing addresses the world view of the learner and what they bring to the learning experience. Emergence addresses the evolution of learning from one-dimensional to multidimensional and existing as multimodal and mixed media (Haythornthwaite & Andrews, 2011).

Despite the innovations for acquiring new knowledge, some institutions still follow a didactic approach to teaching. The didactic approach is a teacher-centered educational approach, where the teacher is the classroom's authority figure and learners passively acquire new knowledge. Research has shown that this approach is ineffective in meeting learners' needs, especially with the rise of technological innovations and the tremendous opportunities they afford. The inception of the digital era is acclaimed for evolving learning dimensions and learner interests towards ubiquitous access, a concept defined by Haniya and Rusch (2017) as learning anywhere, anytime, and any place. Haythornthwaite and Andrews (2011) differentiate the advent of e-learning experiences from traditional learning as a modality that emphasizes learner interactions and the social aspects of learning—collaborative intelligence, active learning, formative assessment, and community building.

To promote digital equity, we should move from the didactic approach to a more transformative learning approach consistent with Bloom's Taxonomy. Using Bloom's Taxonomy as praxis for student development and organizational learning has proved effective (Bidwell & Froebe, 1971; Jagzape et al., 2018; Tractenberg et al., 2019) and can be applied in the digital era to mitigate the persistence of digital inequities among marginalized groups. Consequently, individuals can take advantage of the knowledge economy yielded by the digital era to become active knowledge makers, seeking flexible access to career pathways.

9.4 UNDERSTANDING BLOOM'S CONTRIBUTIONS TO LEARNING

Benjamin Samuel Bloom (1913–1999) was an academic researcher who believed that all students could learn at a high standard of excellence given the proper learning conditions (Anderson, 2002; Bloom, 1978; Brandt, 1985). Kropp et al. (1966) and Seaman (2011) depicted Benjamin S. Bloom as a progressive academic researcher who, while spending years as an examiner, took an interest in designing a theoretical framework that sought to facilitate better communications among examiners about student behaviors. In addition, the taxonomy was initially conceptualized as a guide for understanding the specific meaning of broad goals (i.e., national, state, and local educational goals) as a point of reference for aligning educational objectives, activities, and assessments, and as a scale of educational possibilities for any course or curriculum (Krathwohl, 2002). Additionally, Bloom studied changes in human characteristics and their evolution through learning experiences (Bloom, 1978; Brandt, 1985; Seaman, 2011). Bloom (1978) shared his concerns for developing student learning capabilities and equitable learning opportunities, presented in the Taxonomy and later explained by Seaman (2011) as the categorization of educational objectives and their hierarchy for evaluation. While working as an examiner with the University of Chicago's Board of Examinations, Bloom took the lead in conceptualizing the *Taxonomy of Educational Objectives, The Classification of Educational Goals, Handbook I: Cognitive Domain*, which was published in 1956 (Anderson, 2002; Bloom et al., 1956; Seaman, 2011).

Seddon (1978) explained that as a resource, the handbook guides examiners in creating test questions and assessments that address student cognition based on prior learning experiences. As a taxonomy with educational and psychological properties, the handbook presents the six categories of cognitive outcomes achieved through student learning experiences—knowledge, comprehension, application, analysis, synthesis, and evaluation (Kropp et al., 1966; Seaman, 2011; Seddon, 1978). Seaman (2011) clarified the taxonomy as not a sequence of instruction but a classification system that communicates knowledge development based on the educational objective, assessment, and instruction. Krathwohl (2002) further explained the taxonomy as a guide for creating actionable objectives that express the intended learning outcomes. Using the taxonomy to create broad learning objectives, instructional leaders would express the subject matter content as a noun phrase and describe the cognitive process as a verb phrase (Krathwohl, 2002). For example, learners will understand e-learning ecologies in new learning and assessment. In order to achieve this broad objective, we can rely on the six categories with the relatable subcategories listed as action verbs. These verbs create student-centered learning outcomes that descriptively communicate the cognitive process for achieving the learning objective (Krathwohl, 2002; Kropp et al., 1966). In doing so, we can have several learning outcomes from these subcategories, such as:

1. The learner will classify e-learning ecologies in new learning and assessment.
2. The learner will compare and contrast the dimensions of e-learning that are useful in corporate and community education settings.

In this example, the action verbs *classify, compare*, and *contrast* are the taxonomy's subcategories and outcomes for cognitively achieving the objective "understand."

From another perspective, the taxonomy is categorized from least complex to most complex orders of cognition. The six unique categories classify the intended outcomes of educational objectives—knowledge, comprehension, application, analysis, synthesis, and evaluation (Kropp et al., 1966; Seaman, 2011; Seddon, 1978). The hierarchy of Bloom's Taxonomy was examined by Miller et al. (1979) and can arguably be divided into two dimensions: (1) concrete intelligence and (2) applied intelligence. According to Bloom's order of the cognitive outcomes, lower-order thinking (knowledge, comprehension, and application) and higher-order thinking (analysis, synthesis, and evaluation) are synonymous with Miller et al.'s (1979) examination and conclusion of the hierarchy as a two-dimensional analysis of intelligence (Seaman, 2011).

The psychological perspective of the taxonomy suggests the order of cognitive outcomes in the hierarchy is theoretically relevant to accepted psychological principles (Seddon, 1978). Bloom's Taxonomy of the educational objectives posits that manipulators of subject matter must conclude or assume a student's prior learning experiences before introducing new learning objectives to achieve the next level of cognitive outcomes (Seaman, 2011; Seddon, 1978). Bloom (1978), Seaman (2011), and Seddon (1978) maintain that the learning spectrum can start and end at any position on the hierarchy of the taxonomy.

9.5 DIGITAL EQUITY THROUGH THE LENS OF BLOOM'S TAXONOMY

The competition between education and technology continues (Goldin & Katz, 2008), and because of this, educators are adjusting teaching and learning practices towards differentiated knowledge acquisitions. The change makes learning equitable and inclusive for all learner types. Brandt (1985) explained Bloom's ideology for student development as equitable. Bloom (1978) expressed his belief that schools should not select students for special learning experiences based on aptitude. Instead, they should focus on performance and achievement. Benjamin S. Bloom spent much of his career studying human characteristics and behaviors. In studying human behaviors, Bloom (1978) posits that favorable learning conditions improve student motivations for learning and learning abilities and reduce external distractions. Students must be provided with the appropriate conditions and placed on a mastery scale based on cognitive outcomes. According to Bloom (1978) this will inspire students' learning abilities in ways they would ordinarily give up. Bloom (1978) presents keen insights for improving educational achievement and student assessment globally, even considering a focus on mental health as a factor for student learning behaviors. Bloom's ideology, cultural perspectives, studies in human behavior, and belief that learning should be vivid and fulfilling were foundational in developing the taxonomy for the cognitive domain (Bloom et al., 1956, 1978; Brandt, 1985; Seaman, 2011). In what follows, we will discuss how Bloom's use would promote student development, faculty development, and lifelong organizational learning in a knowledge economy and digital society.

9.5.1 Student Development

The innovative use of Bloom's Taxonomy can be applied to mitigate inadequate student transitions into higher education in underinvested K-12 school systems, specifically among secondary school systems in rural communities and communities of color. Chandra (1966), Heifetz and Laurie (1997), Kotter (2008), and Lewin (1946) agreed that implementing a social and cultural change like using the cognitive domain of Bloom's Taxonomy to overcome digital inequities requires disrupting the system to perform the adaptive work before "re-freezing" it. In this example, the adaptive work involves using Bloom's Taxonomy as the developmental pathway for the appropriate use and application of digital learning technologies, such as tablets, PCs, mobile devices, gamification devices, and headsets used for virtual reality and the metaverse. The metaverse is the newest introduction to digital learning that bridges virtual three-dimensional (3D) spaces with human interactions. In the metaverse, students learn and collaborate in real-time as an avatar—their digital representation. Angel-Urdinola et al. (2022) explained how national colleges in the eastern Caribbean decided to design a virtual campus after enduring the learning losses and declines in student success since the school closures resulting from the COVID-19 outbreak. On May 27, 2022, Talladega College, Alabama's first private liberal arts HBCU founded in 1865, announced its partnership with EON Reality (EON-XR) to introduce students and faculty to the knowledge metaverse, an in-kind grant program valued at $4,462,913. Morehouse College, located in Atlanta, Georgia, is a private liberal arts HBCU established in 1867 to prepare Black men for distinguished careers in innovation, healthcare, and government relations. The college recently announced the virtual Morehouse campus using the metaverse (Fink, 2021). "The future of education is global and will combine physical and digital spaces to provide students with better educational opportunities" (Angel-Urdinola et al., 2022).

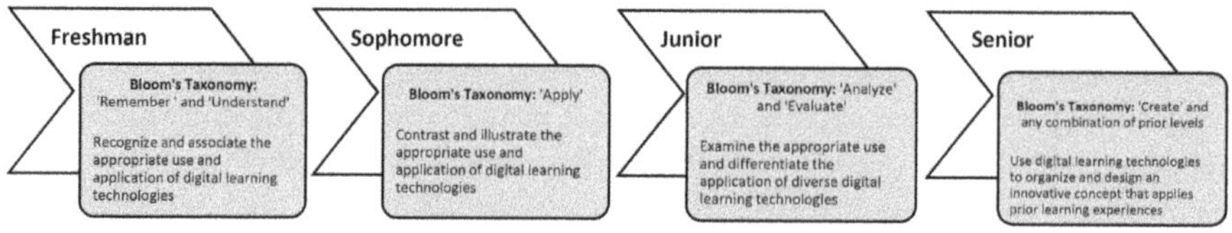

FIGURE 9.1 Applying Bloom's Taxonomy as a praxis for student development in digital learning technologies.

Note: The "appropriate use and application of digital learning technologies" can be based on any technology or concept deemed useful for any course taught during the high school years.

Applying Bloom's Taxonomy to develop students' digital skills is a social change strategy with transformative implications. Before students can use digital learning technologies, education practitioners must inform them of their appropriate use and application in a real-world context. As with the example of the metaverse, workplaces and career-related events (e.g., conferences, tradeshows, job fairs, and others) are also using virtual spaces to engage their target audiences. For this reason, students gain access to a more resourceful quality of life by overcoming digital inequities. For example, in the first year of high school, assuming underinvested school systems receive investments, students learn the use and application of digital learning technologies from Bloom's remember and understand cognitive level. This practice would then continue throughout the high school years. In the sophomore year of high school, students learn the use and application of digital learning technologies from Bloom's apply cognitive level. In the junior year of high school, they learn the use and application of digital learning technologies from Bloom's analyze and evaluate cognitive level. In the senior year of high school, students learn the use and application of digital learning technologies from Bloom's create cognitive level. At the create stage, students are active producers of knowledge and project deliverables, and they are more prepared to contribute to global conversations about technological innovations and their evolution.

A conceptual model of student development in digital learning technologies is illustrated in Figure 9.1. If implemented and applied effectively, students within the underinvested and developing school systems can experience improvements in motivation and learning abilities (Bloom, 1978; Harper et al., 2009) and the willingness to engage in collaborative digital learning experiences, thereby improving student persistence rates and mobility towards more significant economic opportunities (Hammond et al., 2021; Mwananchi Digital, 2022).

9.5.2 Faculty Development

Student-centered learning using digital technologies is only as effective as the faculty's development of the best practices for using digital technologies in the classroom. Just as learners change, so does faculty. The current state of workplace dynamics includes the five generations in the workplace—traditionalists, baby boomers, Gen Xers, millennials, and Gen Zers. Among the generational differences are diverse access levels, usability, interests, and skills for introducing technology-mediated learning in the classroom. This workplace dynamic presents challenges for preparing students to overcome digital skills gaps. In other words, faculty are the lifeline of educational institutions and research and must also receive investments in their professional and skills development for using 21st-century pedagogy and technological tools. Further, quicker access to knowledge is resourceful for faculty, and they also value learning communities, both traditional and online communities, where digital access is provided and stable. Verizon Innovative Learning (2021) depicted several perspectives among K-12 educators who shared their frustrations about students' limited access to broadband and the school systems' limited access to stable and secure broadband for better facilitating course lessons. The digital divide not only affects students but also affects the faculty's role in teaching and learning.

Bloom's perspective for education practices considers the student-centered and teacher-centered approaches, particularly for assessment and evaluation. He was motivated to improve teaching and learning techniques globally (Bloom et al., 1956). Anderson (2002) gives an account of Benjamin S. Bloom's cultural lens in education, detailing his accomplishment in founding the International Association for the Evaluation of Educational Achievement (IEA). The IEA focuses on designing, conducting, and reporting cross-national studies on enhanced educational achievement (IEA, n.d.). The IEA is an international cooperative of scholars, government research agencies, national research institutions, and analysts working to evaluate and improve education worldwide (IEA, n.d.). Anderson (2002) summarizes that Benjamin S. Bloom fulfilled his academic career publishing research in testing, measurement, and evaluation. He co-authored books addressing human characteristics in school learning, evaluation to improve learning, compensatory education, the home environment, and others (Anderson, 2002). Anderson (2002) further highlighted a lasting contribution of Benjamin S. Bloom's research, the book *Stability and Change in Human Characteristics* (Bloom, 1966). This book informed the federal Head Start program (Anderson, 2002). Another excellent contribution for education practitioners to review. The following case study illustrates the use of Bloom's Taxonomy for teaching in the e-learning environment and as a tool for increasing faculty engagement in online learning communities. This case proves that Bloom's is a helpful resource for teaching and learning and that faculty are willing to engage in skills and professional development in the digital era.

9.5.2.1 Case Study: Using Bloom's Taxonomy for Group-Based Asynchronous e-Learning

In this case study, Jagzape et al. (2018) detailed the application of the Revised Bloom's Taxonomy (RBT) for group-based asynchronous e-learning activities, which are a component of the Faculty Development Program facilitated by the Foundation for Advancement of International Medical Education and Research (FAIMER). Jagzape et al. (2018) and Schoenfeld-Tacher et al. (2001) posit that asynchronous communications, while flexible in the e-learning community, must also be focused and intentionally build a learning culture. The course media and teaching methods used significantly influence student learning abilities. In the asynchronous learning environment, its essential to maintain the learner-learner, learner-instructor, and learner-content interactions through probing discussion questions that engage critical thinking, student reflections, practical application, and formative assessments (Bloom, 1978; Guskey, 2007; Jagzape et al. 2018; Schoenfeld-Tacher et al., 2001; Mukhopadhyay et al., 2020). In doing so, Jagzape et al. (2018) detailed the case study's focus on applying the cognitive domain of RBT to discussions, thereby promoting active learning among faculty.

Jagzape et al. (2018) indicated the study was a qualitative study conducted over four weeks evaluating feedback from 16 participants. The study participants were culturally diverse and represented both males and females (Jagzape et al., 2018). During week one, participants were asked questions from the remember and understand level of the RBT cognitive process dimension. During week two, participants were asked questions from the apply and analyze level of the taxonomy. During week three, participants were asked questions from the analyze and evaluate level, and during week four, participants were asked questions from the create level of the taxonomy (Jagzape et al., 2018). Jagzape et al. (2018) detailed how each week presented a new cognitive outcome level. The study results indicate that instructional methods and mixed-media approaches improve learner engagement, particularly in technology-focused use.

In another study, Alexander et al. (2010) detailed the ten guiding principles used by the North Carolina Center for Public Health Preparedness (NCCPHP) for implementing technology-enhanced training using an e-learning platform to facilitate continuing education courses for public health workers. They explained that the educational offerings were designed based on Bloom's cognitive learning levels to increase learner engagement and opportunity. The action was taken in response to the public health workforce's challenges with obtaining continuing education credits—lack of access, cost, limited opportunities, work schedules, and others (Alexander et al., 2010). As a result of adopting the e-learning platform, Alexander et al. (2010) discussed how workers of the NCCPHP have on-demand access to education and training opportunities and can confidently fulfill their continuing education requirements.

Both studies imply that Bloom's Taxonomy has a great potential to positively impact the learner's ability to "think, learn, apply, [analyze], evaluate the situation and create a particular situation which promoted active learning and interaction" (Jagzape et al., 2018, p. 5).

9.5.3 Lifelong Organizational Learning and the Future of Work

Brown (2013) and Brown et al. (2013) explained the new knowledge economy, with its changes in knowledge acquisitions, is igniting a performance-based approach to career pathways preceding meritocracies in the workplace and placing greater emphasis on lifelong organizational learning. In doing so, knowledge and workforce talents are retained and transferred among peer learning communities.

The spread of COVID-19 abruptly moved business and industry into the virtual workspace. During this time, organizations were forced into virtual learning and presentation platforms only to discover that new experiences for organizational learning would follow. The future of work is ubiquitous. Acemoglu and Restrepo (2019) discussed the new tasks for the workplace, explaining that automation changes the *task content* of production—using technology instead of humans to perform work. Chia (2021) argued the *post-work society* is a society dominated by technological unemployment, vast work-life balance, and gamification used for completing work tasks. And Bessant and Watts (2021) reported that 4.3 million people, or 32% of the Australian workforce, began working digitally when COVID-19 spread in 2020. The workplace impacts are resounding and yet to be resolved, just as the learning losses experienced globally. Digital working is an evolutionary process for managing business operations; however, by engaging a new experience of digital equity, Globalization 3.0 can more easily be realized for working-class citizens to participate in lifelong learning.

Bloom's Taxonomy is illustrated by Bidwell and Froebe (1971) as a practical guide for lifelong organizational learning. In addition to developing course objectives, curriculum, and assessments, Bloom's Taxonomy has been used for developing and evaluating practical career skills in fields like nursing (Bidwell & Froebe, 1971; Tractenberg et al., 2019). For example, Tractenberg et al. (2019) designed a Mastery Rubric (MR) for the nurse practitioner program curriculum. The purpose of the MR is to operationalize the competencies taught by advanced practice registered nurse (APRN) educators (Tractenberg et al., 2019). Tractenberg et al. (2019) explained that the MR for nurse practitioner (MR-NP) education would advance the student from novice to apprentice and journeyman—lifelong practice skills and mastery. Guided by the cognitive domain of Bloom's Taxonomy, Tractenberg et al. (2019) illustrated that competency-based educational experiences will help the nursing industry achieve its outcomes for student development. Competency-based education has been a focus of the industry since the 1980 publication of *Guidelines for Family Nurse Practitioner Curricular Planning* and is noted as essential but challenging to promote among medical educators worldwide (Tractenberg et al., 2019). The MR-NP serves as a curriculum development and evaluation tool promoting continuous learning beyond the classroom that translates into career skills (Tractenberg et al., 2019).

Tractenberg et al. (2019) classified the nurse practitioner curriculums designed using the MR-NP increase the educator's ability to engage the learner's metacognitive development, identify learning and skills gaps, improve active learner engagement and student development on learning objectives, and advance instructor evaluation metrics and curriculum planning. The MR-NP was recognized by Tractenberg et al. (2019) as the practical guide for developing curriculum for advanced practice registered nursing programs and has been used to accelerate student development and career achievement globally.

9.6 NEW PERSPECTIVES OF BLOOM'S TAXONOMY

9.6.1 Opposing Perspective of Bloom's Cognitive Domain

Although Bloom's Taxonomy has great potential for promoting equity, several challenges and critiques are associated with it. In a review of Seddon's (1978) analysis of the educational and psychological properties of Bloom's Taxonomy, Furst (1981) analyzed Bloom's neutrality, comprehensiveness, cumulative hierarchical structure, and usefulness. He questioned the validity and practical use of Bloom's Taxonomy. Furst (1981) considered the taxonomy's epistemology, claiming that focusing on student behaviors creates challenges for learning leaders. From his perspective, a focus on student behaviors confuses the outcomes with their objectives since the taxonomy relies on empirical data not easily observed as overt behavior. And because the empirical observation seeks a change in student learning ability, competency, and understanding—a fundamental to education—Furst (1981) argues that the concept of "understanding" is omitted from the taxonomy.

Furst (1981) further argued that the taxonomy's categorization should be a classification of cognitive processes and not a classification of cognitive outcomes and educational objectives. He believes the taxonomy targets instructional outcomes rather than teaching techniques to examine student perspectives and knowledge that facilitate in-class discussions. Likewise, Miller et al. (1979) had similar concerns. Furst's opinion (1981) was that the taxonomy's hierarchy is one-dimensional and simplistic posing philosophical opposition, and "evaluation" should be in higher order than "synthesis." He considered the taxonomy as an inventory of educational customs since he believed it lacked theoretical constructs for a valid taxonomy like in the natural sciences. Bloom's Taxonomy was later revised to include much of the concerns presented by Furst.

9.6.2 Revision of Bloom's Taxonomy

Efforts to revise Bloom's Taxonomy began in the late 20th century, towards the 21st century. According to Seaman (2011), David R. Krathwohl and seven scholars began revising the taxonomy in 1994. As a group, Seaman (2011) noted, they were interested in refocusing educational leaders' attention on the significance of the original handbook and incorporating the new school of thought and current societal perspectives into the framework. In 2001, the group published the revised version of the taxonomy: *A Taxonomy for Learning, Teaching, and Assessing: A Revision of Bloom's Taxonomy of Educational Objectives*. Krathwohl (2002) detailed the changes as follows:

- Established a two-dimensional taxonomy using the knowledge dimension and the cognitive process dimension;
- Developed a six-tier hierarchy categorized of less rigid learning outcomes with more emphasis on the subcategories (cognitive processes), whereas the original hierarchy was more rigid with a greater focus on cognitive development;
- Renamed the categories to the more relevant and useful verb form of the original categories—remember, understand, apply, analyze, evaluate, and create;
- Reversed the order of synthesis and evaluation and renamed synthesis to create;
- Replaced the original subcategories with gerunds and noted them as cognitive processes.

Krathwohl (2002) explained that the revised taxonomy focuses on the teacher's development, curriculum, instructional delivery, and assessment. It provides teachers with up-to-date guidance for identifying missed learning opportunities, classifying learning activities and course objectives, assessing the quality of individual learning objectives, determining the appropriateness of learning activities to facilitate learning outcomes, and determining the appropriateness of assessments to evaluate the intended learning outcome (Krathwohl, 2002; Seaman, 2011). In a later article posted in the *Educational Psychologist*, Merlin C. Wittrock received acknowledgment as the thought leader for replacing the category of comprehension with understanding and changing the synthesis category to create—concluding that create best describes actively establishing meaning and plans of action (Krathwohl & Anderson, 2010).

The revised taxonomy is highly recommended by leading educational associations such as the Association for College and University Educators (ACUE); ACUE uses the revised taxonomy for teaching the micro-credential "Designing Learning-Centered and Equitable Courses" (Association of College and University Educators [ACUE], 2016a, 2016b, 2022a). This course helps to promote equity by preparing post-secondary educators to design and implement evidence-based teaching practices and learner-centered course outcomes. Designing learning through this approach does not merely benefit educators but also the learners those teachers will teach in the future (ACUE, 2022a, 2022b).

9.7 DISCUSSION

The need for digital equity is upon us. New learners of the 21st century are immersed in a high-tech digital world. They take full advantage of ubiquitous access to digital tools and new knowledge to thrive. These learners place a greater value on access to diversifying global careers and flexibility in the work-life and learning balance. They also seek a sense of belonging (Ross, 2017), as digital access is now considered a social dimension of lifestyle and should be fulfilled (Ragnedda, 2018; Ragnedda, 2019). Otherwise, 21st-century learners feel limited in their ability to engage in the digital economy—where technology and commerce intersect with upward economic opportunity. Brown (2013) and Brown et al. (2013) said it best: social mobility is the repositioning of lower-class families to participate in the middle- and upper-class financial earnings and lifestyle. This paradigm shift forgoes the deficit-based perspectives of historically marginalized people groups, seeing them as assets with acquired education and skills used as workforce collateral. Of course, the move to the middle class must first be addressed within the education system, proving a more equitable practice for all learners to achieve and experience a sense of belonging. Therefore, transformative approaches like Bloom's Taxonomy can reignite in the learning environment as the education landscape shifts towards digital equity.

Bloom's Taxonomy is central to teaching and learning for faculty development through ACUE's course in "Effective Teaching Practices" (2022). Institutions completing micro-credentials report greater faculty confidence in teaching online courses, improvements in students' course completion outcomes, educational equity advancements, and student performance and progress in test scores. Bloom's vision for the taxonomy at its inception was to develop an evaluation model for understanding student cognitive levels at each assessment stage. The model gave Bloom and his colleagues an equitable point of reference for discussing the next levels in student development (Bloom et al., 1956; Brandt, 1985; Seaman, 2011; Seddon, 1978). ACUE's course in effective teaching embodies this practice leading faculty towards mastery of its concepts and successful outcomes in both the traditional and online classroom environments.

In the Jagzape et al. (2018) case example of asynchronous e-learning for faculty development, researchers of the study proved that using Bloom's Taxonomy for achieving learner outcomes in a digital learning environment promoted active learning and learner engagement. It also established a learning community not reliant upon the teacher-student interaction. In this example, participants of the e-learning course engaged with multimodality and collaborative intelligence, thereby applying the social and collaborative dimensions to learning (Cope & Kalantzis, 2017)—a necessity for new learners and faculty development.

In an exploratory study, Halawi et al. (2009) evaluated the use of e-learning based on Bloom's Taxonomy for teaching and learning effectiveness. The study considered three reputable learning management systems of the early 21st century (WebCT, Blackboard, and eCollege) with similar functionality for facilitating e-learning courses. The researchers performed a regression analysis to understand the relationship between learner factors, instructional factors, and learning through a web-based platform. The study proved using Bloom's Taxonomy as the evaluation method that e-learning is an effective learning modality compared to traditional in-class instruction (Halawi et al., 2009). But of course, the progressive results of this study are contingent upon access to digital technologies used for new learning.

As the knowledge economy continues to experience fast-paced evolutions in learning and the representation of epistemic artifacts like the newest inclusion of the metaverse, Bloom's Taxonomy maintains a practical approach for developing academic objectives, assessments, and evaluation. With it as a praxis for digital inclusion, the education system has a great propensity to move towards digital equity.

9.8 CONCLUSION AND FUTURE SCOPE

In this chapter, we aimed to transform learning and promote digital equity via the integration of Bloom's Taxonomy in the age of the knowledge economy and digital innovations. Transforming learning is essential to respond to the ongoing social-cultural changes we are presently witnessing in the education ecosystem. Learning should be more flexible, social, and responsive to society's needs. For that reason, Bloom's Taxonomy can be a critical teaching and learning tool in accommodating the societal and cultural changes in education by facilitating newer conversations about student levels of development in technology-mediated epistemology and establishing learner-centered curriculums and assessments for all learner types. The notion would emphasize differentiation. Bloom categorized the cognitive outcomes to reach mastery into six processes—remember, understand, apply, analyze, evaluate, and create (Krathwohl, 2002). While Bloom's Taxonomy has been scrutinized and studied since the early years of its inception, it is still highly recommended among educators worldwide for developing mastery learning.

Previous research proved the practical application and adaptability of Bloom's Taxonomy in student development, faculty development, lifelong organizational learning, and the future of work to promote digital equity. We believe that Bloom's Taxonomy is beneficial and equitable for developing the digital technology skills needed to engage in e-learning experiences. The taxonomy can serve as praxis for student development in the effective use and application of e-learning technologies, thereby overcoming digital inequities, disrupting social norms across communities of color, rural communities, and HBCUs, and mitigating their disenfranchisement from the digital revolution.

In the near future, we aim to develop a framework to guide education practitioners towards integrating digital technology more effectively among populations marginalized by the digital divide. We are also interested in collecting data from faculty, learners, and organizational leaders to see the impact of using Bloom's Taxonomy to transform their teaching and learning practices.

REFERENCES

Acemoglu, D., & Restrepo, P. (2019). Automation and new tasks. *The Journal of Economic Perspectives*, *33*(2), 3–30.

ACS, Z. J. (2013). The wealth of nations. In Z. J. ACS (ed.), *Why philanthropy matters: How the wealthy give, and what it means for our economic well-being* (pp. 86–120). Princeton University Press.

Adhikari, R. (2020). *Fourth industrial revolution: From least developed countries to knowledge societies.* Sustainable Development Policy Institute.

African Intellectuals. (2022, May 13). *The role of innovation for sustainable development* [Video]. YouTube. https://youtu.be/CYL4BMVtzW4.

Alexander, L. K., Horney, J. A., Markiewicz, M., & MacDonald, P. D. M. (2010). 10 guiding principles of a comprehensive internet-based public health preparedness training and education program. *Public Health Reports*, *125*(5), 51–60.

Amina, T. (2017). Active knowledge making: Epistemic dimensions of e-Learning. In B. Cope, & M. Kalantzis (eds.), *e-Learning ecologies: Principles for new learning and assessment* (pp. 65–87). Routledge.

Anderson, L. (2002). Benjamin S. Bloom (1913–1999). *American Psychologist*, *57*(1), 63.

Angel-Urdinola, D., Marchioni, C., & Vainstein, J. (2022, April 4). Education meets the metaverse in eastern Caribbean national colleges. *World Bank Blogs*. https://blogs.worldbank.org/latinamerica/education-meets-metaverse-eastern-caribbean-national-colleges.

Association of College and University Educators. (2016a). *Action verbs for writing powerful outcomes.* [Handout]. Canvas.

Association of College and University Educators. (2016b). *Selecting teaching methods and moves.* [Handout]. Canvas.

Association of College and University Educators. (2022a). *Designing learner-centered and equitable courses.* https://acue.org/?acue_courses=designing-student-centered-courses.

Association of College and University Educators. (2022b). *The ACUE impact.* https://acue.org/impact/efficacy-studies-report/.

Bessant, J., & Watts, R. (2021). COVID, capital, and the future of work in Australia. *Australian Quarterly, 92*(1), 20–28.

Bidwell, C. M., & Froebe, D. J. (1971). Development of an instrument for evaluating hospital nursing performance. *The Journal of Nursing Performance, 1*(5), 10–15.

Bill & Melinda Gates Foundation. (2022). *Foundation fact sheet*. www.gatesfoundation.org/about/foundation-fact-sheet.

Bloom, B. S. (1966). *Stability and change in human characteristics*. John Wiley.

Bloom, B. S. (1978). New views of the learner: Implications for instruction and curriculum. *Educational Leadership, 35*(7), 563–576.

Bloom, B. S., Engelhart, M. D., Furst, E. J., Hill, W. H., & Krathwohl, D. R. (1956). *Taxonomy of educational objectives, the classification of educational goals, handbook I: Cognitive domain*. Longmans.

Brandt, R. S. (1985). On talent development: A conversation with Benjamin Bloom. *Educational Leadership, 43*(1), 33–35.

Brown, P. (2013). Education, opportunity and the prospects for social mobility. *British Journal of Sociology and Education, 34*(5/6), 678–700.

Brown, P., Reay, D., & Vincent, C. (2013). Introduction: Education and social mobility. *British Journal of Sociology and Education, 34*(5/6), 637–643.

Campbell, S., Castro, J. R., & Wessel, D. (2021, August 18). *The benefits and costs of broadband expansion*. Brookings. www.brookings.edu/blog/up-front/2021/08/18/the-benefits-and-costs-of-broadband-expansion/.

Centers for Disease Control and Prevention. (2020, July 6). *Coronavirus Disease 2019 (COVID-19): Social distancing keep a safe distance to slow the spread* [Press Release]. https://stacks.cdc.gov/view/cdc/90522.

Chandra, S. (1966). Lewin's theory of social change. *Indian Psychological Review, 2*(2), 139–141.

Chia, A. (2021). Self-making and game making in the future of work. In O. Sotamaa & J. Svelch (eds.), *Game production studies* (pp. 47–64). Amsterdam University Press.

Chou, S.-Y. (2019). The fourth industrial revolution: Digital infusion with internet of things. *Journal of International Affairs, 72*(1), 107–120.

Ciuriak, D. (2019). *The data-drive economy: Implications for Canada's economic strategy* [Policy Brief]. Center for International Governance Innovation.

Cope, B., & Kalantzis, M. (2017). *e-Learning ecologies: Principles for new learning and assessment*. Routledge.

The Economist Intelligence Unit. (2021). *Connecting learners: Narrowing the educational divide: The benefits from, and barriers to, improved school connectivity and access to digital learning*. https://connecting-learners.economist.com/data/EIU_Ericsson_Connecting.pdf.

Edmond, C. (2021, December 15). These startups are making education accessible using phone calls, texts and WhatsApp. *World Economic Forum*. www.weforum.org/agenda/2021/12/education-learning-accessible-phone-technology/.

Elkholm, B., & Fore, H. H. (2021, December 10). We need to connect every school to the internet. Here's how. *World Economic Forum*. www.weforum.org/agenda/2021/12/covid-19-education-digital-divide/.

Fink, C. (2021, March 9). *Morehouse college starts VR classes with VictoryXR*. Forbes. www.forbes.com/sites/charliefink/2021/03/09/morehouse-college-starts-vr-classes-with-victoryxr/?sh=3a7a9a5e2ba3.

Fletcher, M. (2000, March/April). The PUSH for diversity in silicon valley. *US Black Engineer and Information Technology, 24*(1), 74–75, 77.

Frederick D. Patterson Research Institute. (2022). *HBCUs making America strong: The positive economic impact of historically black colleges and universities*. United Negro College Fund (UNCF). https://cdn.uncf.org/wp-content/uploads/HBCU_Consumer_Brochure_FINAL_APPROVED.pdf?_ga=2.101771398.688845693.1656184664-2102309352.1656184664.

Friedman, T. L. (2007). *The world is flat: A brief history of the twenty-first century*. Picador. (Original work published in 2005).

Furst, E. J. (1981). Bloom's taxonomy of educational objectives for the cognitive domain: Philosophical and educational issues. *Review of Educational Research, 51*(4), 441–453.

Goldin, C., & Katz, L. F. (2008). *The race between education and technology*. Harvard University Press.

Greenstein, D. (2019). The future of undergraduate education: Will differences across sectors exacerbate inequality? *Daedalus, 148*(4), 108–137.

Guskey, T. R. (2007). Closing achievement gaps: Revisiting Benjamin S. Bloom's "learning for mastery". *Journal of Advanced Academics, 19*(1), 8–31.

Ha, N. H., Nayyar, A., Nguyen, D. M., & Liu, C. A. (2019). Enhancing students' soft skills by implementing CDIO-BASED integration teaching mode. In *The 15th international CDIO conference* (p. 569).

Halawi, L. A., McCarthy, R. V., & Pires, S. (2009). An evaluation of e-Learning on the basis of Bloom's taxonomy: An exploratory study. *Journal of Education for Business, 84*(6), 374–380.

Hammond, M., Owens, L., & Gulko, B. (2021). *HBCUs transforming generations: Social mobility outcomes for HBCU alumni.* UNCF. https://cdn.uncf.org/wp-content/uploads/Social-Mobility-Report-FINAL.pdf?_ga=2.225610650.1203443287.1637257494-1067485201.1637257494.
Haniya, S., & Rusch, A. (2017). Ubiquitous learning: Spatio-temporal dimensions of e-Learning. In B. Cope & M. Kalantzis (eds.), *e-Learning ecologies: Principles of new learning and assessment* (pp. 46–64). Routledge.
Harper, S. R., Patton, L. D., & Wooden, O. S. (2009). Access and equity for African American students in higher education: A critical race historical analysis of policy efforts. *The Journal of Higher Education, 80*(4), 389–414.
Haythornthwaite, C., & Andrews, R. (2011). *e-Learning theory & practice.* Sage.
Heifetz, R. A., & Laurie, D. L. (1997). The work of leadership. *Harvard Business Review, 75*(1), 124–130.
IEA. (n.d.). *About us.* www.iea.nl/about.
Jackman, L. W. (1999). *Information literacy: An issue of equity for new majority students* (UMI No. 9934618) [Doctoral dissertation, Lesley College]. UMI.
Jackson, L. M., & Rudin, T. (2019). Minority serving institutions: America's overlooked STEM asset. *Issues in Science and Technology, 35*(2), 53–55.
Jagzape, A. T., Shigli, K., & Patel, K. (2018). Group-based asynchronous e-Learning incorporating revised Bloom's taxonomy: An innovative approach. *Journal of Clinical & Diagnostic Research, 12*(1), 1–6.
Kotter, J. P. (2008). Developing a change-friendly culture: An interview with John P. Kotter. *Leader to Leader, 48, 33–38.*
Krathwohl, D. R. (2002). A revision of Bloom's taxonomy: An overview. *Theory into Practice, 41*(4), 212–218.
Krathwohl, D. R., & Anderson, L. W. (2010). Merlin C. Wittrock and the revision of Bloom's taxonomy. *Educational Psychologist, 45*(1), 64–65.
Kropp, R. P., Stoker, H. W., & Bashaw, W. L. (1966). The validation of the taxonomy of educational objectives. *The Journal of Experimental Education, 34*(3), 69–76.
Kumar, A., Krishnamurthi, R., Bhatia, S., Kaushik, K., Ahuja, N. J., Nayyar, A., & Masud, M. (2021). Blended learning tools and practices: A comprehensive analysis. *IEEE Access, 9*, 85151–85197.
Lewin, K. (1946). Action research and minority problems. *Journal of Social Issues, 2*(4), 34–46.
Miller, W. G., Snowman, J., & O'Hara, T. (1979). Application of alternative statistical techniques to examine the hierarchical ordering of Bloom's taxonomy. *American Educational Research Journal, 16*(3), 241–248.
Mukhopadhyay, M., Pal, S., Nayyar, A., Pramanik, P. K. D., Dasgupta, N., & Choudhury, P. (2020, February). Facial emotion detection to assess learner's State of mind in an online learning system. *5th International Conference on Intelligent Information Technology*, Hanoi, Vietnam.
Mwananchi Digital. (2022, January 24). *Bridging the digital divide in Tanzania* [Video]. YouTube. https://youtu.be/5jE9B_Ut-xI.
National Academies of Sciences, Engineering, and Medicine. (2019). *Minority serving institutions: America's underutilized resource for strengthening the STEM workforce.* The National Academies Press. https://doi.org/10.17226/25257.
National Center for Education Statistics. (2022). Number of public school districts and public and private elementary and secondary schools: Selected years, 1869–70 through 2010–11 (Table 98) [Data set]. Digest of Education Statistics. https://nces.ed.gov/programs/digest/d12/tables/dt12_098.asp.
National Digital Inclusion Alliance. (2022). *Definitions.* Retrieved June 7, 2022, from www.digitalinclusion.org/definitions/.
Philbeck, T., & Davis, N. (2019). The fourth industrial revolution: Shaping a new era. *Journal of International Affairs, 72*(1), 17–22.
Ragnedda, M. (2018). Tackling digital exclusion: Counter social inequalities through digital inclusion. In G. W. Muschert, K. M. Budd, M. Christian, B. V. Klocke, J. Shefner, & R. Perrucci (ed.), *Global agenda for social justice* (pp. 152–157). Bristol University Press.
Ragnedda, M. (2019). Conceptualising the digital divide. In B. Mutsvairo & M. Ragnedda (eds.), *Mapping digital divide in Africa: A mediated analysis* (pp. 27–43). Amsterdam University Press.
Richardson, V. (2022, June 12–16). *Digital solutions—HBCUv hackathon* [conference session]. UNCF Unite 2022 Conference.
Ross, K. A. (2017). *Breakthrough strategies: Classroom-based practices to support new majority college students.* Harvard Education Press.
Ruyter, A., Brown, M., & Burgess, J. (2019). Gig work and the fourth industrial revolution. *Journal of International Affairs, 72*(1), 37–50.
Schoenfeld-Tacher, R., McConnell, S., & Graham, M. (2001). Do no harm-A comparison of the effects of online vs. traditional delivery media on a science course. *Journal of Science Education and Technology, 10*(3), 257–265.

Seaman, M. (2011). Bloom's taxonomy: Its evolution, revision, and use in the field of education. *Curriculum and Teaching Dialogue*, *13*(1–2), 29–43.
Seddon, G. M. (1978). The properties of Bloom's taxonomy of educational objectives for the cognitive domain. *Review of Educational Research*, *48*(2), 303–323.
Shade, L. R. (2014). Missing in action: Gender in Canada's digital economy agenda. *Signs*, *39*(4), 887–896.
Skoll Foundation. (2021). *Powering social innovators to transform our world.* Skoll Foundation. https://skoll.org/about/.
Smith, A., & Kennett, K. (2017). Multi-modal meaning: Discursive dimensions of e-Learning. In B. Cope & M. Kalantzis (eds.), *e-Learning ecologies: Principles for new learning and assessment* (pp. 88–117). Routledge.
Sraders & Lambert. (2020, December 15). *Nearly 100,000 establishments that temporarily shut down due to the pandemic are now out of business.* Fortune. https://fortune.com/2020/09/28/covid-buisnesses-shut-down-closed/.
Talladega College. (2022, May 27). *To the metaverse, and beyond.* www.talladega.edu/news/to-the-metaverse-and-beyond/.
Tractenberg, R. E., Wilkinson, M. R., Bull, A. W., Pellathy, T. P., & Riley, J. B. (2019). A developmental trajectory supporting the evaluation and achievement of competencies: Articulating the master rubric for the nurse practitioner (MR-NP) program curriculum. *PLoS One*, *14*(11), 1–23.
UNICEF. (2021, December 06). *Learning losses from covid-19 could cost this generation of students close to $17 trillion in lifetime earnings: World Bank-UNESCO-UNICEF report lays out the magnitude of the education crisis.* www.unicef.org/press-releases/learning-losses-covid-19-could-cost-generation-students-close-17-trillion-lifetime.
Verizon. (2017, September 26). *Without a net: The digital divide in America, a new documentary from Academy Award nominee Rory Kennedy and Verizon premieres in national geographic on Tuesday, September 26.* Verizon. www.verizon.com/about/news/without-net-digital-divide-america-new-documentary-academy-award-nominee-rory-kennedy-and.
Verizon. (2021, September 17). *Verizon|Verizon Innovative Learning|Without a net* [Video]. YouTube. https://youtu.be/47c4nerUEk8.
Watson, V. B. (2020). The fourth industrial revolution and its discontents: Governance, big tech, and the digitization of geopolitics. In A. L. Vuving (ed.), *Hindsight, insight, foresight: Thinking about security in the Indo-Pacific* (pp. 37–48). Daniel K. Inouye Asia-Pacific Center for Security Studies.
The World Bank. (2021, July 1). *Ending learning poverty.* www.worldbank.org/en/topic/education/brief/ending-learning-poverty.
The World Bank, United Nations Educational, Scientific, and Cultural Organization, United Nations International Children's Emergency Fund, United States Agency for International Development, Foreign Commonwealth and Development Office, & Bill & Melinda Gates Foundation. (2022, June 23). *The state of global learning poverty: 2022 update* [Conference Edition]. www.unicef.org/media/122921/file/State%20of%20Learning%20Poverty%202022.pdf.

10 The Empirical Investigation of Artificial Intelligence for Enhancing the Learner–Instructor Interaction towards Online Learning Using Multiple Regression Analysis

Ajay Sidana and Neeru Sidana

10.1 INTRODUCTION

The advent of the pandemic put to test the resilience of the world at large. In no other sector was this change more evident than in education; almost overnight, the way of learning transformed at warp speed. Despite already being forecasted as a rapidly accelerating market valued at USD 300 billion by 2025 (Majumdar and Calhoun, 2020), this assessment was quickly re-evaluated to new heights after COVID-19. The pandemic has given a new direction and focus to the advancement in the context of online learning (Zhang and Lin, 2020; Hwang and Tu, 2021), promoting the transfer of offline curriculum into online learning ways. Online learning has become viable only via the application of modern computer technologies (Dhawan and Batra, 2020), and it has further enabled greater innovation in learning methods (Tang et al., 2021). Digital technologies and multimedia have also escalated the usage of online system (Mukhopadhyay et al., 2020). As millions of new learners across all groups and sectors enter the world of online learning, the scope and reach of technology is unparalleled even in this nascent stage (Seo et al., 2021).

Traditional learning practices include face-to-face interaction and directing the students to learn through memorizing and reciting techniques (Kumar et al., 2021). While the most apparent and discussed usage of advanced learning technology has been the use of smart devices in classrooms, or facilitation of online learning via file-sharing and communication applications, what has been equally noteworthy is the broadening scope of artificial intelligence (AI) in this field. AI enables technological tools to develop a human like intelligence characterized by the showcase of cognitive ability, adaptability, learning and decision-making. As (Sharma et al., 2019) puts it, AI refers to machines that have the capacity to approximate human reasoning. With its application in education sector, AI has the power to transform online learning process for the learner as much as the instructor. Instructors in the online learning field can leverage AI enabled technology to dispense their duties at a wider scale with relatively greater ease and efficiency, an impossible feat without digitalization. The impact of AI may be visible in instruction process, administration of learning, and also review of the effectiveness upon the learner (Chen et al., 2020). Instructors can now perform the strenuously repetitive tasks of their job such as grading tests and detecting plagiarism with the support of AI, making the process quicker and more efficient. While conducting any online learning sessions, the use of AI can help the instructors by analysing the learning history as well

DOI: 10.1201/9781003425779-10

as abilities of an online learner. The present technology offers several highly reliable AI functions that facilitate the online learning process right from building learner's profile to the assessment and evaluation of learner's performance (Abdulmunem Alshehhi et al., 2021). Technologies like face and speech recognition, virtual labs provide the opportunity to conduct a smart learning system authentically despite being remote. Use of content maps and adaptive learning systems enabled by AI aids the instructor in not only detection but also resolution of learning gaps among the students. The effective use of AI in online education can help in both grading as well as automating all the activities and their assessment using different filling blanks and questions related to multiple-choice options. Moreover, the proper use of AI also can help online tutors while preparing students' report cards and their automation as well while conducting online learning. The instructors can get a clear and vast detailed picture regarding particular subjects as well as lessons that need to be taught and evaluated from learners' perception. In several more of these ways, AI has been embraced by instructors in online learning scenarios, with a deep knowledge of its vast ability to optimize usual instruction methods.

From the learner's perspective, AI provides supplementary support to the existing learning capacity, leading to the argument by several researchers that AI can also lead to higher education levels and better academic performance (Kuprenko, 2020). AI also provides a more flexible learner support system than conventional check-ins by the instructor. AI-propelled interactions offer space for more liberating interactions between learners and instructors, as well as reducing time and space limitations in the learning network models (Jiang et al., 2020). Technologies such as virtual personalized assistants and real-time analysis of instructions gives the learners ready support while eliminating the need for the instructor's constant availability.

An investigation regarding the use of AI on online learning has also reflected that the advanced process can at once equalize different virtual opportunities for effective learning. Besides, it has been also traced that the applications of proper AI technology can at once enhance the learner-instructor relationship and interactions while conducting effective online learning. In contrast to that, it can be determined that using numerous AI technologies can escalate numerous skills and ability differences regarding polarizing suitable teaching jobs.

Presently, while there exists relevant literature reviews in the field of AI applications in online learning, it may be seen that a majority of such reviews are focused solely on a particular discipline such as science or maths (Hwang and Tu, 2021), or restricted to a certain field (George and Lal, 2019). Additionally, the existing literature in this field has also been left suddenly outdated due to the vast changes brought in by the pandemic. This development has rendered the existing research lacking relevance to the present scenario (Sharma et al., 2019; Kim et al., 2019; Wartman and Combs, 2019). Additionally, these studies have not explored the impact of integrating AI into online learning while differentiating the perspective and experiences of instructors and learners involved. Last, as the post-pandemic world begins to transition into a hybrid mode of learning, it is of great importance to re-establish research into the development of AI in online learning in this current scenario.

Therefore, considering the discussion above, the pre-existing research in this field was extracted and analysed in this study. By applying the literature methodology, this chapter has pondered four major research questions, namely:

R1: How has AI integration facilitated learner-instructor interactions towards online learning?

R2: How can the impact of AI in facilitating learner-instructor interactions towards online learning be assessed?

R3: What has been the overall impact of AI in developing learner-instructor interactions towards online learning?

R4: What are the ways in which AI technology can be used to sustainably ameliorate learner-instructor interactions towards online learning?

The findings of this study will have potential benefits to several stakeholders in the online learning field. The study will be a worthy addition to further research regarding the impact of AI on the online learning process, particularly vis-à-vis the attitude of instructors and students towards the same. It has been identified that AI implementation on the online learning process can at once enhance the attitudes of receptiveness towards online learning methods and aid in effective teaching and obtaining a proper education. The findings will have practical implications for administrators, teachers and coaches, leadership and management in online learning institutions by enabling evidence-based decisions regarding integration of AI into online learning. Furthermore, the use of AI for online learning also can be implemented for dealing with potential online challenges in various educational institutions. At a broader scale, the data-backed findings of this study can also have usefulness in influencing policy decisions around AI with the objective being enhancing both learner and instructor attitudes towards online learning.

10.1.1 Organization of the Chapter

The chapter is organized as follows. Section 10.2 highlights literature review which provides a comprehensive overview of research already existing in this field. In this section, detailed analysis on the merits of using AI for enhancing interactions towards online learning during the global pandemic is discussed from a dual perspective of learners and instructors. Section 10.3 discusses the research methodology where a survey has been conducted which collected the data from some respondents which has been further analysed for drawing an evaluation and conclusion. Using multiple regression analysis, the importance and impact of applying AI on online learning has been evaluated in respect to the effective learning and interactions between the instructor and the learner. SPSS regression analysis has been conducted as well to assess the entire data for understanding the significant relationship between the variables. Section 10.4 presents the analysis and interpretation of the data, where relationship between the dependent and independent variables of online learning is analysed. Section 10.5 presents a discussion based on findings obtained from the regression analysis conducted in the study. And, finally section 10.6 concludes the chapter with future scope.

10.2 LITERATURE REVIEW

Discussions around AI and its applications in the modern day have begun to be associated with conducting an effective online learning process that can aid both the instructor and the learner. In this section, a comprehensive review of relevant literature in this field is presented in a structure by explaining the nature of AI in learning, the impact of AI implementation in online learning, AI implementation and the instructor's perspective, and AI implementation and the learner's perspective. At the end of the review, some research gaps have been highlighted. These gaps in the existing literature have laid the foundation for the present chapter.

10.2.1 Nature of AI in Learning

To understand the implementation of AI into the learning processes, it is important to first establish the meaning of AI as perceived in this study. The present subsection seeks to establish the meaning and nature of AI and its role in learning.

The study builds upon the understanding of AI as per its meaning laid out in Chassignol et al. (2018). In the study, the researchers defined AI to be a theoretical framework which may be used to effectively guide the usage of computer systems, but with the added intelligence and ability to perform tasks with a likeness to human beings themselves. This presence of artificial cognitive abilities, or intelligence, allows a computer to perform certain guided tasks involving perception, decision-making, translation, recognition and so on. Additionally, AI must be inclusive of the ability to adapt to an immediately changing environment, thus mimicking human actions even further. This definition, along with several similar others (Fukui et al., 2019), forms the tenets and features that lay down the basic characteristics of what constitutes AI implementation today.

The implementation of AI into education and learning comprises approaches towards smarter learning, improved input processing, data analysis, results prediction and providing adaptive learning outcomes. As explained by Fukui et al. (2019), the triple-pronged approach to AI in learning must yield three key results: (1) educating people about AI and its scope; (2) tackling challenges in the education sector with the judicious use of AI; and (3) prioritizing the development of our own human intelligence through the benefits of AI-aided learning. To achieve these objectives, Fukui et al. (2019) suggested collaboration between educators and AI developers for building AI technology which is specially designed for improving training and education.

The integration of AI-enabled technologies such as speech recognition, prediction systems, data mining, analytics, virtual assistants, chatbots and so forth offers possibilities of improved attitudes towards education in every scenario. Chen et al. (2020) highlighted how education scenarios of varying kinds, such as students or school assessments, exam conduction and grading, personalized coaching and instruction, can utilize specific sets of AI tools which can significantly better their experience and results. The study suggested that AI techniques are not one-size-fits-all but rather offer a cornucopia of benefits that can be chosen as per necessity and objective of a particular education scenario. As per the research done by Chassignol et al. (2018), AI is extensively applicable in the development of educational curriculum and offers personalization of content within. AI's range of implementation also enables improved pedagogy and instruction, and the quality of assessment. The research also highlighted that AI improves the communication capacity between students and instructors by providing an environment for the same. By providing benefits such as expedition and automation of administrative tasks like grading essays or maintaining attendance rolls, the AI systems help the instructors to free their personal time and mind space for interacting with students on a personal level. The researchers have given instances of multiple AI applications on different platforms, calling them interactive learning environments (ILEs) that facilitate exchanges between students and teachers. These AI-aided environments can be used by instructors to efficiently evaluate and manage the performance of learners for giving actionable feedback. Chen et al. (2020) also identified that AI systems create individualized learning digital interfaces between the instructor and learner so that instructors are able to gain better students insights with the tools at their disposal.

According to a research by Sharma et al. (2019), the role of AI has gradually taken the shape of adaptive learning and intelligent tutoring systems. These improved systems have immense utility in ameliorating the quality of regular administration of education, the instructions process, and learning outcomes. The findings of this study are in sync with the observations made by Pokrivčáková (2019). In the latter study, the researcher states that AI is an intelligent system which takes on adaptive capabilities. The introduction of these capabilities is what allows AI in education to be multidimensional; it can take on multiple different roles played by an instructor in the classroom or the administration. The traditional duties performed by instructors can be aided or improved upon by AI. Along with managing this, AI can simultaneously improve the learning experiences of students by smoothly adapting to their personal needs and expectations from the learning programs.

As pointed out in the study by Wartman and Combs (2019), education is gradually transforming in form and methods as per the shifting scenario in the professional sector. This necessitates the implementation of constantly adapting and evolving learning models. The implementation of AI in learning can result in higher applicability of instructions due to the immediate relevance in such changing environments. The study done by Mikropoulos and Natsis (2011) provided another aspect of AI implementation in education and learning. The study provided insights into the development of virtual reality and three-dimensional technology in the learning process, and how the same adds wider opportunities for the instructor to conduct learning. The additional layer of AI techniques thus aids the instructor in facilitating experiential learning for the students by providing simulations for more effective instructions.

Such intelligent systems help in increasing timeliness and reliability of feedback and instruction, thus improving the overall effectiveness of learning. AI-aided techniques suggested by the study in improving learning include computer vision and image recognition for grading answer sheets faster and with more accuracy. In a similar vein, an adaptive learning method and parallel designed approach provides ease of assessment for schools and students. Intelligent data mining systems backed with reliable patterns predicted by learning analytics further find applications in improving the outcomes of personalized coaching.

AI in learning thus lends itself to the development of holistic learning models which are based on well-established structures and rules of association to collect the requisite data and build data maps. Kim et al. (2019) elaborated upon the technological structure that is followed in order to accommodate AI into learning. The researchers outlined that AI-enabled learning systems are first founded upon an emotionally intelligent algorithm which relies on learning maps, content maps, and knowledge metadata to propose learning models and profile. This accumulated knowledge is then processed via the use of AI techniques and tools including machine learning, natural language processing, computer vision and others in order to provide complete benefits of a personalized and adaptive learning outcome.

10.2.2 Impact of AI Implementation in Online Learning

As the modern world becomes increasingly technology driven, there is much supporting evidence of how macro-operating environments across all sectors are gradually transitioning from plain computer-based practices to online or virtual technologies, with a parallel increase in dependency on AI or intelligent systems. As per Ally (2019), it had been evaluated that using AI technology in the virtual learning process has several advantages that can be highly beneficial for all online learners. This subsection focuses on the integration of AI systems into online learning environments and the existing research that supports this development. Particularly during and after the pandemic, this field has shown an exponential growth and encouraged meaningful research. The subsection will provide insights into the existing studies which have brought out the impact of AI implementation in online learning process.

According to Kahraman et al. (2010), the integration of the technology and principles of AI improves learners' experiences. The study explored the utility of AI in replacing the bland leveraging and use of internet and World Wide Web by adaptive and intelligent web-based education. In a similar vein, Pedro et al. (2019) also emphasized the impact of integration of AI into web-based platforms more than conventional learning tools. The study proposed that intelligent web-based learning is taking the position of being a crucial component of modern-day education, especially with the growing scope of online education. The study discussed the development of AI into online education within the context of the great power yielded by online education platforms as a pedagogical tool which can incorporate and leverage AI and also include other intelligent tools, methods, and theories. The study also explores deeper how engineering agent-based technologies can be incorporated into web-based education with intelligent systems. According to an empirical study by Edwards and Cheok (2018), it was found that enormous learning hubs have shown preference towards utilizing AI when conducting online learning programs. This preference had been justified by citing enhanced virtual learning efficiency as a result of AI implementation in online learning.

According to Ciolacu et al. (2018), AI has the potential to foster greater access to education. The researchers suggested that AI fosters learning by elimination of barriers to learning. It also aids in the automation of administration and management tasks in educational institutions and helps in the optimization of learning. Furthermore, AI implementation paves the way for evidence-based, analytical, and empirical decisions in chalking out the progression of the education process. These benefits have led to overall positive impact in installing a better professional environment for learners and instructors.

From the analysis in the study by Holstein et al. (2018), it was concluded that the application of AI in learning provides avenues to dismantle the physical barriers that are placed by national and international borders with learning materials getting domiciled across the internet. The researchers argued that learning online or with the use of web-based learning platforms means that the material is accessible from anywhere in the world, and leveraging other aspects of AI, such as language translation tools, makes it possible for students to learn best within the context of their individual abilities.

During the time of the pandemic, instructors sought to apply numerous AI tools and software in order to enhance the efficiency of online learning (Pedro et al., 2019). On the other hand, through efficient use of all these artificial intelligent software, the communication process between both the teachers and the students can be enhanced while processing any online learning program (Mohammed and Watson, 2019). One of the most interesting merits of using AI in the virtual learning process is conducting personalized learning. In contrast to that, while conducting an adaptive learning process, the usefulness of AI implementation for online learning also can be effective for the learners during the time of the current pandemic.

It is also important to consider the factors which encourage the integration of AI into online education process. The same was analyzed in a study by Pedro et al. (2019). According to the findings of their study, the incorporation of AI is dependent on several factors, including but not limited to the knowledge and skill level of the learners, their learning prowess, their capabilities to perform, the overall level of compatibility with AI and so forth. These factors can be leveraged in the development and usage of online education platforms with improved experiences for both teachers and learners.

10.2.3 The Negative Impact of AI Implementation in Learning

Several authors explained that, besides positive impacts, AI systems in education may have some negative impacts as well. For example, students have mentioned that data assessment by AI systems can breach personal data on the internet and personal data may lose privacy protection (Yang et al., 2019). Moreover, students can perceive algorithms and data bias when AI is implemented. This suggests that algorithms in AI are trained using biased data. An example of AI bias that can be explained apart from the teaching and learning is developing a human face diagram using AI where AI develops the white-faced man rather than a person with a dark-toned skin colour. Various other types of societal and algorithmic biases are implemented inside AI which is a major drawback of the AI system in education (Leavy, 2018).

According to Criollo-C et al. (2018), high dependence on AI systems for answering questions and solving problems reduces the critical thinking ability of a student. Authors suggested that AI is an interesting and attractive technology that attracts students to use AI for solving simple to complex problems. As previously mentioned, AI saves the time of a teacher and student, and thus students are attracted towards AI without using critical thinking. This is another major drawback of the AI system in education. Kumar (2019) suggested that how the AI system will be used depends on the institution and the teacher. Thus, when teachers limit the use of AI in class and students are not exposed to advanced AI technologies, it will reduce the dependency on AI (Criollo-C et al., 2018).

In their study, Kumar (2019) suggested that the AI system affects the connection between the learner and the instructor. This suggests that lethargy and not being interested to use critical thinking skills lead to use of AI in classes (Kumar, 2019). This ultimately reduces the interaction between the teacher and the student. Moreover, AI systems may have an excessive impact inside the classroom or in online classes which include problems in building effective cognitive relationships between the learner and instructor, changing the relationships and so on.

10.2.4 AI Implementation and the Instructor's Perspective

This subsection delves into the literature which has supported the utility of AI tools and models to develop an instructor's experience. Several studies in the past have reported that the AI technology and its useful applications have several benefits from an instructor's perspective.

The vast use of AI technologies also can be traced while investigating the effective use of learning through processing multiple analyses of regression. Using proper AI tools and software for learners can be highly beneficial for instructors because AI technologies can offer multiple opportunities in order to track weaknesses in the learning process. According to Holstein et al. (2018), the entire process using artificial technologies can help tutors to improve their subject contents continuously in order to process a better efficiency regarding relevant resources. Apart from this, an increased return on investment can be measured and applied for the betterment of students' learning process through using various AI technologies. Thus, these factors are essential for strengthening the instructor interactions during teaching.

In the study by Mohammed and Watson (2019), the researchers discussed the utility of AI implementation in discovering learning gaps. Using AI techniques, instructors can conduct numerous training courses that can aid in identifying learning gaps between the instructors' methods and the knowledge-gaining activities of the students. In order to fill the gaps between learner-instructors' interactions for conducting more effective engagement, instructors mainly focus on applying AI methods efficiently. AI also helps in creating curriculum automatic methods for learners so that they can be able to fix all the gaps traced during the teaching process.

Along with the resolution of learning gaps, the study by Ally (2019) elaborated that AI can be effectively used to pose intelligent solutions to other learning problems. The use of AI is also effective for the instructors because it can provide desired solutions regarding various teaching-related issues, including recognition of learning speech, effective language translations, various educational decision-making approaches and so on.

According to Ocana-Fernandez et al. (2019), the applications of AI in education can offer automatic learner assessments that can at once help in strengthening active communication between both the teachers and the students regarding any subject issues. AI also deals with the implementation of numerous learning tools in order to support global virtual learning. Besides, online instructors while teaching their students primarily throw some effective light on the built-in creation of stealth assessments that help learners recognize essential aspects of an online test. AI and its applications on different opportunities related to online learning can use essential resources regarding educational approaches that provide help to the instructors.

According to Sandu and Gide (2019), the implementation of numerous AI technologies while teaching students mediums can enhance educational productivity. The main reason behind this factor is that AI technological advantages can accelerate the rate of the entire learning process. Thus, applying for AI benefits with teaching, instructors can effectively utilize a better assessment of teacher time.

Researchers found that applying AI technologies over the learning process can conduct as well as condense more than one educational lecture at a time. This process can at once enhance effective interaction between the teachers and the students by using numerous guidelines (García-Peñalvo, 2020).

As per Pereira et al. (2020), using numerous flashcards along with smart guides for studies can also aid a tutor in processing effective learning. It had been identified that using these factors according to the problems faced by various students can be highly effective. On the other hand, AI technology applied in these systems can help both learners and instructors to adapt to a vast range of learning styles. In contrast to that, developing a learning program through using AI technologies is also essential for education that is mainly based on the preferences of personal educational guides.

According to García-Peñalvo (2020), these technologies at once help them increase the learning efficiency to almost 67% by creating short and engaging educational courses while conducting virtual teaching. From various surveys and reports, it has been also evaluated that these AI methods of learning can influence professionals to build an effective learning platform for further automation.

According to Putnam and Conati (2019), while discussing the impacts of using AI across the learning process, it can be analysed that AI can at once automate all the basic tasks related to education. One of the important uses of AI for enhancing virtual learning can be vastly seen in the overall grading system of the learners. Through using numerous AI software and tools, students can prepare desired online classes towards effective professional development. On the other hand, AI technology also aids in enhancing the students-teachers communication towards education by focusing more on various activities related to in-class assessments. Besides, AI can also help in improving the quality of online courses. AI and its applications in education are necessary for analysing course patterns from an effective perspective. However, by alerting all the instructors to these particular course patterns, AI can improve their teaching abilities with time.

Samek and Müller (2019) listed several advantages for educators and institutions by incorporating a greater role of AI in learning. According to the researchers, the primary advantage of AI in learning is custom curriculum formation. AI can aid educators in developing personalized curriculums for every student that can adapt to their strengths and weaknesses. The presence of AI makes this mental process more manageable and evidence based, rather than relying on the educators' observations and judgment alone. At the same time, AI allows educators to delve deeper into the education process by sparing time and effort required for lesson plan development and data analysis of the students' output. AI's role is also extended to detection of students' limitations and shortcomings which may occur as a repetitive pattern. By bringing it to the educator's notice, AI can potentially help in diagnosis of divergent learning styles in a student. Additionally, AI technologies can then assist the educational institution in finding the best teacher for a particular learning style.

According to Jocas et al. (2019), AI-based learning provides answers to the simple questions of the students quickly, which saves time over conventional methods and suggested that AI assistants are used by the instructors to save time for providing answers to simple formula-based questions. Questions with 'Yes and No' answers, formulas and short answers are managed by implementing AI.

Edwards and Cheok (2018) suggested that an AI system helps an instructor to analyse students' progress, performance and click-stream data. Ciolacu et al. (2018) posited that hybridized deep neural network (HDNN) technology is used to assess the student's performance. By making use of deep learning, HDNN technology in AI can distinguish human action patterns far better than conventional methods of data analysis. The HDNN method is a better technology than any other method for analysing students' performance and progress. Table 10.1 explains the various instruction objectives achieved through adapting AI tools for improving learner efficiency.

TABLE 10.1
Summary of Suggested Artificial Intelligence–Aided Techniques Which Can Assist the Instructor in the Learning Process

Instruction Objective	AI Tools for Improved Efficiency
Analysis of curriculum and course materials	Gradescope AI, data analytics systems
Instruction effectiveness and accessibility	Humanoid robots, automatic speech transcription
Practical instructions and models	3-D modelling, virtual reality, augmented reality
Customized teaching and aids based on personal metadata	Gamified learning, chatbot
Data analysis of student performance	Gradescope AI, virtual learning assistants, hybridized deep neural network
Grade assessment	Plagiarism detection, grammar correction, hybridized deep neural network
Supervision	Plagiarism detection

Source: Chen et al. (2020), Sharma et al. (2019).

10.2.5 AI Implementation and the Learner's Perspective

On the flip side, AI implementation yields several benefits from the learner's perspective as well. In this subsection, the study provides a review of the current research into AI implementation vis-a-vis its impact on a student during the learning process.

It can be also analysed that AI and its utilization of learning processes can provide several benefits to the students. While conducting educational programs, learners can apply a personalized approach towards effective learning by using AI technology based on their preferences and learning experiences and preferences. Besides, students also can get help from various virtual AI tutors (Chen et al., 2020). According to Samek and Müller (2019), learners can search for answers to their queries in seconds through artificial automation as well as conversational intelligence learning. One of the essential advantages of AI-powered tools is that they can make the online learning process accessible for all learners from anywhere and anytime they need. On the other hand, AI applications also help the instructors to answer frequently asked questions and task automation (Putnam and Conati, 2019). Thus, the effective use of AI for enhancing online learning can be conducted broadly across the globe while processing online education.

According to Sie et al. (2018), network learning is achieved by connectedness. The connectedness here defines the connections between resources, ideas and people. Authors suggested that effective learning is achieved when an affordable multitude is provided for the social exchange of knowledge between the instructor and students.

On the other hand, Alencar and Netto (2020) suggested that effective learning is achieved through an openness between the student, instructor and learning processes. The authors also stated that online learning is dependent on self-determination, affordances, community building and sense of purpose. Other than these, supporting learning platforms are required for providing guidance at every problem of the student (Jiang et al., 2020). Therefore, online learning requires more than the resources which include the social presence (visible social presence) where both teacher and student will be engaged in a face-to-face manner. Studies suggest that facial impressions are important for the learning process because 90% of human communications are nonverbal (Stevens et al., 2021).

A study by Stevens et al. (2021) also stated that 41% of face-to-face interaction had a significant benefit in online learning. However, the study was carried out to understand the importance of online learning where the respondents agreed with the benefits of face-to-face learning. The study did not compared face-to-face and no face-to-face interactions. Thus, it can be concluded that online teaching is a beneficial practice to some extent where face-to-face engagement is more important.

Dynamic network learning requires cognitive and teaching presence where student-teacher interaction is essential for effective learning (Edwards and Cheok, 2018). This suggested that visible human interaction is important to build a strong network connection between the learner and the instructor. As previously mentioned, more than 90% of the conversations occur non-verbally and thus, cognitive presence is necessary to share maximum knowledge along with gaining access to resources and ideas. Apart from this, cognitive and visible online teaching practices help the students and teachers to feel a group of connected environments which develop trust and safety among the people (Saputro and Susilowati, 2019).

Seo et al. (2021) provided a model that outlines the beneficial impact of AI and supportive systems into learning and teaching. Using a circular model, the study discussed how influence of AI supports the development of learning activities such as the development and grading of tasks and activities, and enhances the teaching presence of the instructors. This support to the learners is reflected in enhanced teaching as well with improved engagement, classroom discussions and interaction between pupil and master. Development of AI in the online learning process also completes the missing element of social and cognitive presence which is otherwise conspicuously absent from virtual learning.

The study by Chen et al. (2020) supported the argument that integration of AI technologies like virtual reality can facilitate the learning process beyond a physical learning space. With the addition of virtual reality environments, students can experience a global classroom by connecting via AI. Additionally, the experience can also benefit from AI-based chatbots, which provide personalized online learning and convert instructions into more digestible chat conversations for increased engagement. The technology can also be used to assess the understanding level of the students. Table 10.2 explains the AI-aided techniques which can assist the instructor in learning process.

10.2.6 Learner-Instructor Interactions

The present subsection of this study shows a review of the existing studies on learner-instructor's interactions towards online learning. This review of the literature will provide insight into the attitude of instructors towards online learning in general.

Since decades, researchers have generally agreed upon the importance of interaction as a key variable in the level of satisfaction and learning progress in distance or online education (Wanstreet, 2006). According to Wanstreet (2006), the variable interaction can be defined through its scope as instructional exchange between multiple entities. It includes interactions between the user and the interface, or user and information (Sabry and Baldwin, 2003), and also the process of communication as facilitated by computer-mediated technologies (Wanstreet, 2006). It can also refer to learner-instructor interactions, which poses as a social and psychological connection across two different perspectives with the objective to foster learning. The study has also discussed Vygotsky's (1978) model on learner-instructor interactions known as the zone of proximal development. In this model, Vygotsky (1978) posits the instructor to act as the bridge between the learner's existing knowledge and capacity and the learner's desired level of knowledge and capacity (Ng'ambi and Hardman, 2004). The research overall concluded that while there exist several nuanced definitions of the term interaction, there is a general agreement throughout the field on the conceptual definition of the term.

The satisfaction of learner-instructor interactions was based upon the number of times informational communication as initiated by the instructors (Kang and Im, 2013). The study by Lee and Gibson (2003) found that learner-instructor interactions were influenced by learning style preferences. One of the measures for learner-instructor interactions effectiveness by the number of queries resolved within a given interactive setup (Appana, 2008). Similarly, the research by Wanstreet

TABLE 10.2
Summary of Artificial Intelligence–Aided Techniques Which Can Assist the Learners in the Learning Process

Learning Objective	AI Tools for Improved Efficiency
Pattern analysis of learning behaviour	Multi-agent systems (MAS)
Customization of course selection for learners	Library assistants, virtual tutors
Data predictions regarding school attendance and longevity	Data analytics
Detection of ongoing learning state and assessment of improvement	Learning behaviour assessment, data analytics
Simulate practical aspects of learning	Virtual reality, stimulation
Repetitive practice and improved questions	Speech recognition, machine learning
Information-seeking, problem-solving	Chatbots, cobots, intelligent tutoring systems (ITS)
Writing and translating, automatic grade assessment	Immersive reader, optical character recognition, computer-assisted language learning (CALL)

Source: Chen et al. (2020), Sharma et al. (2019).

(2006) also found that reciprocal communication was a key determinant of learner-instructor interaction success. Instructor updating knowledge and reading material are also a determinant factor of effective learning (Ha et al., 2019).

According to Kang and Im (2013), interaction serves as a critical element in online learning environments. The study relates the satisfaction by learner-instructor interactions to successful learning outcomes online. It was found that instructional interaction led to greater perceived learning achievements and learner's confidence. According to Appana (2008), online or distanced learning separates the learner and instructor by geographical distance or time, thus making student readiness limited in the learning environment. The study also listed the benefits of online learning on the instructor-learner relationship as improved learning quality, and increased access to resource sharing. These findings were supported by the study by Andersen (2013), which found that learner-instructor interactions were determinant factors for general course satisfaction levels. The study highlighted that online learning environments were learner centric instead of faculty centered, which directly shapes the teaching methodology employed in these learning processes.

10.2.6.1 Research Gaps

It is evident from the current review of literature that abundant research is available on the applications of AI in virtual learning. However, some key research gaps can be identified which makes the current research lacking.

Firstly, currently available research is insufficient in exploring the relationship between AI and online learning from the perspective of improving existing interactions with online learning. The current study has delved into the direct impact of AI implementation on interactions towards online learning.

Secondly, in the few studies which have been undertaken in this field, the relationship has not been analysed from the split perspective of instructors and learners. This poses the problem of generalization in our understanding regarding the impact of AI implementation in interactions towards online learning. The current study addresses this differentiation by separately assessing the perspective of learner and instructor in their interactions towards online learning.

10.3 RESEARCH METHODOLOGY

The research method is based on primary quantitative data collection from students and instructors. The pandemic situation has resulted in the prohibition of human movements, and thus the researcher has chosen an online survey–based data collection technique Survey data helps to collect quantitative information based on individual judgements. Moreover, primary sources help a researcher to collect raw and practical data which can be further analysed to draw a conclusion. The primary data was analysed by assessing recently available online journal articles and authentic sources. The journal articles were selected from Google Scholar, PubMed and Scopus. The research was carried forward by assessing articles published in the last 5 years (2018–2022). Articles published earlier than 2018 may have conventional and less-defined information about the new technologies. Thus, to assess the current technologies, the researcher used the most recent five-year period.

Besides, authentic internet sources have been analysed for completing the incomplete judgements from journal articles. Authentic internet sources included BBC.com, some websites with the suffix '.org' and country-based websites ('.uk' and so on). Moreover, international websites will be assessed as well when required.

The *purposive sampling technique* has been used to conduct the research. This technique allows a researcher to draw a judgement based on primary quantitative data. The primary data has been collected by a survey on 25 students and 25 instructors via Google Forms. The survey form was given and asked whether AI technology has significance on Responsibility, Quality and Quantity, Connections between the instructor and student, Surveillance and Support in education. These factors have been selected as dependent variables, and Gender and AI implementation have been selected as independent variables. Therefore, the research will assess whether AI implementation has a significant benefit for the dependent variables. The students and teachers have provided their satisfaction level depending on whether the dependent variables are achieved through AI implementation. Therefore, regression tests were carried out to understand whether AI implementation has any significance on education.

Output values of the regression test have been evaluated for further interpretation. When the significance value is below 0.05 ($p < 0.05$) between two variables, it means there is a significant relationship between the two variables (dependent and independent). *P*-value > 0.05 has been considered as an insignificant relationship between the variables. Other than this, the *R*-square value has been considered as well.

After interpreting the data, the researcher has moved forward to further evaluate the output data where secondary research will be carried out to draw a judgement based on the primary data. Judgments and reasons behind the responses have not been collected from the respondents; rather the researcher has drawn the judgement using available journal articles.

10.4 ANALYSIS AND INTERPRETATION

Table 10.3 shows the coefficient and regression values where the *t* value, significance value (*p*) and *R*-square values were selected (Figure 10.1). The *t* value has been selected due to its ability to reject the null hypothesis. The null hypothesis, in this case, is 'Students are not receiving any impact by the implementation of AI'. Thus, the alternative hypothesis is students are positively or negatively affected by the implementation of AI in education. Twenty-five students were selected to understand how many times they were exposed to AI in their education. Researchers identified that the number ranged between 0 and 40. After that, based on the expositing numbers, researchers asked them to rate their satisfaction level according to Quality and Quantity of education, Responsibility in AI, Support by AI, Connection maintained with AI and Surveillance system. The satisfaction levels ranged between 0 and 5, where 0 defines satisfaction level as lowest and 5 defines satisfaction level as highest.

Table 10.3 shows that the coefficient *t* value is much higher when Quality and Quantity is considered in AI learning. Moreover, the *p*-value is less than 0.001 ($p < 0.001$), which suggests a presence of greater significance between the number of AI exposures and satisfaction level based on Quality and Quantity of education. A higher *R*-square value (*R*-square = 0.756) interprets the two variables as highly correlated with each other. An *R*-square value above 0.9 is taken as standard; however, in this case, the value is close to 0.8. Therefore, a significant correlation is present between the two

TABLE 10.3
Regression Analysis of Student's Perception

	Coefficients (*t* value)	Significance (*p*-value)	*R*-square value
Times of AI Implementation (0–40) [independent variable]	0.00	0.00	0.00
Quality and Quantity[a]	8.447	0.000	0.756
Responsibility[a]	–1.972	0.061	0.145
Support[a]	0.180	0.859	0.001
Connection[a]	4.236	0.000	0.438
Surveillance[a]	–4.679	0.000	0.488

[a] = Satisfaction level on a 5-point Likert scale with 0 = lowest satisfaction and 5 = highest satisfaction.

Source: Created by the researcher.

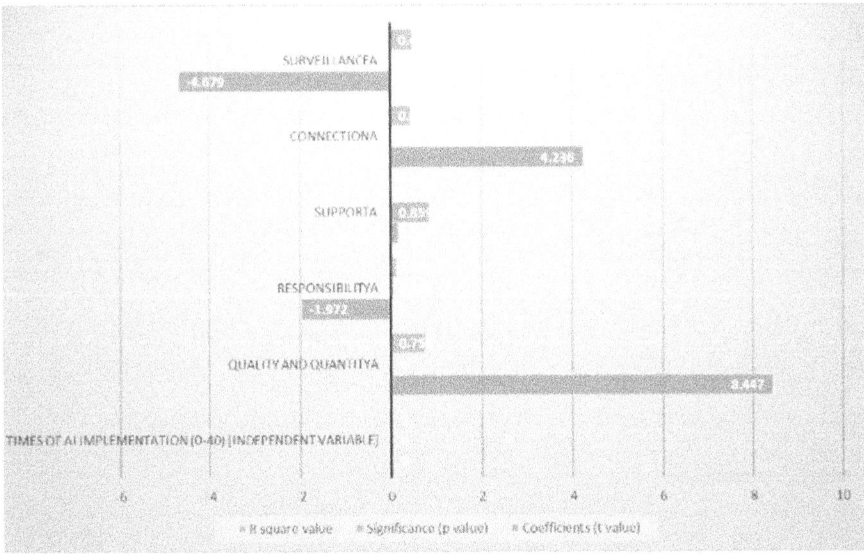

FIGURE 10.1 Regression analysis diagram of students' responses.

Source: Created by the researcher.

variables. The *t* value here is 8.447, which indicates that the *t* value is much greater and is positive. Usually, a positive *t* value indicates the two variables change with each other proportionally. To simplify, when the exposure to AI increases, the satisfaction level also increases in the case of 'Quality and Quantity' of education and vice versa. Thus, a positive *t* value indicates AI implementation has satisfied the students' need on Quantity and Quality of education. Moreover, a greater *t* value (8.447) indicates the correlation is highly significant. This suggests that when AI exposure is increased among students, they receive high quality and quantity of education. Thus, it shows AI has a positive impact on the quantity and quality of education.

On the other hand, instructors have provided their satisfaction level on this matter (Table 10.4; Figure 10.2). The *R*-square value is quite low (*R*-square < 0.2), which suggests that AI exposure did not significantly impact the instructors on a basis of Quality and Quantity of education. The satisfaction level among instructors is highly variable. However, the significance level is less than 0.05 ($p < 0.05$), which suggests that an average significant relationship is present between the two variables. Last, the *t* value is 2.259, which is larger than 1; therefore, the null hypothesis can be rejected and the alternative hypothesis can be accepted. The null hypothesis states that no significant correlation is present between the two variables. More specifically, AI does not satisfy the instructors in education based on quality and quantity. Thus, a positive $t < 2.3$ indicates AI exposure positively impacts the instructors' behaviour towards education quality and quantity.

When satisfaction level was measured among students based on the Responsibility of AI, the significance was average ($p < 0.062$). This suggests that Responsibility and exposure to AI have an average correlation with each other. However, the *t* value is negative (–1.972), which suggests that AI exposure harms students' perception. Students believe AI exposure did not benefit the satisfaction level based on Responsibility. This will be further discussed in the discussion section. The *R*-square value is average as well and is much lower than 0.4, which suggests that the correlation between the two variables is not quite significant. The null hypothesis is not rejected in this case. On the other hand, the *t* value of instructors showed –2.942, which is highly negative and shows a strong negative correlation between the two variables. This suggests that AI exposure reduces the responsibilities.

TABLE 10.4
Regression Analysis of Instructor's Perception

	Coefficients (t value)	Significance (p-value)	R-square value
Times of AI Implementation (0–40) [independent variable]	0.00	0.00	0.00
Quality and Quantity[a]	2.259	0.034	0.182
Responsibility[a]	−2.942	0.007	0.273
Support[a]	5.927	0.000	0.604
Connection[a]	7.546	0.000	0.712
Surveillance[a]	−1.665	0.110	0.108

[a] = Satisfaction level on a 5-point Likert scale with 0 = lowest satisfaction and 5 = highest satisfaction.

Source: Created by the researcher.

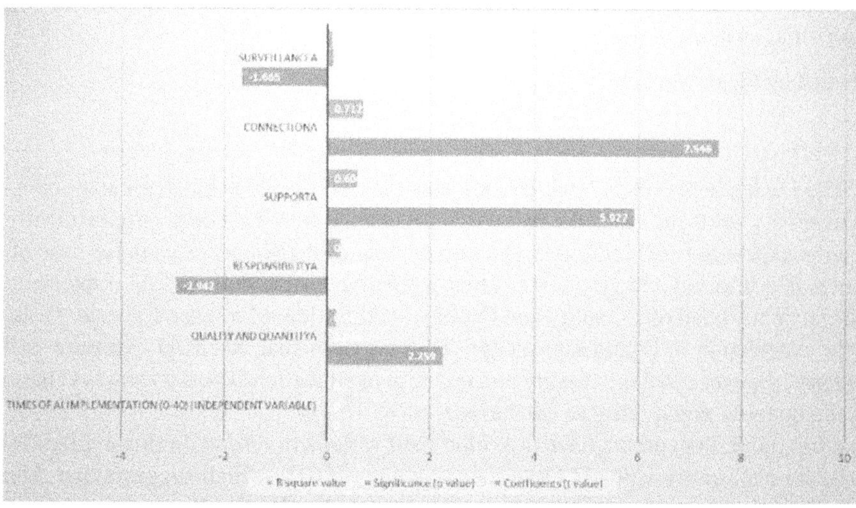

FIGURE 10.2 Regression analysis diagram of instructors' responses.

Source: Created by the researcher.

The significance value is much lower; $p < 0.008$, which suggests that a strong and significant relationship is present between the two variables.

When satisfaction level on Support is determined, students showed that AI exposure did not significantly impact the support. Significance value is 0.859 ($p > 0.8$), which is greater than 0.05. Therefore, the null hypothesis is accepted and it can be concluded that satisfaction based on support by AI is not determined by the number of AI exposure. A smaller t and R-square value (0.180 and 0.001, respectively) also indicates the correlation is much lower. In the case of instructors, the Satisfaction level based on support is highly significant ($p < 0.001$). Moreover, the t value is positive and much higher (5.927), which suggests instructors were satisfied with AI exposure based on providing support to the student. The R-square value is greater than 0.6, which also suggests a good correlation is present between the two variables.

In the case of maintaining a connection between instructor and students, students highly agreed with building helpful connections between them and instructors. This is suggested by observing the *R*-square value, which is 4.236. Moreover, the significance value is less than 0.001 ($p < 0.001$), which defines a strong correlation between the two variables. The *R*-square value is greater than 0.43, which also suggests the null hypothesis is rejected. In the case of instructors, the connection is maintained positively using AI. Here, significance is less than 0.001 ($p < 0.001$) as well, which suggests a strong correlation is present between the two variables. Moreover, the *t* value is positive and much higher (7.546), which suggests that AI exposure satisfied the instructors based on maintaining a healthy connection between them and students.

Last, satisfaction level on Surveillance has been measured among students and instructors. Both instructors and students have shown a negative correlation between the two variables. *T* values of instructors and students are −4.679 and −1.665, respectively, which suggests that AI technology was unable to integrate the surveillance feature effectively which can positively benefit the students and instructors. Further discussion will be explained in the discussion section. *P*-value is much lower in the case of students' perception ($p < 0.001$), which suggests that students are highly dissatisfied with AI surveillance and the more AI exposure, the more dissatisfaction they receive in terms of surveillance. However, in the case of the instructor, the significance is greater than 0.1 ($p > 0.1$), which suggests that the correlation is not significant between the two variables. Here, the null hypothesis is accepted to some extent.

10.5 DISCUSSION AND FINDINGS

Tables 10.3 and 10.4 suggested the satisfaction levels and the correlation between the independent variable (number of AI exposures) and dependent variables. Students have observed that AI exposure has positively impacted the quality and quantity of online education. After learners go through the basics of their online learning with AI systems, the conversations between the educator and learners becomes more meaningful. This happens because instructors can spend their time in more complex and fruitful discussions instead of simple repetitive tasks in administration and basic classroom operations. Thus, AI exposure has a positive impact on the quality and quantity of education (Kumar, 2019).

In the case of responsibility, both students and instructors stated that AI exposure has a negative impact on the responsibility of giving valuable answers. Students perceive that AI systems can provide unreliable explanations for a particular subject which will affect their examination marks. Other studies suggested that AI system is biased at many algorithms which can negatively impact their psychology (Stevens et al., 2021). Instructors also stated that AI exposure has a negative impact on responsibility. A conflict between different answers may arise because the perception by AI and the instructor may vary to some extent.

In the case of maintaining a connection between instructor and students, students highly agreed with building helpful connections between them and instructors. This suggests that the AI system has allowed them to be friendlier with the online learning system. Both students and instructors were satisfied with AI exposure in terms of connection. According to Sie et al. (2018), network learning is achieved by connectedness. This defines the connections between the resources, ideas and people. Andersen (2013) suggested that effective learning is achieved through openness between the student, instructor and learning processes. AI systems provide social cues and are more aware of the needs of students, which when conveyed to the instructors helps to build a valuable connection.

In the case of support, students perceive no correlation is present between the AI exposure and support in learning. This suggests that AI systems have a standardized support system which does not directly affect their cognitive behaviour towards learning. Thus it did not play a role in increasing the support mechanism around online learning. On the other hand, instructors believed that AI systems have a positive support system for the students. This shows that AI systems help and guide online educators on a real-time basis; however it may not be perceived thusly by the students. Alencar and Netto (2020) also stated that online learning is dependent on self-determination, affordances, community building and sense of purpose.

Last, both students and instructors felt dissatisfied with the surveillance feature of AI. Students suggested that the surveillance system in AI feels uncomfortable because of its unconscious behaviour and facial expression tracking system. On the other hand, instructors suggested that the AI system does not provide valuable cues of social interaction for students.

The findings of this study can be corroborated by similar results in previous studies and research experiments. As demonstrated by Criollo-C et al. (2018), prior to AI implementation, students felt embarrassed and uncomfortable asking multiple questions in online classes. They feared judgement and ridicule on the part of their peers as well as the educators. However, students can ask as many questions to the AI systems as they wish to, without any negative apprehensions. Moreover, students were hesitant to ask simple questions due to self-consciousness, and thus AI exposure helped them to ask any type of questions without any second thought. In their study, Seo et al. (2021) also suggested that instructors are more satisfied in online learning with greater AI exposure. According to them, the greater the exposure to AI, the better the quality and quantity of education. Instructors have found that AI can answer repetitive and simple questions of the students, decreasing their time and effort involved. Kumar (2019) has also highlighted the importance of AI assistance in classroom administrative tasks like maintenance of attendance rolls and exam grading, and the consequent improvement in the quality of instructor-learner relationship.

10.6 CONCLUSION AND FUTURE SCOPE

The present study has focused on finding the impact of AI implementation on the effectiveness of learner-instructor attitudes towards embracing online learning. Using empirical data the study has identified that enhanced role of AI can indeed result in more positive learner-instructor attitudes towards reception of online learning methods. The study has analysed this phenomenon through testing on five dependent variables. It may be interesting to see future studies replicate this model in more particular streams of education, such as medicine or law. There remain several more under-researched aspects of AI implementation in education which can provide scope for future studies. For instance, future researchers may find it valuable to research how privacy and data-sharing in AI-aided learning can influence the attitudes towards online learning. Additionally, the present study has researched the use of AI-aided systems, with gradual increase in the exposure to AI within conventional online learning. To further explore the effectiveness of AI in online learning, there may be future research on the improvement of instructor-learner relationship where AI systems in learning are self-sufficient and devoid of human interaction entirely. The present study will also benefit from supporting research into discomfort experienced by learners and instructors while adapting to new technologies.

To conclude, the study has observed that AI implementation in education has benefited the students and instructors in terms of providing Quantity and Quality of education, Support, and Connection. However, AI systems have disadvantages and limitations as well. For example, AI systems provide unreliable explanations of some problems which vary with the explanation of instructors. This can affect the examination marks of the students. Other than this, AI systems build social interaction between the student and instructor. In the case of surveillance, the students have observed that the facial expression tracking feature on AI systems is uncomfortable for them. Therefore, the AI system can be helpful to some extent; however, the system needs to be rejected at some point where it can harm the education system.

REFERENCES

Abdulmunem Alshehhi, P., Mansoor, W., Alshehhi, M. A., AlMulla, H., & Mansoor, M. D. (2021). Impact of artificial intelligence on online learning during COVID-19: A framework. *Psychology and Education*, *58*(2), 9581–9587.

Alencar, M., & Netto, J. F. (2020). Measuring student emotions in an online learning environment. In *Proceedings of the 12th international conference on agents and artificial intelligence* (Vol. 10, p. 0008956505630569).

Ally, M. (2019). Competency profile of the digital and online teacher in future education. *International Review of Research in Open and Distributed Learning*, *20*(2).

Andersen, J. C. (2013). *Learner satisfaction in online learning: An analysis of the perceived impact of learner-social media and learner-instructor interaction* (Doctoral dissertation, East Tennessee State University).

Appana, S. (2008). A review of benefits and limitations of online learning in the context of the student, the instructor and the tenured faculty. *International Journal on E-learning*, *7*(1), 5–22.

Chassignol, M., Khoroshavin, A., Klimova, A., & Bilyatdinova, A. (2018). Artificial intelligence trends in education: A narrative overview. *Procedia Computer Science*, *136*, 16–24.

Chen, L., Chen, P., & Lin, Z. (2020). Artificial intelligence in education: A review. *IEEE Access*, *8*, 75264–75278.

Ciolacu, M., Tehrani, A. F., Binder, L., & Svasta, P. M. (2018, October). Education 4.0-Artificial Intelligence assisted higher education: Early recognition system with machine learning to support students' success. In *2018 IEEE 24th international symposium for design and technology in electronic packaging (SIITME)*, 23–30.

Criollo-C, S., Luján-Mora, S., & Jaramillo-Alcázar, A. (2018, March). Advantages and disadvantages of M-learning in current education. In *2018 IEEE world engineering education conference (EDUNINE)*, 1–6.

Dhawan, S., & Batra, G. (2020). Artificial intelligence in higher education: Promises, perils, and perspective. *Expanding Knowledge Horizon. OJAS*, *11*, 11–22.

Edwards, B. I., & Cheok, A. D. (2018). Why not robot teachers: Artificial intelligence for addressing teacher shortage. *Applied Artificial Intelligence*, *32*(4), 345–360.

Fukui, H., Hirakawa, T., Yamashita, T., & Fujiyoshi, H. (2019). Attention branch network: Learning of attention mechanism for visual explanation. *Proceedings of the IEEE/CVF Conference on Computer Vision and Pattern Recognition*, 10705–10714.

García-Peñalvo, F. J. (2020). Learning analytics as a breakthrough in educational improvement. In *Radical solutions and learning analytics*, 1–15. Singapore: Springer.

George, G., & Lal, A. M. (2019). Review of ontology based recommender systems in e-Learning. *Computers & Education*, *142*, 103642.

Ha, N. H., Nayyar, A., Nguyen, D. M., & Liu, C. A. (2019). Enhancing students' soft skills by implementing CDIO-based integration teaching mode. In *The 15th International CDIO Conference*, 569.

Holstein, K., McLaren, B. M., & Aleven, V. (2018, June). Student learning benefits of a mixed-reality teacher awareness tool in AI-enhanced classrooms. In *International conference on artificial intelligence in education*, 154–168. Cham: Springer.

Hwang, G. J., & Tu, Y. F. (2021). Roles and research trends of artificial intelligence in mathematics education: A bibliometric mapping analysis and systematic review. *Mathematics*, *9*(6), 584.

Jiang, R., Mou, X., Shi, S., Zhou, Y., Wang, Q., Dong, M., & Chen, S. (2020). Object tracking on event cameras with offline–online learning. *CAAI Transactions on Intelligence Technology*, *5*(3), 165–171.

Jocas, M., Kurrek, P., Zoghlami, F., Gianni, M., & Salehi, V. (2019, July). Ai-based learning approach with consideration of safety criteria on example of a depalletization robot. In *Proceedings of the design society: International conference on engineering design*, *1*(1), 2041–2050. Cambridge University Press.

Kahraman, H. T., Sagiroglu, S., & Colak, I. (2010, October). Development of adaptive and intelligent web-based educational systems. In *2010 4th international conference on application of information and communication technologies*, 1–5. IEEE.

Kang, M., & Im, T. (2013). Factors of learner–instructor interaction which predict perceived learning outcomes in online learning environment. *Journal of Computer Assisted Learning*, *29*(3), 292–301.

Kim, N. Y., Cha, Y., & Kim, H. S. (2019). Future English learning: Chatbots and artificial intelligence. *Multimedia-Assisted Language Learning*, *22*(3), 32–53.

Kumar, A., Krishnamurthi, R., Bhatia, S., Kaushik, K., Ahuja, N. J., Nayyar, A., & Masud, M. (2021). Blended learning tools and practices: A comprehensive analysis. *IEEE Access*, *9*, 85151–85197.

Kumar, N. S. (2019). Implementation of artificial intelligence in imparting education and evaluating student performance. *Journal of Artificial Intelligence*, *1*(01), 1–9.

Kuprenko, V. (2020). Artificial intelligence in education: Benefits, challenges, and use cases. *Medium. com*. https://medium. com/towards-artificialintelligence/artificial-intelligence-in-education-benefits-challenges-and-use-cases-db52d8921f7a [accessed 15 January 2022].

Leavy, S. (2018, May). Gender bias in artificial intelligence: The need for diversity and gender theory in machine learning. In *Proceedings of the 1st international workshop on gender equality in software engineering*, 14–16.

Lee, J., & Gibson, C. C. (2003). Developing self-direction in an online course through computer-mediated interaction. *American Journal of Distance Education*, *17*(3), 173–187.

Majumdar, M., & Calhoun, C. (2020, April 28). *Being resilient: e-Learning is now serious*. Infosys Knowledge Institute. www.infosys.com/iki/perspectives/being-resilient-learning.html [accessed 10 January 2022].

Mikropoulos, T. A., & Natsis, A. (2011). Educational virtual environments: A ten-year review of empirical research (1999–2009). *Computers & Education*, *56*(3), 769–780.

Mohammed, P. S., & Nell Watson, E. (2019). Towards inclusive education in the age of artificial intelligence: Perspectives, challenges, and opportunities. In *Artificial intelligence and inclusive education*, 17–37. Singapore: Springer.

Mukhopadhyay, M., Pal, S., Nayyar, A., Pramanik, P. K. D., Dasgupta, N., & Choudhury, P. (2020, February). Facial emotion detection to assess Learner's State of mind in an online learning system. In *Proceedings of the 2020 5th International Conference on Intelligent Information Technology*, 107–115.

Ng'ambi, D., & Hardman, J. (2004). Towards a knowledge-sharing scaffolding environment based on learners' questions. *British Journal of Educational Technology*, *35*(2), 187–196.

Ocaña-Fernández, Y., Valenzuela-Fernández, L. A., & Garro-Aburto, L. L. (2019). Artificial intelligence and its implications in higher education. *Journal of Educational Psychology-Propositos y Representaciones*, *7*(2), 553–568.

Pedro, F., Subosa, M., Rivas, A., & Valverde, P. (2019). Artificial intelligence in education: Challenges and opportunities for sustainable development. In *Working Paper by UNESCO*, France.

Pereira, F. D., Oliveira, E. H., Oliveira, D. B., Cristea, A. I., Carvalho, L. S., Fonseca, S. C., & Isotani, S. (2020). Using learning analytics in the Amazonas: Understanding students' behaviour in introductory programming. *British Journal of Educational Technology*, *51*(4), 955–972.

Pokrivčáková, S. (2019). Preparing teachers for the application of AI-powered technologies in foreign language education. *Journal of Language and Cultural Education, 7*(3), 135–153.

Putnam, V., & Conati, C. (2019, March). Exploring the need for explainable artificial intelligence (XAI) in intelligent tutoring systems (ITS). *IUI Workshops*, *19*.

Sabry, K., & Baldwin, L. (2003). Web-based learning interaction and learning styles. *British Journal of Educational Technology*, *34*(4), 443–454.

Samek, W., & Müller, K. R. (2019). Towards explainable artificial intelligence. In *Explainable AI: Interpreting, explaining and visualizing deep learning*, 5–22. Cham: Springer.

Sandu, N., & Gide, E. (2019, September). Adoption of AI-Chatbots to enhance student learning experience in higher education in India. *2019 18th international conference on information technology based higher education and training (ITHET)*, 1–5. IEEE.

Saputro, B., & Susilowati, A. T. (2019). Effectiveness of learning management system (LMS) on in-network learning system (Spada) based on scientific. *Journal for the Education of Gifted Young Scientists*, *7*(3), 481–498.

Seo, K., Tang, J., Roll, I., Fels, S., & Yoon, D. (2021). The impact of artificial intelligence on learner–instructor interaction in online learning. *International Journal of Educational Technology in Higher Education*, *18*(1), 1–23.

Sharma, R. C., Kawachi, P., & Bozkurt, A. (2019). The landscape of artificial intelligence in open, online and distance education: Promises and concerns. *Asian Journal of Distance Education*, *14*(2), 1–2.

Sie, R. L., Delahunty, J., Bell, K., Percy, A., Rienties, B., Cao, T., & De Laat, M. (2018, December). Artificial Intelligence to enhance learning design in UOW online, a unified approach to fully online learning. In *2018 IEEE international conference on teaching, assessment, and learning for engineering (TALE)*, 761–767. IEEE.

Stevens, G. J., Bienz, T., Wali, N., Condie, J., & Schismenos, S. (2021). Online university education is the new normal: But is face-to-face better? *Interactive Technology and Smart Education, 18*(3), 278–297.

Tang, Y. M., Chen, P. C., Law, K. M., Wu, C. H., Lau, Y. Y., Guan, J., . . . Ho, G. T. (2021). Comparative analysis of Student's live online learning readiness during the coronavirus (COVID-19) pandemic in the higher education sector. *Computers & Education*, *168*, 104211.

Vygotsky, L. S. (1978). *Mind in society: The development of higher psychological processes* (M. Cole, V. John-Steiner, S. Schribner, & E. Souberman, Eds. & Trans.). Cambridge, MA: Harvard University Press.

Wanstreet, C. E. (2006). Interaction in online learning environments: A review of the literature. *Quarterly Review of Distance Education*, *7*(4), 399.

Wartman, S. A., & Combs, C. D. (2019). Reimagining medical education in the age of AI. *AMA Journal of Ethics*, *21*(2), 146–152.

Yang, K., Zeng, Z., Peng, H., & Jiang, Y. (2019). Attitudes of Chinese cancer patients toward the clinical use of artificial intelligence. *Patient Preference and Adherence*, *13*, 1867.

Zhang, Y., & Lin, C. H. (2020). Student interaction and the role of the teacher in a state virtual high school: What predicts online learning satisfaction? *Technology, Pedagogy and Education*, *29*(1), 57–71.

11 Effect of Digital Competence and Pedagogies on Gender Orientation of Pedagogues

A Quantitative Study with Regression Modeling of Higher Education Institutions

Muhammad Mujtaba Asad, Syeda Sumbul Shah, Prathamesh Churi, Norah Almusharraf, and Anand Nayyar

11.1 INTRODUCTION

In less than a decade, the rapid growth and development of information communication technologies (ICT) have led to major changes which influence every field of life; education is no exception. In this digital era usage of ICT is everywhere: according to UNESCO, ICT is important factor for education to survive in digital world. Therefore, 21st-century education requires ICT skills to compete in the world. Therefore, educational institutes need to include new learning theories, models, pedagogies, materials, resources, and devices for replacing traditional classrooms with a digital classroom where students develop skills and competencies for their future (Roblizo and Cózar, 2015). As a result, society requires well-trained teachers who are at ease with technology and can integrate and use a variety of materials, tools, and digital applications in their teaching (Asad et al., 2021). Therefore, the development of digital competencies of teachers are very essential within the idea of lifelong learning. The fourth industrial revolution also stresses that in the future, most jobs require digital skills (Williamson et al., 2019). To survive in the future, researchers and educationists are working to develop digital competencies of teachers who will transfer these skills to the new generation (Tafazoli et al., 2019a). According to the study of Roblizo and Cózar (2015), 21st-century teachers must have knowledge of digital content and digital pedagogies for this; digital competencies are important to ensure their implementation.

During the past ten years, the digital education revolution has been steadily gaining steam as more and more educators use cutting-edge teaching strategies to engage their pupils. Pakistan is one of the most populous nations on earth, and it is one of the nations that are using digital tools and are curious to adopt digital education instead of traditional. Therefore, the use of digital tools to address the problems with conventional education is known as "digital education" in Pakistan. Despite this, there are a variety of reasons why Pakistani instructors are not implementing digital pedagogies. A study by Aslan et al. (2018) found that teachers are reluctant to implement technology in the classroom because they question its efficacy. Some are concerned that using technology in the classroom won't genuinely enhance students' learning and might potentially be a time waster. Some teachers also think that computers will never totally take the role of interpersonal connection in the classroom. They believe that adopting technology will only serve to further separate pupils from the teacher and that there is no alternative for a teacher's in-person interactions with students. They

DOI: 10.1201/9781003425779-11

believe that adopting technology will only serve to further separate pupils from the teacher and that there is no alternative for a teacher's in-person interactions with students. Moreover, in Pakistan few teachers are using digital pedagogies in their classrooms, which affects overall effectiveness of the education. Hence, the aim of this study is to measure the effect of innovative pedagogies on developing the digital skills of male and female teachers in public universities of Pakistan.

11.1.1 Objectives of the Chapter

The objectives of the chapter are:

1. To identify the level of digital competencies of male and teachers at public universities of Pakistan;
2. To analyze the effect of innovative pedagogies on developing the digital skills of male and female teachers in public universities of Pakistan.

11.1.2 Organization of the Chapter

The rest of the chapter is organized as follows. Section 11.2 enlists problem statement. Section 11.3 highlights theoretical framework. Section 11.4 elaborates literature review. Section 11.5 illustrates methodology, and section 11.6 stresses on results and findings. Section 11.7 enlightens the discussion. And, finally section 11.8 concludes the chapter with future scope.

11.2 PROBLEM STATEMENT

It is crucial that educational institute learn how to respond to students' needs in an educational, didactic, and safe manner because new generations in today's society are expected to have a high level of digital competence (Mirete et al., 2020). This is because they are constantly changing, their learning habits have changed, and their needs and circumstances are different than they were ten years ago. In order to accomplish this, it is necessary for teachers to carry out the teaching-learning process of students and to encourage the acquisition of critical competences in pupils (Nouri et al., 2020). Moreover, instructors will assist the educational system in meeting this need by successfully engaging and instructing generation Z students. ICT resources must be a minimum requirement for educational institute systems, and curricula must be created to encourage a collaborative, learner-centered environment that kids can relate to and respond to (Skantz-Åberg et al., 2022). Therefore, teachers need professional development in using innovative pedagogies classrooms. Additionally, advancement of technology requires digital competencies to store, retrieve, evaluate, exchange, present information, and also have knowledge to collaborate through internet and social networking tools (Tafazoli et al., 2019b; Ruiz Mezcua, 2019). But people are facing problems in operating digital resources due to lack of digital competencies. Vázquez-Cano et al. (2020) highlighted that digital competency is necessary because advancement in technology presents digital content which sometimes can be fake but seems real. Similarly, López-Meneses et al. (2020) posited that this problem is not constant but new dimensions of the problem emerged day by day just as with the development of technology. Moreover, lack of teacher training is also a major issue that creates hindrance in developing teacher's digital competencies. In addition to this, Akcaoglu et al. (2015) highlighted that intensity of workload negatively affects teacher's innovative pedagogy and technology in class. Apart from Western researchers, there are some Pakistani researchers that highlighted issues and challenges while developing teachers digital competencies, as Farid et al. (2015) highlighted some obstacles such as lack of technical skills, attitude towards ICT, inadequate resources for the growth of teaching staff, and lack of awareness are some major challenges. Similarly, another researcher also revealed that a lack of teachers' attitude towards technology is the major barrier in developing teachers' digital competencies (Caliskan et al., 2017). In Pakistan, most teachers don't know about basic knowledge of using technological devices; teachers even don't know how to use technological resources effectively (Pirani & Hussain, 2019). However, Jan (2018) highlighted another factor which is gender discrimination in the usage of technology. In Pakistan males use more technology as compared to females, because males are provided more opportunities as compare to females. Moreover, Pakistan is ranked 143 out of 144 countries in the gender inequality index according to the World Economic Forum's global gender gap report (2015). In Pakistan most females are facing problems in usage of digital tools due to some factors such as negative stereotypes about technology for females and negative social cultural attitudes (Khan et al., 2020). Furthermore, some common challenges faced by male and female teachers are infrastructure, instructional, technical skill and attitude, interest, lack of trainings, and teachers' perception about technology (Shaikh & Khoja, 2011). Hence, this study aimed to identify the digital competencies of male and female teachers of public universities of Sindh, Pakistan.

11.3 THEORETICAL FRAMEWORK

11.3.1 European Digital Competence Framework for Educators

In this study, the European Digital Competence Framework for educators has been used. The framework consists of six core elements which are elaborated below.

1. *Professional engagement of teachers*: The first core component of this framework focuses on the working environment where teachers practice and enhance their competencies. Digital competencies of teachers are one of the characteristics of teachers and these competencies can be nourished and improved by providing a proper and professional environment where teachers practice their digital skills in their pedagogy. Additionally, this framework also emphasizes professional interaction with staff, peers, family members, and different people for educational purposes (Cabero-Almenara et al., 2020). However, without continued professional development of teachers, professional engagement is almost impossible. Hence, training and workshops are necessary for developing teacher's digital competencies. Moreover, it is essential for teachers to update themselves about technology innovation and also learn how to integrate these inventions in their pedagogy. Technological literacy of teachers is also important because teachers are those who directly interact with students and are also responsible for their future. Hence teachers should be technologically literate in order to meet the current needs and demands of the digital world (Tondeur et al., 2017).
2. *Technological resource*: This framework also stressed proper and adequate resources including distribution of resources, availability of resources, and selection of resources. Furthermore, it is essential for teachers to know how to select, adapt, arrange, and develop technological resources and integrate them into their pedagogy. Moreover, while selecting resources teachers keep in mind the learning style of the pupils and the learning outcomes of their lessons (Tang, 2021). The study of Zaidieh (2012) emphasized that teachers should know how to use different resources, digital platforms, and tools such as wikis, blogs, social networks and, other technological material in their teaching practice. At the same time, teachers should be technologically smart in using authentic, reliable information and also respect copyrights and personal data (From, 2017). Moreover, any technical tools that are accessible can be a helpful aid to the learning process. Some schools are able to provide laptops for every student or even computers in every classroom. If so, teachers should make as much use of this equipment as they can. Students can utilize these in resources for better learning. However, the majority of teacher are not aware about the technological resources, and they don't how to recognize trustworthy websites and pertinent information by using computers. So, for better digital education,

teachers must be familiar about technological resources and also must have accesses to those resources.

3. *Teaching and learning*: Another core component of this framework is the process of teaching and learning. This model elaborates how to design, plan, choose, and implement digital resources in teaching practices, as shown in Figure 11.1. This model suggests some teaching approaches, methods, and strategies to enhance teachers' digital skills (Shi et al., 2017). Teachers must receive individualized, continuing professional development in order to successfully instruct in a digital learning environment. Despite the fact that some teaching techniques are appropriate for both traditional and digital learning, teachers will need professional development opportunities to support the use of particular techniques and technologies in digital learning.
4. *Assessment*: Assessment of technology is very important in the process of teaching and learning; monitoring is an important factor that helps to improve any system. Hence, different assessments give direction to improve digital resources, tools, and usage in education Cabero-Almenara et al. (2020). In addition to this, it refers to all assessment tasks that require the use of technology for design, performance, and feedback. Moreover, it is a technique for assessing students' cognitive performance and ability that primarily relies on anytime, anywhere access to individualized instruction, test preparation resources, and feedback, all of which are supposed to make it more effective than the standard assessment. Digital assessment is the presenting of data used to evaluate student performance and is carried out using computer technology. Moreover, digital assessments have important additional layers of security that paper assessments lack. Also, it might lessen the demand on institutions to keep paper files secure both during and after tests. The assessment items can be secured and encrypted by being created and stored digitally in an item bank. There is always a chance of influence after exam papers have been printed and sent out. Exam papers may be compromised if a consignment is lost or appears to have been tampered with upon arrival, in which case awarding organizations will need to think about purchasing expensive and time-consuming replacement papers.
5. *Empowering teaching and learning*: Another essential factor of the European Digital Competence Framework for teachers is to enhance the attitude and perception of learners in the usage of technology. Hence, teachers use the internet, video resources during instructions, group work, and assignments, also allowing students to use smart gadgets when preparing group work (Donovan, 2014). Moreover, technological resources also offer different digital platforms which help students to adapt according to their learning needs, interests, and levels (Cabero-Almenara et al., 2020). Technology has also contributed to bettering the educational process. With the aid of technology, students can now take more pleasure in learning because they are exposed to a more engaging and interactive learning environment. Learners can be engaged by technology to maintain their attention on what they are studying; this promotes empowering teaching and learning process. In addition to this, being an empowered teacher entails having the freedom and resources necessary to provide each student the education they deserve. Therefore, this framework supports empowering teaching and learning for better education.
6. *Facilitating learner's digital competencies*: For enhancing student's digital competencies, a number of strategies and technological resources have been suggested with the help of the European Digital Competencies Framework. Moreover, the agenda of the European Commission was taking the initiative for European strategies on new jobs and skills which require these competencies (Prestridge, 2017). Furthermore, another study revealed that the European Digital Competencies Framework for education is considered as the most authentic, appropriate, and reliable framework because it presents extensively pedagogical competencies as well as technological competencies; these are presented in Table 11.1.

TABLE 11.1
Descriptive Results

Statements	Mean	Std. Deviation
Record and edit audio (REA)		
Teacher knows how to create and record audio clips.	2.0125	1.02493
Teacher knows basic editing to content produced by others.	2.3000	1.26691
Teacher has skills to add effect in audio clips and recording.	2.3125	1.08609
Create annotated, interactive content (CAIN)		
Teacher prefers to create video content.	2.3125	1.07437
Teacher feels confident putting video content.	2.4000	1.23862
Teacher creates video conference.	2.5250	1.26266
Use social networking and websites (UNW)		
Teacher prefers to utilize social networks as source of information.	2.2875	1.16046
Teacher uses different social networks to preparer class material.	2.3125	1.05054
Teacher uses online resources to prepare lessons.	2.4250	1.21983
Create presentation (CP)		
Teacher uses different platforms to make effective presentations.	2.6375	1.08200
Teacher uses presentation software for instructions.	2.8500	1.11492
Teacher uses presentations for directing class activities.	2.7250	1.11350
Create digital portfolio (CDP)		
Teacher prefers to create digital portfolio.	2.9875	1.18529
Teacher regularly updates portfolio content.	2.9875	1.18529
Teacher has ability to develop interactive content in e-portfolio.	2.8375	1.17402
Create non-traditional quizzes (CTQ)		
Teacher uses different digital tools to assess students.	2.9875	3.77364
Teacher creates online assessments, quizzes, and activities.	2.4375	1.11200
Teacher creates digital platform to submit project report.	3.0250	3.69391
Use social media (USM)		
Teacher is accessible through different platforms.	2.6125	1.53023
Teacher uses emails to communicate with students.	2.4375	1.13454
Teacher has ability to share media and material with students.	2.5500	1.28181
Use blogs and wikis (UBW)		
Teacher extracts information from wikis.	2.7625	2.49680
Teacher prefers to design blogs.	2.6456	1.29137
Teacher uses blogs for class discussion.	2.5750	2.51967
Create visual content (CVC)		
Teacher creates info graphics and posters.	2.1750	1.19889
Teacher creates simple digital content using digital tools.	2.4250	1.20940
Teacher uses graphs figure and tables to explain different concepts.	2.1500	1.02005

Moreover, it is crucial that institutions must learn how to respond to students' needs in an educational, didactic, and safe manner because new generations in today's society are expected to have a high level of digital competence. This is because they are constantly changing, their learning habits have changed, and their needs and circumstances are different than they were ten years ago. In order to accomplish this, it is necessary for teachers to carry out the teaching-learning process of students and to encourage the acquisition of critical competences in pupils.

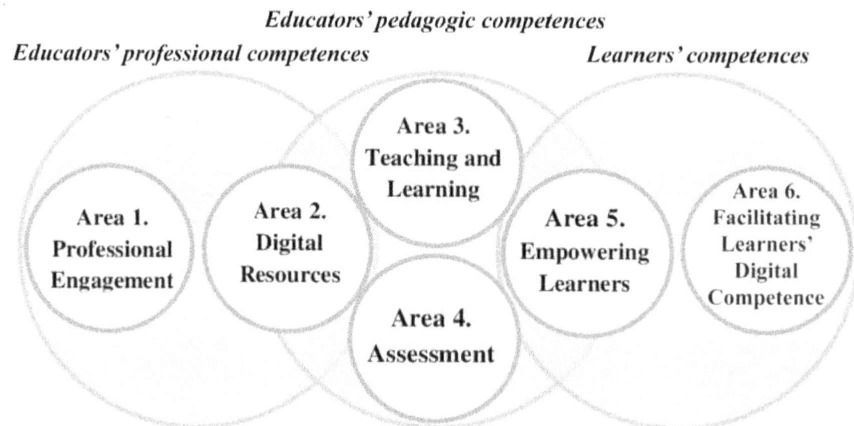

FIGURE 11.1 Educators' pedagogical competence.

11.4 LITERATURE REVIEW

Some serious changes have been noticed in the world. Futurists, sociologists, and educationists are talking about new generations. The study of Rutkowski et al. (2011) highlighted some serious changes in the teaching and learning process; in this era educational space is expanding beyond the classroom. Almost all educationists and researchers agreed that teachers use the internet and video resources during instructions and allow students to use smart gadgets in classroom.

In other hand, teachers have diametrically refused how to respond technological changes in their pedagogies from traditional to digitalization, and teach children in the same manner as practicing in the last century (Ertmer et al., 2015). Therefore, the complete restructuring of the education system is necessary to meet the current demand of the world. In this current scenario, futurist, sociologies, and educationists suggested some innovative pedagogies for teachers, which are described below

Moreover, the study of Alammary (2019) highlighted one of the innovative pedagogies named as blended learning, it is the way of teaching is to combine online learning opportunities with online educational materials and traditional classroom courses in the classroom, it requires the physical presence of both the teacher and the student, some element of the student's control over path, place and, time. In this approach, the presence of teachers and students is necessary for combining classroom practices with digital-mediate activities regarding content and its delivery (Singh, 2021).

In addition to this the second innovative pedagogy is flipped learning, which is explained in the study of Supo (2019) as a teaching strategy. Considered a type of blended learning, it aims to increase learning and engagement of students by having students complete reading at their homes and work on problem-solving during class time. It transmits activities, including those that were traditionally considered homework, in a flipped classroom, students collaborate in an online discussion, watching online lectures, or in-home research processes.

Moreover, e-learning is also considered as innovative way of teaching. It has been explained in the study of Meskhi et al. (2019) as a teaching and learning approach that makes use of an information network such as internet and extranet. Whether fully or partially, for instruction or course delivery, web-based learning is also a subset of e-learning.

Similarly, mobile learning is also a part of innovative pedagogy which can be defined as Mobile learning means learning through mobile devices like tablets, PCs, or smartphones. Additionally, mobile learning has changed the environment of the educational system by presenting an opportunity to involve learners in digitalization.

However, digital competencies is another key term used by educationists when talking about innovative pedagogies. The concept of digital competencies suggested by Jay Cross in 1999.

Digital competencies were defined by Holzberger et al. (2013) to facilitate teaching and upgrade the experience of teaching including skill development by using internet-based media like text, video, and graphics. Likewise, Uerz et al. (2018) describe teacher digital competencies as the ability and skills of teachers to utilize digital resources in their pedagogy not only supporting their existing practice but also transform them as per need and demand of the current education system. Additionally, the use of technology and electronic devices like computers were incorporated in assessing the parameters like time, schedule, and location, which influence the teaching process in different scenarios such as instruction and professional and personal development (Kaklamanou et al., 2012). Currently, digital education encompasses abundant knowledge and information in various sectors. This alters the meaning and perception of digital education, also an explanation provided by the American Society of Training and Education (ASTD) is widely accepted. It says that the usage of digital media in the teaching process is known as digital teaching. Among the common components of digital media are computers, satellite broadcasting, the internet, corporate network, compact disk, interactive TV, audiotapes, and videotapes (Kaklamanou et al., 2012). Moreover, Andrews and Shabani (2012) described several parts of digital teaching: digital teaching materials, e-books, podcasting, blogs and wikis, web tools, digital video, creative presentation, and interactive whiteboards. Its main purpose is to allow students to learn using digital content. The second point is digital tools: these are the set of tools to help teachers to access digital content, smartphones, notebook computers, tablet computers, and desktop computers. The third point is all about digital delivery, the various channels to provide the teachers materials to teach can be internet examples like satellite broadcasting, internet, and intranet. The last point is autonomous learning: just like self-study doesn't need any supervision, autonomous learning allows the learners to pursue the tasks on their own but using digital tools, digital delivery, and digital teaching material.

Furthermore, Andrews and Shabani (2012) explained teacher's digital competences are defined as teachers' capacity and skills to use digital resources in their pedagogy to not only support but also modify their existing practices to meet the needs and demands of the present educational system. Moreover, these competencies of teachers can be defined as skills and abilities, and the capacity of each teacher to solve the educational problem by integrating ICT (Blau & Shamir-Inbal, 2017). Currently, educational institutes are facing challenges to finding innovative ways to develop teacher's digital competencies, especially in the light of the recent social, economic, and technological changes that are taking place rapidly (Cabero-Almenara et al., 2020). Because of this situation educators train and educating new generation for a disconnecting, alarming, and uncertain future (Cabero-Almenara et al., 2020). In the 21st century, technology is progressing rapidly and so many innovations have been done such as display of media content across different devices, fake material and data is available which seems real (Vazquez et al., 2020). This problem is not constant but new dimensions of the problem emerged day by day just as with the development of technology. Hence, the development of digital competencies is very essential within the idea of lifelong learning. Moreover, the fourth industrial revolution stressed that in the future most of the jobs require digital skills (Williamson et al., 2019). To survive in the future, researchers and educationists are working to develop digital competencies in teachers who will transfer these skills to the new generation (Tafazoli et al., 2019b). As a result, digital competencies will be essential for our society, which directly affect employability, success, innovation, creativity and, the prosperity of each individual. Hence, all these scenarios demand that teachers possess digital competencies and also require mastery in ICT and its usage in their pedagogy and learning process (Hatlevik et al., 2018; Roig-Vila et al., 2015). Additionally, in literature, some factors are present as mobilizing variables of teacher digital competencies, which are mentioned below.

The first key component of explained teacher's digital competences is training of teachers. The fundamental factor for developing a teacher's digital competencies is initial training: teacher's working experience and degree of knowledge of the technological tools and skills to operate them properly (Beneyto-Seoane, & Collet-Sabé, 2017).

The second component of explained teacher's digital competences is resources, which is availability of technological resources such as digital devices tools are very important to develop the digital competencies of teachers because without these resources teachers cannot practice their theories in practice (Flores -Lueg and Roigvilla, 2016). However, some teachers arrange resources to integrate ICT into teaching and learning processes, if they provided sufficient resources they utilize and integrate effectively (Cela-Ranilla et al., 2017).

Usage of time is third component, explained by Penalva Velez et al. (2018) as the dedication to use technology in and out of the classroom. It is also necessary because sufficient time to prepare lesson plan is very important and encourage teachers to use ICT in their pedagogy. Likewise, lack of time to prepare any lesson to affect negatively on the usage of technology (Hilliger et al., 2020).

Moreover, interest and attitude towards technology is last component of TDCs: in terms of skills provided by ICT for teachers, there are important critical variables in teachers' perception, attitude, beliefs, and interests that determine the ICT addition to the teacher's teaching process, not only addition but also manner in which they are applying, adopting, and introducing the function assigned to them (Aslan & Zhu, 2018; Scherer & Siddiq, 2019). Hence, attitude and interest are considered as essential factors of developing and adopting TDCs (Choi et al., 2018; Penalva Velez et al., 2018). The current education system emphasized the usage of technology in classrooms. Hence, educational policies also promote usage of technology didactic and pedagogic trends (Vazquez-Cano et al., 2020). Empirically, TDCs are related to knowledge, skills, attitude necessary for teachers in a digital world (Gutierrez-Castillo et al., 2017).

In addition to this, the current literature suggests to develop innovative pedagogies of teachers. Therefore, researchers and educators are aiming to create digital competences of teachers who will pass these abilities to next generation in order to survive in the future (Tafazoli et al., 2019a). There are number of tools available on the internet that teacher can choose effectively and use wisely and properly in their pedagogy. The nine fundamental competencies encompass a range of skills necessary for leveraging technology and digital tools to enhance content creation, networking, professional growth, resource sharing, and assessment practices. These competencies include creating visually compelling content, utilizing social networking platforms for content creation, establishing and nurturing personal learning networks (PLNs), engaging in continuous professional development, utilizing social bookmarking platforms, creating and sharing resources with classes, crafting engaging presentations, building digital portfolios, and creating non-traditional quizzes. By mastering these competencies, individuals can effectively communicate ideas, generate engaging content, foster connections, stay updated with industry trends, curate valuable resources, facilitate meaningful learning experiences, captivate audiences with interactive presentations, showcase professional achievements, and design innovative assessments that promote learner engagement and comprehension.

The study of De Leon-Abao et al. (2015) posited that teachers having knowledge and skill of social media can quickly and easily contact their students not only in their localities and each other but also help them to interact with cultural, social, and political networks and find multiple ways of communication. Additionally, electronic social networking such as Facebook, Twitter, and Myspace, and others are very popular among the young generation. Therefore, teacher must know the usage of such application to get the interest of students. Similarly, Zaidieh (2012) highlighted nowadays people frequently use globally famous social networks. Therefore, teachers should know different social networks to create content and grow themselves professionally. The second feature of NFDC is having knowledge about blogging, there are some blogging websites such as Tumbler and LinkedIn which are very famous among young teachers (Zaidieh, 2012; Duffy & Bruns, 2006). Therefore, blogs considered as a platform to communicate and discuss topics online, and teacher needs to know how to create blogs to help students collaborate with one another, sharing ideas and constructing knowledge. Third feature of NFDC is having knowledge about wikis, mostly wikis utilized as learning resources for collaboration of projects and assignments. These wikis are more convenient in terms of availability, accessibility, updating, reviewing, and editing teaching and learning material, anytime and anywhere (Abreu et al., 2012).

The fourth feature of NFDC is familiarity with how to create interactive audio and video content. The concept of audio and visual aids in education is considered as educational material at both sense of sight and sense of hearing, recording, and video clips. Visual representation of anything used in classroom makes the instruction and teaching and learning process effective (McCarthy, 2015). It is obvious that audiovisual aids are crucial teaching and learning tools. Students learn and retain knowledge better and for longer periods of time, and the teacher can more effectively present the lesson; the use of audiovisual aids enhances students' ability to think critically and analytically (Al Mamun, 2014). Moreover, there are different types of audios and video material such as projects, educational DVDs, PowerPoints, multimedia, Facebook, YouTube, and other online material (Clark, 2020). The core purpose of audiovisual aids is to increase teachers' ability to make lessons effective and easy for students to understand (Abreu et al., 2012). Hence, the digital competencies of teachers are an essential factor, which directly influence success, innovation, creativity, and the prosperity of each individual.

In addition to this, create engaging presentations is fifth feature of NFDC. PowerPoint is a Microsoft office program which allows people to create slide-based presentations. PowerPoint is mostly used as a pedagogical tool to create visual content-rich presentation with multimedia (Priya, 2017). Students' cognitive abilities can be raised through a PowerPoint presentation. Additionally, it supports teachers in their instructional strategies. Different fonts, visual effects, and highlighting can help students learn new information quicker. The sixth feature of NFDC is to create info graphics and posters. Different leaners and students have various learning preferences. Some of them respond fast to verbal and written messages. Others like tactile or visual techniques. People can easily comprehend information when it is presented to them in an infographic. Supporting processes for attention, memory, and recall entails presenting text, visuals, and even interactive aspects. Infographics can be used alongside written content as a supplementary tool. As a result, students can learn effectively and acquire knowledge properly (Davidson, 2014). Therefore, 21st-century teachers must know how to create infographics and posters for better learning and support of the students.

The last feature of NFDC is to create digital portfolios. Digital portfolios help develop soft skills because they require people to articulate their experiences and present them in a way that is easily digestible to others. It gives individuals the opportunity to reflect on projects, goals, and track growth over time (Kilbane & Milman, 2017). Therefore, teachers must know how to create digital portfolios for professional development.

In addition to this, in this section of literature the role of gender in digital competencies has been discussed. The problem of gender inequality was identified in the early 2000s. The stereotype has been developed that technological and computer-based skills are suitable for male (Charles & Bradley, 2009). The toys of boys are technology and action based and girls' toys are based on beauty and domestic things (Kollmayer et al., 2018). Moreover, parents also play a role in this gender inequality: they provide more opportunity to boys as compared to girls to use technological resources, girls are expected to use digital tools only for reading and socially interacting with their peers (Eccles, 2009). Moreover, negative gender stereotypes about technology also influence females and create hindrance to pursue ICT in their educational field. Additionally, Khan et al. (2020) also found some factors which create gender gaps such as socio-cultural attitude, perception of parents and society, and providing less opportunity to girls as compared to male. Moreover, Britner and Pajares (2001) revealed that perception of girls towards ICT is less positive as compared to males and they are also less confident about their digital ability. Because of this issue. The study of Perkowski and Nicewicz (2013) revealed that Pakistani social cultural attitudes towards women are also gender biased and create negative stereotypes for females. Moreover, Tanwir and Khemka (2018) posited that female teachers use fewer digital tools as compared to males and are less digitally competent. Hence, Pakistani researchers and education must take some serious steps to resolve the issue of gender inequality.

11.5 METHODOLOGY

The aim of this study is to analyze the level of digital competencies of male and female teachers at public universities of Pakistan and to measure the effect of innovative pedagogies on developing the digital skills of male and female teachers in universities of Pakistan.

To achieve the aim and objective of this study, two major questions have been generated including

1. What is the level of digital competencies of male and teachers at public universities of Pakistan?
2. What is the effect of innovative pedagogies on developing male and female teachers' digital skills in public universities of Pakistan?

To address these questions, quantitative research methodology has been used in the form of a survey using questioner. Purposive sampling technique has been utilized in this research, as Kozleski (2017) highlighted that a purposive sampling is the best technique to understand the phenomena perspectives and points of view participants. A total of 384 teachers participated in the research from two different institutes. This study targeted those participants who practice technology in their pedagogy. About 50% male participants were selected from one institute and 50% were female participants from another institute. According to Morgan and Berrie's (1970), the minimum number for a population of 88 is 84. The data has been gathered by using set of instruments, the instrument having been adopted from Oriogu et al. (2018) and modified as per nature of the study. The questioner contains 27 items using a 5-point Likert scale ranging from 1 (strongly agree) to 5 (strongly disagree). The components of the instruments were record and edit audio, create annotated, interactive content, use social networking and websites, create presentation, digital portfolio, non-traditional quizzes, use social media, use blogs and wikis, and visual content. The instrument has been validated from two language experts and three subject matter experts. The pilot study was conducted on 30 teachers to ensure reliability of the instrument. Additionally, a reliability analysis was done by using Cronbach's alpha. The result showed the questionnaire/instrument is $\alpha = .782$, which indicate that the instrument is reliable. The data was analyzed by using SPSS v.27.0 using descriptive (mean and standard deviation) and inferential statistics (linear regression).

Moreover, on the basis of research objectives and questions, the major hypotheses are as follows:

- Alternative hypothesis: There is positive effect of innovative pedagogies on developing male and female teachers' digital skills.
- Null hypothesis: There is no positive effect of innovative pedagogies on developing male and female teachers' digital skills.

11.6 RESULTS AND FINDINGS

In this section, the results based on the collected data are reported. Descriptive and inferential results are specified below. The findings are based on 384 teachers from two different institutes who took part in the study. The participants in this study were teachers who use technology in their teaching.

The descriptive findings as shown in Table 11.1, indicate the first construct, Record and Edit Audio (REA) shows that 2.0125, 2.3000, 2.3125 lies under the moderate level of mean table according to mean level of Hassam et al. (2015). Similarly, the highest standard derivation is 1.02493, 1.26691, and 1.08609. Likewise, second construct named Create Annotated, Interactive Content (CAIN), mean shows 2.3125, 2.4000, and 2.5250 which also indicate moderate level of mean with having 1.07437, 1.23862, and 1.26266 which also states the highest standard derivation. Using

Social Networking and Websites (UNW) is the third construct have 2.2875, 2.3125, 2.4250 that displays moderate level of mean with highest values of standard division 1.16046, 1.05054, 1.21983. The fourth construct is Create Presentation (CP), which also illustrates mean level moderate and possesses the highest standard division. Here the moderate level came across as 2.6375, 2.8500 and 2.7250 whereas the highest level was found as 1.08200, 1.11492 and 1.11350. Likewise, the fifth construct Create Digital Portfolio (CDP) also show that 2.9875, 2.9875, 2.8375 lies under the moderate level of mean and possess the highest standard division 1.18529, 1.18529, 1.17402. The sixth construct named Create Non-traditional Quizzes (CTQ) indicates high as well as moderate level of mean 3.0250, 2.4375, and 2.9875, having moderate and high standard division 3.77364, 1.11200, 3.69391.

Standard deviation, here the moderate level came across as 2.6125, 2.4375, and 2.5500 whereas the highest level was found as 1.53023, 1.13454, and 1.28181. The eighth construct, Use blogs and wikis (UBW) mean result shows 2.7625, 2.6456, and 2.5750 which also indicate moderate level of mean with having moderate and high standard derivation 2.49680, 1.29137, 2.51967. The last construct is Create visual content (CVC) which also indicate moderate level of mean 2.1750, 2.4250, with highest standard division 1.19889, 1.20940, 1.02005. From the findings, it can conclude that all the means are in the range of moderate and highest level with having a high value of standard division.

In Table 11.2, the R value represents the simple correlation and is .662a, which indicates high correlation. Likewise, the ANOVA table indicates that there is significance difference in the regression model of digital competencies among male and female teachers. Here p is < .000, which is less than 0.05. Overall, the regression model statistically significantly predicts the outcome variable. The four-predictor model has been identified from the results. The first predictor identified according to model summary was UNW, having R value of 0.554, which indicated moderate correlation, whereas the significance value was found to be 0.000 which indicates the significance of the predictor. Similarly, the R value for the second predictor (UNW, CP) was found to be 0.591 having a significance value of 0.014 which also show moderate correlation. For the third predictor of the model (UNW, CP, UBW), R value was found to be 0.62 having a significance value of 0.42 which indicate high correlation. For the fourth predictor (UNW, CP, UBW, CTQ), the R value was found to be 0.648 with a significance level of 0.034. From the findings, it can be concluded that all the predictors are significant having a high value of R as shown in Table 11.2.

Hence, the statistic of the linear regression shows that there is a significant difference between male and female teachers, which indicates that both male and female are different in terms of their digital competencies. Therefore, the null hypothesis is rejected and the alternative hypothesis is accepted.

11.7 DISCUSSION

This study broadly aimed to identify the effect of innovative pedagogies on developing male and female teachers' digital skills. The findings of this study revealed that there is positive effect of innovative pedagogies on developing teachers' digital skills. The results of this study are in line with previous studies on this topic. The review of the current literature also indicates that gender bias is the main factor which creates hindrance to developing digital competencies of teachers. Khan et al. (2020) explored that in Pakistan socio-cultural attitude is a key factor which create gender gap and because of this gap females are less confident and lose their interest in ICT. Jan (2018) also said in his study that in Pakistan females are less digital literate compared to males. Additionally, according to preliminary study, men are more knowledgeable and skilled in technology than women are, and they also have more positive attitudes toward ICT. However, current study indicates that as women gain more knowledge and training in ICT, their favorable attitudes are more or less comparable (Casillas et al., 2017). Innovative pedagogies help

TABLE 11.2
Regression Analysis

Model Summary									
Model	R	R Square	Adjusted R Square	Std. Error of the Estimate	Change Statistics				
					R Square Change	F Change	df1	df2	Sig. F Change
1	.662[a]	.296	.287	.41998	.296	32.837	1	78	.000
2	.591[b]	.349	.332	.40647	.053	6.273	1	77	.014
3	.620[c]	.384	.360	.39804	.035	4.294	1	76	.042
4	.648[d]	.420	.389	.38874	.036	4.681	1	75	.034

[a] Predictors: (Constant), UNW.
[b] Predictors: (Constant), UNW, CP.
[c] Predictors: (Constant), UNW, CP, UBW.
[d] Predictors: (Constant), UNW, CP, UBW, CTQ.

teachers to develop their digital competencies. As Williamson et al. (2019) highlighted in his study, the development of digital competencies of teacher is very essential to compete this digital world and fulfilled current need of the students because in future most jobs require digital skills. Researchers and educators are stressing the development of digital competencies in teachers who will impart these abilities to the next generation in order to survive in the future. (Tafazoli et al., 2019b; Ruiz Mezcua, 2019). Moreover, the study of Williamson et al. (2019) posited that digital competencies play vital role educational reforms and inventions. Additionally, digital competencies of teachers are necessary because there is the number of tools available on the internet that teacher can choose effectively and use wisely and properly in their pedagogy (Williamson et al., 2019). Moreover, number of researchers suggested that teachers prepare themselves with nine fundamental digital competencies: creating visual content, using social networking websites to create content, creating PLNs, growing professionally, using social bookmarking websites, creating and sharing resources with classes, creating engaging presentations, creating digital portfolios, and creating non-traditional quizzes (Hussin, 2018). Moreover, De Leon-Abao et al. (2015) posited that teachers having knowledge and skill of social media can quickly and easily contact their students not only in their localities and each other but also interact with cultural, social, and political networks and find multiple ways of communication. Social networking also helps teachers to integrate technology in their teaching process it also enables them to be aware of the social issues of the student. Additionally, electronic social networking such as Facebook, Twitter, and Myspace quickly increases usage and fame. Hence, Zaidieh (2012) highlights that some tools are outdated such as search engine to search information or communicate, nowadays people frequently use globally famous social networks. Therefore, teachers should know different social networks to create content and grow themselves professionally. Apart from Western researchers, Pakistan is also realizing the importance of digital competencies and introduced number of trainings and programs to enhance digital competencies of teachers (Zaidieh, 2012). The study of Shehzadi et al. (2020) highlighted those trainings play a vital role in developing digital skill, but the readiness of teachers to attend trainings and implement that knowledge in their pedagogy is also the main barrier. Hence, this situation needs to take some major efforts at the administrative and individual levels to develop digital competencies in teachers, education commission, and ministry of education develop plan and policy to enhance digital competencies of teachers. However, Salam et al. (2017) highlighted that number of education plan related to ICT are there, but the need is to make sure it is implemented. So policymakers make sure to implement these polices in educational institutes.

11.8 CONCLUSION AND FUTURE SCOPE

In this digital era usage of ICT is everywhere, according to UNESCO, the usage of ICT increases day by day in every field, therefore it is considered as an important technology, management technique, and engineering discipline used to control information and its application related to economic, social, and cultural issues. Additionally, ICT helps to take maximum benefit from various technologies, and utilize resources. The World Wide Web, which is very essential, the globally accepted service e-mail, and IRC are some common examples of this service. Digital teaching and learning are at the forefront of education in the digital age. Digital skills are required by emerging technology, artificial intelligence, and other technical resources in education. Moreover, technology considered as an extraordinary tool to shape and enhance education. Hence, technological skills are necessary to ensure the usage of technology in education to meet the current need and demands of the world. Researchers and educators are attempting to increase teachers' digital competencies in order for them to survive in the future. Many countries realized this importance like, Australia, Spain, Brazil, Jordan, and the United Kingdom have introduced more than a thousand training programs for developing digital competencies among teachers. Pakistan also working to enhance the digital competencies of the teacher. Hence, the aim of this study is to identify the effect of innovative pedagogies on developing male and female teacher's digital skills in a public university. The finding of this study shows there is a significant difference between male and female teachers in terms of their digital competencies. Additionally, based on findings it is recommended that teachers should undergo training on proper usage of technology and other social media tools, resources, and applications. Additionally, conducting researches is a powerful tool for developing and knowing a master plan for better pedagogical practices, enhancement of digital competencies, and ICT integration.

Moreover, in future the content of this study will be beneficial to educators who seek to implement innovative pedagogies in the contemporary educational system. This study can also be useful as a baseline reference to know the effect of innovative pedagogies of university teachers on their digital competencies. Moreover, this study will be a road map for policymakers and administration of the universities to ensure the usage of innovative pedagogies in classrooms, and also for teachers to challenge their skills with the usage of innovative pedagogies.

REFERENCES

Abreu, P., Castro Silva, D., Mendes, P., & Vinhas, V. (2012). Effect of the usage of wikis on an educational context. Computer Applications in Engineering Education, 20(4), 646–653.

Akcaoglu, M., Gumus, S., Bellibas, M. S., & Boyer, D. M. (2015). Policy, practice, and reality: Exploring a nation-wide technology implementation in Turkish schools. Technology, Pedagogy and Education, 24(4), 477–491.

Al Mamun, M. (2014). *Effectiveness of audio-visual aids in language teaching in tertiary level* (Doctoral dissertation, BRAC University).

Alammary, A. (2019). Blended learning models for introductory programming courses: A systematic review. PLoS One, 14(9), e0221765.

Andrews, J., & Shabani, B. (2012). Re-envisioning the role of hydrogen in a sustainable energy economy. International Journal of Hydrogen Energy, 37(2), 1184–1203.

Asad, M. M., Hussain, N., Wadho, M., Khand, Z. H., & Churi, P. P. (2021). Integration of e-learning technologies for interactive teaching and learning process: an empirical study on higher education institutes of Pakistan. *Journal of Applied Research in Higher Education*, 13(3), 649–663.

Aslan, A., & Zhu, C. (2018). Starting teachers' integration of ICT into their teaching practices in the lower secondary schools in Turkey. Educational Sciences: Theory & Practice, 18(1), 23–25.

Beneyto-Seoane, M., & Collet-Sabé, J. (2017). Análisis de la actual formación docente en competencias TIC. Por una nueva perspectiva basada en las competencias, las experiencias y los conocimientos previos de los docentes.

Blau, I., & Shamir-Inbal, T. (2017). Digital competences and long-term ICT integration in school culture: The perspective of elementary school leaders. Education and Information Technologies, 22(3), 769–787.

Britner, S. L., & Pajares, F. (2001). Self-efficacy beliefs, motivation, race, and gender in middle school science. Journal of Women and Minorities in Science and Engineering, 7(4), 15–30.

Cabero-Almenara, J., Gutiérrez-Castillo, J. J., Palacios-Rodríguez, A., & Barroso-Osuna, J. (2020). Development of the teacher digital competence validation of DigCompEdu check-in questionnaire in the university context of Andalusia (Spain). Sustainability, 12(15), 6094.

Caliskan, A., Bryson, J. J., & Narayanan, A. (2017). Semantics derived automatically from language corpora contain human-like biases. Science, 356(6334), 183–186.

Casillas, S., Cabezas, M., Ibarra, M. S., & Rodríguez, G. (2017, October). Evaluation of digital competence from a gender perspective. In *Association for Computing Machinery (ACM),* New York, United States, (pp. 1–5).

Charles, M., & Bradley, K. (2009). Indulging our gendered selves? Sex segregation by field of study in 44 countries. American Journal of Sociology, 114(4), 924–976.

Choi, M., Cristol, D., & Gimbert, B. (2018). Teachers as digital citizens: The influence of individual backgrounds, internet use and psychological characteristics on teachers' levels of digital citizenship. Computers & Education, 121, 143–161.

Clark, J. T. (2020). Distance education. In *Clinical engineering handbook* (pp. 410–415). Academic Press.

Davidson, R. (2014). Using infographics in the science classroom. The Science Teacher, 81(3), 34.

De Leon-Abao, E., Boholano, H. B., & Dayagbil, F. T. (2015). Engagement to social networking: Challenges and opportunities to educators. European Scientific Journal, 11(16), 55–68.

Donovan, L., Green, T. D., & Mason, C. (2014). Examining the 21st century classroom: Developing an innovation configuration map. Journal of Educational Computing Research, 50(2), 161–178.

Duffy, P., & Bruns, A. (2006). The use of blogs, wikis and RSS in education: A conversation of possibilities. In *Learning on the move: Proceedings of the online learning and teaching conference 2006* (pp. 31–38). Australia, Queensland University of Technology.

Eccles, J. (2009). Who am I and what am I going to do with my life? Personal and collective identities as motivators of action. Educational Psychologist, 44(2), 78–89.

Ertmer, P. A., Ottenbreit-Leftwich, A. T., & Tondeur, J. (2015). Teachers' beliefs and uses of technology to support 21st-century teaching and learning. *International handbook of research on teacher beliefs*, 403.

Farid, S., Ahmad, R., Niaz, I. A., Arif, M., Shamshirband, S., & Khattak, M. D. (2015). Identification and prioritization of critical issues for the promotion of e-Learning in Pakistan. Computers in Human Behavior, 51, 161–171.

Flores-Lueg, C., & Roig Vila, R. (2016). Design and validation of a scale of self-assessment digital skills for students of education. Pixel-Bit, Revista de Medios y Educacion, 48, 209–224.

From, J. (2017). Pedagogical digital competence–between values, knowledge and skills. Higher Education Studies, 7(2), 43–50.

Gutiérrez-Castillo, J. J., Cabero-Almenara, J., & Estrada-Vidal, L. (2017). Design and validation of an instrument for evaluation of digital competence of University student. Revista espacio critico, 38, 1–27.

Hassam, S., Ficara, E., Leva, A., & Harmand, J. (2015). A generic and systematic procedure to derive a simplified model from the anaerobic digestion model No. 1 (ADM1). Biochemical Engineering Journal, 99, 193–203.

Hatlevik, O. E., Throndsen, I., Loi, M., & Gudmundsdottir, G. B. (2018). Students' ICT self-efficacy and computer and information literacy: Determinants and relationships. Computers & Education, 118, 107–119.

Hilliger, I., Ortiz-Rojas, M., Pesántez-Cabrera, P., Scheihing, E., Tsai, Y. S., Muñoz-Merino, P. J., . . . & Pérez-Sanagustín, M. (2020). Identifying needs for learning analytics adoption in Latin American universities: A mixed-methods approach. The Internet and Higher Education, 45, 100726.

Holzberger, D., Philipp, A., & Kunter, M. (2013). How teachers' self-efficacy is related to instructional quality: A longitudinal analysis. Journal of Educational Psychology, 105(3), 774.

Hussin, A. A. (2018). Education 4.0 made simple: Ideas for teaching. International Journal of Education and Literacy Studies, 6(3), 92–98.

Jan, S. (2018). Gender, school and class wise differences in level of digital literacy among secondary school students in Pakistan. Issues and Trends in Educational Technology, 6(2), 15–27.

Kaklamanou, D., Nelson, M., & Pearce, J. (2012). *Food and academies: A qualitative study* (pp. 1-23). School Food Trust.

Khan, A. A., Niazi, S., & Saif, S. K. (2020). *Universities unprepared for switch to remote learning*. University World News. [Online]. Available: https://www.universityworldnews.com/post.php?story=20200326141547229

Kollmayer, M., Schober, B., & Spiel, C. (2018). Gender stereotypes in education: Development, consequences, and interventions. European Journal of Developmental Psychology, 15(4), 361–377.

Kozleski, E. B. (2017). The uses of qualitative research: Powerful methods to inform evidence-based practice in education. Research and Practice for Persons with Severe Disabilities, 42(1), 19–32.

López-Meneses, E., Sirignano, F. M., Vázquez-Cano, E., & Ramírez-Hurtado, J. M. (2020). University students' digital competence in three areas of the DigCom 2.1 model: A comparative study at three European universities. Australasian Journal of Educational Technology, 36(3), 69–88.

Maria Cela-Ranilla, J., Esteve Gonzalez, V., Esteve Mon, F., Gonzalez Martinez, J., & Gisbert-Cervera, M. (2017). Teachers in the digital society: A proposal based on transformative pedagogy and advanced technology. *Profesorado-revista de curriculum y formacion de profesorado*, 21(1), 403–422.

McCarthy, J. (2015). Evaluating written, audio and video feedback in higher education summative assessment tasks. Issues in Educational Research, 25(2), 153–169.

Meskhi, B., Ponomareva, S., & Ugnich, E. (2019). E-learning in higher inclusive education: Needs, opportunities and limitations. International Journal of Educational Management, 33(3), 424–437.

Mirete, A. B., Maquilón, J. J., Mirete, L., & Rodríguez, R. A. (2020). Digital competence and university teachers' conceptions about teaching. A structural causal model. Sustainability, 12(12), 4842.

Morgan, S. F., & Berrie, A. M. M. (1970). Development of dormancy during seed maturation in Avena ludoviciana winter wild oat. Nature, 228(5277), 1225–1225.

Nouri, S., Khoong, E. C., Lyles, C. R., & Karliner, L. (2020). Addressing equity in telemedicine for chronic disease management during the Covid-19 pandemic. NEJM Catalyst Innovations in Care Delivery, 1(3), 1–13.

Oriogu, C. D., Chukwuemeka, A. O., & Oriogu-Ogbuiyi, D. C. (2018). Faculty awareness, perception and use of information resources and services in a private university in Nigeria. Covenant Journal of Library and Information Science, 1(2), 32–44.

Peñalva Vélez, A., Fraile, M. N., & Lacambra, A. M. M. (2018). Digital competence and digital literacy of adults (educators and families). International Journal of New Education, 1, 1–13 .

Perkowski, A. J., & Nicewicz, D. A. (2013). Direct catalytic anti-Markovnikov addition of carboxylic acids to alkenes. Journal of the American Chemical Society, 135(28), 10334–10337.

Pirani, S., & Hussain, N. (2019). Technology is a tool for learning: Voices of teachers and parents of young children. Journal of Education & Social Sciences, 7(1), 55–66.

Prestridge, S. (2017). Examining the shaping of teachers' pedagogical orientation for the use of technology. Technology, Pedagogy and Education, 26(4), 367–381.

Priya, M. M. (2017). PowerPoint use in teaching. Retrieved From, 7, 1–3.

Roblizo, M. J. & Cózar, R. (2015). Usos y competencias en TIC en los futuros maestros de Educación Infantil y Primaria: hacia una alfabetización tecnológica real para docentes. Pixel-Bit. *Revista de Medios y Educación*, 47, 23–39. Doi: http://dx.doi.org/10.12795/pixelbit.2015.i47.02

Roig-Vila, R., Mengual-Andrés, S., & Quinto-Medrano, P. (2015). Primary teachers' technological, pedagogical and content knowledge. Comunicar, 45, 151–159.

Ruiz Mezcua, A. (2019). Digital competence and ICT in interpretation: "To renew or to perish". EDMETIC, 8(1), 55–71.

Rutkowski, D., Rutkowski, L., & Sparks, J. (2011). Information and communications technologies support for 21st-century teaching: An international analysis. Journal of School Leadership, 21(2), 190–215.

Salam, S., Jianqiu, Z., Pathan, Z. H., & Lei, W. (2017, December). Strategic barriers in the effective integration of ICT in the public schools of Pakistan. In *Association for Computing Machinery (ACM)*, New York, United States, (pp. 169–172).

Scherer, R., & Siddiq, F. (2019). The relation between students' socioeconomic status and ICT literacy: Findings from a meta-analysis. Computers & Education, 138, 13–32.

Shaikh, Z. A., & Khoja, S. A. (2011). Role of ICT in shaping the future of Pakistani higher education system. Turkish Online Journal of Educational Technology-TOJET, 10(1), 149–161.

Shehzadi, S., Nisar, Q. A., Hussain, M. S., Basheer, M. F., Hameed, W. U., & Chaudhry, N. I. (2020). The role of digital learning toward students' satisfaction and university brand image at educational institutes of Pakistan: A post-effect of COVID-19. Asian Education and Development Studies, 2, 276–294.

Shi, L., Stickler, U., & Lloyd, M. E. (2017). The interplay between attention, experience and skills in online language teaching. Language Learning in Higher Education, 7(1), 205–238.

Singh, H. (2021). Building effective blended learning programs. In *Challenges and opportunities for the global implementation of e-learning frameworks* (pp. 15–23). IGI Global.

Skantz-Åberg, E., Lantz-Andersson, A., Lundin, M., & Williams, P. (2022). Teachers' professional digital competence: An overview of conceptualisations in the literature. Cogent Education, 9(1), 2063224.

Stickler, U., & Shi, L. (2017). Eyetracking methodology in SCMC: A tool for empowering learning and teaching. ReCALL, 29(2), 160–177.

Supo, V. E. G. (2019). El Aprendizaje Flip Learning centrado en el estudiante como generador de calidad educativa. Revista Arbitrada Interdisciplinaria Koinonía, 4(8), 427–450.

Tafazoli, D., Gómez Parra, M. ª. E., & Huertas Abril, C. A. (2019a). Attitude towards computer-assisted language learning: Do gender, age and educational level matter? Teaching English with Technology, 19(3), 22–39.

Tafazoli, D., Huertas Abril, C. A., & Gómez Parra, M. E. (2019b). Technology-based review on computer-assisted language learning: A chronological perspective. Pixel-Bit: Revista de Medios y Educación, 54, 29–43.

Tang, H. (2021). Implementing open educational resources in digital education. Educational Technology Research and Development, 69(1), 389–392.

Tanwir, M., & Khemka, N. (2018). Breaking the silicon ceiling: Gender equality and information technology in Pakistan. Gender, Technology and Development, 22(2), 109–129.

Tondeur, J., Scherer, R., Siddiq, F., & Baran, E. (2017). A comprehensive investigation of TPACK within pre-service teachers' ICT profiles: Mind the gap! Australasian Journal of Educational Technology, 33(3), 46–60.

Uerz, D., Volman, M., & Kral, M. (2018). Teacher educators' competences in fostering student teachers' proficiency in teaching and learning with technology: An overview of relevant research literature. Teaching and Teacher Education, 70, 12–23.

Vázquez-Cano, E., Gómez-Galán, J., Infante-Moro, A., & López-Meneses, E. (2020). Incidence of a non-sustainability use of technology on students' reading performance in Pisa. Sustainability, 12(2), 749.

Williamson, B., Potter, J., & Eynon, R. (2019). *New research problems and agendas in learning, media and technology: The editors' wishlist.* Taylor & Francis.

Zaidieh, A. J. Y. (2012). The use of social networking in education: Challenges and opportunities. World of Computer Science and Information Technology Journal (WCSIT), 2(1), 18–21.

12 Artificial Intelligence in Sustainable Education

Benefits, Applications, Framework, and Potential Barriers

V. Harish, Ravindra Sharma, Geeta Rana, and Anand Nayyar

12.1 INTRODUCTION

The development of technology has had a significant impact on the field of education, resulting in numerous modifications to the ways in which students learn and teachers instruct. Traditional teaching and learning methods have become more interactive, engaging, and efficient as a result of technological advancements over time. From the invention of the printing press to the introduction of computers and the internet, technology has revolutionised the education system by providing students and teachers with new learning tools and resources (Li, 2020). Recent technological advancements have continued to revolutionise the field of education, creating new learning and teaching opportunities. With the proliferation of digital technologies such as artificial intelligence, machine learning, virtual and augmented reality, and mobile applications, educators now have access to a vast array of tools and resources to increase student engagement and enhance learning outcomes. These new technologies have made personalised learning possible, allowing students to learn at their own pace and in accordance with their specific needs (Devagiri et al., 2022; Rana & Sharma, 2019). In this chapter, we will investigate the recent technologies impacting education, their benefits and challenges, as well as their potential future implications. We will also discuss how these technologies can be integrated into the educational system in order to improve learning outcomes and better prepare students for the demands of the future workforce.

In recent years, the incorporation of artificial intelligence (AI) into education has garnered considerable attention due to the potential benefits it can offer (Sharma et al., 2021). AI refers to the use of intelligent machines that can perform tasks that normally require human intelligence, such as learning, problem-solving, and making decisions. In the field of education, artificial intelligence can aid in areas such as personalised learning, intelligent tutoring systems, automated grading, and adaptive assessment. The use of AI in education has been shown to improve student outcomes such as retention rates, academic performance, and learning process engagement (Ouyang et al., 2022; Chen et al., 2020). In addition, AI can provide educators with data-driven insights for identifying student strengths and weaknesses and customising instruction to meet individual requirements (Bates et al., 2020; Prakash et al., 2021). However, the incorporation of AI into education also raises ethical concerns, such as data privacy, algorithmic bias, and the possibility of human teachers being replaced (Masters, 2019). Therefore, it is essential to carefully consider the potential benefits and challenges associated with the incorporation of AI in education and to implement the necessary policies and practices to ensure its responsible and ethical use.

By promoting sustainability, artificial intelligence (AI) has the potential to revolutionise the field of education. Sustainability is defined as the capacity to meet present needs without compromising future generations' ability to meet their own needs. Sustainable education entails the development of an educational system that meets the needs of the present without compromising the capacity of

DOI: 10.1201/9781003425779-12

future generations to learn and realise their full potential (Moore et al., 2017). AI can help achieve this objective in multiple ways.

12.1.1 Objectives of the Chapter

The objectives of the chapter are:

- To investigate the potential of AI in promoting sustainable education and learning;
- To provide an overview of the various AI applications that can be used to promote sustainable practices, as well as the benefits and potential barriers associated with its adoption;
- To conduct a literature review to shed light on the growing interest in the use of artificial intelligence in educational settings and the potential for AI to help solve sustainability-related problems;
- To discuss variety of technologies and their potential applications in sustainable education, including individualised instruction, the creation of curricula, the evaluation of student progress, the distribution of resources, and environmental monitoring;
- To provide a framework for educational institutions to integrate AI into their teaching and learning processes, while also addressing the ethical and responsible use of AI to ensure that its adoption will not have unintended consequences;
- And, to encourage the adoption of AI in promoting sustainable education and learning, as well as to provide educational institutions with guidance on the effective and responsible incorporation of AI into the curriculum.

12.1.2 Organisation of the Chapter

The rest of the chapter is organised as follows. Section 12.2 offers a literature review, followed by benefits of AI in sustainable education in section 12.3. Section 12.4 elaborates the potential of AI to solve sustainability-related problems in education. Section 12.5 focuses on applications of AI in sustainable education. Section 12.6 highlights the framework for integrating AI into sustainable education to meet future demands. Section 12.7 highlights potential barriers for implementing AI in sustainable education. And, finally section 12.8 concludes the chapter with future scope.

12.2 LITERATURE REVIEW

Education has undergone significant change throughout history, with technological advancements and societal norm shifts influencing how teaching and learning are conducted (Huang et al., 2020). In this literature review, the evolution of education from ancient times to the present will be examined, with a focus on the key developments and factors that have contributed to this evolution.

12.2.1 Historical Overview of Education: From Ancient Times to Modernity

Ancient education: Education in ancient times emphasised the transmission of cultural and religious knowledge from one generation to the next (Altekar, 2009). In ancient Greece, for example, philosophy, music, and athletics were central to education. The vast majority of the population remained illiterate, with the vast majority of the elites possessing access to education (Sokoloff & Engerman, 2000).

Mediaeval education: Education in mediaeval times was dominated by the church, with monasteries and cathedral schools educating the elite. Latin was the language of instruction, with the curriculum focusing on religious and moral education. Only the sons of nobility and the wealthy had access to education, which was extremely exclusive (Perkin, 2007).

Modern education: With the establishment of public schools and universities during the Age of Enlightenment in the 18th century, the modern education system emerged. With the introduction of literacy campaigns and mandatory education laws, education became more widely available. The curriculum was broadened to include science, mathematics, and the social sciences (Gruzdeva et al., 2020).

12.2.2 Technology and Education

The incorporation of technology into education has significantly altered how teaching and learning are conducted. Technology has transformed conventional teaching practices and revolutionised the student learning experience (Kharatova et al., 2022). The advantages of technology in education include its ability to improve the learning experience, increase access to educational resources, and provide students with personalised learning opportunities.

In recent years, artificial intelligence (AI) integration in education has evolved rapidly, with the potential to transform traditional teaching methods and personalise student learning experiences. In this literature review, we will examine the evolution of AI in the education sector, focusing on the key developments and innovations that have contributed to its growth (Olszewski & Crompton, 2020).

The development of intelligent tutoring systems (ITS) was one of the earliest applications of AI in education (Guo et al., 2021). These systems were created to provide students with personalised feedback and instruction, as well as to accommodate their unique learning styles. During the 1970s, Donald Norman and his colleagues created the Intelligent Computer-Aided Instruction (ICAI) system, which used natural language processing to interact with students and provide feedback based on their responses (Kommers, 2022).

The emergence of educational data mining (EDM) and learning analytics was another significant step in the evolution of AI in education. These disciplines involve the analysis of large datasets to identify patterns and trends in student performance, which can inform teaching and learning practices. The development of early warning systems that use predictive analytics to identify students at risk of falling behind is one application of EDM in education (Romero & Ventura, 2020).

In recent years, the development of machine learning algorithms has significantly contributed to the expansion of artificial intelligence in education. These algorithms enable the creation of personalised learning experiences for students, based on their specific learning preferences and needs. For instance, the Smart Sparrow platform uses machine learning to customise the content and level of difficulty of learning activities for each student (Aggarwal et al., 2022).

The emergence of chatbots and virtual assistants is another significant development in the evolution of AI in education. These tools interact with students and provide them with support and guidance using natural language processing and machine learning. IBM Watson Education Advisor is one example of a system that uses machine learning to answer students' questions and provide them with personalised recommendations (Hannan & Liu, 2023).

The use of artificial intelligence in assessment and feedback is another area of significant growth within the education sector. Automated grading systems analyse student work using machine learning algorithms and provide feedback based on predefined criteria. For instance, EdX uses automated grading systems to grade assignments and provide students with feedback (Guan et al., 2020).

Last, the advancement of natural language processing and speech recognition technologies has facilitated the incorporation of AI in education. These technologies enable the development of conversational agents and virtual tutors that can interact with students in natural language and offer them individualised support and instruction (Haldorai et al., 2021).

In conclusion, the evolution of AI in education has been marked by a number of significant innovations and developments, such as the emergence of intelligent tutoring systems, educational data mining and learning analytics, machine learning algorithms, chatbots and virtual assistants, automated grading systems, and natural language processing and speech recognition technologies. These technologies have the potential to revolutionise traditional teaching methods, personalise students' learning experiences, and provide educators with invaluable insight into student performance. As AI continues to advance, it is likely to become an increasingly important tool in the education sector, influencing the delivery and experience of teaching and learning.

12.2.3 Significant Studies in the Area of AI in Sustainable Education

Popenici and Kerr (2017) illustrated a literature review on AI in education and discussed the various AI tools currently used in higher education, such as intelligent tutoring systems, chatbots, and adaptive learning systems. In addition, they examined the potential benefits and obstacles associated with the use of AI in education, such as increased personalised learning, improved student engagement, and ethical considerations pertaining to data privacy and algorithmic bias. The authors conclude with recommendations for educators and policymakers to maximise the potential positive effects of AI while minimising its potential negative effects.

Butler-Adam (2018) examined how the fourth industrial revolution (4IR) affects schooling. The author explained how the 4IR could disrupt existing sectors and restructure the global economy. The article discussed the 4IR's effects on education, emphasising the necessity for schools to adapt to changing employment needs and equip students with new economic skills. The author advocated for introducing digital literacy, critical thinking, and problem-solving skills into education programmes and using technology to enhance student learning rather than replace it. The study urged policymakers and educators to collaborate to prepare education systems for 4IR challenges and opportunities.

Pedro et al. (2019) examined the potential of AI in education and its effects on sustainable development. Authors covered individualised learning, intelligent tutoring, and educational data mining using AI and also noted ethical concerns about data privacy and algorithmic bias, as well as the necessity to employ AI to enhance classroom engagement rather than replace it. AI can improve education in developing nations and reduce educational institutions' carbon footprint, according to the paper. Last, governments and educators are advised to employ AI in education ethically, sustainably, and equitably.

Zawacki-Richter et al. (2019) conducted a systematic review of AI research in higher education. The authors examined 71 peer-reviewed articles on AI applications in higher education from 2000 to 2018, concentrating on educators' roles in AI system development and implementation. The article lists student evaluation, learning analytics, and personalised learning as AI applications in higher education. The authors concluded by urging educators and AI developers to work together to use AI to enhance learning rather than replace it.

Papadopoulos et al. (2020) in their study discussed on socially assistive robots (SARs) in pre-tertiary education are reviewed in this systematic review. The review examines SARs in education from 2010 to 2019. SARs can improve students' academic results, social-emotional development, and learning experiences by offering tailored and engaging interactions. Technical issues, ethical concerns, and little scientific evidence are also obstacles.

Tanveer et al. (2020) believed that academic policies and practices must examine the effects of AI on the environment, society, and economy to be sustainable. AI's effects on labour, privacy, and energy usage are examined in the essay. Ethical considerations in AI development and application are also stressed. They recommend that academic institutions incorporate sustainability into AI policies and practises like research funding, curriculum creation, and industrial relationships.

Chiu and Chai (2020) in their work discussed the adoption of self-determination theory is used to provide a sustainable AI education curriculum planning framework. To motivate and engage students, AI curriculum design should incorporate autonomy, competence, and relatedness. A sustainable AI curriculum should teach critical thinking, problem-solving, and ethical decision-making while addressing AI's impact on society and the environment, according to the authors. K-12 and higher education AI education examples are provided in the article. Sustainable AI education can help create responsible AI practitioners who employ AI for social and environmental good, according to the authors.

Bozkurt et al. (2021) discussed the review 50 years of education AI research and elaborated how AI is used in teaching, learning, assessment, and administration. They also debate AI ethics and its benefits and drawbacks in schooling. AI can improve personalised and adaptable learning, student outcomes, and teacher and administrative decision-making. The authors also note technical obstacles, data privacy concerns, and the possibility for biases and discrimination in AI-based teaching. The study concluded that sustainable and equitable AI development and deployment in education requires a critical and ethical perspective.

Lee and Lee (2021) addressed how artificial intelligence (AI) could change physical education (PE). AI's tailored and adaptive education, feedback, and assessment can improve PE learning, according to the authors. Authors demonstrated how AI can be utilised in fitness monitoring, skill analysis, and game design in PE. The authors emphasized data privacy, bias, and justice in AI development and use in PE and how AI can help create a more inclusive and equitable PE environment by giving various learners the chance to play. To progress AI in PE, researchers, instructors, and industry professionals must collaborate and design a framework and build upon to achieve significant transformation in the field.

12.2.4 Additional Studies in 2022

A number of academic papers investigating the potential of AI in education for sustainable development were published in 2022. A systematic review argued that while AI has the potential to significantly enhance education for sustainable development, its application must address ethical and social issues, data privacy, and biases. Another study investigated the potential of artificial intelligence in alleviating poverty and its implications for management education and sustainable development. The study recommended using AI to improve financial inclusion, healthcare access, and educational outcomes in order to reduce poverty.

Other papers published in 2022 investigated the use of AI in engineering study programmes, the implementation of AI in China's education policy, the role of digital technologies in education, and learning design to facilitate student–AI collaboration. These papers employed various methodologies, such as case studies, qualitative research, and systematic reviews. The papers emphasised the significant potential of AI to improve education for sustainable development, increase access to education, facilitate personalised learning, and increase student engagement. However, the papers also identified potential barriers, such as ethical and social issues, data privacy, and biases, that must be addressed for AI to be implemented effectively in education for sustainable development.

In conclusion, these studies suggest that artificial intelligence has the potential to improve sustainable education by providing personalised learning experiences, enhancing teacher efficiency, and optimising resource management. AI can reduce education's carbon footprint by promoting paperless learning and reducing waste. However, the implementation of AI in education requires careful consideration of ethical and privacy issues, as well as the training and development of teachers and infrastructure. To fully explore the potential of AI in promoting sustainable education, additional research is required.

12.3 BENEFITS OF AI IN SUSTAINABLE EDUCATION

Personalised learning is one of the potential applications of AI for promoting sustainable education (Pataranutaporn et al., 2021). Personalised learning is the use of technology to tailor education to the unique needs of each student. AI algorithms are capable of analysing a student's learning style, their preferences, and their strengths and weaknesses in order to create a personalised learning plan for each student. This strategy can help reduce educational waste by ensuring that each student is learning at their own pace and is not wasting time on topics they have already mastered. By reducing the use of paper, textbooks, and other resources, this can help reduce the environmental impact of education (Haleem et al., 2022).

TABLE 12.1
Review of Recent Articles

Author(s)	Title	Objective	Methodology	Findings
Goralski & Tan (2022)	"Artificial intelligence and poverty alleviation: Emerging innovations and their implications for management education and sustainable development"	The objective of the paper is to explore the potential of AI in poverty alleviation and its implications for management education and sustainable development.	Literature review	The research suggests employing AI to increase financial inclusion, healthcare access, and education results to reduce poverty.
Paulauskaite-Taraseviciene et al. (2022)	"Assessing education for sustainable development in engineering study programs: A case of AI ecosystem creation"	The objective of the paper is to assess the ESD in engineering study programs by analysing the case of AI ecosystem creation.	Case study	The paper illustrates that the engineering study program's AI environment has promoted interdisciplinary collaboration, student engagement, and innovation for ESD.
Campbell (2022)	"Artificial intelligence for education policy in Wuhan City, China"	The objective of the paper is to examine the use of AI in education policy in Wuhan City, China.	Case study	The study reveals that Wuhan City's education strategy uses AI to increase teaching quality, student performance, and individualised learning.
Haleem et al. (2022)	"Understanding the role of digital technologies in education: A review"	The objective of the paper is to review the literature on the role of digital technologies in education and its potential impact on sustainable operations and computers.	Systematic review of the literature	The paper identifies several potential advantages of digital technologies in education, including increasing access to education, fostering personalised learning, and enhancing student engagement.
Kim et al. (2022)	"Learning design to support student–AI collaboration: Perspectives of leading teachers for AI in education"	The objective of the paper is to explore the perspectives of leading teachers for AI in education on learning design that supports student–AI collaboration.	Qualitative study that involved semi-structured interviews	The paper demonstrates that prominent AI educators recognise the significance of designing learning environments that facilitate student–AI collaboration.

Lamb et al. (2022)	"Real-time prediction of science student learning outcomes using machine learning classification of hemodynamics during virtual reality and online learning sessions"	The objective of the paper is to investigate the feasibility of using machine learning classification of hemodynamics to predict science student learning outcomes in real-time during virtual reality and online learning sessions.	Study of 23 participants wearing a hemodynamic monitoring device	The paper demonstrates the viability of utilising machine learning classification of hemodynamics to predict real-time science student learning outcomes during virtual reality and online learning sessions.
Ouyang et al. (2022)	"Artificial intelligence in online higher education: A systematic review of empirical research from 2011 to 2020"	The objective of the paper is to conduct a systematic review of empirical research on the use of AI in online higher education from 2011 to 2020.	Systematic review of empirical research	This paper examines the current state of artificial intelligence in online higher education and emphasises the potential of AI to improve the quality and efficiency of online learning. AI has been utilised in various facets of online higher education, including student assessment, personalised learning, and course design, according to the authors.

The use of virtual and augmented reality is an additional potential application of AI in promoting sustainable education. Using virtual and augmented reality, immersive educational simulations of real-world environments can be created (Daniela & Lytras, 2019). This can reduce the need for travel and other resources typically required for hands-on learning opportunities. Using virtual field trips, for instance, students can learn about ecosystems without having to physically visit a forest or wetland. By reducing the need for transportation and other resources, this can help to reduce the carbon footprint of education.

AI can also be used to make educational systems more efficient. For instance, AI algorithms can be utilised to optimise student transportation routes, thereby reducing the time and fuel required to transport students to and from school (Chen et al., 2020). By automatically adjusting heating, cooling, and lighting systems based on occupancy and usage patterns, AI can also be used to optimise energy usage in schools. This can reduce the environmental impact of education by decreasing energy consumption and greenhouse gas emissions.

There are already a number of instances in which AI has been used to promote sustainable education. For instance, IBM's Watson Education platform uses AI to personalise students' learning experiences (Firat, 2023). The platform analyses student data to identify problem areas and generates individualised learning plans to help students improve. Another example is the use of virtual reality in science education, in which students can explore complex scientific concepts in a safe and immersive environment using VR technology (Hamilton et al., 2021).

By promoting sustainability, AI has the potential to revolutionise the field of education. We can reduce the environmental impact of education and ensure that future generations have access to high-quality education by using AI to create personalised learning experiences, immersive educational experiences, and efficient educational systems. However, it is important to ensure that AI is used ethically and responsibly, and not to replace human educators or perpetuate existing inequalities in education. AI can be a potent tool for promoting sustainable education if it is carefully planned and implemented (Borenstein & Howard, 2021).

Education that is sustainable is crucial for numerous reasons. First, it contributes to a more equitable and just society by ensuring that all individuals, regardless of socioeconomic status, have access to a high-quality education. Second, it promotes environmental sustainability by decreasing the environmental impact of education, such as waste and energy consumption. Last, it helps prepare future generations for the challenges of a world that is rapidly changing, such as climate change, technological advancements, and global economic shifts (Nousheen et al., 2020).

In addition, AI can aid in the creation of immersive educational experiences that simulate real-world environments, such as virtual field trips, thereby reducing the need for travel and other resources typically required to provide hands-on learning opportunities (Meccawy, 2022). By reducing the need for transportation and other resources, this can help to reduce the carbon footprint of education.

Last, AI can assist in preparing students for the challenges of a world that is rapidly changing, such as climate change, technological advancements, and global economic shifts (Oliveira & de Souza, 2022). AI can foster creativity, innovation, and critical thinking, which are essential for success in the 21st century, by providing students with access to cutting-edge technologies and tools.

In conclusion, sustainable education is necessary for creating a more equitable and just society, promoting environmental sustainability, and preparing future generations for the challenges of a world that is rapidly changing. Artificial intelligence can play a crucial role in achieving sustainable education by providing innovative solutions to some of the challenges facing education today. We can reduce the environmental impact of education and ensure that future generations have access to high-quality education by using AI to create personalised learning experiences, immersive educational experiences, and efficient educational systems.

Table 12.2 highlights the benefits of AI in sustainable education.

TABLE 12.2
Benefits of Artificial Intelligence in Sustainable Education

Benefits	Description	Author(s)
1. Personalised learning	AI can support personalised learning experiences, which can be tailored to individual students' needs and learning styles. This can promote student engagement and motivation, leading to better learning outcomes.	Hamilton et al. (2021)
2. Environment monitoring	AI can be used to monitor the environment, such as air quality, water quality, and energy consumption. This can help to identify areas for improvement and promote sustainable behavior.	Huang et al. (2023) Zawacki-Richter et al. (2019)
3. Efficient resource allocation	AI can support efficient allocation of resources, such as energy, water, and materials. This can help to reduce waste and improve sustainability performance.	Bates et al. (2020)
4. Objective evaluations	AI can provide objective evaluations of student progress, which can help to identify areas where further support is needed and measure the impact of sustainability initiatives.	González-Calatayud et al. (2021)
5. Creation of environmentally friendly curricula	AI can be used to develop curricula that incorporate sustainability-related topics and themes. This can help to raise awareness and understanding of environmental issues and promote behavior change among students.	Campbell (2022) Tanveer et al. (2020)
6. Early detection of learning difficulties	AI can detect early signs of learning difficulties and provide personalised interventions, which can help to prevent students from falling behind and improve learning outcomes.	Chen et al. (2020)
7. Efficient grading	AI can automate the grading process, which can save teachers time and enable more frequent and detailed feedback for students.	Bozkurt et al. (2021)
8. Enhanced accessibility	AI can support accessibility for students with disabilities, such as by providing closed captions for videos and audio descriptions for images.	Firat (2023)

12.4 POTENTIAL OF AI TO SOLVE SUSTAINABILITY-RELATED PROBLEMS IN EDUCATION

Artificial intelligence (AI) is emerging as a transformative technology with the potential to revolutionise education and solve problems associated with sustainability. AI has the potential to support sustainable education by creating personalised learning environments, automating administrative tasks, enhancing student engagement, and providing both students and teachers with real-time feedback.

The following are the seven ways in which AI can solve education-related sustainability issues:

Individualised educational experiences: By analysing a student's individual learning patterns, preferences, and strengths, AI can personalise their educational experiences. This method is more effective than the standard, one-size-fits-all method, which can be less engaging and less effective for some students. Adaptive learning platforms powered by AI use data to personalise the learning process, adjust the level of difficulty of assignments, and recommend learning resources based on the student's progress. These platforms allow students to learn at their own pace, which can increase motivation, engagement, and academic achievement (Kim et al., 2022).

Administrative tasks that are performing automatically: Administrative tasks such as grading, attendance tracking, and course scheduling can be automated by AI. By automating these tasks, teachers can concentrate on teaching and providing students with individualised support. Additionally, AI can optimise course schedules to reduce energy consumption and transportation expenses (Ahmad et al., 2022). AI can analyse data on student attendance patterns and transport availability to generate schedules that minimise energy consumption and travel time, for instance.

Real-time response: Students and teachers can receive real-time feedback from AI, which can enhance the learning experience and boost academic achievement. For instance, chatbots powered by AI can provide immediate feedback and improvement suggestions on students' assignments (Lamb et al., 2022). Similarly, AI-powered analytics tools can provide teachers with real-time data on student performance, allowing them to adapt their teaching strategies to better meet their students' needs. These tools can also help teachers identify struggling students and provide them with additional assistance.

Improved student engagement: By creating more interactive and immersive learning environments, AI can enhance student engagement. For instance, virtual reality (VR) powered by AI can simulate real-world scenarios and allow students to explore complex concepts in a safe, supervised environment, making it more engaging and entertaining. AI can increase student motivation and interest in sustainability-related topics by making learning more engaging.

Personalised assistance for students with special needs: AI can offer individualised assistance to students with special needs, such as those with learning disabilities or sensory impairments. For instance, speech recognition powered by AI can assist students with hearing impairments by converting spoken words to text. Similarly, AI-powered language translation can assist multilingual students by translating lectures and homework into their native tongue. Such assistance can enable students with special needs to fully engage in the learning process and achieve academic success (Bhutoria, 2022).

Environmental footprint reduction: AI can reduce the environmental impact of education by optimising energy consumption and decreasing waste. AI can optimise classroom temperature and lighting, for instance, to reduce energy consumption. AI-powered waste management systems can also assist schools in reducing waste by monitoring and analysing waste patterns and recommending strategies for waste reduction. These measures can aid schools in reducing their carbon footprint and fostering a more sustainable future (Shumskaia, 2022).

Enhancement of learning outcomes: By providing students with more personalised, engaging, and effective learning experiences, AI can improve learning outcomes. AI can assist students in identifying their strengths and weaknesses, setting goals, and tracking their progress by analysing student data and providing real-time feedback (Meng et al., 2023). Similarly, by automating administrative tasks and providing teachers with real-time data, AI can allow teachers to focus on achieving learning outcomes as opposed to performing mundane tasks.

12.5 APPLICATIONS OF AI IN SUSTAINABLE EDUCATION

The application of AI in education has the potential to address sustainability-related issues, such as promoting personalised learning, creating environmentally friendly curricula, conducting objective evaluations of student progress, allocating resources efficiently, and monitoring the environment. The following points elaborate the applications of AI in sustainable education as shown in Figure 12.1

Potential of AI to Solve Sustainability related problems in education	Individualized Educational Experiences
	Administrative Tasks That Are Performing Automatically
	Real-Time Response:
	Improved Student Engagement
	Personalized Assistance for Students with Special Needs
	Environmental Footprint Reduction
	Enhancement of Learning Outcomes

FIGURE 12.1 Potential of artificial intelligence to solve sustainability-related issues in education.

Individualised instruction for students: Personalised learning has been identified as a crucial component of sustainable education because it enables instruction to be tailored to the needs of individual students, resulting in improved academic outcomes and lower dropout rates (Arun Kumar et al., 2022). AI can aid in the creation of personalised learning experiences by analysing individual student data, such as learning styles, academic performance, and engagement levels, and providing content and support that is tailored to meet their specific needs (Lillywhite & Wolbring, 2020).

Environmentally friendly curriculum development: Another potential application of AI in sustainable education is the development of eco-friendly curricula. AI can be used to evaluate existing curricula and recommend modifications to include sustainability concepts and practices (Ceylan, 2021). This strategy would enable educators to equip students with the knowledge and skills required to address sustainability challenges, such as climate change and environmental degradation, and prepare them for a sustainable future.

Objective assessments of student development: Using AI, it is also possible to conduct objective assessments of student progress. Traditional forms of assessment, such as multiple-choice tests, may not accurately evaluate students' problem-solving skills, creativity, or critical thinking abilities in real-world situations (González-Calatayud et al., 2021). AI can be used to develop and administer adaptive assessments that provide more comprehensive and accurate evaluations of student progress, taking into account factors such as previous performance and learning styles.

Effective resource management: Another potential application of AI in sustainable education is resource allocation. AI can be used to analyse data on resource utilisation, such as energy and water consumption, to identify inefficiencies that can be addressed to reduce waste and enhance sustainability. For instance, AI can analyse classroom usage data and recommend scheduling changes that reduce energy consumption (Huang, 2021).

Environmental surveillance: Monitoring the environment is another potential AI application in sustainable education. AI can analyse sensor data to monitor environmental parameters such as air quality, temperature, and humidity in schools. This data can be used to identify and address potential health hazards, such as high levels of indoor air pollution. AI can also analyse energy consumption data and identify areas where energy conservation measures can be implemented to reduce the carbon footprint of the school (Zawacki-Richter et al., 2019).

AI can also help promote sustainable practices beyond the classroom, such as waste reduction and recycling. These systems can also provide students and staff with feedback on their efforts to reduce waste, encouraging behaviour modification and promoting sustainability. AI has the potential to address sustainability-related issues in education by promoting personalised learning, creating environmentally friendly curricula, conducting objective evaluations of student progress, allocating resources efficiently, and monitoring the environment. These potential AI applications in education hold great promise for advancing sustainable development and preparing students for a sustainable future. However, the implementation of AI in education must be conducted with caution, taking into account ethical concerns such as data privacy and security, as well as the need for adequate teacher training to ensure that AI is used effectively to achieve the desired results.

12.6 FRAMEWORK FOR INTEGRATING AI INTO SUSTAINABLE EDUCATION: MEETING FUTURE DEMANDS

The generic framework for integrating AI into sustainable education is as follows (Al-Youbi et al., 2020; Wilson & Van Der Velden, 2022; Pedro et al., 2019; Di Vaio et al., 2020).

12.6.1 Needs Assessment and Goal Setting

This entails identifying the specific sustainability-related issues that must be addressed, establishing improvement goals, and determining how AI can support these efforts. According to Al-Youbi et al. (2020), conducting a needs assessment and establishing sustainability goals are indispensable for the development of effective sustainability strategies. In addition, AI can support these efforts by providing data-driven insights and recommendations.

12.6.2 Data Collection and Analysis

Collecting and analysing data pertaining to sustainability, such as energy consumption, waste production, and carbon emissions, can be accomplished with AI. This information can then be used to identify patterns, trends, and improvement opportunities. Wilson and Van Der Velden (2022) explain further that AI can streamline data collection and analysis, making it easier to monitor sustainability performance and identify areas for improvement. In addition, AI provides more precise and timely data analysis than conventional methods.

12.6.3 AI-Enabled Teaching and Learning

AI can support personalised learning experiences that are tailored to the needs and learning styles of individual students. This can increase student engagement and motivation, leading to improved academic outcomes. According to Pedro et al. (2019), AI can also support adaptive learning, in which the system adjusts the material's difficulty based on the student's performance. This can ensure that the learning experience is both challenging and manageable, resulting in more effective learning outcomes.

12.6.4 AI-Enabled Curriculum Development

AI can be used to develop curricula that include topics and themes related to sustainability. This can help to increase student awareness and comprehension of environmental issues and promote behaviour modification. AI can support curriculum development by analysing student data, identifying knowledge gaps, and recommending relevant learning resources, according to Ceylan (2021). This can ensure that sustainability-related topics are incorporated into the curriculum and that students have access to high-quality learning resources.

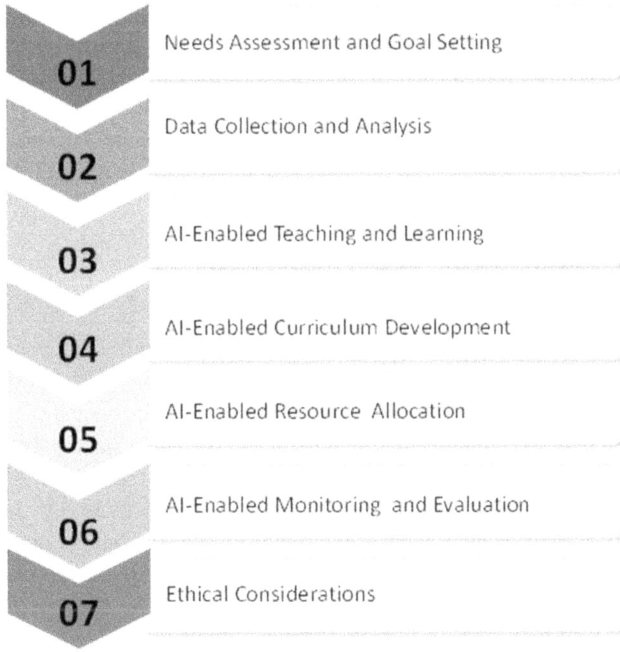

FIGURE 12.2 Framework for integrating artificial intelligence into sustainable education.

12.6.5 AI-Enabled Resource Allocation

AI can facilitate the efficient allocation of resources like energy, water, and materials. This can contribute to waste reduction and improved sustainability performance. Bates et al. (2020) explain that AI can be used to optimise resource allocation by analysing data on resource utilisation and identifying improvement opportunities. AI can be used to identify energy-saving opportunities, such as turning off lights when they are not needed or adjusting the temperature of a room to reduce energy consumption.

12.6.6 AI-Enabled Monitoring and Evaluation

AI can be used to monitor and evaluate sustainability performance, providing real-time feedback and enabling continuous improvement. This can aid in identifying areas requiring additional action and measuring the impact of sustainability initiatives. AI can support monitoring and evaluation, according to Bozkurt et al. (2021), by analysing data on sustainability performance and providing recommendations for improvement. In addition, AI can be used to predict future sustainability performance, allowing organisations to take preventative measures to address potential problems.

12.6.7 Ethical Considerations

It is crucial to consider the ethical implications of AI in sustainable education, including privacy, bias, and transparency concerns. Borenstein & Howard (2021) explained that AI systems must be designed to protect the privacy of students and to eliminate bias in data analysis and decision-making. Additionally, it is essential to be transparent about how AI is used and how decisions are made in order to ensure accountability and build trust among stakeholders.

This framework provides a structured approach for the incorporation of artificial intelligence in sustainable education, addressing key areas such as needs assessment, data collection and analysis, teaching and learning, curriculum development, resource allocation, monitoring and evaluation, and ethical considerations. By adopting this framework, educational institutions will be able to harness the potential of artificial intelligence to address sustainability-related challenges and foster a more sustainable future. This framework is consistent with the UN Sustainable Development Goals (SDGs), specifically SDG 4 (Quality Education) and SDG 13 (Climate Action), which highlight the importance of education for sustainable development and climate change mitigation.

12.7 POTENTIAL BARRIERS OF IMPLEMENTING AI IN SUSTAINABLE EDUCATION

Various research indicates integrating AI into education has the potential to revolutionise teaching and learning, thereby contributing to a more sustainable future. However, a number of potential obstacles must be overcome in order to successfully implement AI in sustainable education. The following seven points illustrate the potential obstacles to the implementation of AI in sustainable education.

Cost: Cost is one of the most significant obstacles to AI implementation in sustainable education. Development, maintenance, and implementation of AI systems may be prohibitively expensive for many educational institutions, especially those in developing nations or with limited resources. In addition, the cost of AI systems may exacerbate the digital divide between affluent and disadvantaged communities, which can have a substantial effect on educational equity.

Privacy and data security: Privacy and data security concerns are an additional potential barrier to implementing AI in sustainable education. As AI systems rely heavily on data collection and analysis, there is a possibility that students' and instructors' privacy could be compromised. Moreover, the data collected by AI systems may be susceptible to infiltration and misuse, which can have severe repercussions for educational institutions.

Lack of trust: The dearth of trust in AI systems can also be a significant barrier to their implementation in sustainable education. Many individuals are sceptical that AI can effectively support and improve education, and they may be hesitant to adopt AI systems without a thorough comprehension of their potential benefits and risks.

Bias and discrimination: AI systems are only as effective as the data on which they are trained with regards to bias and discrimination. If the data used to develop AI systems is prejudiced or discriminatory, the AI systems will be biased and discriminatory as well. This can have grave implications for educational equity, as AI systems may unjustly disadvantage certain student groups.

Lack of understanding: A dearth of understanding of AI systems and their potential benefits and risks can be a significant barrier to their implementation in sustainable education. Many educators may be unfamiliar with AI systems or unsure of how to implement them effectively in the classroom.

Resistance to change: Change resistance can also be a significant barrier to the implementation of AI in sustainable education. Due to either a lack of comprehension or a fear of change, many educators may be resistant to incorporating AI systems into their teaching methods.

Ethical concerns: Ethical concerns can also be a significant barrier to the implementation of AI in sustainable education. As AI systems become more advanced, there is a possibility that they will completely supplant human educators. This raises significant ethical concerns regarding the role of technology in education and the potential impact of artificial intelligence on the teaching profession.

To ensure that AI systems are effectively integrated into education and contribute to a more sustainable and equitable future, it will be crucial to address these obstacles.

12.8 CONCLUSION AND FUTURE SCOPE

Education is no longer restricted to textbooks and classrooms in the modern era. With technological advancements, the education system has witnessed a radical transformation, paving the way for innovative learning approaches. Incorporating AI into education provides a new paradigm for sustainable education. This chapter examines the benefits, prospective applications, framework, and potential barriers of artificial intelligence in sustainable education.

There are numerous advantages to incorporating AI into education, including personalised learning experiences, increased pupil engagement, and decreased resource consumption. AI has the potential to transform the traditional one-size-fits-all approach to education by providing adaptive learning experiences that are tailored to the specific requirements and abilities of each student. Providing access to digital resources and decreasing the need for paper-based materials, AI-powered educational tools can also help to reduce resource consumption.

In addition to its numerous advantages, AI has the potential to solve education-related sustainability issues. Educators can identify patterns in student behaviour and learning outcomes with the assistance of AI, thereby optimising teaching strategies and improving student outcomes. Moreover, AI-powered assessment tools can help identify and resolve learning gaps in real time, thereby enhancing student retention and reducing dropout rates.

The framework for integrating AI into sustainable education provides guidelines for the responsible integration of AI into education, addressing potential obstacles and emphasising ethical considerations. The framework emphasises the significance of collaboration between educators, policymakers, and industry to ensure that AI is incorporated in a way that promotes sustainability and equity. In addition, it emphasises the significance of transparency, accountability, and responsible data use in mitigating potential risks and ensuring that the benefits of AI are realised.

Nevertheless, the incorporation of AI into education is not without obstacles. Ethical and privacy concerns, a dearth of funding and infrastructure, and resistance to change are potential obstacles. Ethical concerns include bias, impartiality, and transparency, which can affect the precision and dependability of educational tools powered by AI. Privacy concerns involve the acquisition and use of personal information, which must be handled in an open and accountable manner.

In addition to ethical and privacy concerns, integrating AI into education requires substantial infrastructure and resource investments. Numerous educational institutions lack the infrastructure required to support AI-powered educational tools, which can be costly and require extensive technical knowledge to implement. In addition, resistance to change can be a significant barrier to the incorporation of AI in education. Educators and administrators may be hesitant to implement new technologies, especially if they view them as a threat to conventional teaching methods.

While artificial intelligence is increasingly being incorporated into sustainable education, there are still a number of unexplored areas. Among the possible future research areas in AI and sustainable education are:

- *Developing and implementing AI-based assessment tools*: AI can be used to more objectively and accurately assess and evaluate student learning. Future research could investigate the potential of artificial intelligence-based assessment tools and their influence on student performance.

  AI has the potential to personalise learning experiences for students, but additional research is required to optimise and enhance these experiences. Future research could investigate ways to further individualise learning with AI while ensuring that students receive a well-rounded education.
- *Enhancing AI-enabled curriculum development*: The use of artificial intelligence in curriculum development is still in its infancy. Future research may investigate how AI can be utilised to develop more engaging and effective curricula that promote sustainability.

AI can support teachers' professional development by providing real-time feedback and assistance. Future research may investigate how AI can be utilised to enhance the efficacy of teacher professional development programmes.

- *Investigating the ethical implications of AI in sustainable education*: As AI is incorporated into sustainable education, it is essential to consider its ethical implications. In the context of AI-enabled sustainable education, future research may examine ethical issues such as privacy, bias, and transparency.

  AI has the potential to promote behaviour change among students, resulting in more sustainable practices. Future research could investigate how artificial intelligence can be utilised to encourage students to adopt more sustainable behaviours.
- *Analysing the impact of AI on sustainability performance*: Given that AI is used to monitor and evaluate sustainability performance, it is essential to comprehend its impact on sustainability outcomes. Future research could investigate the efficacy of AI-enabled sustainability initiatives and the effect they have on sustainability performance.

  Exploring the potential of AI to reduce educational institutions' carbon footprint educational institutions are significant contributors to greenhouse gas emissions. Future research could investigate how AI can be utilised to reduce educational institutions' carbon footprint and promote more sustainable practices.

There is substantial potential for AI to support sustainable education in numerous ways. Future research can aid in optimising the use of AI in sustainable education and ensuring its positive impact on students, teachers, and the environment.

REFERENCES

Aggarwal, K., Mijwil, M. M., Al-Mistarehi, A. H., Alomari, S., Gök, M., Alaabdin, A. M. Z., & Abdulrhman, S. H. (2022). Has the future started? The current growth of artificial intelligence, machine learning, and deep learning. Iraqi Journal for Computer Science and Mathematics, 3(1), 115–123. https://doi.org/10.24897/ijcsm.v3i1.164.

Ahmad, S. F., Alam, M. M., Rahmat, M. K., Mubarik, M. S., & Hyder, S. I. (2022). Academic and administrative role of artificial intelligence in education. Sustainability, 14(3), 1101. https://doi.org/10.3390/su14031101.

Al-Youbi, A. O., Al-Hayani, A., Bardesi, H. J., Basheri, M., Lytras, M. D., & Aljohani, N. R. (2020). The King Abdulaziz University (KAU) pandemic framework: A methodological approach to leverage social media for the sustainable management of higher education in crisis. Sustainability, 12(11), 4367. https://doi.org/10.3390/su12114367.

Altekar, A. S. (2009). *Education in ancient India*. New Delhi: Gyan Publishing House.

Arun Kumar, U., Mahendran, G., & Gobhinath, S. (2022). A review on artificial intelligence based e-Learning system. In P. Vikram, N. Gupta, N. Kumar, & V. K. Singh (eds.), Pervasive computing and social networking: Proceedings of ICPCSN 2022 (pp. 659–671). Singapore: Springer. https://doi.org/10.1007/978-981-17-3453-3_61.

Bates, T., Cobo, C., Mariño, O., & Wheeler, S. (2020). Can artificial intelligence transform higher education? International Journal of Educational Technology in Higher Education, 17(1), 1–12. https://doi.org/10.1186/s41239-020-00198-8.

Bhutoria, A. (2022). Personalized education and artificial intelligence in United States, China, and India: A systematic review using a human-in-the-loop model. Computers and Education: Artificial Intelligence, 100068. https://doi.org/10.1016/j.caeai.2022.100068.

Borenstein, J., & Howard, A. (2021). Emerging challenges in AI and the need for AI ethics education. AI and Ethics, 1, 61–65. https://doi.org/10.1007/s43681-021-00005-7.

Bozkurt, A., Karadeniz, A., Baneres, D., Guerrero-Roldán, A. E., & Rodríguez, M. E. (2021). Artificial intelligence and reflections from educational landscape: A review of AI studies in half a century. Sustainability, 13(2), 800. https://doi.org/10.3390/su13020800.

Butler-Adam, J. (2018). The fourth industrial revolution and education. South African Journal of Science, 114(5–6), 1–1. https://doi.org/10.17159/sajs.2018.

Campbell, C. (2022, March). Artificial intelligence for education policy in Wuhan City, China. In IOP Conf. Series: Earth and Environmental Science (Vol. 717, p. 012037). https://doi.org/10.1088/1755-1315/717/1/012037.

Ceylan, S. (2021). Artificial intelligence in architecture: An educational perspective. In CSEDU (Vol. 1, pp. 100–107). https://doi.org/10.5220/0010401501000107.

Chen, L., Chen, P., & Lin, Z. (2020). Artificial intelligence in education: A review. IEEE Access, 8, 75264–75278. https://doi.org/10.1109/ACCESS.2020.2988616.

Chiu, T. K., & Chai, C. S. (2020). Sustainable curriculum planning for artificial intelligence education: A self-determination theory perspective. Sustainability, 12(14), 5568. https://doi.org/10.3390/su12145568.

Daniela, L., & Lytras, M. D. (2019). Themed issue on enhanced educational experience in virtual and augmented reality. Virtual Reality, 23(4), 325–327. https://doi.org/10.1007/s10055-019-00409-6.

Devagiri, J. S., Paheding, S., Niyaz, Q., Yang, X., & Smith, S. (2022). Augmented reality and artificial intelligence in industry: Trends, tools, and future challenges. Expert Systems with Applications, 118002. https://doi.org/10.1016/j.eswa.2022.118002.

Di Vaio, A., Palladino, R., Hassan, R., & Escobar, O. (2020). Artificial intelligence and business models in the sustainable development goals perspective: A systematic literature review. Journal of Business Research, 121, 283–314. https://doi.org/10.1016/j.jbusres.2020.09.041.

Firat, M. (2023). Integrating AI applications into learning management systems to enhance e-Learning. Instructional Technology and Lifelong Learning, 4(1), 1–14. https://doi.org/10.4018/itlll.2023010101.

González-Calatayud, V., Prendes-Espinosa, P., & Roig-Vila, R. (2021). Artificial intelligence for student assessment: A systematic review. Applied Sciences, 11(12), 5467. https://doi.org/10.3390/app11125467.

Goralski, M. A., & Tan, T. K. (2022). Artificial intelligence and poverty alleviation: Emerging innovations and their implications for management education and sustainable development. The International Journal of Management Education, 20(3), 100662. https://doi.org/10.1016/j.ijme.2022.100662.

Gruzdeva, M. L., Vaganova, O. I., Kaznacheeva, S. N., Bystrova, N. V., & Chanchina, A. V. (2020). Modern educational technologies in professional education. Growth Poles of the Global Economy: Emergence, Changes and Future Perspectives, 1097–1103. https://doi.org/10.1007/978-3-030-49158-2_148.

Guan, C., Mou, J., & Jiang, Z. (2020). Artificial intelligence innovation in education: A twenty-year data-driven historical analysis. International Journal of Innovation Studies, 4(4), 134–147. https://doi.org/10.1108/IJIS-06-2020-0197.

Guo, L., Wang, D., Gu, F., Li, Y., Wang, Y., & Zhou, R. (2021). Evolution and trends in intelligent tutoring systems research: A multidisciplinary and scientometric view. Asia Pacific Education Review, 22(3), 441–461. https://doi.org/10.1007/s12564-021-09699-8.

Haldorai, A., Murugan, S., & Ramu, A. (2021). Evolution, challenges, and application of intelligent ICT education: An overview. Computer Applications in Engineering Education, 29(3), 562–571. https://doi.org/10.1002/cae.22460.

Haleem, A., Javaid, M., Qadri, M. A., & Suman, R. (2022). Understanding the role of digital technologies in education: A review. Sustainable Operations and Computers. Advance online publication. https://doi.org/10.1007/s40515-022-00149-5.

Hamilton, D., McKechnie, J., Edgerton, E., & Wilson, C. (2021). Immersive virtual reality as a pedagogical tool in education: A systematic literature review of quantitative learning outcomes and experimental design. Journal of Computers in Education, 8(1), 1–32. https://doi.org/10.1007/s40692-021-00188-4.

Hannan, E., & Liu, S. (2023). AI: New source of competitiveness in higher education. Competitiveness Review: An International Business Journal, 33(2), 265–279.

Huang, A. Y., Lu, O. H., & Yang, S. J. (2023). Effects of artificial intelligence–enabled personalized recommendations on learners' learning engagement, motivation, and outcomes in a flipped classroom. Computers & Education, 194, 104684. https://doi.org/10.1016/j.compedu.2022.104684

Huang, C., Yang, C., Wang, S., Wu, W., Su, J., & Liang, C. (2020). Evolution of topics in education research: A systematic review using bibliometric analysis. Educational Review, 72(3), 281–297.

Huang, S. (2021). Design and development of educational robot teaching resources using artificial intelligence technology. International Journal of Emerging Technologies in Learning, 15(5).

Kharatova, S. K., & Ismailov, T. X. O. G. L. (2022). Use of innovative technologies in the educational process. Science and Education, 3(3), 713–718.

Kim, J., Lee, H., & Cho, Y. H. (2022). Learning design to support student-AI collaboration: Perspectives of leading teachers for AI in education. Education and Information Technologies, 27(5), 6069–6104.

Kommers, P. (2022). Navigation in Hypertext. In *Sources for a better education: Lessons from research and best practices* (pp. 137–174). Cham: Springer International Publishing.

Lamb, R., Neumann, K., & Linder, K. A. (2022). Real-time prediction of science student learning outcomes using machine learning classification of hemodynamics during virtual reality and online learning sessions. Computers and Education: Artificial Intelligence, 3, 100078.

Lee, H. S., & Lee, J. (2021). Applying artificial intelligence in physical education and future perspectives. Sustainability, 13(1), 351.

Li, L. (2020). Education supply chain in the era of industry 4.0. Systems Research and Behavioral Science, 37(4), 579–592.

Lillywhite, A., & Wolbring, G. (2020). Coverage of artificial intelligence and machine learning within academic literature, Canadian newspapers, and twitter tweets: The case of disabled people. Societies, 10(1), 23.

Masters, K. (2019). Artificial intelligence in medical education. Medical Teacher, 41(9), 976–980.

Meccawy, M. (2022). Creating an immersive XR learning experience: A roadmap for educators. Electronics, 11(21), 3547.

Meng, L., Xin, Q., & Fan, Q. (2023). Application of artificial intelligence in pre-school education professional talent training in the era of big data. In *e-Learning, e-Education, and online training: 8th EAI international conference, eLEOT 2022, Harbin, China, July 9–10, 2022, proceedings, Part II* (pp. 654–670). Cham: Springer Nature Switzerland.

Moore, J. E., Mascarenhas, A., Bain, J., & Straus, S. E. (2017). Developing a comprehensive definition of sustainability. Implementation Science, 12(1), 1–8.

Nousheen, A., Zai, S. A. Y., Waseem, M., & Khan, S. A. (2020). Education for sustainable development (ESD): Effects of sustainability education on pre-service teachers' attitude towards sustainable development (SD). Journal of Cleaner Production, 250, 119537.

Oliveira, K. K. D. S., & de Souza, R. A. (2022). Digital transformation towards education 4.0. Informatics in Education, 21(2), 283–309.

Olszewski, B., & Crompton, H. (2020). Educational technology conditions to support the development of digital age skills. Computers & Education, 150, 103849. https://doi.org/10.1016/j.compedu.2020.103849

Ouyang, F., Zheng, L., & Jiao, P. (2022). Artificial intelligence in online higher education: A systematic review of empirical research from 2011 to 2020. Education and Information Technologies, 27(6), 7893–7925.

Papadopoulos, I., Lazzarino, R., Miah, S., Weaver, T., Thomas, B., & Koulouglioti, C. (2020). A systematic review of the literature regarding socially assistive robots in pre-tertiary education. Computers & Education, 155, 103924. https://doi.org/10.1016/j.compedu.2020.103924

Pataranutaporn, P., Danry, V., Leong, J., Punpongsanon, P., Novy, D., Maes, P., & Sra, M. (2021). AI-generated characters for supporting personalized learning and well-being. Nature Machine Intelligence, 3(12), 1013–1022.

Paulauskaite-Taraseviciene, A., Lagzdinyte-Budnike, I., Gaiziuniene, L., Sukacke, V., & Daniuseviciute-Brazaite, L. (2022). Assessing education for sustainable development in engineering study programs: A case of AI ecosystem creation. Sustainability, 14(3), 1702.

Pedro, F., Subosa, M., Rivas, A., & Valverde, P. (2019). *Artificial intelligence in education: Challenges and opportunities for sustainable development.* Dordrecht, Netherlands.

Perkin, H. (2007). History of universities. In *International handbook of higher education* Springer International Handbooks of Education (vol. 18, pp. 159–205). Dordrecht: Springer. https://doi.org/10.1007/978-1-4020-4012-2_10

Popenici, S. A., & Kerr, S. (2017). Exploring the impact of artificial intelligence on teaching and learning in higher education. Research and Practice in Technology Enhanced Learning, 12(1), 1–13.

Prakash, C., Saini, R., & Sharma, R. (2021). Role of internet of things (IoT) in sustaining disruptive businesses. In R. Sharma, R. Saini, C. Prakash, & V. Prashad (eds.), *Internet of things and businesses in a disruptive economy* (1st ed.). New York: Nova Science Publishers.

Rana, G., & Sharma, R. (2019). Emerging human resource management practices in Industry 4.0. Strategic HR Review, 18(4), 176–181.

Romero, C., & Ventura, S. (2020). Educational data mining and learning analytics: An updated survey. Wiley Interdisciplinary Reviews: Data Mining and Knowledge Discovery, 10(3), e1355.

Sharma, R., Saini, A. K., & Rana, G. (2021). Big data analytics and businesses in industry 4.0. Design Engineering, 2021(02), 238–252.

Shumskaia, E. I. (2022). Artificial intelligence—reducing the carbon footprint? In *Industry 4.0: Fighting climate change in the economy of the future* (pp. 359–365). Cham: Springer International Publishing.

Sokoloff, K. L., & Engerman, S. L. (2000). History lessons: Institutions, factor endowments, and paths of development in the new world. Journal of Economic Perspectives, 14(3), 217–232.

Tanveer, M., Hassan, S., & Bhaumik, A. (2020). Academic policy regarding sustainability and artificial intelligence (AI). Sustainability, 12(22), 9435.

Wilson, C., & Van Der Velden, M. (2022). Sustainable AI: An integrated model to guide public sector decision-making. Technology in Society, 68, 101926. https://doi.org/10.1016/j.techsoc.2022.101926.

Zawacki-Richter, O., Marín, V. I., Bond, M., & Gouverneur, F. (2019). Systematic review of research on artificial intelligence applications in higher education–where are the educators? International Journal of Educational Technology in Higher Education, 16(1), 1–27.

Index

Note: Page numbers in *italics* indicate a figure and page numbers in **bold** indicate a table on the corresponding page.

A

AAA (anytime, anywhere, anyone) approach, 148
Academic Bank of Credits (ABC), 143
accelerated mobile pages (AMP), 69
access
  hybrid learning, 9–10
  on-demand, 170
accreditation, 145
action verbs, 174
active learning strategies, 158
ACUE (Association for College and University Educators), 179–180
Adaptive Hypermedia Knowledge Management E-Learning Platform (AHKME), 77
adaptive learning, 188–189, 222–223
administrative tasks
  AI assistance in, 188, 200, 227–228
  automation of, 228
adult education, 144
AHKME (Adaptive Hypermedia Knowledge Management E-Learning Platform), 77
AI, *see* artificial intelligence (AI)
algorithmic bias, 190, 219, 222
All India Radio, 159
American Society of Training and Education (ASTD), 209
AMP (accelerated mobile pages), 69
Anderson & Krathwohl Taxonomy of Learning (A&KTL), 158
Anderson's online learning model, 156–157, *157*
Andhra Pradesh, e-learning initiatives in, 141
animated presentation platform, 172
annotation homogeneity, 79
Annual Refresher Programme in Teaching (ARPIT), 116
anxiety, 23–24, 28, 30, 38, 89
anytime, anywhere, anyone (AAA) approach, 148
AR (augmented reality), 78, 154, 162, 171, 219, 226
artificial intelligence (AI)
  Education 4.0, 73
  e learning 3.0, 77
  empirical investigation of AI for enhancing interaction, 185–200
  instructor's perspective on AI implementation, 190–192, **192**
  learner-instructor interactions, 194–195
  learner's perspective on AI implementation, 193–194, **194**
  literature review, 187–195
  meaning of, 187–188
  nature of AI in learning, 187–189
  negative impact of implementation in online learning, 190
  positive impact of implementation in online learning, 189–190
  Society 5.0, 155
  Web 3.0, 69–71
artificial intelligence (AI) in sustainable education, 219–234
  applications of, 228–230
  benefits, 219, 223, 226, **227**, 233
  ethical considerations, 219, 222, 226, 231–234
  evolution, 221
  framework for integrating, 230–233, *231*
  future scope, 233–234
  introduction, 219–220
  literature review, 220–223, **224–225**
  physical education, 223
  potential barriers of implementing, 232
  potential to solve problems in education, 227–228, **229**, 233
artificial intelligence (AI) integration into education, 230–233, *231*
  AI-enabled curriculum development, 229–230
  AI-enabled resource allocation, 231
  AI-enabled teaching and learning, 230
  AI-monitoring and evaluation, 231
  data collection and analysis, 230
  ethical considerations, 231
  needs assessment and goal setting, 230
assessment
  artificial intelligence use, 191–192, 221, 229, 233
  digital, 206
  security issues, 206
  stealth, 191
Association for College and University Educators (ACUE), 179–180
ASTD (American Society of Training and Education), 209
asynchronous learning, 5, 13–14, 110–111
  Bloom's Taxonomy use for group-based e-learning (case study), 177–178, 180
  communication tools, 44
  courses, 116
  dialogue, 111
  Education 4.0, 74
  flipped classroom, 107
  media, 111
asynchronous teaching, 160
attitude, and e-learning continuance intentions, 43–49, 55–60, **56**, *58*
audio content, creating interactive, 211
augmented reality (AR), 78, 154, 162, 171, 219, 226

B

Berners-Lee, Timothy John, 69, 170
bias, and AI, 190, 219, 222, 231–232
big data, 69, 79, 152, 155, 162–163, 163
Bihar, e-learning initiatives in, 141
Blackboard, 110, 117, 159, 163, 172, 180
blended learning, 5, 42, 60, 116, 157, *158*, 208, *see also* hybrid learning
blockchain, 69, 71–72, 80

blogs, 210
Bloom, Benjamin Samuel, 174–175, 177
Bloom's Taxonomy
categories of cognitive outcomes, 174–175, 181
digital equity through lens of, 175–178
faculty development, 176–177
hierarchy, 174–175, 179
inclusive approach, 168
lifelong organizational learning, as guide for, 178
mastery learning, 168, 181
opposing perspective on, 178–179
revision of, 179–180
student development promoted by, 175–176, *176*
transformative learning approach, 168, 173, 180
using for group-based asynchronous e-learning (case study), 177–178, 180
browsers, 170
Byju's, 135

C

carbon footprint, 222–223, 226, 228–229, 234
CBSE podcast, 138
CDIO-based technical teaching mode, 42
censorship, 68
CFA (confirmatory factor analysis), 50
Chamilo, 163–164
chatbots, 188, 221–222
classroom
design for hybrid learning, 13
flipped, 13, 107, 208
cloud computing, 149, 151–152, 162
e-Learning 3.0, 77, 79
Web 2.5, 68
collaboration
between educators and AI developers, 188
flipped classroom, 208
by instructors, 73
video-based services, 134
collaborative learning, 87–88, 90–92, **96**, 96–97, 115
collaborative workspaces, 172
college students
psychological effects of COVID-19 on, 22–39
undergraduates' learning preference, *94*, 97–101, **98**, *99–100*
undergraduates' perception towards e-learning, 87–101, *94*, **96**, *98*
Community of Inquiry Framework, 91
Competence, *see* digital competence
competency-based education, 178
conference calls, 16
confirmatory factor analysis (CFA), 50
connectedness, 164, 193, 199
connectivism, 66–67
Connectivism and Connective Knowledge, 118
constructivist, 87, 90
content
digital, 209
for online learning, 113–114
visual, creating, 210–211, 214
continuance intentions, 42–60
continuous learning, 16, 110, 148–149, 178
convenience, of hybrid learning, 9
cost effectiveness, and continuance intentions, 42, 44, 49, 58
costs, of hybrid learning, 9
co-teaching, 88
course plan
hybrid learning, 14, 16
session-wise, 16
COVID-19 pandemic
e-learning adoption during, 45
e-learning continuance after, 42–60
ICT-based approach use during, 115–119
importance of online teaching/learning technology adoption during, 110–113
instructional strategy implications, 113–115
online learning in Nigeria (case study), 119–124
online teaching sustainability and strategies during, 106–127
quantitative view of, 134–135
teaching and learning technologies amidst (Indian perspective), 133–149
undergraduate perception towards e-learning during, 87–101, *94*, **96**, *98*
COVID-19 pandemic, impact of, 2
challenges in teaching and learning, 2–4, *3*
digital inequities/divide, 22–39, 168
over education, 67–68
psychological effects on college students, 22–39
school closures, 24–25, 67, 82, 90, 106–107, 117–118, 171, 175
virtual workspace, 178
COVID-19 pandemic challenges in teaching and learning
lack of training, 4
paradigm shift, 3
paucity of infrastructure and resources, 3–4
reduction in interaction and motivation, 3
creativity, by instructors, 73
critical thinking, 72, 143, 151–152, 177, 190, 222, 226, 229
culture, building hybrid learning, 13
curriculum development
AI-enabled, 229–230, 233–234
design challenges, in hybrid learning, 17
environmental friendly, 229
personalized, 192
cybergogy, 74

D

data mining, 69, 77, 163, 188–189, 221–222
data privacy, 190, 219, 222, 231–234
data security, 232
decentralized computing, 71
deep learning, 192
Delhi, e-learning initiatives in, 141
delivery model, for hybrid learning, 13
depression, 23–24, 30, 38
design, classroom, 13
didactic approach to teaching, 173
diffusion of innovation theory, 47
digital competence, 43–44, 60, 153, 203–215
components of, 209–210
definition, 209
facilitating learner's, 206–207
gender differences, 211–214
study discussion, 213–214
study methodology, 212
study results and findings, 212–213

digital content, 209
digital divide, 168–172
barriers, 23
bridging, 147, 181
cost of AI, 232
definition, 27
faculty, affect on, 176
literature review, 27–31
negative effects, kinds of, 23
in Nigeria, 119
psychological effects of COVID-19 on college students, 22–39
urban and rural divide, 23, 27–28
digital education
components, 209
in Pakistan, 203–205, 212–215
digital equity, 168–181
need for, 180
through lens of Bloom's Taxonomy, 175–178
digital inequities, 168–171, 173, 175–176, 181, *see also* digital divide
gender, 24
social aspects, 23
digital infrastructure, 27–28, 42, 146
for hybrid learning, 9
in India, 138, 146
for knowledge sharing (DIKSHA), 138
Digital Infrastructure for Knowledge Sharing (DIKSHA), 138, *139–140*
digital learner, 152–173
digital learning, professional development of teachers for, 206
digital pedagogies, 203–204, 208–215
digital platforms, for hybrid learning, 9
digital portfolios, 210–211, 214
digital teaching, 209
digital tools, 209
Ding Talk, 137
distance learning, 1–2, 42, 111, *see also* e-learning; hybrid learning; remote learning; web-based learning
benefits of Web 3.0 in, 81
Education 4.0 and Web 3.0 technologies application, 66–83
e-learning in, 81, *81*
enhancement, 66–83
student satisfaction, 97
Web 3.0 benefits in, 81, *81*
Doordarshan, 159

E

ease of use, perceived, 44, 46–47
EDM (educational data mining), 221–222
Ed-Tech companies, 134–136, 148–149
education
financing, 144
historical overview, 220–221
history of, 151
Education 4.0, 72–74, 82
educational innovation, 153–154
educators, 72–73
e-learning advancements, 74
e-learning enhancement, 74
evolution of, *161*
facilitators of digital revolution in, 153
framework to integrate, 151–165
Industry 4.0, impact of, 151–153
skills, *161*
students, 72
educational data mining (EDM), 221–222
educational innovation, and Education 4.0, 153–154
education sustainable development (ESD), 109–111
educators, *see* teachers
Educomp, 135
EdX, 221
EFA (exploratory factor analysis), 50
Ekstep, 136
e-learning, 208
adoption during COVID-19, 45
advancements with Education 4.0, 74
advantages of, 77, 87, 160
benefits, 42, 58, 90–91
Blooms' Taxonomy learning outcomes, 174–175
Bloom's Taxonomy use for group-based asynchronous (case study), 177–178, 180
critical success factors of Web technologies for, 77–79, *78*
definition, 42, 44, 74, 87, 90
disadvantages of, 88, 160
Education 4.0 enhancement of, 74
environment, 75
evolution (*see* e-learning evolution)
framework development, 75–76
framework to integrate 4.0 to enhance, 151–165
future tools of education, 82, *83*82
global market, 82
intelligent agents, 71
platforms, 117
reasons for preferring, 99–100, *100*, **100**
satisfaction, 88, 92, **96**, 96–97
undergraduate perception towards, 87–101, *94*, **96**, *98*
Web 3.0 influence on, 78–81
e-learning continuance intentions, 42–60
attitude, 43–49, 55–60, **56**, *58*
cost effectiveness, 42, 44, 49, 58
data analysis and interpretation, 53–54, 53–58, *55–56*, **56–57**, *58*
habit, 44–45, 49, 58
hedonic motivation, 44, 49
literature review, 44–49
massive open online course (MOOC), 46
perceived ease of use, 44, 46–47
perceived usefulness, 44–48
questionnaire, 49–53, **51–53**
research methodology, 49–53
self-efficacy, 44–48
social factors, 46
student satisfaction, 43, 45–48, 55–57, 59–60
web quality, 45, 48, 55–57, 59–60
e-learning evolution, 76–77
e-learning 1.0, 76
e-learning 2.0, 76
e-learning 3.0, 77
Web evolution relationship, 72
e-learning framework development, 75–76
assemblage of instructional designs, 75
evaluation, 76
requirements analysis, 75
use and development phase, 75–76

engagement
AI improvement of, 222, 228
as challenge, 147
challenge in hybrid learning, 18
flipped learning, 208
hybrid learning, 9–10, 14–16, *15*
importance of face-to-face, 193
of learners by technology, 206
presentations, creating, 211
professional of teachers, 205
reduction with online learning, 43
tools for, 15
environmental footprint, reduction with AI, 228
environmental surveillance, 229–230
e-PG Pathshala, 138
equity
concept, 110
digital, 168–181
Ericsson, 171
ESD (education sustainable development), 109–111
e-ShodhSindhu, 140
ethics, and artificial intelligence, 219, 222, 226, 231–234
European Digital Competence Framework for Educators, 205–207, **207**, *208*
assessment, 206
empowering teaching and learning, 206
facilitating learner's digital competencies, 206–207
professional engagement of teachers, 205
teaching and learning, 206
technological resource, 205–206
evaluation, *see also* assessment
web-based learning, 147, 149
evolution of education
AI in sustainable education, 222–223
historical overview, 220–221
literature review, 220–223, **224–225**
technology incorporation, 221
exploratory factor analysis (EFA), 50
eyesight problems, 43, 59–60

F

Facebook, 30–31, 36, 49, 68, 76, 89, 116–117, 141, 210–211, 214
face recognition, 186
face-to-face instruction, as undergraduates' learning preference, 97–101, **98**, *99–100*
faculty development
Bloom's Taxonomy, 176–177
professional development, 176–177, 192, 204–206, 209–211, 234
fear of non-performance, 148
feedback
actionable, 188
artificial intelligence use, 188–189, 221
real-time, 149, 228
web-based learning, 147, 149
flipped classroom, 13, 107, 208
Foundation for Advancement of International Medical Education and Research (FAIMER), 177
fourth industrial revolution (4IR), 152–153, 158, 161, 203, 209, 222

G

Gates Foundation, 172
gender discrimination, 24
gender inequality, 205, 211–212
Generation Z, 2, 152, 158, 204
GER (Gross Enrolment Ratio), 143, 145
Gigi initiative, 171
globalization, 108, 169–170, 178
Google Classroom, 42, 89, 96, 116–117, 121, **121**, 123, 134, **136**, 137, 149, 163–164
Google Forms, 30, 38, 49, 149, 195
Google Meet, 9, 30–31, **31**, 36, 74, 116, 119, 136, **136**, 172
Google Scholar, 136, 195
Google Teams, 115
grading systems, automated, 221
Green Libraries, 113
Gross Enrolment Ratio (GER), 143, 145

H

habit, and continuance intentions, 44–45, 49, 58
Hangouts, 76, 134, 136, **136**, 149
HDNN (hybridized deep neural network) technology, 192
hedonic motivation, 44, 49
heutagogy, 74
higher education for sustainability, review of, 108–110
higher education institutions (HEIs)
Industry 4.0 effect over, 158–159
stakeholders of e-learning implementation, 159
historically black colleges and universities (HBCUs), 168, 170–171, 175, 181
Hiuen Tsang, 133
H1N1 flu, 106
holistic teaching, 73
HTML (Hypertext Markup Language), 170
HTTP (Hypertext Transfer Protocol), 170
humor, sense of, 73
hybridized deep neural network (HDNN) technology, 192
hybrid learning, 1–8, 157
artificial intelligence, 186
benefits, 9–10, *10*
challenges of system, 16–18, *17*
components, 4, *4*
courses, 116–117
definition, 4–5
elements of, *8*, 8–9
engagement, tips for effective, 14–16, *15*
future scope, 18
implementation roadmap, 12–14, *14*
introduction, 1
literature review, 4–8, **6–7**
need for, 21–8
pathway, 10–12
hybrid learning pathway, 10–12
determine and design, 11
evaluate and act, 11–12
planned execution, 11
understanding and conceive, 11

I

IBM Watson Education Advisor, 221, 226
ICAI (Intelligent Computer-Aided Instruction) system, 221

ICTs, *see* information communication technologies (ICTs)
IEA (International Association for the Evaluation of Educational Achievement), 177
IIT-PAL, 139
ILEs (interactive learning environments), 188
illiteracy, digital, 147
inclusion, 110, 223
inclusiveness in teaching and learning process amidst COVID-19 pandemic, 133–149
India
  challenges and gains due to web-based learning, 146–148
  gains due to web-based learning, 148–149
  government initiatives, 137–141
  history of online education in, 159
  history of teaching-learning process in, 133–134
  initiatives of Indian states, 141–142
  National Education Policy (NEP), 133, 142–146
  paradigm shift towards online learning, 137–142
  regulatory bodies of higher education, 144
  schemes of higher education, 142
  teaching and learning technologies amidst COVID-19, 133–149
Indian Institute of Translation and Interpretations (IITI), 143
Indian languages, promotion of, 143–144
Indira Gandhi National Open University (IGNOU), 66
individualised educational experiences, *see* personalised learning
Industry 4.0, 72, 82
  Education 4.0, impact on, 151–153
  evolution of Industry 1.0 to, 162–163
  framework, 161–162, *162*
  learning factory 4.0, *163*
  online teaching-learning methods, effect over, 158–160
information age, 169, 172
information communication technologies (ICTs), 74, 82, 170
  as backbone of IR 4.0, 159
  digital education, 203–204, 213–215
  Education 3.0, 151
  e-learning, 87, 90
  expectations towards educational use of, 107
  gender gap in perception and use, 211–214
  in Nigeria, 119
  teacher's digital competences, 209–215
  use during COVID-19 pandemic, 115–119
information system success model (ISSM), 43–45, 47–48, *50*, 59
information technology (IT), 112
information technology support, for hybrid learning, 9
infrastructure, digital, 27–28, 42, 146
  for hybrid learning, 9
  for knowledge sharing (DIKSHA), 138
institutions
  accreditation, 145
  advantages of AI incorporation, 192
  challenges, in hybrid learning, 17
  critical success factors for e-learning, 79
  financial support, 145
  Industry 4.0 effect over, 158–159
  sustainability, 109–110
instructional strategies, 113–115, *114*
  course content, 113–114
  learning activities, 114
  learning supports, 114–115
instructors, *see* teachers
integrated fairness theory, 46
intelligence
  AI (*see* artificial intelligence (AI))
  concrete and applied, 174
Intelligent Computer-Aided Instruction (ICAI) system, 221
intelligent systems, 188–189
intelligent tutoring systems (ITS), 188, 219, 221–222
intelligent web, 70
intentions, continuance, 42–60
interaction, as challenge, 147
interaction equivalence theorem, 92
interactive learning environments (ILEs), 188
interactive teaching process, 16
interactivity, 111
International Association for the Evaluation of Educational Achievement (IEA), 177
internet
  access to, 154
  connectivity issues, 135, 146
  number of users in the world, *154*
Internet of Things (IOT), 71, 74, 81, 149, 154, 162
internet service provider, 170
interoperability, 78
IR 4.0 (fourth industrial revolution), 152–153, 158, 161, 203, 209, 222
ISSM (information system success model), 43–45, 47–48, *50*, 59
ITS (intelligent tutoring systems), 188, 219, 221–222

J

Jammu, e-learning initiatives in, 142

K

Kang, Li, 135
Kashmir, e-learning initiatives in, 142
Kessler-10 distress scale (K-10), 24, 30
KEWL (Knowledge Environment for Web-based Learning), 159
knowledge economy, 180–181
  digital learner, 172–173
  evolution of, 169–173
  Globalization 3.0, 170
  lifelong organizational learning, 178
knowledge management, 154

L

Lanka Education and Research Network (LEARN), 89
Lark, 137
Learnable, 171
learner-instructor interaction, AI facilitation of, 185–200
learners, *see also* students
  challenges of web-based learning, 147
  decline in soft skills, 147
  digital, 172–173
  perspective on AI implementation, 193–194, **194**
  removal of psychological barriers between tutor and, 148
learning
  adaptive, 188–189, 222–223
  barriers, elimination of, 189–190
  collaborative, 87–88, 90–92, **96**, 96–97, 115
  components, 173

connectivism theory, 66–67
continuous, 16, 110, 148–149, 178
Covid pandemic challenges, 2–4, *3*
definition, 173
distance (*see* distance learning)
hybrid (*see* hybrid learning)
lifelong, 74, 109, 178, 203, 209
lifelong organizational, 175, 178, 181
machine, 69, 79, 189, 221
mastery, 168, 181
nature of artificial intelligence (AI), 187–189
passive study, 18
self-paced, 4, 74, 157
student-centered, 74, 83, 87, 91, 115, 152, 174, 176–177
transformative, need for, 173
learning activities, 114
learning analytics, 153, 162, 189, 221–222
learning communities, 91, 176–178
learning gaps, identification of, 191
learning management system (LMS), 14, 42, 48, 110, 115–117, 172
Education 4.0 and Web 3.0 technologies application, 66–83
in e-learning evolution, 76
Moodle-based, 89
overview, 117
software systems for online learning, 117
students unprepared for use of, 147
technically oriented education, use in, 163–164
learning outcomes
Bloom's Taxonomy, 174–175
improvement with AI, 228
learning preference, undergraduates', *94*, 97–101, **98**, *99–100*
learning styles, 5, 42, 73, 116, 119, 191–192, 194, 205, 221, 223, 229–230
learning supports, 114–115
lifelong learning, 74, 109, 178, 203, 209
lifelong organizational learning, 175, 178, 181
Likert scale, 30, 50, 94, 212
literacy
computer, 88, 97, 160
digital, 27, 79, 93, 158, 168, 170, 222
information, 169, 172
technological, 205
LMS, *see* learning management system (LMS)

M

machine learning, 69, 79, 189, 221
marginalized populations, 23–24, 137, 169–170, 173, 180–181
mashups, 77
massive open online course (MOOC), 46, 116–118
mastery learning, 168, 181
Mastery Rubric for nurse practitioner education, 178
mental health
addressed by teachers, 73
psychological effects of COVID-19 on college students, 22–39
mental stress, 27, 29–30, 32, 34, **35**, 36–39
metaverse, 175–176, 180
Microsoft Teams, 30, 119, 163, 172
mobile learning, 208
mobile phones, *see* smartphones
MOOC (massive open online course), 46, 116–118
Moodle, 89, 117, 159, 163–164, 172
motivation
hedonic, 44, 49
of hybrid learning stakeholders, 12
lack among learners, 147
Myspace, 210, 214

N

Nalanda University, 133
National Council for Education Research and Training (NCERT), 138
National Digital Library of India, 139
National Education Policy (NEP), of India, 133, 142–146
challenges before, 145–146
objectives, 143–144
overview, 142–143
National Mission on Education through ICT (NME-ICT), 138
natural language processing, 189, 221
NCCHP (North Carolina Center for Public Health Preparedness), 177
NCERT (National Council for Education Research and Training), 138
needs assessment, 75
Netscape, 170
network learning, 193, 199
NFDC, 210–211
Nigeria, online learning case study, 119–124
NME-ICT (National Mission on Education through ICT), 138
nonverbal communication, 193
North Carolina Center for Public Health Preparedness (NCCHP), 177
nurse practitioner curriculums, 178

O

OECD (Organisation for Economic Co-operation and Development), 158
on-demand access, 170
One App, One Platform, Many Government Services principle, 141
online education, *see also* online learning
benefits, **122**, 122–124
challenges of, 124
effectiveness, 26, **35**, 36
e-learning continuance intentions, 42–60
interruptions during, 43
limitations, **122**, 122–124
problems, 25–26, 34–36, **35**
psychological effects of COVID-19 on college students due to digital divide, 22–39
student opinions, 32–34, **34**, 37
technology adoption during COVID-19 pandemic, importance of, 110–113
online education methods, **31**, 31–34, *32–33*, **33–34**
applications used, 31, **31**, 36–37
devices used, 32, *33*, **33**
internet connection types, 32, *33*, **34**, 37
methods adopted, 31–32, **31–32**

online learning, *see also* distance learning; hybrid learning
empirical investigation of AI for enhancing interaction, 185–200
environment, 114
history of, 159
instructional strategies, 113–115, *114*
learner-instructor interactions, 195
in Nigeria (case study), 119–124
paradigm shift towards, 137–142
online learning applications
learning management systems (LMS), 117
massive open online course (MOOC), 117–118
student information systems (SIS), 117
video conferencing, 118–119
online learning experience, 92–93, **96**, 96–97
online learning model, Anderson's, 156–157, *157*
online learning sustainability, 111–113
online learning types, 116–117
asynchronous courses, 116
hybrid courses, 116–117
synchronous courses, 116
online platforms, 121, **121**, 123
online teaching-learning, 156–160, *157–158*
effect of Industry 4.0 over methods, 158–160
online teaching sustainability and strategies during COVID-19 pandemic, 106–127
Organisation for Economic Co-operation and Development (OECD), 158
ownership issues
Web 2.0, 68
Web 3.0, 69

P

Pakistan, 203–205, 212–215
Pandit Madan Mohan Malviya Mission on Teachers and Training (PMMMNMTT), 142
passive study, 18
pedagogies, digital, 203–204, 208–215
peeragogy, 74
perceived usefulness, and e-learning continuance intentions, 44–48
personalised learning, 221–223, 226–229, 233
personalization, 71, 77–80
and AI, 188–189, 193
personalized curriculum, 192
personal learning environments (PLEs), 77
personal learning networks (PLNs), 210, 214
persons with disabilities, integration of, 142
physical education, and AI, 223
plan-do-check-act philosophy, 14
PLEs (personal learning environments), 77
PLNs (personal learning networks), 210, 214
podcast, CBSE, 138
political interference, 145–146
polling and quizzes, live interactive, 172
portfolios, digital, 210–211, 214
post-work society, 178
prediction systems, 188
presentations, creating engaging, 210, 214
privacy, 190, 219, 222, 231–234
professional development, 176–177, 192, 204–206, 209–211, 234
professional education, 144
progressive web apps (PWA), 69
psychological effects of COVID-19 on college students, 22–39
discussion of study findings, 37–38
introduction, 22–27
literature review, 27–29
methodology of study, 29–31
results of study, **31**, 31–36, *32–33*, **33–35**
Punjab, e-learning initiatives in, 141
purposive sampling, 185, 212
purposive sampling method, non-probability-based, 29
PWA (progressive web apps), 69

Q

questionnaire
e-learning continuance intentions, 49–53, **51–53**
online, 29–30
online learning in Nigeria (case study), 120–124
undergraduate perception towards e-learning during pandemic, 93–97, **95–96**
questions
answered by AI, 190, 192–193, 200
students' fear of asking, 200
quizzes
creating non-traditional, 210–214
live interactive, 172

R

Rastriya Uchatter Sikasha Abhiyan (RUSA), 142
Read-Only Web (Web 1.0), 68, 72
Read-Write-Execute Web, 69
Read-Write Web (Web 2.0), 68, 72
remote learning, 82, 87, 117, *see also* distance learning; e-learning
completely, 13
Covid impact, 24–25
definition, 5
e-learning, 66, 74–76
isolation, 90
video conferencing, 119
requirements analysis, 75
resource management, AI use in, 229, 231
resources
creating and sharing with classes, 210, 214
educator familiarity with technological, 205–206, 210
lack of, 89
uneven distribution of, 171
responsibility, impact of AI exposure, 199
robots, intelligent, 153

S

SARS, 106
satisfaction
AI in education, **196**, 196–200, **198**
learner-instructor interactions, 194–195
student (*see* student satisfaction)
SDG, *see* Sustainable Development Goal (SDG)
self-determination theory, 222
self-efficacy, and e-learning continuance intentions, 44–48
self-paced learning, 4, 74, 157
semantics, 79
Semantic Web, *see* Web 3.0
SIS (student information systems), 117

Skoll Foundation, 172
Skype, 76, 119, 134
smart agents, 71, 80
SMART goals, 12
smartphones, 2, 20, 26, 32, **33**, 36–38, 46, 89, 96, 111, 116, 120–124, 146, 148, 171, 208–209
Smart Sparrow platform, 221
social bookmarking platforms, 210, 214
social cognitive theory, 92
social identity, 111
social inequality, 23, 27–28
social integration theory, 92
social isolation, 24, 42–44, 59–60
socially assistive robots, 222
social media
  connectivism, 66
  in e-learning, 76
  information communication technology-based learning, role in, 115
  ownership issues, 68
  teacher knowledge and skill with, 210, 214
  Web 2.0, 68
social networking platforms, 115, 210, 214
social presence, 88, 91, **96**, 96–97, 111
Social Web (Web 2.0), 68, 72
Society 4.0 (informational society), 155–156
Society 5.0, 154–156
  digital transformations in, *155*
  evolution of Society 1.0 to, 156, *156*
  significance of, 155–156
Socio-Semantic Web, 70
soft skills, 147, 211
special needs, personalised assistance for, 228
speech recognition technologies, 186, 188, 221, 228
Stability and Change in Human Characteristics (Bloom), 177
stress, mental, 27, 29–30, 32, 34, **35**, 36–39
student-centered learning, 74, 83, 87, 91, 115, 152, 174, 176–177
student development, promoted by Bloom's Taxonomy, 175–176, *176*
student information systems (SIS), 117
students, *see also* learners
  in Education 4.0, 72
  hybrid learning challenges, *17*, 17–18
  impact of Web 3.0-based learning on, 80
  perception of AI in education, **196**, 196–200, *197*
  undergraduate perception towards e-learning, 87–101, *94*, **96**, *98*
student satisfaction, 28, 37
  definition, 88, 92
  with e-learning, 88, 92, **96**, 96–97
  e-learning continuance intentions, 43, 45–48, 55–57, 59–60
  factors responsible, 25
  video conferencing, 119
Sunbird, 138
support in learning, impact of AI exposure on, 199
supports, learning, 114–115
surveillance feature of AI, 200
survey, online, 195
SurveyMonkey, 120
sustainability
  definition, 219
  online teaching sustainability and strategies during COVID-19 pandemic, 106–127
  review of higher education for, 108–110
  teaching and learning process amidst COVID-19 pandemic, 133–149
sustainable development, 108–110
Sustainable Development Goal (SDG), 108–109, 113, 154, 232
sustainable education, artificial intelligence (AI) in, 219–234
SWAYAM (Study Webs of Active-Learning for Young Aspiring Minds), 116, 137–138, 143
Swayam Prabha DTH channel, 139–140
synchronous learning, 5, 13–14
  communication tools, 44
  courses, 116
  Education 4.0, 74
  video conferencing, 118–119
synchronous teaching, 160
Syntactic Web, 68

T

TAM (technology acceptance model), 46–47
task-technology-fit (TTF) model, 43–44, 46–48, *50*, **51**, 55–57, 59–60
TCT (technology continuance theory), 43–45, 47–48, 59
teacher-centered approach, 173, 177
teachers
  AI benefits, 185–186
  attitudes and skills needed, 73
  digital competencies, 203–215, *208*
  digital pedagogies, 203–204, 208–215
  in Education 4.0, 72–73
  as e-Learning 3.0 stakeholders, 79
  empowering teaching and learning process, 206
  empowerment of, 12
  European Digital Competence Framework for Educators, 205–207, **207**, *208*
  hybrid learning challenges, 17, *17*
  impact of Web 3.0-based learning on, 80
  instructional strategies, 113–115, *114*
  interest and attitude toward technology, 210
  lack of trained, 147
  learner-instructor interactions, 194–195
  perception of AI in education, 197–200, *198*, **198**
  perspective on AI implementation, 190–192, **192**
  satisfaction, 12
  training of, 209
teaching-learning process, 1–12, 18, 107, 133, 142, 144, 146, 153, 204, 207
  effect of Industry 4.0, 158–160
  literature review, **6–7**
  theoretical model for online, 156–160
technological literacy, 205
technology
  adoption during COVID-19 pandemic, importance of, 110–113
  gender discrimination in usage, 205

identifying appropriate, 12–13
incorporation into education, 221
interest and attitude toward, 210
technology acceptance model (TAM), 46–47
technology continuance theory (TCT), 43–45, 47–48, 59
teleconferencing, 115–116, 159
Telegram, 117, 119
telehealth, 28
teleworking, 22–23
thinking process, developing students', 16
transformative learning, need for, 173
transparency, 231, 233–234
TTF (task-technology-fit) model, 43–44, 46–48, *50*, **51**, 55–57, 59–60
Twitter, 46, 68, 76, 116, 210, 214

U

UMANG (Unified Mobile Application for New Age Government), 141
undergraduate perception towards e-learning, 87–101, *94*, **96**, *98*
background, 89–90
introduction, 87–88
literature review, 90–93
proposed model illustrating, *94*
study methodology, 93–94, *94*
study results and discussion, 94–100, **95–96**, *98–100*
undergraduates' learning preference, *94*, 97–101, **98**, *99–100*
UNESCO, 24, 67, 109–111, 203, 215
UNICEF, 171
unified theory of acceptance and use of technology (UTAUT), 43–44, 47, 49, *50*, 59
United Nations Educational, Scientific and Cultural Organization (UNESCO), 24, 109–111, 203, 215
Uplink, 171
URL (Uniform Resource Locator), 170

V

verbs, action, 174
Verizon Innovative Learning, 171–172, 176
video calls, 15–16
video conferencing, 118–119
Vidwan, 140
virtual assistants, 186, 188, 221
virtual campus, 175
virtual communities, 45, 111–112, 119, 171
virtual field trips, 226
virtual interaction applications, **136**, 136–137
virtualization, 71, 74, 160
virtual labs, 69, 148, 186
virtual learning, 44, 58–60, 72, 74, 111–113, 119, 160, 162, 168, 178, 189–195
virtual learning environment (VLE), 112
virtual reality (VR), 154, 188, 194, 226, 228
visual content, creating, 210–211, 214
visualization, 78

W

Web 1.0 (Read-Only Web), 68, 72
Web 2.0 (Read-Write/Social Web), 68, 72, 76, 124
Web 3.0 (Semantic Web), 66–69
characteristics, 69–72
distance learning, benefits in, 81, *81*
e-learning, 78–81
impact for instructors, 80
impact for learners, 80
technologies, 70–71
terminologies, 71–72
tools, 69–70
Web 4.0, 82–83, 152
web-based learning, 208
challenges and gains due to, 146–148
evolution of, 135–137
framework for, *135*
gains due to, 148–149
Web evolution, 68–72, *70*
relationship with e-learning evolution, 72
Web 1.0 (Read-Only Web), 68, *72*
Web 2.0 (Read-Write/Social Web), 68, 72
Web 2.5 (Social and Semantic Web), 68–69, 72
Web 3.0 (Semantic Web), 66–69
Web 4.0, 82–83
web quality, influence on e-learning, 45, 48, 55–57, 59–60
web technologies and critical success factors for e-learning, 77–79, *78*
WhatsApp, 29–31, 49, 89, 96, 116–120, 141
whiteboards, digital, 172
wikis, 210–211
Without a Net: The Digital Divide in America (film), 171
work, future of, 178
work-life balance, 22, 173, 178, 180
World Bank, 169
World Economic Forum, 158, 171, 205
World Wide Web, 169–170

Y

YouTube, 30–31, 36, 46, 68, 76, 89, 96, 136, 141, 211

Z

Zoom, 9, 30–31, **31**, 42, 89, 96, 115–116, 119, 121, **121**, 123, 136, **136**, 172

For Product Safety Concerns and Information please contact our EU
representative GPSR@taylorandfrancis.com
Taylor & Francis Verlag GmbH, Kaufingerstraße 24, 80331 München, Germany

www.ingramcontent.com/pod-product-compliance
Ingram Content Group UK Ltd.
Pitfield, Milton Keynes, MK11 3LW, UK
UKHW052052230926
475702UK00025B/1119

* 9 7 8 1 0 3 2 5 4 4 6 4 9 *